Developmen

Development

A Cultural Studies Reader

Edited by

Susanne Schech and Jane Haggis

Flinders University of South Australia

Blackwell Publishers

© 2002 by Blackwell Publishers Ltd
a Blackwell Publishing company
except for editorial arrangement and introduction © 2002 Susanne Schech and Jane Haggis

Editorial Offices:
108 Cowley Road, Oxford OX4 1JF, UK
    Tel: +44 (0)1865 791100
350 Main Street, Malden, MA 02148-5018, USA
    Tel: +1 781 388 8250

First published 2002 by Blackwell Publishers Ltd

Library of Congress Cataloging-in-Publication Data has been applied for

ISBN 0-631-21916-1 (hbk)
ISBN 0-631-21917-X (pbk)

A catalogue record for this title is available from the British Library.

Set in Palatino, 10 on 12pt
by SetSystems, Saffron Walden, Essex
Printed and bound in Great Britain by MPG Books Ltd, Bodmin, Cornwall

For further information on
Blackwell Publishers, visit our website:
www.blackwellpublishers.co.uk

Contents

Part III   Development as Discourse

Part IV   Development, Culture, and Human Rights

Part V   Global/Local

Part VI   Place and Space

Acknowledgments

We are very grateful to Monique Mulholland, who labored long and hard to assemble the readings and permissions, and to Amy Specht for coming on board at the last minute to assist her.

The authors gratefully acknowledge the following for permission to reproduce copyright material:

1 "The Grocer and the Chief: A Parable" by Daniel Lerner (1958). Reprinted with the permission of The Free Press, a Division of Simon and Schuster, Inc. from *The Passing of Traditional Society: Modernizing the Middle East* by Daniel Lerner. Copyright © 1958 by The Free Press.
2 "Modernization Ideals" (excerpts from chapter 2 titled "The Value Premises Chosen"). Reprinted from *Asian Drama: An Enquiry into the Poverty of Nations* (3 vols.). Vol. 1. by G. Myrdal with permission from The Century Foundation, Inc. Copyright © 1968, New York.
3 "A Universal Civilization? Modernization and Westernization" by Samuel P. Huntington (1996). Abridged version. In *The Clash of Civilizations and the Remaking of World Order*. New York: Simon and Schuster, 66–78. Reprinted with permission of Simon and Schuster and Georges Borcharat, Inc. Copyright © 1996 by Samuel P. Huntington.
4 "Divided Market Cultures in China: Gender, Enterprise, and Religion" by Robert P. Weller (1998). Abridged version. In R. W. Hefner (ed.), *Market Cultures: Society and Morality in New Asian Capitalisms*. St. Leonards, NSW: Allen and Unwin, 78–103. Copyright © 1997 by Westview Press. Reprinted by permission of Westview Press, a member of Perseus Books, L.L.C.
5 "Orientalism" (originally titled "Introduction") by Edward W. Said (1995). Abridged version. In *Orientalism: Western Conceptions of the Orient*. London:

Penguin, 1–28. Reprint of the 1991 version with a new afterword. Originally published in 1978 titled *Orientialism*, New York: Pantheon Books.

6   "The West and the Rest: Discourse and Power" by Stuart Hall (1992). Abridged version. In S. Hall and B. Gieben (eds.), *Formations of Modernity*. Cambridge: Polity Press, 275–331. Reprinted with permission.

7   "Black Bodies, White Bodies: Toward an Iconography of Female Sexuality in the Late Nineteenth Century" (originally titled "Black Bodies, White Bodies: Toward an Iconography of Female Sexuality in Late 19th Century Art, Medicine and Literature") by Sander L. Gilman (1985). Abridged version. In *Critical Inquiry*, 12, 259–74. Reproduced with permission of the author and University of Chicago Press.

8   "The Problematization of Poverty: The Tale of Three Worlds and Development" by Arturo Escobar (1995). Abridged version. In *Encountering Development: The Making and Unmaking of the Third World*. Princeton, NJ: Princeton University Press.

9   "The Constitution of the Object of 'Development': Lesotho as a 'Less Developed Country'" (originally titled "Conceptual Apparatus. The Constitution of the Object of 'Development': Lesotho as a 'Less Developed Country'") by James Ferguson (1994). Abridged version. In *The Anti-Politics Machine. "Development," Depoliticisation, and Bureaucratic Power in Lesotho*. Minneapolis and London: Oxford University Press. Revision of the author's doctoral thesis at Harvard University (1985). First published Cambridge and New York: Cambridge University Press (1990).

10 "Becoming a Development Category" by Nanda Shrestha (1995). In J. Crush (ed.), *Power and Development*. London and New York: Routledge, 266–77.

11 "Knowledge for Development" (originally titled "Overview") by World Bank (1999). Abridged version. In *World Development Report 1988/99. Knowledge for Development*. Oxford: Oxford University Press. Copyright © 1998 by the International Bank for Reconstruction and Development/The World Bank. Used by permission of Oxford University Press, Inc.

12 "Universalism, Particularism, and the Question of Identity" by Ernesto Laclau (1995). Abridged version. In J. Rajchman (ed.), *The Identity in Question*. London: Routledge, 93–108. Copyright 1995. Reproduced by permission of Routledge, Inc., part of The Taylor & Francis Group.

13 "Human Rights as Cultural Practice: An Anthropological Critique" by Ann-Belinda S. Preis (1996). Abridged version. In *Human Rights Quarterly*, 18 (2), 286–315. © The Johns Hopkins University Press. Reprinted with permission of The Johns Hopkins University Press.

14 "Women's Rights, Human Rights, and Domestic Violence in Vanuatu" (originally titled "Women Ikat Raet Long Human Raet O No? Women's Rights, Human Rights and Domestic Violence in Vanuatu") by Margaret Jolly (1996). Abridged version. In *Feminist Review*, 52, 169–90.

15 "Disjuncture and Difference in the Global Cultural Economy" by Arjun Appadurai (1996). Abridged version. In *Modernity at Large: Cultural Dimensions of Globalization*. Minneapolis: University of Minnesota Press.

16 "Capitalisms, Crises, and Cultures II: Notes on Local Transformation and Everyday Cultural Struggles" by Allan Pred (1992). Abridged version. In

Reworking Modernity: Capitalisms and Symbolic Discontent. Copyright © 1992 by A. Pred and M. J. Watts. Reprinted by permission of Rutgers University Press.

17 "Narratives of Masculinity and Transnational Migration: Filipino Workers in the Middle East" by Jane A. Margold (1995). Abridged version. In A. Ong and M. G. Peletz (eds.), *Bewitching Women, Pious Men: Gender and Body Politics in Southeast Asia* (Berkeley, Los Angeles, and London: University of California Press, 1995), 274–94.

18 "Learning to be Local in Belize: Global Systems of Common Difference" by Richard Wilk (1995). Abridged version. In D. Miller (ed.), *Worlds Apart: Modernity through the Prism of the Local*. London: Routledge, 110–33.

19 "Geography as Destiny: Cities, Villages, and Khmer Rouge Orientalism" by Kevin McIntyre (1996). Abridged version. In *Comparative Studies in Society and History*, 38 (4), 730–58.

20 "Contesting Cultures: Westernization, Respect for Cultures, and Third World Feminists" by Uma Narayan (1997). Abridged version. In *Dislocating Cultures: Identities, Traditions and Third World Feminism*. New York: Routledge. Copyright 1997. Reproduced by permission of Routledge, Inc., part of The Taylor & Francis Group.

21 "Gender, Place, and Networks: A Political Ecology of Cyberculture" by Arturo Escobar (1999). Abridged version. In W. Harcourt, *Women@Internet: Creating New Cultures in Cyberspace*. London and New York: Zed Books, 31–55.

22 "Maya Hackers and the Cyberspatialized Nation-state: Modernity, Ethnostalgia, and a Lizard Queen in Guatemala" by Diane M. Nelson (1996). Abridged version. In *Cultural Anthropology*, 11 (3), 287–308. Reproduced by permission of the American Anthropological Association from *Cultural Anthropology* 97:4. Not for sale or further reproduction.

23 "CyberResistance: Saudi Opposition Between Globalization and Localization" by Mamoun Fandy (1999). In *Comparative Studies in Society and History* 41 (1999), 124–47. Reprinted with the permission of Cambridge University Press.

24 "The Invention of Tradition Revisited: The Case of Colonial Africa" by Terence Ranger (1993). Abridged version. In T. Ranger and O. Vaughan (eds.), *Legitimacy and the State in Twentieth-century Africa*. Basingstoke: Macmillan, in association with St. Anthony's College, Oxford, 62–111. Copyright © Macmillan, in association with St. Anthony's College, Oxford, 1993. Reprinted with permission from Macmillan Ltd.

25 "Contentious Traditions: The Debate on *Sati* in Colonial India" by Lata Mani (1987). Abridged version. In *Cultural Critique*, 7, 119–56.

26 "When the Earth is Female and the Nation is Mother: Gender, the Armed Forces, and Nationalism in Indonesia" by Saraswati Sunindyo (1998). Abridged version. In *Feminist Review*, 58 (Spring), 1–21.

27 "The Objects of Soap Opera: Egyptian Television and the Cultural Politics of Modernity" by Lila Abu-Lughod (1995). Abridged version. In D. Miller (ed.), *Worlds Apart: Modernity through the Prism of the Local*. London: Routledge, 190–210.

28 "The Credible and the Credulous: The Question of 'Villagers' Beliefs' in Nepal" by Stacy Leigh Pigg (1996). Abridged version. Reproduced by permission of the American Anthropological Association from *Cultural Anthropology*, 11 (2), 160–201. Not for sale or further reproduction.

29 "Modernizing the Malay Mother" by Maila Stivens (1998). Abridged version. In K. Ram and M. Jolly (eds.), *Maternities and Modernities: Colonial and Post-colonial Experiences in Asia and the Pacific*. Cambridge: Cambridge University Press, 50–80. Copyright © Cambridge University Press, 1998. Reprinted with the permission of Cambridge University Press.

The publishers apologize for any errors or omissions in the above list and would be grateful to be notified of any corrections that should be incorporated in the next edition or reprint of this book.

Introduction: Pathways to Culture and Development

Jane Haggis and Susanne Schech

Development studies' love affair with political economy and neoliberal economics is beginning to wane. Culture is coming back onto the agenda, displaced by the centrality of the market over the last twenty years. The readings presented in this book are intended to provide an introduction to the ways in which culture has assumed a visibility again within development studies.

In the 1950s and 1960s, the role of culture in development received considerable attention within a development studies dominated by modernization theory. These sorts of explanations were based on a notion of culture as bounded, "a self-contained system of traits which distinguishes one community from another" (Bauman 1973: 35). A very different way of defining culture guided our approach to compiling this Reader. Drawing from the relatively new discipline of cultural studies, many of the selected texts are informed by a definition of culture that places power at the center of the concept. The consequence is a much more dynamic and broad definition of culture as "a network of representations – texts, images, talk, codes of behaviour, and the narrative structures organising these – which shapes every aspect of social life" (Frow and Morris 1993: viii). This introduction provides an overview of the key influences from cultural studies informing contemporary development studies.

Stuart Hall's (1992) formulation of "the West and the Rest" is probably the best-known articulation of this definition of culture applied to global inequality. Hall's phrase captures a distinctive way of conceiving the power imbalance between the affluent industrialized societies of Western Europe and North America and the developing countries. He describes this relationship in terms of the ways in which a pervasive system of representing the non-West as inferior to the West underpins the political economy of underdevelopment. To break the cycle of global inequality requires strategies that challenge the taken-for-granted meanings embedded in economic, political, and social knowledge about the world. This knowledge is dominated by Western constructions that image the world in terms of itself. Crucially, it is not only the Third World that is constructed through the lens of Western knowledge but also the West itself. Thus Hall differs from Samuel Huntington's (1996) conception of Western civilization as rooted in an essential core originating in ancient Greek and Roman civilization.

In setting up the dualism of the "West and the Rest," Hall explains the concept of "the West" functioning as a tool of categorization. It operates as a standard of comparison; the criterion for evaluating other cultures in relation to the West; and an image which condenses a number of characteristics such as urban, advanced, developed. The West's self-depiction becomes the norm by which the "Rest" are identified. In development studies, the West becomes the model to be emulated by Third World societies. How has the West been able to impose its view of the world on "the Rest"? Hall answers this question by revealing how European colonialism established a regime of truth which embedded a cultural vocabulary of Western superiority, institutionalized through law, education, economic relations, and political forms.

Foucault and Power/Knowledge

Hall draws on the work of the French philosopher and historian, Michel Foucault, in combination with a culturalist tradition within Western European Marxism. The colonial regime of truth Hall identifies relates to Foucault's notion of discourse, defined as a group of statements that provide a language for talking about – i.e., a way of representing – a particular kind of knowledge about a topic. A discourse provides the boundaries within which shared meanings about, for example, development are constructed in ways which are regular, systematic, and which are taken as truth at a particular time and place.

Underwriting the ability of a discourse to attain the status of a general truth is a matrix of power/knowledge. While in the liberal model *true* knowledge is seen as innocent of power, Foucault argues that knowledge always expresses a will to power because it represents "this" and not "that" (Ransom 1997: 19). Foucault explains this through the use of an amusing example, apparently drawn from an ancient Chinese encyclopedia cited by Jorge Luis Borges, which classifies animals as:

> (a) belonging to the Emperor, (b) embalmed, (c) tame, (d) sucking pigs, (e) sirens, (f) fabulous, (g) stray dogs, (h) included in the present classification, (i) frenzied, (j) innumerable, (k) drawn with a very fine camelhair brush, (l) *et cetera*, (m) having just broken the water pitcher, (n) those that from a long way off look like flies. (Foucault 1985: xv)

Foucault goes on: "in the wonderment of this taxonomy, the thing we apprehend ... the thing that ... is demonstrated in the exotic charm of another system of thought, is the limitation of our own, the stark impossibility of thinking *that*" (Foucault 1985: xv). Here Foucault addresses the constructed character of "reality." The "Chinese" typology of animals is based on the view from the imperial throne. Today we distinguish animals by the view from the microscope, in terms of skeletal structure and so on. The animals have not changed, but the discourse by which the animals are known and understood has.

In his writings, Foucault traces just such a shift from one discursive regime to another; the shift in Europe from premodern to modern during the Enlightenment of the seventeenth and eighteenth centuries. A worldview that saw God's power embodied in the figures of king and priest was displaced by a view of power vested in humans who produced knowledge through disinterested scientific observation. This shift involved, Foucault argues, new instruments of power, which normalize on the one hand, and discipline on the other. Importantly, he sees the modern individual as produced by these new instruments of power. In this sense, power is productive rather than an instrument wielded by one agent over another.

Power/Knowledge and Colonialism

Foucault's formulation of discourse and power/knowledge is taken up by Edward Said in his seminal work, *Orientalism* (1978), and applied to the relations between the "West" and the "Rest." As Said points out, the Orient has since antiquity been known in the West as its complementary opposite, but it was during the nineteenth century that this knowledge became systematized and institutionalized through academic scholarship. The crux of this knowledge was its binary opposition of the West and the Orient, which presumed the superiority of the West. Said also observes that colonialism was based not only on military power but also on the knowledge base of academic Orientalism. This was an authoritative way of knowing the Orient as fundamentally different from the West, and inherently inferior. Orientalism in fact operated as the discourse through which the West and the non-West were constructed:

> The Orient that appears in Orientalism, then, is a system of representations framed by a whole set of forces that brought the Orient into Western learning, Western consciousness, and later, Western empire. (Said 1995: 203)

Said gives the example of Napoleon's Egyptian expedition in 1798–9, in which Orientalist scholars were used to manage the emperor's contacts with the native population as well as to create a multi-volume encyclopedia describing Egypt to the West in the language of modern European science. These texts were not simply descriptive but had very material effects. An example is the myth of the "lazy native," embedded in the depiction by European anthropologists of people in Southeast Asia (Alatas 1977). It became a self-fulfilling prophecy in Malaya, where the British colonial administrations effectively prevented the indigenous peoples from entering the more dynamic sectors of the colonial capitalist economy (Lim 1976). The consequent segregation of economic activity by ethnicity is still evident in contemporary Malaysia, with at times unfortunate political consequences. Thus, a European observation regarding an indigenous people became the basis for organizing an economy and its labor force. In this way we can see how Foucault's notion of discourse and power/knowledge, and Said's critique of Orientalism, indicate the importance of the cultural in the structuring of dominance. The amazement with which a Western academic greets the revelation that veiled Islamic women seriously discuss feminism is a case in point. The fact of the veil as an Oriental stereotype of female oppression underpins this surprise (Hirschmann 1998; Haggis and Schech 2000).

The other important point Said makes is that this representation of a superior West and inferior Orient actually becomes the means by which each knows itself. Frantz Fanon, a psychiatrist from Martinique working in colonial Algeria, analyzed the psychological effects of this discourse as enslaving the negro by his inferiority, and the white man by his superiority. He illustrates this in a graphic description of a chance encounter between a white child and a black man:

> My body was given back to me sprawled out, distorted, recoloured, clad in mourning in that white winter day. The negro is an animal, the negro is bad, the negro is mean, the negro is ugly; look, a nigger, it's cold, the nigger is shivering, the nigger is shivering because he is cold, the little boy is trembling because he is afraid of the nigger, and the nigger is shivering with cold, that cold that goes through your bones, the handsome little boy is trembling because he thinks the nigger is quivering with rage, the little white boy throws himself into his mother's arms: Mama the nigger's going to eat me up. (Fanon 1968: 80)

What Fanon is describing here is the way in which the stereotype of the black man as primitive and threatening takes on a life of its own in the colonial engagement. The child of the colonizer cannot see the person in front of him, only the monster of racist colonial discourse. For the man, although he knows himself not as a monster but as an educated Frenchman, this self-identity is ruptured by the child's terror, his fear of black skin. The black man becomes the colonized – the stereotype. Fanon uses these insights to articulate a powerful rejection of the colonial relationship, and argues for the importance of reclaiming "negro" as a self-determining identity. This raises the issue of counter-discourse or resistance to dominant power/knowledge. The Negritude movement, of which Fanon was one leading proponent, reverses the binary underlying colonial racism by replacing the negative "black" with a positive assertion of "blackness."

Post-Marxism and Postcolonialism

A criticism leveled at Said's work is that he assumes that power/knowledge is always possessed by the colonizer, while the colonized are powerless. Homi Bhabha argues that this runs counter to Foucault's idea of power/knowledge, which "places subjects in a relation of power and recognition that is not part of a symmetrical or dialectical relation – self/other, master/slave – which can then be subverted by being inverted" (Bhabha 1994: 72). As Ransom (1997) suggests, Foucault's coupling of power/knowledge refigures terrains of resistance. The idea that certain knowledge could provide a platform from which power can be denounced is revealed as illusory, as all knowledge is implicated in the will to power. Yet by revealing the productivity of power/knowledge, Foucault breaks down the "big ball of domination" and "points to the oppositional possibilities present in the tentative and shifting nature of their alliance" (Ransom 1997: 21).

However, it is precisely these possibilities which for other writers raise major concerns about the usefulness of Foucault's work for elucidating the continuing power imbalance between the cultural West and the Rest. As mentioned above, a culturalist trajectory of Marxism has been an important influence on the return of culture. Of particular significance is the work of Antonio Gramsci (1971), an Italian communist whose prison notebooks, written in the 1930s under Musso-lini's fascist regime, introduced the concept of hegemony to explain the ideologi-cal strength of bourgeois power. Gramsci focused specifically on how working-class consent in the maintenance of bourgeois control was achieved through the cultural institutions of civil society. He emphasized the role of organic intellectuals and a politicized vanguard in constructing a revolutionary consciousness. With the translation of Gramsci's work into English in the 1960s and 1970s, the notion of hegemony and the importance of culture as a site of class struggle began to transform the ways in which left-wing intellectuals conceived of challenging the dominant order. In Britain, the works of Raymond Williams (1961), E. P. Thompson (1978), and Eric Hobsbawm (1968) were crucial in laying the foundations for what is now called cultural studies. Stuart Hall and the Birmingham Centre for Contemporary Cultural Studies pioneered the appli-cation of Gramsci's ideas to the complex class, race, and gender relations constitutive of British society in the 1970s. Hall made the linkage between Gramsci and Foucault, building on their shared focus on the production of knowledge and its power (Hall 1997).

These poststructuralist formulations of Marxism are characterized by an uncomfortable marriage between hegemony and Foucault's conceptualization of discourse. The notion of hegemony assumes an emancipatory knowledge is possible, whereas Foucault's idea of discourse, as Ransom (1997: 22) explains, assumes that "[t]he role that knowledge usually plays, including in many cases the kind that claims to be emancipatory, is that of companion to the constructs of power which shape our world." While this precludes a simple recipe for universal emancipation, it allows for resistance in a more contingent, plural, and open-ended way.

The complex machinations of power and knowledge in the postcolonial era are explored in the work of Indian historian Partha Chatterjee (1986, 1993), a key member of the subaltern studies group of Indian historians. Drawing on Gram-sci's notion of hegemony, this group has explored the subaltern narratives hidden behind the hegemonic discourses of Indian nationalist history. These subaltern histories are embedded in a more continuous indigenous trajectory than the new colonial middle class, from which anticolonial nationalism emerged. Chatterjee's work traces how Indian nationalists accepted the colonial-ist critique of India as "a society fallen into barbarism and stagnation, incapable of progress or modernity," while at the same time affirming "the superiority of the East's spiritual heritage" (Chatterjee 1992: 194–5). The claims of anticolonial nationalism to a politics of emancipation are revealed as constrained by their own complicity in the discourses of Western colonialism and modernity. In Chatterjee's work, Said's arguments are extended to reveal the nuances inform-ing resistance to colonial rule. Subaltern studies, however, avoids the trap Said falls into in Orientalism (1978), by suggesting subaltern groups are not powerless

victims of a relentless colonizing discourse but remained outside the anticolon-
ial/colonial binary, as a repository of alternative indigenous conceptions of
community and identity.

Somewhat ironically, given Chatterjee's intentions, Aihwa Ong (1999) argues
that his own work continues precisely one of the binaries he accuses nationalists
and colonialism of sharing. By placing the subaltern as external to colonial
modernities and as authentic holders of counter-discourse he unwittingly dupli-
cates the tradition/modern couplet of colonizing discourse. The subaltern is
outside time, somehow managing to escape engagement with the events of
colonialism or postcolonialism. As Ong points out, "it is as if Chatterjee believes
the West is not present in Indian elites who champion narratives of the indigenous community" (Ong 1999: 34). This point can also be applied to the location
of the subaltern intellectuals themselves. Their role is assumed to be that of
unmediated representation of the subaltern voice. However, as Spivak (1988)
makes clear, the subaltern does not speak – her voice is always refracted through
the power/knowledge grid. Subaltern studies intellectuals and academics cannot
escape their own placement within this grid.

Postcolonial Feminisms

These questions of voice, location, and power have been explored extensively in
the debates between first and Third World feminists, dating back to at least the
mid-1980s. In a seminal article, Mohanty (1991) brought postcolonial and poststructuralist critiques to bear on feminist development writings. Mohanty analyzed how these writings universalized Western feminists' own particular
perspectives as normative, and essentialized Third World women as tradition-
bound victims of timeless patriarchal cultures. Thus, she charged Western
feminist scholarship with reproducing and continuing the colonizing discourses
of mainstream development. The effect was to create a stereotype of the "Third
World woman" as Other to Western woman, the latter represented in feminist
discourse as the educated liberated woman who has escaped the bonds of
tradition.

One response to postcolonial feminist critique is a relativist perspective, which
seeks to undermine the hierarchical representation of the West and the Rest by
focusing on respect for cultural difference. However, as Narayan explains, this
has its own pitfalls: "Seemingly *universal* essentialist generalizations about 'all
women' are replaced by *culture-specific* essentialist generalizations that depend
on totalizing categories ... The resulting portraits of 'Western women,' 'Third
World women,' ... or the like, as well as the pictures of the 'cultures' that are
attributed to these various groups of women, often remain fundamentally
essentialist" (Narayan 1998: 87–8). The feminist politics that results from this can
turn up some strange bedfellows. A view of cultures and identities as bounded,
coherent, and autonomous, which underlies the relativist argument, replicates
the discourse of conservative fundamentalism, which uses the same argument to
cast patriarchal practices as essential to cultural preservation (e.g., the Taliban
regime in Afghanistan). It can also stereotype feminism as a specifically Western

knowledge, leaving Third World feminists vulnerable to the charge of being cultural traitors.

Another response to postcolonial feminist critiques, which is more constructive, locates feminist agencies and culture within the grid of power/knowledge. This picks up on Bhabha's (1994) point that there are multiple relations of power and difference, such as class, race, and ethnicity. Feminist politics is then constructed out of contingent and contextual negotiations, based on the contestability of all knowledges and power relations (see especially Marchand and Parpart 1995).

Alternative Modernities

East Asia's economic development has put to the test many of the assumptions underpinning development thinking. This success has challenged beliefs that such high rates of economic growth and standards of living could be "realisable only within the framework of Occidental civilization" (Hefner 1998: 1). Many commentators have ascribed the success of these economies to the distinctive features of Confucian social ideas embedded within Chinese cultural systems (e.g., Brook and Luong 1997; Clark 1997; Sheridan 1999). Similar claims have been effectively used by political leaders, such as Singapore's Lee Kwan Yew and Malaysia's Dr. Mahathir, to argue for a distinctive set of Asian values underpinning their country's economic success and distinguishing them from Western normative modernity. Aihwa Ong argues, however, that the cultural essentialism underpinning such claims is a strategic reworking of state hegemonies and forms of governmentality, within the context of globalization and transnational flows of people and capital. There is nothing primordial about the cultural distinctiveness of "Asian values," she suggests. They are "an amalgam of indigenous ideas, Western concepts, and self-orientalizing representations by Asian leaders" (Ong 1999: 81). This is not surprising, she continues, given the geopolitical and historical construction of the Asian Pacific region by Western discourses of imperialism and capitalism. The alternative quality she identifies in Asian modernities is not a difference in content. Rather, "alternative" expresses the self-confident political assertion of Asian development as a refutation of the inevitability of Western domination.

Importantly for our arguments here, Ong sees these alternatives as distinct power/knowledge complexes in their own right, which serve to invigorate and extend state relations of ruling against the challenges of globalization and transnationalism. Hence the state in Asia is not in retreat but in strategic adaptation to the new forms of capitalist economy and cultures. Ong's depiction of Asian alternative modernities refutes the "orientalist definitions of modernity [that] suggest that modern societies 'have' culture, while non-modern societies 'are' culture" (Lowe and Lloyd 1997: 23). Here we have examples of non-Western societies employing culture to strategic political and economic purpose.

East Asia is often seen as an anomaly in an otherwise gloomy picture of worsening global inequality. We do not necessarily refute the argument regarding inequality but do dispute East Asia's anomalous status. Alternative modernities are the consequence of a long process of engagement between "the West and the Rest" framed by colonialism, imperialism, and more recently, globalization. A case in point is the deployment of witchcraft and sorcery in some contemporary African contexts. Geschiere (1998) asks the question why there is such a strong tendency in many parts of Africa for people to interpret modern processes of change in terms of witchcraft. He argues against the explanation that these are cultural residues of tradition or the effects of Western colonial stereotypes of African "superstition." Rather, he sees this as a phenomenon of the present, and cites the growth of spirit cults in Taiwan, an Asian Tiger, in support of his point. He goes on to suggest the role of globalization in this process: "Witchcraft in general is about the horrors and the enticements of new circuits of people and goods that seem to be open-ended. It is also an attempt to definitely clarify the true identity of people within one's close surroundings" (Geschiere 1998: 133; see also Appadurai 1998).

Post-development, Anti-development, and Alternative Development

So far in this Introduction, we have identified some of the new ways of looking at culture, power, and global inequality that have emerged within the social sciences over the past few decades. In this section, we briefly address how these approaches have been taken up within development studies. Foucault's notion of power/knowledge, and the work of Said and Hall, have been explored most comprehensively in Arturo Escobar's work. In *Encountering Development* (1995), he analyzes how development has operated as a discourse of power/knowledge to construct the hierarchical relationship between the First World and the Third World. He calls for a post-development praxis, arguing that "the dream of Development is over"; what is required is "not more Development, but a different regime of truth and perception" (Escobar 1992: 412–14).

The post-development position has been criticized because to date it has failed to identify what this different regime of truth might be, and how to build it. In the face of this absence, various writers (e.g., Grillo and Stirrat 1997; Jackson 1997; Pieterse 2000) have accused post-development of throwing the baby out with the bath water. By essentializing development as a unitary construct of power/knowledge, Escobar and others have discarded the alternative models of development that have emerged over the past decades. It is often precisely the local where the dream of development is most active. As Escobar (1995) discusses, a number of studies have shown how the ideals of modernity and development are dynamic parts of the social imaginaries of the majority world. In this sense, we agree with Pieterse's point that the agenda of post-development ignores the ways in which visions of development are embedded in the alternative modernities Ong (1999) and others (e.g., Pigg 1996; Reynolds 1998) describe. Pieterse suggests, therefore, that instead of post-development we should talk about alternative development, thus retaining development as a meaningful concept. However, Escobar's call for new regimes of truth is crucial to shifting the power/knowledge complex of "Development." This is the point that is missed in Pieterse's critique of post-development, which remains caught in an understanding of structural agency, either in the guise of a progressive state or radical NGOs, able to resolve development problems. Perhaps the question is not so much "So what to do?" (Pieterse 2000: 182) but rather one about the process by which agenda and action are arrived at. We disagree with the accusation made against post-development that it leads to an apolitical inertia on the part of development activists, alternative or otherwise. What it does mean is that a radical praxis of engagement with global inequality and poverty must begin with addressing its own embeddedness in relations of power/knowledge that are themselves constitutive of global inequality (Schech and Haggis 2000).

Again, feminist scholars are leading the way in addressing these issues. Ann Ferguson's (1998) idea of "building bridge identities" is an attempt to overcome the expert trap by which progressive development practitioners are caught in the pincers of development discourse and development institutions. Self-reflexivity is, she argues, a necessary aspect of any practitioner approach to participatory development processes. This means confronting the dominant aspects of one's own identity and revealing its "horizons of ignorance," as a prelude to according a critical authority to "other knowledges" to "talk back" in ways which give full meaning to democratic participatory development processes. Ferguson's feminist approach arrives at a similar point to that of post-development theorists in that they both emphasize the necessity to particularize and localize the theory and practice of what we currently call development.

Locating the Reader

This Introduction provides a background to the readings we have selected for this book. The process of selecting from a rich and diverse field was, as ever, a difficult one. We were guided by the Reader's companion volume, *Culture and Development: A Critical Introduction* (Schech and Haggis 2000), which provides a much fuller exegesis of the ways in which cultural studies, postcolonial critiques, and poststructuralism have brought home the extent to which culture is deeply embedded in visions of development. Key texts discussed in that book are included in the present volume. However, the Reader has been organized to reflect the thematic areas these literatures open up, rather than following the structure of the companion volume. In this way, we seek to avoid the compartmentalization that a book structure necessarily imposes on any subject matter, as well as seeking to make the Reader useful to a broader audience. Thus, rather than having a separate section in the Reader on feminist writings, we decided to highlight the contribution of these feminist texts to broader debates. We thought long and hard whether to include a separate section on post-development and its responses, but concluded that this area of debate is in its early stages, and the field is changing rapidly. Hence our section in this Introduction attempts instead to pinpoint some of the current contributions to this field and provide a guide for readers who wish to pursue it further.

References

Alatas, S. H. 1977: *The Myth of the Lazy Native: A Study of the Image of the Malays, Filipinos and Javanese from the 16th to the 20th Century and its Function in the Ideology of Colonial Capitalism*. London: F. Cass.

Appadurai, A. 1998: "Dead Certainty: Ethnic Violence in the Era of Globalization." *Development and Change* 29, 905–25.

Bauman, Z. 1973: *Culture as Praxis*. London: Routledge and Kegan Paul.

Bhabha, H. 1994: *Locations of Culture*. London: Routledge.

Brook, T. and Luong, H. V. 1997: *Culture and Economy: The Shaping of Capitalism in Eastern Asia*. Ann Arbor: University of Michigan Press.

Chatterjee, P. 1986: *Nationalist Thought and the Colonial World: A Derivative Discourse*. London: Zed Books.

Chatterjee, P. 1992: "Their Own Words? An Essay for Edward Said." In M. Sprinker (ed.), *Edward Said: A Critical Reader*. Cambridge, MA: Blackwell, 194–220.

Chatterjee, P. 1993: *The Nation and its Fragments: Colonial and Postcolonial Histories*. Princeton, NJ: Princeton University Press.

Clark, C. 1997: *Comparing Development Patterns in Asia*. Boulder, CO: Lynne Rienner.

Escobar, A. 1992: "Reflections of 'Development: Grassroots Approaches and Alternative Politics in the Third World'". *Alternatives* 10, 411–36.

Escobar, A. 1995: *Encountering Development: The Making and Unmaking of the Third World*. Princeton, NJ: Princeton University Press.

Fanon, F. 1968: *Black Skin, White Masks*, trans. Charles Lam Markmann. London: MacGibbon and Kee.

Ferguson, A. 1998: "Resisting the Veil of Privilege: Building Bridge Identities as an Ethico-politics of Global Feminisms." *Hypatia: Special Issue. Border Crossings: Multicultural and Postcolonial Feminist Challenges to Philosophy, Part 2*, 13 (3), 95–114.

Foucault, M. 1985: *The Order of Things: An Archaeology of the Human Sciences*. London: Tavistock Press.

Frow, J. and Morris, M. (eds.) 1993: *Australian Cultural Studies: A Reader*. St. Leonards, NSW: Allen and Unwin.

Geschiere, P. 1998: "Globalization and the Power of Intermediate Meaning: Witchcraft and Spirit Cults in Africa and East Asia." *Development and Change* 29, 811–37.

Gramsci, A. 1971: *Selections from the Prison Notebooks*. New York: International Publishers.

Grillo, R. D. 1997: "Discourses of Development: The View from Anthropology." In R. D. Grillo and R. L. Stirrat (eds.), *Discourses of Development: Anthropological Perspectives*. Oxford: Berg, 1–34.

Grillo, R. D. and Stirrat, R. L. (eds.) 1997: *Discourses of Development: Anthropological Perspectives*. Oxford: Berg.

Haggis, J. and Schech, S. 2000: "Meaning Well and Global Good Manners: Reflections on White Western Feminist Cross-cultural Praxis." *Australian Feminist Studies* 16, 387–99.

Hall, S. 1992: "The West and the Rest: Discourse and Power." In S. Hall and B. Gieben (eds.), *Formations of Modernity*. Cambridge: Polity Press.

Hall, S. (ed.) 1997: *Representation: Cultural Representations and Signifying Practices*. London: Sage/The Open University.

Hefner, R. W. 1998: "Introduction: Society and Morality in the New Asian Capitalisms." In R. W. Hefner (ed.), *Market Cultures: Society and Morality in the New Asian Capitalisms*. St. Leonards, NSW: Allen and Unwin, 1–40.

Hirschmann, N. J. 1998: "Western Feminism, Eastern Veiling, and the Question of Free Agency." *Constellations* 5 (3), 345–68.

Hobsbawm, E. 1968: *Industry and Empire*. London: Weidenfeld and Nicolson.

Huntington, S. 1996: *The Clash of Civilizations and the Remaking of World Order*. New York: Simon and Schuster.

Jackson, C. 1997: "Post-poverty, Gender and Development?" *Institute of Development Studies (IDS) Bulletin* 28 (3), 145–53.

Lim, T. G. 1976: *Peasants and their Agricultural Economy in Colonial Malaya, 1874–1941*. Kuala Lumpur and New York: Oxford University Press.

Lowe, L. and Lloyd, D. 1997: Introduction. In L. Lowe and D. Lloyd (eds.), *The Politics of Culture in the Shadow of Capital*. Durham, NC: Duke University Press, 1–32.

Marchand, M. H. and Parpart, J. (eds.) 1995: *Feminism/Postmodernism/Development*. London and New York: Routledge.

Mohanty, C. T. 1991: "Under Western Eyes: Feminist Scholarship and Colonial Discourses." In C. T. Mohanty, A. Russo, and L. Torres (eds.), *Third World Women and the Politics of Feminism*. Bloomington and Indianapolis: Indiana University Press, 51–80. (Earlier versions were published in *Boundary 2*, 12 (3)/13 (1) (Fall/Spring 1984) and in *Feminist Review* 30, 61–88 (Autumn 1988).)

Narayan, U. 1998: "Essence of Culture and a Sense of History: A Feminist Critique of Cultural Essentialism." *Hypatia: Special Issue. Border Crossings: Multicultural and Postcolonial Feminist Challenges to Philosophy, Part 1*, 13 (2), 86–107.

Ong, A. 1999: *Flexible Citizenship: The Cultural Logics of Transnationality*. Durham, NC: Duke University Press.

Pieterse, J. Nederveen 2000: "After Post-development." *Third World Quarterly* 21 (2), 175–91.

Pigg, S. L. 1996: "The Credible and the Credulous: The Question of 'Villager's Beliefs' in Nepal." *Cultural Anthropology* 11 (2), 160–201.

Ransom, J. S. 1997: *Foucault's Discipline*. Durham, NC: Duke University Press.

Reynolds, C. J. 1998: "Globalization and Cultural Nationalism in Modern Thailand." In J. S. Kahn (ed.), *Southeast Asian Identities: Culture and the Politics of Representation in Indonesia, Malaysia, Singapore, and Thailand*. London and New York: I. B. Tauris; Singapore: Institute of Southeast Asian Studies, 115–45.

Said, E. W. 1995: *Orientalism*. London: Penguin. (First published in 1978.)

Schech, S. and Haggis, J. 2000: *Culture and Development. A Critical Introduction*. Oxford: Blackwell.

Sheridan, G. 1999: *Asian Values, Western Dreams: Understanding the New Asia*. St. Leonards, NSW: Allen and Unwin.

Spivak, G. C. 1988: "Can the Subaltern Speak?" In C. Nelson and L. Grossberg (eds.), *Marxism and the Interpretation of Cultures*. Illinois: University of Illinois Press, 271–316.

Thompson, E. P. 1978: *The Poverty of Theory, and Other Essays*. London: Merlin Press.

Williams, R. 1961: *The Long Revolution*. London: Chatto and Windus.

Part I

Modernizing Cultures

Introduction

The question of how development processes change the social and cultural makeup of countries has been an important focus of some strands in development studies, particularly in the modernization school that dominated the 1950s and 1960s. While analyses of developing societies in that period were much broader than the more constricted emphasis on political and economic development that followed in subsequent decades, they were based on the assumption that modern and traditional societies could be defined as each other's opposites. The differences between modern and traditional societies were explained in terms of deeply embedded cultural traits. Thus the traditional traits of Third World societies were thought to dissolve through contact with modernity. Daniel Lerner, a sociologist of Middle Eastern societies, worked with this dichotomy in his study of the small village of Balgat, then located on the outskirts of the Turkish city of Ankara. In Balgat, Lerner had identified a microcosm of what was happening throughout the Middle East. In an introduction to Lerner's study, David Riesman describes Lerner's use of the modern/traditional dichotomy as sophisticated:

> Mr Lerner's cast of characters puts the Moderns on the one side – they are cosmopolitan, urban, literate, usually well-off, and seldom devout – and the Traditionals on the other side – they are just the opposite. But in between he puts several categories of transitionals: people who share some of the empathy and psychic mobility of the Moderns while lacking essential components of the Modern style, notably literacy. These Transitionals are the men in motion. (Riesman 1958: 13)

While Lerner represents the North American version of the modernization school in this Reader, Gunnar Myrdal's work stands for the European, social-democratic interpretations of this theoretical strand. His three-volume work, *The Asian Drama*, represents one of the most influential modernization studies on South Asia undertaken in this period, and is characterized by a keen awareness of how class differences and power relations affect the exposure to and diffusion of modernization ideals. In the excerpt chosen here he outlines the "modernization ideals" which form the value premises for this study. These ideals, which stem from the European Enlightenment, had been introduced to the people of South Asia during colonial times, and had become the "official creed" of the new nationalisms after independence. In the first part of the extract Myrdal reflects on the barriers of caste, color, religion, ethnic origin, and so on which prevent the diffusion of modernization ideals from the intellectual elite to the broader population. The second part focuses on those ideals that Myrdal relates to improving social and economic institutions and attitudes, in what he sees as a social revolution that will produce the "modern man."

The third extract in this section is from Samuel Huntington's recent work on the "clash of civilizations." An American political scientist, Huntington has occupied an important place in the political development studies literature since the 1960s, when he was engaged in debates over what political structures were most appropriate for modernizing and developing nations (Huntington 1968). In the extract reproduced here, Huntington argues for a differentiation between modernization and Westernization, pointing out that the concept of a universal civilization is a product of Western civilization, and finds little support in other civilizations. In arguing that non-Western societies, such as Japan, Singapore, and China, are embracing modernity without becoming Western, Huntington retains the Modernization School's view of culture as a bounded and coherent entity which is acted upon by the forces of modernization (Schech and Haggis 2000: 40).

The extract from Robert Weller considers the Asian values debate over the nature of East Asian capitalism. He argues that there is no such entity as a singular core of Asian values shared by all in any given society. He thus differs from Huntington in emphasizing the plural and contested nature of culture in Asian societies, and their long history of contact with the West. Weller also refutes the modernization thesis of cultural convergence implicit in Lerner's account of change in Turkey. Taking Chinese societies as an example, he instead argues that their ability to develop thriving market economies rest on successfully fostering some Chinese cultural resources, and burying others.

References

Huntington, S. P. 1968: *Political Order in Changing Societies*. New Haven, CT: Yale University Press.
Riesman, D. 1958: "Introduction." In D. Lerner, *The Passing of Traditional Society*. Glencoe, IL: Free Press.
Schech, S. and Haggis, J. 2000: *Culture and Development. A Critical Introduction*. Oxford: Blackwell.

1 The Grocer and the Chief: A Parable

Daniel Lerner

The village of Balgat lies about eight kilometers out of Ankara, in the southerly direction. It does not show on the standard maps and it does not figure in the standard histories. I first heard of it in the autumn of 1950 and most Turks have not heard of it today. Yet the story of the Middle East today is encapsulated in the recent career of Balgat. Indeed the personal meaning of modernization in underdeveloped lands can be traced, in miniature, through the lives of two Balgati – The Grocer and The Chief.

My first exposure to Balgat came while leafing through several hundred interviews that had been recorded in Turkey during the spring of 1950. [. . .] Four years later an oversize manuscript on the modernizing Middle East was in hand. To see how close a fit to Middle East reality was given by our picture of it, I went out for a self-guided tour and final round of interviews in the spring of 1954. My odyssey terminated where my ideas originated: in Balgat, on the eve of a second national election. With Balgat, then, our account begins.

Balgat Perceived: 1950

The interviewer who recorded Balgat on the verge – his name was Tosun B. – had detected no gleam of the future during his sojourn there. "The village is a barren one," he wrote. "The main color is gray, so is the dust on the divan on which I am writing now." Tosun was a serious young scholar from Ankara and he loved the poor in his own fashion. He had sought out Balgat to find the deadening past rather than the brave new world. He found it:

Excerpted from D. Lerner, "The Grocer and the Chief: A Parable." In *The Passing of Traditional Society: Modernizing the Middle East* (New York: Free Press, 1958), 19–43.

> I have seen quite a lot of villages in the barren mountainous East, but never such a colourless, shapeless dump. This was the reason I chose the village. It could have been half an hour to Ankara by car if it had a road, yet it is about two hours to the capital by car without almost any road and is just forgotten, forsaken, right under our noses.

Tosun also sought and found persons to match the place. Of the five villagers he interviewed, his heart went straight out to the village shepherd. What Tosun was looking for in this interview is clear from his *obiter dicta*:

> It was hard to explain to the village Chief that I wanted to interview the poorest soul in the village. He, after long discussions, consented me to interview the shepherd, but did not permit him to step into the guest-room. He said it would be an insult to me, so we did the interview in someone else's room, I did not quite understand whose. The Chief did not want to leave me alone with the respondent, but I succeeded at the end. This opened the respondent's sealed mouth, for he probably felt that I, the superior even to his chief, rather be alone with him.

When the shepherd's sealed mouth had been opened, little came out. But Tosun was deeply stirred:

> The respondent was literally in rags and in this cold weather he had no shoe, but the mud and dirt on his feet were as thick as any boot. He was small, but looked rugged and sad, very sad. He was proud of being chosen by me and though limited tried his best to answer the questions. Was so bashful that his blush was often evident under the thick layer of dirt on his face. He at times threw loud screams of laughter when there was nothing to laugh about. These he expected to be accepted as answers, for when I said "Well?" he was shocked, as if he had already answered the question.

His frustration over the shepherd was not the only deprivation Tosun attributed to the Chief, who "imposed himself on me all the time I was in the village, even tried to dictate to me, which I refused in a polite way. I couldn't have followed his directions as I would have ended up only interviewing his family." Tosun did succeed in talking privately with two Balgat farmers, but throughout these interviews he was still haunted by the shepherd and bedevilled by the Chief. Not until he came to interview the village Grocer did Tosun find another Balgati who aroused in him a comparable antipathy. Tosun's equal hostility to these very different men made me curious. It was trying to explain this that got me obsessed, sleeping and waking over the next four years, with the notion that the parable of modern Turkey was the story of The Grocer and The Chief. [. . .]

The Chief was a man of few words on many subjects. He dismissed most of the items on Tosun's schedule with a shrug or its audible equivalent. But he was also a man of many words on a few subjects – those having to do with the primary modes of human deportment. [. . .]

The Chief has so little trouble with first principles because he desires to be, and usually is, a vibrant soundbox through which echo the traditional Turkish virtues. His themes are obedience, courage, loyalty – the classic values of the Ottoman Imperium reincarnate in the Atatürk Republic. For the daily round of village life these are adequate doctrine; and as the Chief has been outside of his village only to fight in two wars he has never found his austere code wanting.

This congruence of biography with ideology explains the Chief's confidence in his own moral judgment and his short definition of a man. When asked what he wished for his two grown sons, for example, the Chief replied promptly: "I hope they will fight as bravely as we fought and know how to die as my generation did." [. . .]

With his life in Balgat, as with the Orphic wisdom that supplies its rationale, the Chief is contented. At 63 his desires have been quieted and his ambitions achieved. To Tosun's question on contentment he replied with another question:

> What could be asked more? God has brought me to this mature age without much pain, has given me sons and daughters, has put me at the head of my village, and has given me strength of brain and body at this age. Thanks be to Him.

The Grocer is a very different style of man. Though born and bred in Balgat, he lives in a different world, an expansive world, populated more actively with imaginings and fantasies – hungering for whatever is different and unfamiliar. Where the Chief is contented, the Grocer is restless. To Tosun's probe, the Grocer replied staccato: "I have told you I want better things. I would have liked to have a bigger grocery shop in the city, have a nice house there, dress nice civilian clothes."

Where the Chief audits his life placidly, makes no comparisons, thanks God, the Grocer evaluates his history in a more complicated and other-involved fashion. He perceives his story as a drama of Self *versus* Village. He compares his virtue with others and finds them lacking: "I am not like the others here. They don't know any better. And when I tell them, they are angry and they say that I am ungrateful for what Allah has given me." The Grocer's struggle with Balgat was, in his script, no mere conflict of personalities. His was the lonely struggle of a single man to open the village mind. Clearly, from the readiness and consistency of his responses to most questions, he had brooded much over his role. He had a keen sense of the limits imposed by reality: "I am born a grocer and probably die that way. I have not the possibility in myself to get the things I want. They only bother me." But desire, once stirred, is not easily stilled. [. . .]

To get out of his hole the Grocer even declared himself ready – and in this he was quite alone in Balgat – to live outside of Turkey. This came out when Tosun asked another of his projective questions: "If you could not live in Turkey, where would you want to live?" The standard reply of the villagers was that they would not live, could not imagine living, anywhere else. The forced choice simply was ignored.

When Tosun persisted ("Suppose you *had* to leave Turkey?") he teased an extreme reaction out of some Balgati. The shepherd, like several other wholly routinized personalities, finally replied that he would rather kill himself. The constricted peasant can more easily imagine destroying the self than relocating it in an unknown, i.e. frightful, setting.

The Chief again responded with the clear and confident voice of traditional man. "Nowhere," he said. "I was born here, grew old here, and hope God will permit me to die here." To Tosun's probe, the Chief replied firmly: "I wouldn't move a foot from here." Only the Grocer found no trouble in imagining himself outside of Turkey, living in a strange land. Indeed he seemed fully prepared, as a man does when he has already posed a question to himself many times. "America," said the Grocer, and, without waiting for Tosun to ask him why, stated his reason: "because I have heard that it is a nice country, and with possibilities to be rich even for the simplest persons."

Such opinions clearly marked off the Grocer, in the eyes of the villagers around him, as heterodox and probably infidel. The vivid sense of cash displayed by the Grocer was a grievous offense against Balgat ideas of tabu talk. In the code regulating the flow of symbols among Anatolian villagers, blood and sex are permissible objects of passion but money is not. To talk much of money is an impropriety. To reveal excessive *desire* for money is – Allah defend us! – an impiety.[1] [. . .]

At the time of Tosun's visit, there was only one radio in Balgat, owned by no less a personage than the Chief. In the absence of any explicit orthodox prohibition on radio, the Chief, former soldier and great admirer of Atatürk, had followed his lead. Prosperous by village standards, being the large landowner of Balgat, he had bought a radio to please and instruct his sons. He had also devised an appropriate ceremonial for its use. Each evening a select group of Balgati foregathered in the Chief's guest room as he turned on the newscast from Ankara. They heard the newscast through in silence and, at its conclusion, the Chief turned the radio off and made his commentary. "We all listen very carefully," he told Tosun, "and I talk about it afterwards." Tosun, suspecting in this procedure a variant of the Chief's containment tactics, wanted to know whether there was any disagreement over his explanations. "No, no arguments," replied the Chief, "as I tell you I only talk and our opinions are the same more or less." Here was a new twist in the ancient role of knowledge as power. Sensing the potential challenge from radio, the Chief restricted the dangers of innovation by partial incorporation, thus retaining and strengthening his role as Balgat's official opinion leader.

Tosun inquired of the Grocer, an occasional attendant at the Chief's salon, how he liked this style of radio session. The grocer, a heretic perhaps but not a foolhardy one, made on this point the shortest statement in his entire interview: "The Chief is clever and he explains the news." Only obliquely, by asking what the Grocer liked best about radio, did Tosun get an answer that had the true resonance. Without challenging the Chief's preference for news of "wars and the danger of wars" – in fact an exclusive interest in the Korean War, to which a Turkish brigade had just been committed – the Grocer indicated that after all *he* had opportunities to listen in the coffee-houses of Ankara, where the audiences exhibited a more cosmopolitan range of interests. "It is nice to know what is happening in the other capitals of the world," said the Grocer. "We are stuck in this hole, we have to know what is going on outside our village." [. . .]

Balgat Revisited: 1954

I reached Ankara in April after a circuitous route through the Middle East. The glories of Greece, Egypt, Lebanon, Syria, Persia touched me only lightly, for some part of me was already in Balgat. Even the Blue Mosque and St. Sophia seemed pallid, and I left Istanbul three days ahead of schedule for Ankara. I had saved this for last, and now here I was. I was half afraid to look.

I called a transportation service and explained that I wanted to go out the following day, a Sunday, to a village some eight kilometers south that might be hard to reach. As I wanted to spend the day, would the driver meet me at 8 a.m. and bring along his lunch?

While waiting for the car, next morning, my reverie wandered back through the several years since my first reading of the Balgat interviews. Was I chasing a phantom? Tahir S. appeared. With solitude vanished anxiety; confidently we began to plan the day. Tahir had been a member of the original interview team, working in the Izmir area. As Tosun had joined the Turkish foreign service and was stationed in North Africa, where he was conducting an inquiry among the Berbers, I had arranged in advance for Tahir to revisit Balgat with me in his place. Over a cup of syrupy coffee, we reviewed the questions that had been asked in 1950, noted the various responses and silences, decided the order in which we would repeat the old questions and interpolate the new ones.

As the plan took shape, Zilla K. arrived. She had no connection with the original survey, but I wanted a female interviewer who could add some Balgat women to our gallery. I had "ordered" her, through a colleague at Ankara University, "by the numbers": thirtyish, semi-trained, alert, compliant with instructions, not sexy enough to impede our relations with the men of Balgat but chic enough to provoke the women. A glance and a word showed that Zilla filled the requisition. We brought her into the plan of operations. The hall porter came in to say our car was waiting. We got in and settled back for a rough haul. Twenty minutes later, as we were still debating the niceties of question-wording and reporting procedure, the driver said briskly: "There's Balgat."

We looked puzzled at each other until Tosun's words of 1950 recurred to *us*: "It could have been half an hour to Ankara if it had a road." Now it did have a road. What was more, a *bus* was coming down the road, heading toward us from the place our driver had called Balgat. As it passed, jammed full, none of the passengers waved or even so much as stuck out a tongue at us. Without these unfailing signs of villagers out on a rare chartered bus, to celebrate a great occasion of some sort, we could only make the wild guess that Balgat had acquired a regular bus service. And indeed, as we entered the village, there it was – a "bus station," freshly painted benches under a handsome new canopy. We got out and looked at the printed schedule of trips. "The bus leaves every hour, on the hour, to Ulus Station. Fare: 20 Kuruş." For about 4 cents, Balgati could now go, whenever they felt the whim, to Ulus in the heart of Ankara. The villagers were getting out of their holes at last. The Grocer, I thought, must be grinning over the fat canary he had swallowed.

We took a quick turn around the village, on our way to check in with the Chief. Things looked different from what Tosun's report had led us to expect. Overhead wires were stretched along the road, with branch lines extended over the houses of Balgat. The village had been electrified. Alongside the road deep ditches had been dug, in which the graceful curve of new water pipe was visible. Purified water was coming to Balgat. There were many more buildings than the

50-odd Tosun had counted, and most of them looked new. Two larger ones announced themselves as a school and a police station. An inscription on the latter revealed that Balgat was now under the jurisdiction of the Ankara district police. They had finally got rid of the *gendarmerie*, scavengers of the Anatolian village and historic blight on the peasant's existence. [. . .]

In Balgat I reported directly to the Chief. He appeared, after a few minutes, steaming and mopping his large forehead. He had been pruning some trees and, in this warm weather, such work brought the sweat to his brow. This was about the only work he did any more, he explained, as he had sold or rented most of his land in the last few years, keeping for himself only the ground in which he had planted a small grove of trees that would be his memorial on earth. Islamic peoples regard a growing and "eternal" thing of nature, preferably a tree, as a fitting monument, and a comfortable Muslim of even diffident piety will usually be scrupulous in observing this tradition – a sensible one for a religion of the desert, where vegetation is rare and any that casts a shade is especially prized. The Chief agreed to show me his trees and as we strolled away from the house he resumed his discourse of yesterday.

Things had changed, he repeated, and a sign of the gravity of these changes was that he – of a lineage that had always been *Muhtars* and landowners – was no longer a farmer. Nor was he long to be *Muhtar*. After the coming election, next month, the incorporation of Balgat into Greater Ankara was to be completed and thereafter it would be administered under the general municipal system. "I am the last *Muhtar* of Balgat, and I am happy that I have seen Balgat end its history in this way that we are going." The new ways, then, were not bringing evil with them?

> No, people will have to get used to different ways and then some of the excesses, particularly among the young, will disappear. The young people are in some ways a serious disappointment; they think more of clothes and good times than they do of duty and family and country. But it is to be hoped that as the *Demokrat* men complete the work they have begun, the good Turkish ways will again come forward to steady the people. Meanwhile, it is well that people can have to eat and to buy shoes they always needed but could not have.

And as his two sons were no longer to be farmers, what of them? The Chief's voice did not change, nor did his eyes cloud over, as he replied:

> They are as the others. They think first to serve themselves and not the nation. They had no wish to go to the battle in Korea, where Turkey fights before the eyes of all the world. They are my sons and I speak no ill of them, but I say only that they are as all the others.

I felt at this moment a warmth toward the Chief which I had not supposed he would permit himself to evoke. His sons had not, after all, learned to fight bravely and die properly. His aspiration which had led him, four years earlier, to buy a radio so his sons would hear the Korean war news and to see movies that would make them "wish more and more their time for military service would come" – had not been fulfilled. Yet the old Chief bore stoically what must have been a crushing disappointment. These two sons through whom he had hoped to relive his own bright dreams of glory had instead become *shopkeepers*.

The elder son owned a grocery store and the younger one owned Balgat's first clothing store. With this news, curiosity overcame sympathy. I rattled off questions on this subject which, clearly, the Chief would rather have changed. As we turned back to the house, he said we would visit the shops after lunch and his sons would answer all my questions. [. . .]

We went first to the elder son's grocery store, just across the road and alongside the village "fountain," where Balgat women did the family wash as in ages past (though this would pass when the new municipal water supply became available at reasonable rates). The central floor space was set out with merchandise in the immemorial manner – heavy, rough, anonymous hemp sacks each laden with a commodity requiring no identity card, groats in one and barley in another, here lentils and there chicory. But beyond the sacks was a distinct innovation, a counter. What is more, the counter turned a corner and ran parallel to two sides of the square hut. Built into it was a cash drawer and above each surface a hygienic white porcelain fixture for fluorescent lighting. Along the walls was the crowning glory – rows of shelves running from "top to floor and side to side, and on them standing myriads of round boxes, clean and all the same, dressed like soldiers in a great parade." The Grocer's words of aspiration came leaping back as I looked admiringly around the store. His dream-house had been built in Balgat – in less time than even he might have forecast – and by none other than the Chief! [. . .]

The afternoon was about over before I got an appropriate occasion to ask about the Grocer. It came when the talk returned to the villagers' favorite topic of how much better life had become during the past four years of *Demokrat* rule. Again they illustrated the matter by enumerating the new shops in Balgat and the things they had to sell that many people could buy. There was even a new barber shop, opened last month by the son of the late Altemur after going for some time to Ankara as apprentice. "How are these new grocery shops better than the old grocery shop of years ago owned by the fat grocer who is now dead?" I asked. The line of response was obvious in advance, but the question served to lead to another: What sort of man had the Grocer been?

The answers were perfunctory, consisting mainly of *pro forma* expressions of goodwill toward the departed. I tried to get back of these ritual references by indirection. How had the Grocer dressed? Why had he been so interested in the life of Ankara? The light finally shone in one of the wiser heads and he spoke the words I was seeking:

> Ah, he was the cleverest of us all. We did not know it then, but he saw better than all what lay in the path ahead. We have none like this among us now. He was a prophet.

As I look back on it now, my revisit to Balgat ended then. I went back several times, once with gifts for the Chief's grandchildren, another time with my camera (as he had coyly suggested) to take his picture. On these visits I felt less tense, asked fewer questions, than during the earlier visits. The last time I went out with the publisher of a prominent Istanbul newspaper ("The New York Times of Turkey"), a dedicated *Demokrat* man, who was eager to see the transformed village I had described to him. He was enchanted with the Chief, the stores, the bus service and electricity and other symbols of the history into which his party had ushered Balgat. He decided to write a feature story about it and asked permission to call it "Professor Lerner's Village." I declined, less from modesty than a sense of anachronism. The Balgat his party needed was the suburb inhabited by the sons of the Chief, with their swaddled children and their proud new clock, their male "corners" and their retail stores, their filiopie-tistic silence and their movies that teach excitement. The ancient village I had known for what now seemed only four short years was passing, had passed. The Grocer was dead. The Chief – "the last *Muhtar* of Balgat" – had reincarnated the Grocer in the flesh of his sons. Tosun was in North Africa studying the Berbers.

Note

1   Silence does not obviate desire. In Turkish villages it is customary for the head of household to bury his hoard of metal coins in a secret garden spot; when he dies there is a frenzied treasure hunt for the cache. Tabu on talk, as Freud suggested, is a way of inhibiting the passage from desires to deeds. Traditional men, like the wise monkeys, find it safer to see no evil, speak no evil, hear no evil. This particular custom has the practical merit of restricting plans for a treasure hunt while papa is still alive.

2 Modernization Ideals

Gunnar Myrdal

[. . .] We shall use as a starting point the incontrovertible fact that the basic social and economic structure of the countries of South Asia is radically different from that existing in advanced Western countries. Conditions in the rich Western countries today are such that, broadly speaking, the social matrix is permissive of economic development or, when not, becomes readily readjusted so as not to place much in the way of obstacles in its path. This is why an analysis in "economic" terms, abstracting from that social matrix, can produce valid and useful results. But that judgment cannot be accurately applied to South Asian conditions. Not only is the social and institutional structure different from the one that has evolved in Western countries, but, more important, the problem of development in South Asia is one calling for induced changes in that social and institutional structure, as it hinders economic development and as it does not change spontaneously, or, to any very large extent, in response to policies restricted to the "economic" sphere.

This view, of course, has been implicit in our criticism of the adequacy of Western conceptual approaches and it forms the essential preconception running through the body of this study. We do not preclude the possibility that, at a future date, the institutional structure of the South Asian countries may be such that some of the Western tools of analysis, at present woefully inadequate, will come into their own. Neither this possibility nor a defense sometimes offered for the current use of Western concepts – their potentiality for defining the targets these countries are seeking to hit – justifies the use of modern Western preconceptions now. The essential first step toward an understanding of the problems of the South Asian countries is to try to discover how they actually function and

Excerpted from Gunnar Myrdal, *Asian Drama: An Inquiry into the Poverty of Nations* (New York: The Twentieth Century Fund, 1968), vol. 1.

what mechanisms regulate their performance. Failure to root analysis firmly in these realities invites both distortions in research and faults in planning.

So our approach is broadly "institutional," and we plead for greatly intensified research efforts along these lines. We should remember that to be really fruitful this new approach cannot be restricted to the insertion of qualifications and reservations meant to take into account the things left out by conventional economic analysis along Western lines. As the very theories and concepts utilized in that analysis guide it away from those "non-economic" factors, what is needed is a different framework of theories and concepts that is more realistic for those societies.[1] [. . .]

[. . .] One might have expected the behavioral disciplines, particularly social anthropology and sociology, to provide the more broadly based system of theories and concepts needed for the scientific study of the problem of development. Unfortunately, they have not done so. The tradition of social anthropology has been to work in static terms, attempting to explain the structure and internal relations of societies in what we now call a state of stagnation or "low-level equilibrium." Much sociological research has remained within this tradition. It is, for instance, surprising how little attention has been devoted in village surveys to the effects of population increase on social stratification. And when studies in these disciplines are focused on change, as they increasingly are, the emphasis is not often placed on development, much less on framing a more comprehensive system of theories and concepts suited to the needs of the planner.

For this there may seem to be an obvious explanation, that the factors abstracted from in the economic analysis – attitudes, institutions, modes and levels of living, and, broadly, culture – are so much more difficult to grasp in systematic analysis than are the so-called economic factors. They undoubtedly are. But if the view propounded in [*Asian Drama*] is correct, it simply follows that the problems of underdevelopment, development, and *planning for* development in South Asia are themselves exceedingly difficult and that they have yet to be mastered. An artificial restriction of "reality" to that which is seemingly easier to grasp misses the central point. For in the South Asian countries the "economic" facts cannot be studied in isolation from other social facts. [. . .]

The Set of Value Premises Selected for This Study:
The Modernization Ideals

Among all the heterogeneous and conflicting valuations that exist in the countries of the region, we have deliberately selected the new ones directed toward "modernization"; they are specified in the next section. These valuations, which for brevity we label "the modernization ideals," were impressed on the nations of South Asia in the Great Awakening following independence, though people there had been gradually conditioned to them by influences from the Western world during colonial times, and more recently by influences from the Soviet Union. They have become the "official creed," almost a national religion, and are one of the powerful strands of the "new nationalism."

Even before independence, the modernization ideals were prominent in the programs of the liberation movements. Later they were often inscribed in the new constitutions. They now appear as the declared main goals in the development plans with which all the countries of the region are equipped and in the introductions to reports by public commissions and committees considering questions of major reform. The programs and general pronouncements of the various political parties regularly adhere to them, or at least avoid contradicting them. They are reiterated in speeches, in leading articles in the press, and in the textbooks for schools and universities. They have, indeed, infiltrated the vocabulary of public discussion. In choosing these ideals as the value premises for our study we are, in a sense, taking these nations, or rather those who speak for them, at their word.

Although the relative homogeneity of this system of valuations is evident, there are differences among the countries in the region and among groups in a single country. The modernization ideals are expressed more clearly and are less confused with other valuations of the traditional type in India, Pakistan, Ceylon, and the Philippines than in Indonesia and Burma. In particular, emphasis on the several elements of the creed varies. In terms of the conventional Western axis of conservatism–radicalism, Pakistan, the Federation of Malaya, Thailand, and the Philippines give a more conservative slant to the modernization ideals, while the official creed of India, Ceylon, Burma, and Indonesia tends to be more radical. There are also movements in time along this axis. At least until recently, Ceylon and, perhaps, Indonesia have moved toward the left, as has Burma, which for a time had tended toward the right. On the whole, India is still moving toward the left in public declarations, though hardly in practical politics.

Viewed in the light of prevailing conditions, however, the creed is radical throughout the South Asian countries, for even modest realization of the ideals would drastically change their economic, social, and political conditions. In fact, when abstractly presented – and very general pronouncements are much more common in South Asia than in the West – the modernization ideals are there ordinarily stated with a more radical flair. On this point there is an interesting parallel with the era of Enlightenment in the Western countries, when radical ideals – notably, but not exclusively, concerning equality – were commonly expressed more uncompromisingly in the literature than at present, although their society was much further from the realization of these ideals than is ours.[2]

As a matter of fact, it turns out that this official creed of the South Asian countries is composed mainly of the ideals long cherished in the Western world as the heritage of the Enlightenment and more recently realized to a large extent in the "created harmony" of the welfare state. These valuations have a long-standing association with thinking in the social sciences, particularly economics, though always with serious opportune compromises and even deviations, and without the methodological clarity of being stated as value premises.[3]

We have noted the relative heterogeneity of the official creed among countries and among groups of intellectuals within the countries. On the general level of valuations, where this creed exists, the ideals are also somewhat vague and indeterminate; at times, moreover, they are internally inconsistent. These logical deficiencies are part of the reality that must be faced; they cannot be disposed of by conceptual tricks that tidy the argument.[4] They indicate that the valuation viewpoint is not really a point but rather a limited space within which the key concepts are often blurred at the edges.

The modernization ideals are mainly the ideology of the politically alert, articulate, and active part of the population – particularly the intellectual elite. The judgments that follow refer to the opinions of these groups. Though their members are trying to spread their ideology to the whole educated class and to the masses of the population, their success in accomplishing this should not be exaggerated. The inclinations of the broader strata of the population, as yet only partially touched by the Great Awakening, greatly influence the prospects for initiating and implementing policies that conform to the modernization ideals. At least the masses can resist and create obstacles.

And we should also be aware that the modernization ideals have to compete with conflicting valuations. Even politically alert and active members of the educated class are often of two minds and engage in awkward and frustrating mental compromises. Although such conflicts are characteristic of ideologies of this nature,[5] in South Asia they are magnified by the vast distance between ideals and reality.

It should be stressed that endowing the modernization ideals with the technical function of serving as value premises for our study does not, in itself, say more about actual valuations and power relations in the countries under study than that these ideals are relevant because they are present among these actual valuations and that they have that significance of being held, or at least expressed, by social strata which exert most of the political power. Still less does this choice imply any *a priori* assumption that events must go in the direction of the realization of those ideals.[6] It means simply that we are looking at conditions and events from the point of view of the stated value premises, and that we are defining our concepts in terms of that viewpoint.

Naturally, the choice of this set of value premises would be more fully justified if our study were to indicate that their realization represented the trend of the future. This finding did not emerge. But one of the convictions we hold as a result of our investigation is that, particularly in view of the accelerating population increase, rapid strides toward the realization of the modernization ideals must be made in order to avoid increasing misery and social upheaval. They all have a rationale [. . .]. This is what gives our set of value premises, or rather a study of the countries in the region undertaken from that angle, practical importance.[7] We should also bear in mind that, in one sense, they have all passed the point of no return. The modernization ideals are in effect in South Asia, at least to the extent of preventing these countries from reverting to their traditional undisturbed status. "Countries may never succeed in becoming modern, but they can never return to a traditional society or polity. A state which, however minimally, advances toward modernity . . . has irreversibly turned its back on the traditional oligarchic alternative."[8] [. . .]

Improved institutions and attitudes. In general, it is held that social and economic institutions and attitudes should be changed, in order to: increase labor efficiency and diligence, effective competition, mobility, and enterprise; permit greater equality of opportunities; make possible higher productivity and well-being; and generally promote development. It is even quite common in all the countries of the region to discuss these desired changes as a social, as well as an economic, "revolution" and to proclaim that such a revolution is necessary for development.

In regard to institutions, perhaps the easiest way to illustrate the prevalent valuations contained in the modernization ideals is to picture the kind of national community implied in reasonings about the need for asocial revolution and in the motivation for specific reform proposals. What is envisaged is a united and integrated national community within which there is solidarity and "free competition" in a much wider sense than the term implies in economic analysis. In such a national community the barriers of caste, color, religion, ethnic origin, culture, language, and provincial loyalties would be broken down, and property and education would not be so unequally distributed as to represent social monopolies. A nation with marked social and economic equality, high social as well as spatial mobility, and firm allegiance of the whole population to the national community is visualized. The desire for such a "modernization" of institutions is most clearly expressed in India,[9] where the barriers to free competition in this wider sense are strongest and most pervasive. The ideal is shared, however, in the whole region, though in Ceylon and Southeast Asia with considerable reservation in regard to foreign ethnic groups.

The modern welfare state in the rich Western countries is, of course, much closer to the realization of this ideal, as are, at lower but rising levels of living, the Communist countries. From the valuation perspective of national consolidation, South Asian countries are all much more amorphous and splintered. The ideal system is viewed as a unified and integrated nation-state, branching out into smaller communities bound together by loyalties to the nation-state. In reality, however, the social and political framework is traversed by lines of interests and allegiances to other types of communities that do not fit into the ideal order but are inimical to it. Although these narrower communities for the most part have no formal existence in a constitutional legal sense, they greatly influence how people feel and think and what they are prepared to do or not do. Many of the proposed and partially enacted reforms of the institutional system – land reforms, tenancy legislation, attempts in India to break up the caste divisions, etc. – should be viewed in this broader perspective, as attempts to eradicate social monopolies and barriers against free competition in the pursuit of happiness, considered inimical to national consolidation, to equalization, and to advances in productivity and levels of living.

Attitudes, in turn, are understood to be supported by and at the same time to uphold established institutions. In regard to attitudes, the general ideal of a social revolution is commonly referred to as the creation of the "new man" or the "modern man," the "citizen of the new state," the "man in the era of science," the "industrial man," and so on. What is implied is illustrated below, though the list should not be regarded as complete, nor should the individual items be viewed as independent of one another:

(1) efficiency;
(2) diligence;
(3) orderliness;

(4)   punctuality;

(5)   frugality;

(6)   scrupulous honesty (which pays in the long run and is a condition for raising efficiency in all social and economic relations);

(7)   rationality in decisions on action (liberation from reliance on static customs, from group allegiances and favoritism, from superstitious beliefs and prejudices, approaching the rationally calculating "economic man" of Western liberal ideology);

(8)   preparedness for change (for experimentation along new lines, and for moving around spatially, economically, socially);

(9)   alertness to opportunities as they arise in a changing world;

(10) energetic enterprise;

(11) integrity and self-reliance;

(12) cooperativeness (not limiting but redirecting egoistic striving in a socially beneficial channel; acceptance of responsibility for the welfare of the community and the nation);

(13) willingness to take the long view (and to forego short-term profiteering; subordination of speculation to investment and of commerce and finance to production, etc.).

The desirability of changing attitudes, though accepted at a very general level, is usually played down in public debate.[10] Least of all does discussion take the form of demands for specific policy measures aimed directly at changing attitudes. Attitudinal changes are glossed over even in the formulation of educational policies.

There are several explanations why a frontal attack on attitudes is avoided. First, it would wound national pride. The educated themselves, including the intellectual elite, are aware of the failure to live up to ideals in this respect. Even more important is the separation of this group from the masses. Conscious of the wide gap between their modes and levels of living, culture, and all circumstances of their life and work and those of the villagers and urban slum dwellers, the intellectual elite compensate for their alienation by romanticizing the plight of the masses. The demand for more efficient labor performance and greater enterprise is often countered by protests that the peasants are rational, intelligent, hard-working, and zealous.[11]

Another important determinant of such thinking is that it developed during the fight for liberation as a protest against colonial theories and stereotypes. Europeans in colonial times typically described the "natives" of these countries as superstitious, lazy, careless, unenterprising, and merely survival-minded. These derogatory views were part of the rationalization of the prerogatives they took to themselves and were able to retain as a super-caste.

It is obvious, moreover, that the attitudes that are thought to need changing are a function of the low levels of living and culture, and that these levels can only slowly be elevated. These attitudes are also fortified by the institutions in which they are molded and which they help to preserve. Together, the modes and levels of living, the attitudes, and the institutions form a complex social system that is difficult to change, particularly as all these countries are reluctant to apply compulsion. In curious juxtaposition to this awareness of the complexity of the problem is the over-optimism, nurtured by Marx's thinking but largely taken over by Western economists – mostly only as an implicit assumption, revealed by immanent criticism – that economic development and, in particular, industrialization will automatically change both institutions and attitudes. The escape from thinking or doing much about institutions and attitudes is made easier by the application in economic analysis and planning of the Western approach, which ordinarily takes into account solely the "economic" factors. Because it serves vested interests in the status quo, this approach appeals to the conservatives at the same time that it permits the radicals to be optimistic.

To sum up: among the articulate groups there is unanimous support, on a very general plane, for changing institutions and attitudes, but there is also much escapism, particularly in regard to specific issues. [. . .]

Notes

1   "We all agree that the basic requirement of any model is that it should be capable of explaining the characteristic features of the economic process as we find them in reality. It is no good starting off a model with the kind of abstraction which initially excludes the influence of forces which are mainly responsible for the behavior of the economic variables under investigation; and upon finding that the theory leads to results contrary to what we observe in reality, attributing this contrary movement to the compensating (or more than compensating) influence of residual factors that have been assumed away in the model. . . . Any theory must necessarily be based on abstractions; but the type of abstraction chosen cannot be decided in a vacuum: it must be appropriate to the characteristic features of the economic process as recorded by experience." (Nicholas Kaldor, "Capital Accumulation and Economic Growth," in *The Theory of Capital* [London: Macmillan, 1961], 177–8.)

2   Gunnar Myrdal, *Economic Theory and Under-developed Regions* (London: Duckworth, 1957), 112 *et passim*.

3   See [. . .] particularly Myrdal, *Economic Theory and Under-developed Regions*, Part 11, "Economic Inequalities, the Public Conscience and Economic Theory."

4   "These conflicts cannot be concealed by such blanket terms as 'maximum welfare.' The main aims of economic policy have to be listed, their compatibility investigated, and where incompatibility remains, preferences have to be stated." (Paul Streeten, *Economic Integration, Aspects and Problems* [Leyden: Sythoff, 1961], 17.)

5   This is a main viewpoint in the writer's *An American Dilemma. [The Negro Problem and Modern Democracy* (New York: Harper, 1944).]

6   The contrast to the writer's study of the Negro problem in America comes readily to mind. Not only were the set of value premises in that study, the "American Creed," much more firmly rooted in actually existing and powerful valuations in the whole population, but those valuations were so strong that – after study – they also stood out as determining the trend in the past and for the future. See ibid., 23 *et passim*.

7   The writer must in honesty add that the distinct aura of Enlightenment surrounding the modernization ideals in South Asia is congenial to him and to his collaborators, who are conservative in their moral allegiances and are personally deeply attached to those inherited radical ideals. Undoubtedly, this attitude made it easier to work with, and stick to, this set of value premises. As instrumental in this study they were

not, however, selected on that personal ground, but rather for their relevance and significance in South Asia. The sympathy of the writer and his collaborators for those ideals may have been psychologically favorable to the conduct of the study but has in principle to be considered as accidental and logically irrelevant.

8 Edward Shils, "The Military in the Political Development of the New States," in John J. Johnson (ed.), *The Role of the Military in Underdeveloped Countries* (Princeton, NJ: Princeton University Press, 1962), 60–1.

9 "Let us be clear about our national objective. We aim at a strong, free and democratic India where every citizen has an equal place and full opportunity of growth and service, where present-day inequalities in wealth and status have ceased to be, where our vital impulses are directed to creative and co-operative endeavour. In such an India communalism, separatism, isolation, untouchability, bigotry, and exploitation of man by man have no place, and while religion is free, it is not allowed to interfere with the political and economic aspects of a nation's life." (Nehru's Convocation Address, Allahabad 'Varsity, December 13, 1947.)

   In his *The Discovery of India* (4th ed. [London: Meridian Books, 1956], 534), Nehru had already pleaded for a "functional organization of society" where "merit is the only criterion and opportunity is thrown open to everybody."

10 Gandhi upbraided his people for wrong attitudes toward life and work much more frankly than have his followers. Occasionally, however, an Indian intellectual does not mince the subject but speaks out: "The young Indian must come round to a rational and objective view of material advancement. He must be able and willing to tear himself away from his family ties; flout customs and traditions; put economic welfare before cow worship; think in terms of farm and factory output rather than in terms of gold and silver ornaments; spend on tools and training rather than on temples and ceremonials; work with the low caste rather than starve with the high caste; think of the future rather than of the past; concentrate on material gains rather than dwell on *Kismet* (destiny). These are extremely difficult changes to envisage in the Hindu social structure and ideas. But they seem unavoidable." (D. K. Rangnekar, *Poverty and Capital Development in India* [London: Oxford University Press, 1958], 81.)

11 This tendency toward romantic pastoralism when viewing subordinate social strata is familiar from European history. It was particularly prominent in the eighteenth century, when the social system in Europe was somewhat closer to a surviving feudal order while the intellectuals were becoming radical in their philosophy.

3 A Universal Civilization? Modernization and Westernization

Samuel P. Huntington

Universal Civilization: Sources

The concept of a universal civilization is a distinctive product of Western civilization. In the nineteenth century the idea of "the white man's burden" helped justify the extension of Western political and economic domination over non-Western societies. At the end of the twentieth century the concept of a universal civilization helps justify Western cultural dominance of other societies and the need for those societies to ape Western practices and institutions. Universalism is the ideology of the West for confrontations with non-Western cultures. As is often the case with marginals or converts, among the most enthusiastic proponents of the single civilization idea are intellectual migrants to the West, such as Naipaul and Fouad Ajami, for whom the concept provides a highly satisfying answer to the central question: Who am I? "White man's nigger," however, is the term one Arab intellectual applied to these migrants,[1] and the idea of a universal civilization finds little support in other civilizations. The non-Wests see as Western what the West sees as universal. What Westerners herald as benign global integration, such as the proliferation of worldwide media, non-Westerners denounce as nefarious Western imperialism. To the extent that non-Westerners see the world as one, they see it as a threat.

   The arguments that some sort of universal civilization is emerging rest on one or more of three assumptions as to why this should be the case. First, there is the assumption [. . .] that the collapse of Soviet communism meant the end of history and the universal victory of liberal democracy throughout the world. This argument suffers from the single alternative fallacy. It is rooted in the Cold War

Excerpted from S. P. Huntington, "A Universal Civilization? Modernization and Westernization." In *The Clash of Civilizations and the Remaking of World Order* (New York: Simon and Schuster, 1996), 66–78.

perspective that the only alternative to communism is liberal democracy and that the demise of the first produces the universality of the second. Obviously, however, there are many forms of authoritarianism, nationalism, corporatism, and market communism (as in China) that are alive and well in today's world. More significantly, there are all the religious alternatives that lie outside the world of secular ideologies. In the modern world, religion is a central, perhaps *the* central, force that motivates and mobilizes people. It is sheer hubris to think that because Soviet communism has collapsed, the West has won the world for all time and that Muslims, Chinese, Indians, and others are going to rush to embrace Western liberalism as the only alternative. The Cold War division of humanity is over. The more fundamental divisions of humanity in terms of ethnicity, religions, and civilizations remain and spawn new conflicts.

Second, there is the assumption that increased interaction among peoples – trade, investment, tourism, media, electronic communication generally – is generating a common world culture. Improvements in transportation and communications technology have indeed made it easier and cheaper to move money, goods, people, knowledge, ideas, and images around the world. No doubt exists as to the increased international traffic in these items. Much doubt exists, however, as to the impact of this increased traffic. Does trade increase or decrease the likelihood of conflict? The assumption that it reduces the probability of war between nations is, at a minimum, not proven, and much evidence exists to the contrary. International trade expanded significantly in the 1960s and 1970s and in the following decade the Cold War came to an end. In 1913, however, international trade was at record highs and in the next few years nations slaughtered each other in unprecedented numbers.[2] If international commerce at that level could not prevent war, when can it? The evidence simply does not support the liberal, internationalist assumption that commerce promotes peace. Analyses done in the 1990s throw that assumption further into question. One study concludes that "increasing levels of trade may be a highly divisive force ... for international politics" and that "increasing trade in the international system is, by itself, unlikely to ease international tensions or promote greater international stability."[3] Another study argues that high levels of economic interdependence "can be either peace-inducing *or* war-inducing, depending on the expectations of future trade." Economic interdependence fosters peace only "when states expect that high trade levels will continue into the foreseeable future." If states do not expect high levels of interdependence to continue, war is likely to result.[4]

The failure of trade and communications to produce peace or common feeling is consonant with the findings of social science. In social psychology, distinctiveness theory holds that people define themselves by what makes them different from others in a particular context: "one perceives oneself in terms of characteristics that distinguish oneself from other humans, especially from people in one's usual social milieu ... a woman psychologist in the company of a dozen women who work at other occupations thinks of herself as a psychologist; when with a dozen male psychologists, she thinks of herself as a woman."[5] People define their identity by what they are not. As increased communications, trade, and travel multiply the interactions among civilizations, people increasingly accord greater relevance to their civilizational identity. Two Europeans, one German and one French, interacting with each other will identify each other as German and French. Two Europeans, one German and one French, interacting with two Arabs, one Saudi and one Egyptian, will define themselves as Europeans and Arabs. North African immigration to France generates hostility among the French and at the same time increased receptivity to immigration by European Catholic Poles. Americans react far more negatively to Japanese investment than to larger investments from Canada and European countries. Similarly, as Donald Horowitz has pointed out, "An Ibo may be . . . an Owerri Ibo or an Onitsha Ibo in what was the Eastern region of Nigeria. In Lagos, he is simply an Ibo. In London, he is Nigerian. In New York, he is an African."[6] From sociology, globalization theory produces a similar conclusion: "in an increasingly globalized world – characterized by historically exceptional degrees of civilizational, societal and other modes of interdependence and widespread consciousness thereof – there is an *exacerbation* of civilizational, societal and ethnic self-consciousness." The global religious revival, "the return to the sacred," is a response to people's perception of the world as "a single place."[7]

The West and Modernization

The third and most general argument for the emergence of a universal civilization sees it as the result of the broad processes of modernization that have been going on since the eighteenth century. Modernization involves industrialization, urbanization, increasing levels of literacy, education, wealth, and social mobilization, and more complex and diversified occupational structures. It is a product of the tremendous expansion of scientific and engineering knowledge beginning in the eighteenth century that made it possible for humans to control and shape their environment in totally unprecedented ways. Modernization is a revolutionary process comparable only to the shift from primitive to civilized societies, that is, the emergence of civilization in the singular, which began in the valleys of the Tigris and Euphrates, the Nile, and the Indus about 5000 BC.[8] The attitudes, values, knowledge, and culture of people in a modern society differ greatly from those in a traditional society. As the first civilization to modernize, the West leads in the acquisition of the culture of modernity. As other societies acquire similar patterns of education, work, wealth, and class structure, the argument runs, this modern Western culture will become the universal culture of the world.

That significant differences exist between modern and traditional cultures is beyond dispute. It does not necessarily follow, however, that societies with modern cultures resemble each other more than do societies with traditional cultures. Obviously a world in which some societies are highly modern and others still traditional will be less homogeneous than a world in which all societies are at comparable high levels of modernity. But what about a world in which all societies were traditional? This world existed a few hundred years ago. Was it any less homogeneous than a future world of universal modernity is likely to be? Possibly not. "Ming China . . . was assuredly closer to the France of the Valois," Braudel argues, "than the China of Mao Tse-tung is to the France of the Fifth Republic."[9]

Yet modern societies could resemble each other more than do traditional societies for two reasons. First, the increased interaction among modern societies may not generate a common culture but it does facilitate the transfer of techniques, inventions, and practices from one society to another with a speed and to a degree that were impossible in the traditional world. Second, traditional society was based on agriculture; modern society is based on industry, which may evolve from handicrafts to classic heavy industry to knowledge-based industry. Patterns of agriculture and the social structure which goes with them are much more dependent on the natural environment than are patterns of industry. They vary with soil and climate and thus may give rise to different forms of land ownership, social structure, and government. Whatever the overall merits of Wittfogel's hydraulic civilization thesis, agriculture dependent on the construction and operation of massive irrigation systems does foster the emergence of centralized and bureaucratic political authorities. It could hardly be otherwise. Rich soil and good climate are likely to encourage development of large-scale plantation agriculture and a consequent social structure involving a small class of wealthy landowners and a large class of peasants, slaves, or serfs who work the plantations. Conditions inhospitable to large-scale agriculture may encourage emergence of a society of independent farmers. In agricultural societies, in short, social structure is shaped by geography. Industry, in contrast, is much less dependent on the local natural environment. Differences in industrial organization are likely to derive from differences in culture and social structure rather than geography, and the former conceivably can converge while the latter cannot.

Modern societies thus have much in common. But do they necessarily merge into homogeneity? The argument that they do rests on the assumption that modern society must approximate a single type, the Western type, that modern civilization is Western civilization and that Western civilization is modern civilization. This, however, is a totally false identification. Western civilization emerged in the eighth and ninth centuries and developed its distinctive characteristics in the following centuries. It did not begin to modernize until the seventeenth and eighteenth centuries. The West was the West long before it was modern. The central characteristics of the West, those which distinguish it from other civilizations, antedate the modernization of the West.

What were these distinguishing characteristics of Western society during the hundreds of years before it modernized? Various scholars have produced answers to this question which differ in some specifics but agree on the key institutions, practices, and beliefs that may legitimately be identified as the core of Western civilization. These include the following.[10]

The Classical legacy. As a third generation civilization, the West inherited much from previous civilizations, including most notably Classical civilization. The legacies of the West from Classical civilization are many, including Greek philosophy and rationalism, Roman law, Latin, and Christianity. Islamic and Orthodox civilizations also inherited from Classical civilization but nowhere near to the same degree the West did.

Catholicism and Protestantism. Western Christianity, first Catholicism and then Catholicism and Protestantism, is historically the single most important characteristic of Western civilization. During most of its first millennium, indeed, what is now known as Western civilization was called Western Christendom; there existed a well-developed sense of community among Western Christian peoples that they were distinct from Turks, Moors, Byzantines, and others; and it was for God as well as gold that Westerners went out to conquer the world in the sixteenth century. The Reformation and Counter-Reformation and the division of Western Christendom into a Protestant north and a Catholic south are also distinctive features of Western history, totally absent from Eastern Orthodoxy and largely removed from the Latin American experience.

European languages. Language is second only to religion as a factor distinguishing people of one culture from those of another. The West differs from most other civilizations in its multiplicity of languages. Japanese, Hindi, Mandarin, Russian, and even Arabic are recognized as the core languages of their civilizations. The West inherited Latin, but a variety of nations emerged and with them national languages grouped loosely into the broad categories of Romance and Germanic. By the sixteenth century these languages had generally assumed their contemporary form.

Separation of spiritual and temporal authority. Throughout Western history first the Church and then many churches existed apart from the state. God and Caesar, church and state, spiritual authority and temporal authority, have been a prevailing dualism in Western culture. Only in Hindu civilization were religion and politics also so distinctly separated. In Islam, God is Caesar; in China and Japan, Caesar is God; in Orthodoxy, God is Caesar's junior partner. The separation and recurring clashes between church and state that typify Western civilization have existed in no other civilization. This division of authority contributed immeasurably to the development of freedom in the West.

Rule of law. The concept of the centrality of law to civilized existence was inherited from the Romans. Medieval thinkers elaborated the idea of natural law according to which monarchs were supposed to exercise their power, and a common law tradition developed in England. During the phase of absolutism in the sixteenth and seventeenth centuries the rule of law was observed more in the breach than in reality, but the idea persisted of the subordination of human power to some external restraint: *"Non sub homine sed sub Deo et lege."* The tradition of the rule of law laid the basis for constitutionalism and the protection of human rights, including property rights, against the exercise of arbitrary power. In most other civilizations law was a much less important factor in shaping thought and behavior.

Social pluralism. Historically Western society has been highly pluralistic. As Deutsch notes, what is distinctive about the West "is the rise and persistence of diverse autonomous groups not based on blood relationship or marriage."[11] Beginning in the sixth and seventh centuries, these groups initially included monasteries, monastic orders, and guilds, but then expanded to include in many areas of Europe a variety of other associations and societies.[12] Associational pluralism was supplemented by class pluralism. Most Western European societies included a relatively strong and autonomous aristocracy, a substantial peasantry, and a small but significant class of merchants and traders. The strength of the feudal aristocracy was particularly significant in limiting the extent to which absolutism was able to take firm root in most European nations. This European pluralism contrasts sharply with the poverty of civil society, the weakness of the aristocracy, and the strength of the centralized bureaucratic empires which simultaneously existed in Russia, China, the Ottoman lands, and other non-Western societies.

Representative bodies. Social pluralism early gave rise to estates, parliaments, and other institutions to represent the interests of the aristocracy, clergy, merchants, and other groups. These bodies provided forms of representation which in the course of modernization evolved into the institutions of modern democracy. In some instances these bodies were abolished or their powers were greatly limited during the period of absolutism. Even when that happened, however, they could, as in France, be resurrected to provide a vehicle for expanded political participation. No other contemporary civilization has a comparable heritage of representative bodies stretching back for a millennium. At the local level also, beginning about the ninth century, movements for self-government developed in the Italian cities and then spread northward "forcing bishops, local barons and other great nobles to share power with the burghers, and in the end often yield to them altogether."[13] Representation at the national level was thus supplemented by a measure of autonomy at the local level not duplicated in other regions of the world.

Individualism. Many of the above features of Western civilization contributed to the emergence of a sense of individualism and a tradition of individual rights and liberties unique among civilized societies. Individualism developed in the fourteenth and fifteenth centuries and acceptance of the right of individual choice – what Deutsch terms "the Romeo and Juliet revolution" – prevailed in the West by the seventeenth century. Even claims for *equal* rights for all individuals – "the poorest he in England has a life to live as much as the richest he" – were articulated if not universally accepted. Individualism remains a distinguishing mark of the West among twentieth-century civilizations. In one analysis involving similar samples from fifty countries, the top twenty countries scoring highest on the individualism index included all the Western countries except Portugal plus Israel.[14] The author of another cross-cultural survey of individualism and collectivism similarly highlighted the dominance of individualism in the West compared to the prevalence of collectivism elsewhere and concluded that "the values that are most important in the West are least important worldwide." Again and again both Westerners and non-Westerners point to individualism as the central distinguishing mark of the West.[15]

The above list is not meant to be an exhaustive enumeration of the distinctive characteristics of Western civilization. Nor is it meant to imply that those characteristics were always and universally present in Western society. Obviously they were not: the many despots in Western history regularly ignored the rule of law and suspended representative bodies. Nor is it meant to suggest that none of these characteristics appeared in other civilizations. Obviously they do: the Koran and the *shari'a* constitute basic law for Islamic societies; Japan and India had class systems paralleling that of the West (and perhaps as a result are the only two major non-Western societies to sustain democratic governments for any length of time). Individually almost none of these factors was unique to the West. The combination of them was, however, and this is what gave the West its distinctive quality. These concepts, practices, and institutions simply have been more prevalent in the West than in other civilizations. They form at least part of the essential continuing core of Western civilization. They are what is Western but not modern about the West. They are also in large part the factors which enabled the West to take the lead in modernizing itself and the world.

Responses to the West and Modernization

The expansion of the West has promoted both the modernization and the Westernization of non-Western societies. The political and intellectual leaders of these societies have responded to the Western impact in one or more of three ways: rejecting both modernization and Westernization; embracing both; embracing the first and rejecting the second.[16]

Rejectionism. Japan followed a substantially rejectionist course from its first contacts with the West in 1542 until the mid-nineteenth century. Only limited forms of modernization were permitted, such as the acquisition of firearms, and the import of Western culture, including most notably Christianity, was highly restricted. Westerners were totally expelled in the mid-seventeenth century. This rejectionist stance came to an end with the forcible opening of Japan by Commodore Perry in 1854 and the dramatic efforts to learn from the West following the Meiji Restoration in 1868. For several centuries China also attempted to bar any significant modernization or Westernization. Although Christian emissaries were allowed into China in 1601 they were then effectively excluded in 1722. Unlike Japan, China's rejectionist policy was in large part rooted in the Chinese image of itself as the Middle Kingdom and the firm belief in the superiority of Chinese culture to those of all other peoples. Chinese isolation, like Japanese isolation, was brought to an end by Western arms, applied to China by the British in the Opium War of 1839–42. As these cases suggest, during the nineteenth century Western power made it increasingly difficult and eventually impossible for non-Western societies to adhere to purely exclusionist strategies.

In the twentieth century improvements in transportation and communication and global interdependence increased tremendously the costs of exclusion. Except for small, isolated, rural communities willing to exist at a subsistence level, the total rejection of modernization as well as Westernization is hardly possible in a world becoming overwhelmingly modern and highly interconnected. "Only the very most extreme fundamentalists," Daniel Pipes writes concerning Islam, "reject modernization as well as Westernization. They throw television sets into rivers, ban wrist watches, and reject the internal combustion engine. The impracticality of their program severely limits the appeal of such groups, however; and in several cases – such as the Yen Izala of Kano, Sadat's assassins, the Mecca mosque attackers, and some Malaysian *dakwah* groups – their defeats in violent encounters with the authorities caused them then to disappear with few traces."[17] Disappearance with few traces summarizes generally the fate of purely rejectionist policies by the end of the twentieth century. Zealotry, to use Toynbee's term, is simply not a viable option.

Kemalism. A second possible response to the West is Toynbee's Herodianism, to embrace both modernization and Westernization. This response is based on the assumptions that modernization is desirable and necessary, that the indigenous culture is incompatible with modernization and must be abandoned or abolished, and that society must fully Westernize in order to successfully modernize. Modernization and Westernization reinforce each other and have to go together. This approach was epitomized in the arguments of some late nineteenth-century Japanese and Chinese intellectuals that in order to modernize, their societies should abandon their historic languages and adopt English as their national language. This view, not surprisingly, has been even more popular among Westerners than among non-Western elites. Its message is: "To be successful, you must be like us; our way is the only way." The argument is that "the religious values, moral assumptions, and social structures of these [non-Western] societies are at best alien, and sometime hostile, to the values and practices of industrialism." Hence economic development will "require a radical and destructive remaking of life and society, and, often, a reinterpretation of the meaning of existence itself as it has been understood by the people who live in these civilizations."[18] Pipes makes the same point with explicit reference to Islam:

> To escape anomy, Muslims have but one choice, for modernization requires Westernization. . . . Islam does not offer an alternative way to modernize. . . . Secularism cannot be avoided. Modern science and technology require an absorption of the thought processes which accompany them; so too with political institutions. Because content must be emulated no less than form, the predominance of Western civilization must be acknowledged so as to be able to learn from it. European languages and Western educational institutions cannot be avoided, even if the latter do encourage freethinking and easy living. Only when Muslims explicitly accept the Western model will they be in a position to technicalize and then to develop.[19]

Sixty years before these words were written Mustafa Kemal Ataturk had come to similar conclusions, had created a new Turkey out of the ruins of the Ottoman empire, and had launched a massive effort both to Westernize it and to modernize it. In embarking on this course, and rejecting the Islamic past, Ataturk made Turkey a "torn country," a society which was Muslim in its religion, heritage, customs, and institutions but with a ruling elite determined to make it modern, Western, and at one with the West. In the late twentieth century several countries are pursuing the Kemalist option and trying to substitute a Western for a non-Western identity. [. . .]

Reformism. Rejection involves the hopeless task of isolating a society from the shrinking modern world. Kemalism involves the difficult and traumatic task of destroying a culture that has existed for centuries and putting in its place a totally new culture imported from another civilization. A third choice is to attempt to combine modernization with the preservation of the central values, practices, and institutions of the society's indigenous culture. This choice has understandably been the most popular one among non-Western elites. In China in the last stages of the Ch'ing dynasty, the slogan was *Ti-Yong*, "Chinese learning for the fundamental principles, Western learning for practical use." In Japan it was *Wakon, Yōsei*, "Japanese spirit, Western technique." In Egypt in the 1830s Muhammad Ali "attempted technical modernization without excessive cultural Westernization." This effort failed, however, when the British forced him to abandon most of his modernizing reforms. As a result, Ali Mazrui observes, "Egypt's destiny was not a Japanese fate of technical modernization *without* cultural Westernization, nor was it an Ataturk fate of technical modernization *through* cultural Westernization."[20] In the latter part of the nineteenth century, however, Jamal al-Din al-Mghani, Muhammad 'Abduh, and other reformers attempted a new reconciliation of Islam and modernity, arguing "the compatibility of Islam with modern science and the best of Western thought" and providing an "lslamic rationale for accepting modern ideas and institutions, whether scientific, technological, or political (constitutionalism and representative government)."[21] This was a broad-gauged reformism, tending toward Kemalism, which accepted not only modernity but also some Western institutions. Reformism of this type was the dominant response to the West on the part of Muslim elites for fifty years from the 1870s to the 1920s, when it was challenged by the rise first of Kemalism and then of a much purer reformism in the shape of fundamentalism.

Rejectionism, Kemalism, and reformism are based on different assumptions as to what is possible and what is desirable. For rejectionism both modernization and Westernization are undesirable and it is possible to reject both. For Kemalism both modernization and Westernization are desirable, the latter because it is indispensable to achieving the former, and both are possible. For reformism, modernization is desirable and possible without substantial Westernization, which is undesirable. Conflicts thus exist between rejectionism and Kemalism on the desirability of modernization and Westernization and between Kemalism and reformism as to whether modernization can occur without Westernization. [. . .]

This hypothetical general model is congruent with both social science theory and historical experience. Reviewing at length the available evidence concerning "the invariable hypothesis," Rainer Baum concludes that "the continuing quest of man's search for meaningful authority and meaningful personal autonomy occurs in culturally distinct fashions. In these matters there is no convergence toward a cross-culturally homogenizing world. Instead, there seems to be invariance in the patterns that were developed in distinct forms during the historical and early modern stages of development."[22] Borrowing theory, as elaborated by Frobenius, Spengler, and Bozeman among others, stresses the extent to which recipient civilizations selectively borrow items from other civilizations and adapt, transform, and assimilate them so as to strengthen and insure the survival of the core values or "paideuma" of their culture.[23] Almost all of the non-Western civilizations in the world have existed for at least one millennium and in some cases for several. They have a demonstrated record of borrowing from other civilizations in ways to enhance their own survival. China's absorption of Buddhism from India, scholars agree, failed to produce the "Indianization" of China. The Chinese adapted Buddhism to Chinese purposes and needs. Chinese culture remained Chinese. The Chinese have to date consistently defeated intense Western efforts to Christianize them. If, at some point, they do import Christianity, it is to be expected that it will be absorbed and adapted in such a manner as to be compatible with the central elements of Chinese culture. Similarly, Muslim Arabs received, valued, and made use of their "Hellenic inheritance for essentially utilitarian reasons. Being mostly interested in borrowing certain external forms or technical aspects, they knew how to disregard all elements in the Greek body of thought that would conflict with 'the truth' as established in their fundamental Koranic norms and precepts."[24] Japan followed the same pattern. In the seventh century Japan imported Chinese culture and made the "transformation on its own initiative, free from economic and military pressures" to high civilization. "During the centuries that followed, periods of relative isolation from continental influences during which previous borrowings were sorted out and the useful ones assimilated would alternate with periods of renewed contact and cultural borrowing."[25] Through all these phases, Japanese culture maintained its distinctive character.

The moderate form of the Kemalist argument that non-Western societies *may* modernize by Westernizing remains unproven. The extreme Kemalist argument that non-Western societies *must* Westernize in order to modernize does not stand as a universal proposition. It does, however, raise the question: Are there some non-Western societies in which the obstacles the indigenous culture poses to modernization are so great that the culture must be substantially replaced by Western culture if modernization is to occur? In theory this should be more probable with consummatory than with instrumental cultures. Instrumental cultures are "characterized by a large sector of intermediate ends separate from and independent of ultimate ends." These systems "innovate easily by spreading the blanket of tradition upon change itself. . . . Such systems can innovate without appearing to alter their social institutions fundamentally. Rather, innovation is made to serve immemoriality." Consummatory systems, in contrast, "are characterized by a close relationship between intermediate and ultimate ends. . . . society, the state, authority, and the like are all part of an elaborately sustained, high-solidarity system in which religion as a cognitive guide is pervasive. Such systems have been hostile to innovation."[26] Apter uses these categories to analyze change in African tribes. Eisenstadt applies a parallel analysis to the great Asian civilizations and comes to a similar conclusion. Internal transformation is "greatly facilitated by autonomy of social, cultural, and political institutions."[27] For this reason, the more instrumental Japanese and Hindu societies moved earlier and more easily into modernization than Confucian and Islamic societies. They were better able to import the modern technology and use it to bolster their existing culture. Does this mean that Chinese and Islamic societies must either forgo both modernization and Westernization or embrace both? The choices do not appear that limited. In addition to Japan, Singapore, Taiwan, Saudi Arabia, and, to a lesser degree, Iran have become modern societies without becoming Western. Indeed, the effort by the Shah to follow a Kemalist course and do both generated an intense anti-Western but not antimodern reaction. China is clearly embarked on a reformist path.

Islamic societies have had difficulty with modernization, and Pipes supports his claim that Westernization is a prerequisite by pointing to the conflicts between Islam and modernity in economic matters such as interest, fasting, inheritance laws, and female participation in the work force. Yet even he approvingly quotes Maxine Rodinson to the effect that "there is nothing to indicate in a compelling way that the Muslim religion prevented the Muslim world from developing along the road to modern capitalism" and argues that in most matters other than economic

> Islam and modernization do not clash. Pious Muslims can cultivate the sciences, work efficiently in factories, or utilize advanced weapons. Modernization requires no one political ideology or set of institutions: elections, national boundaries, civic associations, and the other hallmarks of Western life are not necessary to economic growth. As a creed, Islam satisfies management consultants as well as peasants. The Shari'a has nothing to say about the changes that accompany modernization, such as the shift from agriculture to industry, from countryside to city, or from social stability to social flux; nor does it impinge on such matters as mass education, rapid communications, new forms of transportation, or health care.[28]

Similarly, even extreme proponents of anti-Westernism and the revitalization of indigenous cultures do not hesitate to use modern techniques of e-mail, cassettes, and television to promote their cause.

Modernization, in short, does not necessarily mean Westernization. Non-Western societies can modernize and have modernized without abandoning their own cultures and adopting wholesale Western values, institutions, and practices. The latter, indeed, may be almost impossible: whatever obstacles non-Western cultures pose to modernization pale before those they pose to Westernization. It would, as Braudel observes, almost "be childish" to think that modernization or the "triumph of *civilization* in the singular" would lead to the end of the plurality of historic cultures embodied for centuries in the world's great civilizations.[29] Modernization, instead, strengthens those cultures and reduces the relative power of the West. In fundamental ways, the world is becoming more modern and less Western.

Notes

1   Edward Said on V. S. Naipaul, quoted by Brent Staples, "Con Men and Conquerors," *New York Times Book Review*, May 22, 1994, p. 42.

2   A. G. Kenwood and A. L. Lougheed, *The Growth of the International Economy 1820–1990* (London: Routledge, 3rd ed., 1992), 78–9; Angus Maddison, *Dynamic Forces in Capitalist Development* (New York: Oxford University Press, 1991), 326–7; Alan S. Blinder, *New York Times*, March 12, 1995, p. 5E.

3   David M. Rowe, "The Trade and Security Paradox in International Politics," unpublished manuscript, Ohio State University, September 15, 1994, p. 16.

4   Dale C. Copeland, "Economic Interdependence and War: A Theory of Trade Expectations," *International Security* 20 (Spring 1996), 25.

5   William J. McGuire and Claire V. McGuire, "Content and Process in the Experience of Self," *Advances in Experimental Social Psychology* 21 (1988), 102.

6   Donald L. Horowitz, "Ethnic Conflict Management for Policy-makers," in Joseph V.

Montville and Hans Binnendijk (eds.), *Conflict and Peacemaking in Multiethnic Societies* (Lexington, MA: Lexington Books, 1990), 121.

7   Roland Robertson, "Globalization Theory and Civilizational Analysis," *Comparative Civilizations Review* 17 (Fall 1987), 22; Jeffery A. Shad, Jr., "Globalization and Islamic Resurgence," *Comparative Civilizations Review* 19 (Fall 1988), 67.

8   See Cyril E. Black, *The Dynamics of Modernization: A Study in Comparative History* (New York: Harper and Row, 1966), 1–34; Reinhard Bendix, "Tradition and Modernity Reconsidered," *Comparative Studies in Society and History* 9 (April 1967), 292–3.

9   Fernand Braudel, *On History* (Chicago: University of Chicago Press, 1980), 213.

10 The literature on the distinctive characteristics of Western civilization is, of course, immense. See, among others, William H. McNeill, *Rise of the West: A History of the Human Community* (Chicago: University of Chicago Press, 1963); Braudel, *On History* and earlier works; Immanuel Wallerstein, *Geopolitics and Geoculture: Essays on the Changing World-System* (Cambridge: Cambridge University Press, 1991). Karl W. Deutsch has produced a comprehensive, succinct, and highly suggestive comparison of the West and nine other civilizations in terms of twenty-one geographical, cultural, economic, technological, social, and political factors, emphasizing the extent to which the West differs from the others. See Karl W. Deutsch, "On Nationalism, World Regions, and the Nature of the West," in Per Torsvik (ed.), *Mobilization, Center–Periphery Structures and Nation-building: A Volume in Commemoration of Stein Rokkan* (Bergen: Universitetsforlaget, 1981), 51–93. For a succinct summary of the salient and distinctive features of Western civilization in 1500, see Charles Tilly, "Reflections on the History of European State-making," in Tilly (ed.), *The Formation of National States in Western Europe* (Princeton, NJ: Princeton University Press, 1975), 18ff.

11 Deutsch, "Nationalism, World Regions, and the West," 77.

12 See Robert D. Putnam, *Making Democracy Work: Civil Traditions in Modern Italy* (Princeton, NJ: Princeton University Press, 1993), 121ff.

13 Deutsch, "Nationalism, World Regions, and the West," 78. See also Stein Rokkan, "Dimensions of State Formation and Nation-building: A Possible Paradigm for Research on Variations within Europe," in Tilly (ed.), *The Formation of National States*, 576, and Putnam, *Making Democracy Work*, 124–7.

14 Geert Hofstede, "National Cultures in Four Dimensions: A Research-based Theory of Cultural Differences among Nations," *International Studies of Management and Organization* 13 (1983), 52.

15 Harry C. Triandis, "Cross-cultural Studies of Individualism and Collectivism," in *Nebraska Symposium on Motivation 1989* (Lincoln: University of Nebraska Press, 1990), 44–133, and *New York Times*, December 25, 1990, p. 41. See also George C. Lodge and Ezra F. Vogel (eds.), *Ideology and National Competitiveness: An Analysis of Nine Countries* (Boston: Harvard Business School Press, 1987), *passim*.

16 Discussions of the interaction of civilizations almost inevitably come up with some variation of this response typology. See Arnold J. Toynbee, *Study of History* (London: Oxford University Press, 1935–61), II, 187ff., VIII, 152–3, 214; John L. Esposito, *The Islamic Threat: Myth or Reality* (New York: Oxford University Press, 1992), 53–62; Daniel Pipes, *In the Path of God: Islam and Political Power* (New York: Basic Books, 1983), 105–42.

17 Pipes, *Path of God*, 349.

18 William Pfaff, "Reflections: Economic Development," *New Yorker*, December 25, 1978, p. 47.

19 Pipes, *Path of God*, 197–8.

20 Ali Al-Amin Mazrui, *Cultural Forces in World Politics* (London: James Currey, 1990), 4–5.

21 Esposito, *Islamic Threat*, 55; see generally, 55–62; and Pipes, *Path of God*, 114–20.

22 Rainer C. Baum, "Authority and Identity: The Invariance Hypothesis II," *Zeitschrift für Soziologie* 6 (October 1977), 368–9. See also Rainer C. Baum, "Authority Codes: The Invariance Hypothesis," *Zeitschrift für Soziologie* 6 (January 1977), 5–28.

23 See Adda B. Bozeman, "Civilizations Under Stress," *Virginia Quarterly Review* 51 (Winter 1975), 5ff.; Leo Frobenius, *Paideuma: Umrisse einer Kultur- und Seelenlehre* (Munich: C. H. Beck, 1921), 11ff.; Oswald Spengler, *The Decline of the West* (New York: Alfred A. Knopf, 2 vols., 1926, 1928), II, 57ff.

24 Bozeman, "Civilizations Under Stress," 7.

25 William E. Naff, "Reflections on the Question of 'East and West' from the Point of View of Japan," *Comparative Civilizations Review* 13/14 (Fall 1985/Spring 1986), 222.

26 David E. Apter, "The Role of Traditionalism in the Political Modernization of Ghana and Uganda," *World Politics* 13 (October 1960), 47–68.

27 S. N. Eisenstadt, "Transformation of Social, Political, and Cultural Orders in Modernization," *American Sociological Review* 30 (October 1965), 659–73.

28 Pipes, *Path of God*, 107, 191.

29 Braudel, *On History*, 212–13.

4 Divided Market Cultures in China: Gender, Enterprise, and Religion

Robert P. Weller

[. . .]

On Culture and Convergence

The East Asian response to modernization theories of convergence toward Western market culture has centered around claims that Confucianism, broadly interpreted, offered cultural resources that promoted the adoption of market capitalism.[1] Most authors recognize that Confucian ideas alone are not sufficient cause for capitalist development and that contact with the West helped free Chinese culture from an imperial system that impeded market growth. They thus usually talk about post-Confucianism to distinguish current formulations from the millennium-old neo-Confucianism that formed the ideological base of late imperial rule.

Authors vary widely in just what they mean by post-Confucianism, but the list of most important features usually includes an emphasis on human relations and social harmony based on the idea of filial piety, respect for authority and a strong identity with the organization, and a combination of worldly diligence and fatalism.[2] The contrast with Western individualist atomization is implicit throughout. All but the most naive authors, of course, would admit that this post-Confucian model simplifies a great deal of social, geographic, and historical variation. Yet they would also insist (and I would agree) that on the whole, some such set of ideas and practices does in fact usefully differentiate the Chinese and Western cultural spheres. Although it is certainly possible to trace these views,

Excerpted from Robert P. Weller, "Divided Market Cultures in China: Gender, Enterprise, and Religion." In R. W. Hefner (ed.), *Market Cultures: Society and Morality in New Asian Capitalisms*. St. Leonards, NSW: Allen and Unwin, 78–103.

however loosely defined, back to the thought of Confucius himself, they also pervade many aspects of Chinese culture generally even among people who could say nothing about philosophical Confucianism. I will thus refer more simply to Chinese culture and save references to Confucianism and post-Confucianism to the ongoing philosophical effort that I discuss in the following pages.

A general description of Chinese culture based on Confucian tenets has shaped Western ideas about the growth of market economies in the region throughout the twentieth century. Alarmingly, however, the conclusions social scientists now draw from these features are just the opposite of what people concluded from the same observations for the first sixty or seventy years of the century. From Max Weber's original pessimistic predictions through the modernization theorists of the 1950s and 1960s, the standard arguments considered Chinese culture inimical to capitalism. Weber himself had argued that the Confucian "enchanted world" did not create the drive toward change that allowed Protestantism to catalyze the European economic transformation (Weber 1951). Others argued that family-centered particularism blocked rational economic development (e.g., Levy 1949: 354–9) or that China had religious impediments to economic growth (e.g., Bellah 1965). Now, however, Weber's Confucian world is offered as the key to East Asian economic success, and Levy's traditional particularism is seen as the key to successful family enterprise.[3]

In retrospect, the problems with the earlier version seem clear. Earlier analyses treated Chinese culture as an abstract, clearly formulated set of propositions and were often based on Chinese elite descriptions of cultural ideals. These analyses specified social and economic consequences based on differences between these ideals and an equally idealized version of Western market culture. Instead of placing actual behavior in real contexts, they assumed an automatic translation of a unitary culture into action. The new version, in part because Chinese scholars have taken the lead in its development, grounds its claims in a far better understanding of Chinese culture and history. It also has the good fortune of coming after the fact and so will not suffer the kind of empirical disproof that awaited the modernization version.

The new version of Chinese culture is thus much deeper than the old one but continues to offer a unitary culture largely out of context. Its post facto origins raise the danger of picking only those bits of traditional China most clearly preadapted to capitalism and ignoring the equally interesting question of how its many ill-adapted features have been overcome. Imperial China, after all, included a number of quite different cultural currents. Neo-Confucianism had the blessing of the state, but other elements also played important roles, even among the elite. [. . .]

[. . .] This diversity suggests that we ask how the various faces of Chinese culture influenced the reception of markets and how expanding market economies in turn selectively encouraged or discouraged various cultural elements by pushing them into unfamiliar terrain. In some ways, diversity itself was the most important preadaptation. A genuinely successful neo-Confucian hegemony that crushed all alternatives in support of the imperial state would have had no hope of making the transition in the twentieth century. This suggests that the most fruitful questions about culture and economic change involve not just identifying the successful roots of modern culture but actively looking at the whole range of resources and at how they change and are in turn changed by the market.

Such an examination requires looking beyond philosophical abstractions of Confucianism and beyond Chinese culture more broadly to place the full range of variation into its social and economic context. The diversity of Chinese culture meant that it was not simply preadapted (or ill-adapted, in older readings) to a new economic system but reacted differentially to historical events. The Chinese have thrived in market economies because they have successfully mined and refined some aspects of their cultural resources and successfully buried others.[4] [. . .]

In the remainder of this chapter I will take up the use of personal ties in business and the resurgence of popular religion in Chinese societies. In spite of the vast differences between these areas of life, I will argue that each is undergoing comparable transformations rather than evidencing a realization of a fortunate preadaptation or an inevitable convergence. The transformations involve the development of an argument over market culture with one side both celebrating and reflecting the new economy and the other searching for moral alternatives. Both sides of this argument have traditional cultural roots as well as ties beyond China. And within each camp, women and men have partially different cultural resources to offer and thus see the issues differently.

Personal Ties: Utility Versus Morality

Much of the literature arguing for an alternative Chinese market culture centers around the use of personal ties through community and especially family. Two kinds of evidence have made a convincing case for the central role of these ties in Chinese societies: the frequency of discourse about the family as a model for business and about the importance of "connections" (*guanxi*), and actual behavior.[5] The discursive evidence is especially strong. Managers of large Chinese enterprises (at least outside the People's Republic) claim to act as fathers of large families.[6] They assert the Confucian responsibility the father owes his children and the obedience the children owe their father (see, e.g., Redding 1990: 156–69). Managers and entrepreneurs at all levels also speak regularly of the critical importance of interpersonal ties and explicitly emphasize values such as trust (*xinyong*) and human feelings (*renqing*) in doing business (DeGlopper 1972; Silin 1972).

Discourse need not translate into practice, of course, and the situation is more complex when we turn to behavior. Chinese paternalism can contribute to an inflexible corporate structure, and the family model problematizes succession in business just as family disputes can become contentious and angry in Chinese societies. The existence of these problems, however, also provides indirect evidence that people really are applying a family metaphor even when it creates some difficulties. In addition, real, non-metaphorical family business has been at the heart of the economic boom in Taiwan, Hong Kong, and the People's Republic. This has been especially true for people with limited access to the state

and the opportunities it can create. In Taiwan the state promoted large enterprises but left most people to their own devices. Banks, for example, would not
make loans to small entrepreneurs, who turned to informal credit arrangements
based on their personal connections. In the People's Republic, small entrepreneurs (*geti hu*) also typically have few connections to the vast resources of the
state, which its bureaucrats still control. They thus also rely heavily on kinship
ties. Larger businesses (*siying qiye*), which almost invariably have close ties to the
state, use family ties much less (McEwen 1994). [. . .]

Two problems, however, prevent us from simply declaring that Chinese
societies have established a clear alternative to Western market culture. The first
is that the picture of Western business practice on which the contrast relies is
itself "occidentalized." Family business, for example, drove early Western capitalism in much the same way as people have recently documented for Chinese
society today. Although there has been a gradual (but by no means complete)
move away from that model in the West, it may suggest that family-centered
capitalism works well during the early development of market economies. If so,
then the Chinese evidence may describe an earlier stage of capitalism rather than
a true alternative.[7]

The second problem, clearly related to the first, is that these Chinese economies continue to change very rapidly. With the passing of several decades of
continuous development, business in Taiwan and Hong Kong is only now
beginning to face some of the difficulties that might discourage the family model
and the extensive use of personalistic ties. Small family enterprises are becoming
large firms, labor-intensive production is moving to the high-technology and
service sectors, company founders are searching for successors, and economic
growth elsewhere in Asia is creating a more fiercely competitive marketplace.
Indeed, some new evidence suggests that people are relying less than ever on
traditional interpersonal connections and that the quality of such relations is
becoming progressively thinner. Several studies have suggested a dilution of the
human feelings (*renqing*) implied in relationships (*guanxi*) in the People's Republic since market-oriented economic reforms began in the early 1980s and the
growth of more purely utilitarian ties (Gold 1985; Yan 1993). A recent study of
these issues in Taiwan, Hong Kong, and the People's Republic shows that many
entrepreneurs now explicitly reject the use of kinship ties as old-fashioned and
prefer more "modern" relationships, for instance, with classmates (McEwen
1994). Managers of larger enterprises in the People's Republic particularly like to
emphasize their commitment to "scientific" management (McEwen 1994).

The situation remains very much in flux, yet Chinese have clearly drawn on
their cultural traditions to address new economic opportunities. Confucian ideas
do affect management behavior, and business activity relies heavily on ties
established outside the market. The market itself, however, also puts significant
pressure on those relationships. Competition strains both real family ties (which
threaten to drain business resources) and the family as a metaphor. The result is
not yet completely clear, but there is enough evidence to conclude that Chinese
guanxi do indeed influence market behavior and that they have in turn been
changed.

Women's networks

Much of the literature on Chinese culture and business assumes, in a typically Confucian way, that there are no women, or at best that there are no differences between men and women. If true, this would be surprising indeed. We now have two decades of studies of family and gender clearly showing that women's interests in their families and their views of those fundamental kin relationships at the core of Confucian thought differed significantly from those of their husbands, fathers, and sons. Women's work was in theory confined to the domestic sphere; even when they produced commodities, men mediated access to the market.[8] Wives (who were traditionally called *neiren*, "inside people") had no direct access to their husbands' personal networks, and their own external contacts were confined to their natal families and to other women of their husbands' villages. Women, with their bound feet, did not do agricultural labor; nor did they have any place in the management of corporate properties. They were (and still are in the People's Republic) much more likely to be illiterate than their husbands. Perhaps most important, women had little reason to share their husbands' view of the family as one link in an infinite chain of patrilineal connections. Although most wives dutifully burned incense every morning for their husbands' ancestors, they did not worship their own ancestors. Even if a woman's parents had no other descendants to worship them, her husband's family would probably allow no more than a dusty corner in a back room for their commemorative tablets.[9] Women instead focused on creating a "uterine family" (Wolf 1972: 32–41). The birth of a son in particular solidified her place in her husband's house; fostering his continuing loyalty protected her in the years to come.

The idea of a nurturing mother confined to the household does not sound particularly well adapted to capitalism, but women in fact had resources that would become relevant. Although women's spheres of connections were much smaller than men's, they could also be more reliable. Her own natal family had the advantage of being trustworthy but also socially distant enough to prevent it becoming a drain if problems arose. In addition, the close ties uniting village networks of women could make up for the limited scale of the group. Women thus have made extensive use of rotating credit associations. These have been one of the most important ways of raising entrepreneurial capital but rely on high degrees of trust because it is so easy for members to abscond with all the funds. The closeness of women's networks may help them establish the necessary kinds of ties, whereas men may have broader but more utilitarian ties more open to abuse.

Many women have become entrepreneurs in Hong Kong, Taiwan, and the People's Republic. The legislated end of foot-binding (and other legal changes, especially in marriage rights) early in the twentieth century, much greater access to education, opportunities for wage labor, and other changes have helped open the market directly to women. Some estimate that fully half of the petty entrepreneurs in the People's Republic are women (McEwen 1994: 340). Men still dominate, however, and very few women run manufacturing businesses.

Family can pose a major problem for women entrepreneurs. They continue to face the responsibility of providing their husbands with sons and of taking care of children and the household. Young women in particular may have to choose between family and career, and preliminary evidence suggests a high divorce rate for young married women (McEwen 1994: 162, 254). At the same time, young female entrepreneurs value the new freedoms of their position and its opportunities for self-fulfillment (Gates 1991: 25).

As McEwen makes clear for all three of these Chinese societies, many entrepreneurial women feel cut off from the male world of connections (McEwen 1994: 148, 239, 341–2). They particularly miss the opportunity to cement ties through the endless banqueting in which men indulge. Some of this takes place in hostess bars, in which the women feel uncomfortable, and most of it involves competitive social drinking, an activity in which women have traditionally not been welcome. Taking part in such events would call the woman's character into question. Yet women also have ways of dealing with this problem. In many cases they go into business with their husbands. More creatively, some women use their sons or brothers as fronts at these events. They remain backstage pulling the strings while their men work the male networks (McEwen 1994: 341–2). They thus continue to make use of ties of uterine and natal family, running the business as "inside people" just as they ran the family. Whereas they may have problems meeting traditional family responsibilities, they also draw on traditional family skills in kin management to succeed.

Other women may simply forge their own networks. Some draw on traditional ties to do this, as when they raise capital through a rotating credit association of old friends. Others, however, simply start from scratch by searching out like-minded people. [. . .]

[. . . W]omen's relative lack of access to the opportunities that traditional ties create for men has led them to promote something more like a Weberian version of rational market behavior.

There is no simple evolution here. Women draw both on the traditional resources available to them and on innovative kinds of ties. In the process they set loose a series of contradictory processes – affirming the woman's role in the uterine family but making real family life problematic, drawing on traditionally female ties and skills but promoting a more utilitarian kind of relationship network. For women and men, market culture is not just the affirmation of Confucian tradition or just a convergence toward a single (Western-style) market culture inherent to capitalism itself. Instead it creates a new series of tensions around economic life that have ramifications throughout the entire society. These tensions have roots in people's varied cultural resources and in the pressures of the market itself. [. . .]

Market Religions

Chinese societies provide strong evidence – if we still need more evidence in light of events around the world – against the claim that modernity propels a necessary secularization. Indeed, religion appears to be thriving more than ever before. Religion in the People's Republic has boomed along with the economic reforms of the 1980s and the accompanying loosening of political controls. Even in Taiwan, whose history of religious discouragement ("repression" is too strong a word) never compared with the mainland, popular religion has made a strong comeback since the 1970s (Qu and Yao 1986). If anything, the data suggest that expanding markets have actively encouraged religious growth.

As with the other areas I have discussed, several recent studies have suggested that Chinese popular religious practice has shown an elective affinity for capitalism. Peter Berger, for example, proposed what he called the "Li Yih-yuan hypothesis," which holds that "vulgar Confucianism" (including popular religion) influenced Taiwanese development more than any of the more institutionalized "great traditions" (1988: 8–9). Others have suggested that popular religion supports appropriate market values such as utilitarianism and strengthens the informal social networks critical for raising credit and dealing with related enterprises (Gallin and Gallin 1982: 236–7; Li 1992; Yu 1987).

I believe that Chinese popular religion has in fact long included many themes, some apparently preadapted to capitalist development and others apparently antithetical. Chinese societies are developing new religious forms, rooted in the past, that directly address the market and the problem of values in market societies. Once again, these new forms show a rough correlation with gender: Men favor a Confucianist interpretation of texts, and women give stronger support to social action.

Popular religion, individualism, and markets

I have argued elsewhere that the lack of strong interpretative communities that could control religion in China opened a great deal of free space for variation (Weller 1994: 53–6). Even so, most people in Chinese societies would quickly agree on a few religious basics. Whatever else ancestor worship may accomplish, for example, nearly everyone who practices it talks about it as a way of energizing values of filial piety. Temples also clearly support community solidarity (but sometimes at the expense of larger solidarities like the nation). Gods, at least sometimes, speak to the naturalness of bureaucratic politics and the prevalence of upright officials.

Much of Chinese popular religion thus valorizes community and family, uniting individuals with these larger social circles. This is the most public face of popular practice and the picture painted by large calendrical rituals. This meshing of the individual into larger webs of social relations is quite different from Weber's Protestantism and quite different from the kind of ideology he expected with capitalism. This is one reason Weber and some later followers felt Chinese religion stood as a major impediment to capitalist development (Weber 1951; Bellah 1965). [. . .]

Just behind this communal side of religion, however, lurks a far more thoroughly individualistic and competitive religious personality, especially in ghost worship [. . .]. The ghostly side of Chinese religion in Taiwan (the only area for which we so far have extensive data) grew very rapidly in the 1980s, at the point when many Taiwanese for the first time had achieved some significant wealth but when the market economy also appeared particularly threatening and capricious with few productive outlets for capital (see Weller 1994: 148–53).

In addition, popular worship in Taiwan has always had a strong utilitarian side. Much worship occurs simply to make concrete requests of deities for cures, for help getting pregnant, or for business advice. Gods who do not really help soon lose their followers, and people can always tell stories of lives saved and enemies vanquished by their major community gods. Useless gods sometimes end up smashed or thrown in rivers.

Spirit-medium cults, the members of which usually worship at private altars, provide similarly utilitarian help and have none of the communal functions of major temples. Such cults have greatly increased recently in Taiwan. At the same time, more and more different gods are appearing on these private altars. Community temples usually feature one primary deity, often captured in many images. Other gods may appear on secondary altars or in minor positions on the main altar. The horde of different gods on private spirit-medium altars – as many as forty or fifty different images in recent years – reinforces the utilitarian functions of such cults (Li 1992: 11–13). With each deity having its own specialty, these temples can meet the needs of a wider variety of clients, just like a shop that expands its selection of wares. Not coincidentally, spirit-medium shrines themselves are profit-oriented petty capitalist enterprises.

As for all the areas I have discussed, religion shows less a preadaptation to capitalism than an ability to reproportion itself to the new context. The communal side of religion has easily held its own, reinforcing ties of locality and family that have been important to capitalist development. Yet, at least in Taiwan, ghosts and spirit mediums for (previously) minor gods have taken on a greatly expanded role in a kind of celebration of the individualism and competition of the market. [. . .]

[. . .] I will briefly discuss two major branches of these new religions: pietistic sects like the Way of Unity (Yiguan Dao), which have organized congregations, an interest in explicit interpretation of texts, and largely male leaderships; and new Buddhist groups, especially the Compassionate Relief Merit Association [. . .], whose leadership and membership is largely women.

Many of the pietistic sects claim disproportionate business success. The Way of Unity is the most famous, but all share a pietistic tradition with clearly organized congregations, an active concern for evangelization, and an interest in religious texts. They usually also center on a nurturing goddess and rely on spirit writing to produce new sacred texts. Their interpretations tend toward conservative rhapsodies on harmony and Confucian social relations (Jordan and Overmyer 1986). They also often have a general concern with concrete accomplishments in this world. The Way of Unity alone has about a million regular followers, and perhaps 15–20 percent of the adult population may be members of such sects.[10] Many of the sects have strong business support, and anecdotal evidence suggests that a disproportionate number of businessmen are sectarians (Shenmi 1990; Zhao 1992). Membership also appears to have grown rapidly just during the period of Taiwan's most rapid economic growth, but the statistics may be misleading because the Way of Unity was illegal until 1987. [. . .]

Taiwanese sectarians, just like Weber's Protestants, substitute a self-selected group of credit-worthy comrades for the potential problems of ascribed particularistic ties like kinship or residence. Even their vegetarianism marks them as different kinds of individuals, especially at business or religious feasts, which generally feature overflowing platters of meat. Their regular meetings, spirit-writing or spirit-possession sessions, and greater moral discipline distinguish them from the rest of society and offer them a new kind of social resource in business. Many of the sects, including the Way of Unity and the Hall of Compassion, worship a single primary goddess instead of one of the geographically localized gods that typify popular practice. This practice also cuts off the local community associations of sectarian temples and furthers the sectarian separation of members.

These sectarians also heavily emphasize explicit, textually validated values, unlike most popular religious practice. In particular, they consider themselves to be reviving threatened traditional Chinese values as expressed in Confucian and Daoist classics (Jordan and Overmyer 1986: 276–80; Zheng 1987). [. . .] Constant themes include conservative standards in Taiwan such as filial piety, respect for authority, and appropriate relations of hierarchy between men and women, seniors and juniors, parents and children. At the same time, the sects share the utilitarian concerns of popular practice; they stress health, economic success, and similar issues (Zheng 1987; Qu 1989).

Jordan and Overmyer (1986: 275–6) argue that the confirmation of "traditional" values and the chance for a respected position in the sect create an alternative route to self-esteem for people cut off from modern routes to success, especially people lacking a modern education. Yet the embrace of "tradition" also constitutes a kind of reaction to modernity that can characterize the educated and successful as well. This reaction is the other side of the celebration of individual autonomy and self-interest in ghost worship and spirit-medium altars; it is an attempt to retrieve communal values in an era that has lost them. Although these sects do embrace a kind of individualism, they embed it firmly in Confucian discourse on broader social relations. They are the spirit-writing equivalent of the philosophers trying to reclaim Confucianism as a moral alternative for the modern world.

Women have sometimes played an important role in these sects, but men dominate the leadership and sometimes the membership. Even the Religion of Compassion (Cihui Tang), with many female members, has few female leaders. In part, the appeal to Confucian tradition itself may discourage women. [. . .]

In contrast to these sects, some of the most important new Buddhist organizations appeal directly to women even though membership is open to all. [. . .] The most spectacularly successful such organization is the Compassionate Relief Merit Association (Ciji Gongdehui). It had almost 4 million members (close to 20 percent of Taiwan's population) and gave out over US$20 million in charitable aid in 1991 (Ciji Gongdehui, n.d.). [. . .]

Followers are expected to contribute money and time, and Zhengyan's [the nun who runs the organization] broad following took off with the economic boom of the 1980s. Even token contributions confer membership, but many members contribute as much as NT$1 million (about US$40,000) each year. Women also endure two-year waiting lists to volunteer at the state-of-the-art hospital the group has built. The Compassionate Relief Merit Association now has branches around the world and recently opened a clinic in California.

Medical charity and medical education remain its core activities, but it undertakes a wide range of charity for the poor and moral uplift for its usually wealthy members. The society opposes drinking, which can create a considerable hardship for men in business networks. It also urges a generally ascetic lifestyle, discouraging fancy clothes, makeup, or any form of conspicuous consumption. Members meet frequently to give testimonials about how their lives have changed and to listen to taped lectures by their leader. They often attest to how happy they are now that they have "crossed to the other shore" into the society. Above all they focus on concrete activity. Reading and reciting sutras or a Buddha's name are not core activities, unlike with most other forms of Buddhism. Nor is there any particular concern with establishing doctrinal support for their activities. [. . .]

Conclusion

Business and religion are quite disparate areas of culture, but both are experiencing closely comparable tensions that recall arguments over the expansion of market culture in the West. On the one hand, they are pushed toward increasing commodification and utilitarian exploitation of resources – human, natural, and divine. On the other hand, people are strongly reacting against what they see as the deterioration of shared community and family moralities.

Although this tension is sometimes phrased as an argument between market and antimarket moralities, it may better be viewed as reflecting a divided market culture. Both sides of the argument have roots in tradition, just as both sides are in some ways reflexes of the market itself. Thus Confucianism offers itself simultaneously as the key to capitalist success and as the answer to the resulting moral vacuum. In religion, ghosts and some spirit mediums had always catered to individuals and private profit, even as gods and bodhisattvas offered instead community and universal moral worlds. At the same time, divided market cultures also borrow directly from the West: from economic theory and its critics and even, to a limited extent, from religion, as when Buddhists borrow Christian ideas of social action.

There is thus no single market culture that simply grew from earlier tradition or from the market itself or from the hegemonic power of the West. The sense of tension over market culture itself – which pervades the Western, "Confucian," and Islamic worlds – largely escapes metaphors of convergence toward a single market culture or adaptation of older resources. If there is any global conclusion about market culture, it lies in this tension itself. The divide between secular humanists and religious fundamentalists, profit and community morality, moderns and postmoderns, is part of the system itself. [. . .]

Notes

1   See Jochim (1992) for a useful summary of the Chinese-language literature on this.
2   See Harrell (1985) on the combination of diligence and fatalism. I will not take space

here to discuss the combination, which seems counterintuitive but which is also reminiscent of Weber's (1958: 98–128) discussion of Calvinism's combination of predestination and a work ethic.

3   See, among many others, Huang (1984), Redding (1990), Yang and Cheng (1987), and Yu (1987). Jochim (1992) summarizes this and much other relevant work. A parallel argument has marked discussion of Chinese immigrants in the United States. Chinese "clannishness," for example, was cited early in the century as a reason Chinese would never assimilate, and Chinese "timidity" as a reason they would never be successful entrepreneurs. These cultural features became arguments to halt immigration. By the late twentieth century, however, these same features were read instead as Chinese family loyalty and respect for authority and cited as reasons for their success in American society (Tan 1986).

4   The adaptation of the Chinese to a market-driven economy owes just as much to their long history of commercialization, familiarity with cash (Freedman 1959), experience with accounting (Gardella 1992), and regular use of corporate management (Sangren 1984). I will, however, continue to concentrate on cultural resources related to family and Confucianism in this chapter.

5   See, among many others, Greenhalgh (1989), Hamilton and Kao (1990), Hsieh (1989), Redding (1990), and Wong (1988).

6   This kind of Confucian discourse was long frowned upon in the People's Republic; its recent renewal by the government may encourage its use by managers as well.

7   We know, in addition, that all kinds of personal ties play important roles in Western business, and researchers have not yet attempted a systematic comparison that might reveal just how different the use of connections really is between China and the West in practice.

8   Early wage-labor opportunities for women in the late nineteenth and early twentieth centuries opened up a few opportunities for women to escape this system, but in general their production continued to remain tied to the household and controlled by men (Topley 1975; Bell 1994).

9   Although the theory of ancestor worship was clear, the practice varied widely. Strong lineages in fact kept affines off the main ancestral altar in all circumstances, but poor areas with weak or no lineages often welcomed any ties they could get, and one could easily find villages where altars with tablets of three or four different surnames were not unusual (Weller 1987: 31).

10   Official statistics in 1991 listed about 1.5 million members of such sects, but they do not include sects officially registered as branches of Buddhism or Taoism (Cihui Tang is the most important) or people who still deny membership (Yiguan Dao was illegal until 1987).

References

Bell, Lynda S. 1994: "For Better, for Worse: Women and the World Market in Rural China." *Modern China* 20 (2), 180–210.

Bellah, Robert N. 1965: "Epilogue: Religion and Progress in Modern Asia." In Robert N. Bellah (ed.), *Religion and Progress in Modern Asia*. New York: Free Press, 168–229.

Berger, Peter L. 1988: "An East Asian Development Model?" In Peter L. Berger and Hsin-Huang Michael Hsiao (eds.), *In Search of an East Asian Development Model*. New Brunswick, NJ: Transaction Books, 3–11.

Ciji Gongdehui n.d.: "Wuyuan daci tongti dabei" (Great beneficence to known and unknown, and boundless compassion for all). Brochure, n.p.

DeGlopper, Donald R. 1972: "Doing Business in Lukang." In W. E. Willmott (ed.), *Economic Organization in Chinese Society*. Stanford: Stanford University Press, 297–326.

Freedman, Maurice 1959: "The Handling of Money: A Note on the Background to the Economic Sophistication of Overseas Chinese." *Man* 59, 64–5.

Gallin, Bernard and Gallin, Rita 1982: "Socioeconomic Life in Rural Taiwan: Twenty Years of Development and Change." *Modern China* 8, 205–46.

Gardella, Robert 1992: "Squaring Accounts: Commercial Bookkeeping Methods and Capitalist Rationalism in Late Qing and Republican China." *Journal of Asian Studies* 51 (2), 317–39.

Gates, Hill 1991: "'Narrow Hearts' and Petty Capitalism: Small Business Women in Chengdu, China." In Alice Littlefield and Hill Gates (eds.), *Marxist Approaches in Economic Anthropology*. Lanham, MD: University Press of America, 13–36.

Gold, Thomas B. 1985: "After Comradeship: Personal Relations in China Since the Cultural Revolution." *China Quarterly* 104 (December), 657–75.

Greenhalgh, Susan 1989: "Social Causes and Consequences of Taiwan's Post-war Economic Development." In Kwang-chih Chang, Kuang-chou Li, Arthur P. Wolf, and Alexander Chien-chung Yin (eds.), *Anthropological Studies of the Taiwan Area: Accomplishments and Prospects*. Taipei: National Taiwan University, 351–90.

Hamilton, Gary G. and Cheng-shu Kao 1990: "The Institutional Foundations of Chinese Business: The Family Firm in Taiwan." *Comparative Social Research* 12, 95–112.

Harrell, Stevan 1985: "Why Do the Chinese Work So Hard?" *Modern China* 11 (2), 203–26.

Hsieh Jih-chang 1989: "The Chinese Family Under the Impact of Modernization." In Kwang-chih Chang, Kuang-chou Li, Arthur P. Wolf, and Alexander Chien-chung Yin (eds.), *Anthropological Studies of the Taiwan Area: Accomplishments and Prospects*. Taipei: National Taiwan University, 273–84.

Huang Guangguo 1984: "Rujia lunli yu qiye zuzhi xingtai" (Confucian theory and types of enterprise organization). In Huang Guangguo (ed.), *Zhongguoshi guanli* (Chinese-style management). Taipei: Gongshang Shibao, 21–58.

Jochim, Christian 1992: "Confucius and Capitalism: Views of Confucianism in Works on Confucianism and Economic Development." *Journal of Chinese Religions* 20, 135–71.

Jordan, David K. and Overmyer, Daniel L. 1986: *The Flying Phoenix: Aspects of Chinese Sectarianism in Taiwan*. Princeton, NJ: Princeton University Press.

Levy, Marion J., Jr. 1949: *The Family Revolution in Modern China*. Cambridge, MA: Harvard University Press.

Li Yih-yuan 1992: "Taiwan minjian zongjiao de xiandai qushi: Dui Peter Berger jiaoshou dongya fazhan wenhua yinsu lun de huiying" (The modern tendencies of Taiwan's popular religion: A response to Professor Peter Berger's theory of cultural factors in East Asian development). *Wenhua de Tuxiang* (The image of culture) 2, 117–38.

McEwen, Susan 1994: "Markets, Modernization, and Individualism in Three Chinese Societies." Ph.D. dissertation, Boston University.

Qu Haiyuan 1989: *Minjian xinyang yu jingji fazhan* (Popular beliefs and economic development). Report to the Taiwan provincial government. Taipei: Taiwan Shengzhengfu Minzhengting.

Qu Haiyuan and Yao Lixiang 1986: "Taiwan diqu zongjiao bianqian zhi tantao" (Discussion of religious changes in the Taiwan area). *Bulletin of the Institute of Ethnology, Academia Sinica* 75, 655–85.

Redding, S. Gordon 1990: *The Spirit of Chinese Capitalism*. Berlin: Walter de Gruyter.

Sangren, P. Steven 1984: "Traditional Chinese Corporations: Beyond Kinship." *Journal of Asian Studies* 43 (3), 391–415.

"Shenmi jiaopai chongshi tianri" (A secret sect sees the light of day again) 1990: *Yazhou Zhoukan*, August 5, pp. 28–39.

Silin, Robert H. 1972: "Marketing and Credit in a Hong Kong Wholesale Market." In W. E. Willmott (ed.), *Economic Organization in Chinese Society*. Stanford: Stanford University Press, 327–52.

Tan Hong 1986: "'Orientalism' and Image-Making: Chinese Americans as 'Sojourner' and 'Model Minority.'" Typescript, Durham, NC.

Topley, Marjorie 1975: "Marriage Resistance in Rural Kwangtung." In Margery Wolf and Roxane Witke (eds.), *Women in Chinese Society*. Stanford: Stanford University Press, 67–88.

Weber, Max 1951: *The Religion of China: Confucianism and Taoism.* New York: Free Press.

Weber, Max 1958: *The Protestant Ethic and Spirit of Capitalism.* New York: Scribner's.

Weller, Robert P. 1987: *Unities and Diversities in Chinese Religion.* Seattle: University of Washington.

Weller, Robert P. 1994: *Resistance, Chaos and Control in China: Taiping Rebels, Taiwanese Ghosts and Tiananmen.* London: Macmillan.

Wolf, Margery 1972: *Women and the Family in Rural Taiwan.* Stanford: Stanford University Press.

Wong, Siu-lun 1988: "The Applicability of Asian Family Values to Other Sociocultural Settings." In Peter L. Berger and Hsin-Huang Michael Hsiao (eds.), *In Search of an East Asian Development Model*. New Brunswick, NJ: Transaction Books, 134–52.

Yan Yunxiang 1993: "The Flow of Gifts: Reciprocity and Social Networks in a Chinese Village." Ph.D. dissertation, Harvard University.

Yang Kuo-shu and Cheng Po-shyun 1987: "Chuamong jiazhiguan, geren xiandaixing ji zuzhi xingwei: Hourujia jiashou de yixiang weiguan yanzheng" (Confucianized values, individual modernity, and organizational behavior: An empirical test of the post-Confucian hypothesis). *Bulletin of the Institute of Ethnology, Academia Sinica* 64, 1–49.

Yu Yingshi 1987: *Zhongguo jinshi zongjiao lunli yu shangren jingshen* (Modern Chinese religious ethics and business spirit). Taipei: Lunjing.

Zhao Dingjun 1992: "Yiguan dao caili shen bu ke ce" (The immeasurable wealth of the Yiguan Dao). *Wealth Magazine* 121 (April), 131.

Zheng Zhiming 1987: "Youji lei luanshu suo xianshi zhi zongjiao xin qushi" (The new trend in religious worship as seen from biographical travels, memoirs). *Bulletin of the Institute of Ethnology, Academia Sinica* 61, 105–27.

Part II

Culture/Power/Knowledge

Introduction

The readings in this section elaborate on the concepts of discourse and power/knowledge discussed in the Introduction to this Reader. Edward Said and Stuart Hall extend Foucault's conceptual framework to the discourses of colonialism and race and their impact for colonized peoples. In the extract from *Orientalism*, Said defines his use of the term to describe the specific discourse forged out of European colonialism's powerful ways of knowing the "East."

Said's argument hinges on the ways in which colonial domination is structured not only through political and economic domination but through areas of knowledge such as philosophy, literature, art, and imperial administration. The discourse of Orientalism becomes the way in which both the "Occident" and "Orient" know themselves as essentially different from each other, in ways that assume the superiority of the West. Said argues that the contemporary politics between America and the Middle East is still structured by Orientalism, even though the word itself is no longer used to describe the field of knowledge now referred to as "Middle Eastern Studies."

Hall's piece unpacks the phrase "the West and the Rest," which he deploys to describe the power/knowledge relationship Said calls Orientalism. Like Said, Hall is concerned to identify how "the West and the Rest" operates as an idea rather than as referents of geographical location. Usefully, Hall carefully explains how he understands the meaning and nature of the concept of discourse and why it captures the productive aspects of power/knowledge expressed as "the West and the Rest."

Sander Gilman's detailed case study of the representations of female sexuality in nineteenth-century European art, literature, and medicine extends Said's and Hall's focus on the discourse of colonialism to consider how discourses of race, class, and imperialism intertwine. The case study shows how a discourse is constructed across several areas of knowledge, and how it works to establish truths about black and white female bodies within the metropolitan society. Specifically, the black female and the white working-class prostitute come together in an image of pathological female sexuality powerfully informing modes of surveillance and authority over (black and white) women in late nineteenth-century Europe.

5 Orientalism

Edward W. Said

On a visit to Beirut during the terrible civil war of 1975–1976 a French journalist wrote regretfully of the gutted downtown area that "it had once seemed to belong to . . . the Orient of Chateaubriand and Nerval."[1] He was right about the place, of course, especially so far as a European was concerned. The Orient was almost a European invention, and had been since antiquity a place of romance, exotic beings, haunting memories and landscapes, remarkable experiences. Now it was disappearing; in a sense it had happened, its time was over. Perhaps it seemed irrelevant that Orientals themselves had something at stake in the process, that even in the time of Chateaubriand and Nerval Orientals had lived there, and that now it was they who were suffering; the main thing for the European visitor was a European representation of the Orient and its contemporary fate, both of which had a privileged communal significance for the journalist and his French readers.

Americans will not feel quite the same about the Orient, which for them is much more likely to be associated very differently with the Far East (China and Japan, mainly). Unlike the Americans, the French and the British – less so the Germans, Russians, Spanish, Portuguese, Italians, and Swiss – have had a long tradition of what I shall be calling *Orientalism*, a way of coming to terms with the Orient that is based on the Orient's special place in European Western experience. The Orient is not only adjacent to Europe; it is also the place of Europe's greatest and richest and oldest colonies, the source of its civilizations and languages, its cultural contestant, and one of its deepest and most recurring images of the Other. In addition, the Orient has helped to define Europe (or the West) as its contrasting image, idea, personality, experience. Yet none of this Orient is merely imaginative. The Orient is an integral part of European material

Excerpted from E. W. Said, "Introduction." In *Orientalism: Western Conceptions of the Orient* (London: Penguin, 1995), 1–28.

civilization and culture. Orientalism expresses and represents that part culturally and even ideologically as a mode of discourse with supporting institutions, vocabulary, scholarship, imagery, doctrines, even colonial bureaucracies and colonial styles. In contrast, the American understanding of the Orient will seem considerably less dense, although our recent Japanese, Korean, and Indochinese adventures ought now to be creating a more sober, more realistic "Oriental" awareness. Moreover, the vastly expanded American political and economic role in the Near East (the Middle East) makes great claims on our understanding of that Orient.

[. . . B]y Orientalism I mean several things, all of them, in my opinion, interdependent. The most readily accepted designation for Orientalism is an academic one, and indeed the label still serves in a number of academic institutions. Anyone who teaches, writes about, or researches the Orient – and this applies whether the person is an anthropologist, sociologist, historian, or philologist – either in its specific or its general aspects, is an Orientalist, and what he or she does is Orientalism. Compared with *Oriental studies* or *area studies*, it is true that the term *Orientalism* is less preferred by specialists today, both because it is too vague and general and because it connotes the high-handed executive attitude of nineteenth-century and early-twentieth-century European colonialism. [. . .] The point is that even if it does not survive as it once did, Orientalism lives on academically through its doctrines and theses about the Orient and the Oriental.

[. . . There i]s a more general meaning for Orientalism. Orientalism is a style of thought based upon an ontological and epistemological distinction made between "the Orient" and (most of the time) "the Occident." Thus a very large mass of writers, among whom are poets, novelists, philosophers, political theorists, economists, and imperial administrators, have accepted the basic distinction between East and West as the starting point for elaborate theories, epics, novels, social descriptions, and political accounts concerning the Orient, its people, customs, "mind," destiny, and so on. [. . .]

The interchange between the academic and the more or less imaginative meanings of Orientalism is a constant one, and since the late eighteenth century there has been a considerable, quite disciplined – perhaps even regulated – traffic between the two. Here I come to the third meaning of Orientalism, which is something more historically and materially defined than either of the other two. Taking the late eighteenth century as a very roughly defined starting point Orientalism can be discussed and analyzed as the corporate institution for dealing with the Orient – dealing with it by making statements about it, authorizing views of it, describing it, by teaching it, settling it, ruling over it: in short, Orientalism as a Western style for dominating, restructuring, and having authority over the Orient. [. . .] My contention is that without examining Orientalism as a discourse one cannot possibly understand the enormously systematic discipline by which European culture was able to manage – and even produce – the Orient politically, sociologically, militarily, ideologically, scientifically, and imaginatively during the post-Enlightenment period. Moreover, so authoritative a position did Orientalism have that I believe no one writing, thinking, or acting on the Orient could do so without taking account of the limitations on thought and action imposed by Orientalism. In brief, because of Orientalism the Orient was not (and is not) a free subject of thought or action. [. . . T]his book [. . .] tries to show that European culture gained in strength and identity by setting itself off against the Orient as a sort of surrogate and even underground self.

[. . .] My point is that Orientalism derives from a particular closeness experienced between Britain and France and the Orient, which until the early nineteenth century had really meant only India and the Bible lands. From the beginning of the nineteenth century until the end of World War II France and Britain dominated the Orient and Orientalism; since World War II America has dominated the Orient, and approaches it as France and Britain once did. Out of that closeness, whose dynamic is enormously productive even if it always demonstrates the comparatively greater strength of the Occident (British, French, or American), comes the large body of texts I call Orientalist. [. . .]

I have begun with the assumption that the Orient is not an inert fact of nature. It is not merely *there*, just as the Occident itself is not just *there* either. [. . . A]s both geographical and cultural entities – to say nothing of historical entities – such locales, regions, geographical sectors as "Orient" and "Occident" are manmade. Therefore as much as the West itself, the Orient is an idea that has a history and a tradition of thought, imagery, and vocabulary that have given it reality and presence in and for the West. The two geographical entities thus support and to an extent reflect each other.

Having said that, one must go on to state a number of reasonable qualifications. In the first place, it would be wrong to conclude that the Orient was *essentially* an idea, or a creation with no corresponding reality. When Disraeli said in his novel *Tancred* that the East was a career, he meant that to be interested in the East was something bright young Westerners would find to be an all-consuming passion; he should not be interpreted as saying that the East was *only* a career for Westerners. There were – and are – cultures and nations whose location is in the East, and their lives, histories, and customs have a brute reality obviously greater than anything that could be said about them in the West. About that fact this study of Orientalism has very little to contribute, except to acknowledge it tacitly. But the phenomenon of Orientalism as I study it here deals principally, not with a correspondence between Orientalism and Orient, but with the internal consistency of Orientalism and its ideas about the Orient (the East as career) despite or beyond any correspondence, or lack thereof, with a "real" Orient. My point is that Disraeli's statement about the East refers mainly to that created consistency, that regular constellation of ideas as the pre-eminent thing about the Orient, and not to its mere being. [. . .]

A second qualification is that ideas, cultures, and histories cannot seriously be understood or studied without their force, or more precisely their configurations of power, also being studied. To believe that the Orient was created – or, as I call it, "Orientalized" – and to believe that such things happen simply as a necessity of the imagination, is to be disingenuous. The relationship between Occident and Orient is a relationship of power, of domination, of varying degrees of a complex hegemony, and is quite accurately indicated in the title of K. M. Panikkar's classic *Asia and Western Dominance*.[2] The Orient was Orientalized not only because it was discovered to be "Oriental" in all those ways considered common-

place by an average nineteenth-century European, but also because it *could be* –
that is, submitted to being – *made* Oriental. There is very little consent to be
found, for example, in the fact that Flaubert's encounter with an Egyptian
courtesan produced a widely influential model of the Oriental woman; she never
spoke of herself, she never represented her emotions, presence, or history. *He*
spoke for and represented her. He was foreign, comparatively wealthy, male,
and these were historical facts of domination that allowed him not only to
possess Kuchuk Hanem physically but to speak for her and tell his readers in
what way she was "typically Oriental." My argument is that Flaubert's situation
of strength in relation to Kuchuk Hanem was not an isolated instance. It fairly
stands for the pattern of relative strength between East and West, and the
discourse about the Orient that it enabled.

This brings us to a third qualification. One ought never to assume that the
structure of Orientalism is nothing more than a structure of lies or of myths
which, were the truth about them to be told, would simply blow away. [. . .]
After all, any system of ideas that can remain unchanged as teachable wisdom
[. . .] from the period of Ernest Renan in the late 1840s until the present in the
United States must be something more formidable than a mere collection of lies.
Orientalism, therefore, is not an airy European fantasy about the Orient, but a
created body of theory and practice in which, for many generations, there has
been a considerable material investment. Continued investment made Orientalism, as a system of knowledge about the Orient, an accepted grid for filtering
through the Orient into Western consciousness, just as that same investment
multiplied – indeed, made truly productive – the statements proliferating out
from Orientalism into the general culture.

[. . .] In any society not totalitarian, then, certain cultural forms predominate
over others, just as certain ideas are more influential than others; the form of this
cultural leadership is what Gramsci has identified as *hegemony*, an indispensable
concept for any understanding of cultural life in the industrial West. It is
hegemony, or rather the result of cultural hegemony at work, that gives Orientalism the durability and the strength I have been speaking about so far.
Orientalism is never far from what Denys Hay has called the idea of Europe,[3] a
collective notion identifying "us" Europeans as against all "those" non-Europe-
ans, and indeed it can be argued that the major component in European culture
is precisely what made that culture hegemonic both in and outside Europe: the
idea of European identity as a superior one in comparison with all the non-
European peoples and cultures. [. . .]

[. . .] Orientalism depends for its strategy on this flexible *positional* superiority,
which puts the Westerner in a whole series of possible relationships with the
Orient without ever losing him the relative upper hand. And why should it have
been otherwise, especially during the period of extraordinary European ascend-
ancy from the late Renaissance to the present? The scientist, the scholar, the
missionary, the trader, or the soldier was in, or thought about, the Orient because
he *could be there*, or could think about it, with very little resistance on the Orient's
part. [. . .]

[. . . T]he determining impingement on most knowledge produced in the
contemporary West (and here I speak mainly about the United States) is that it

be nonpolitical, that is, scholarly, academic, impartial, above partisan or small-minded doctrinal belief. One can have no quarrel with such an ambition in theory, perhaps, but in practice the reality is much more problematic. No one has ever devised a method for detaching the scholar from the circumstances of life, from the fact of his involvement (conscious or unconscious) with a class, a set of beliefs, a social position, or from the mere activity of being a member of a society. These continue to bear on what he does professionally, even though naturally enough his research and its fruits do attempt to reach a level of relative freedom from the inhibitions and the restrictions of brute, everyday reality. For there is such a thing as knowledge that is less, rather than more, partial than the individual (with his entangling and distracting life circumstances) who produces it. Yet this knowledge is not therefore automatically nonpolitical.

[. . .] What I am interested in doing now is suggesting how the general liberal consensus that "true" knowledge is fundamentally nonpolitical (and conversely, that overtly political knowledge is not "true" knowledge) obscures the highly if obscurely organized political circumstances obtaining when knowledge is produced. [. . .]

[. . .] Now because Britain, France, and recently the United States are imperial powers, their political societies impart to their civil societies a sense of urgency, a direct political infusion as it were, where and whenever matters pertaining to their imperial interests abroad are concerned. I doubt that it is controversial, for example, to say that an Englishman in India or Egypt in the later nineteenth century took an interest in those countries that was never far from their status in his mind as British colonies. To say this may seem quite different from saying that all academic knowledge about India and Egypt is somehow tinged and impressed with, violated by, the gross political fact – and yet *that is what I am saying* in this study of Orientalism. For if it is true that no production of knowledge in the human sciences can ever ignore or disclaim its author's involvement as a human subject in his own circumstances, then it must also be true that for a European or American studying the Orient there can be no disclaiming the main circumstances of his actuality: that he comes up against the Orient as a European or American first, as an individual second. And to be a European or an American in such a situation is by no means an inert fact. It meant and means being aware, however dimly, that one belongs to a power with definite interests in the Orient, and more important, that one belongs to a part of the earth with a definite history of involvement in the Orient almost since the time of Homer. [. . .]

[. . .] My idea is that European and then American interest in the Orient was political according to some of the obvious historical accounts of it that I have given here, but that it was the culture that created that interest, that acted dynamically along with brute political, economic, and military rationales to make the Orient the varied and complicated place that it obviously was in the field I call Orientalism.

Therefore, Orientalism is not a mere political subject matter or field that is reflected passively by culture, scholarship, or institutions; nor is it a large and diffuse collection of texts about the Orient; nor is it representative and expressive of some nefarious "Western" imperialist plot to hold down the "Oriental" world.

It is rather a *distribution* of geopolitical awareness into aesthetic, scholarly, economic, sociological, historical, and philological texts; it is an *elaboration* not only of a basic geographical distinction (the world is made up of two unequal halves, Orient and Occident) but also of a whole series of "interests" which, by such means as scholarly discovery, philological reconstruction, psychological analysis, landscape and sociological description, it not only creates but also maintains; it *is*, rather than expresses, a certain *will* or *intention* to understand, in some cases to control, manipulate, even to incorporate, what is a manifestly different (or alternative and novel) world; it is, above all, a discourse that is by no means in direct, corresponding relationship with political power in the raw, but rather is produced and exists in an uneven exchange with various kinds of power, shaped to a degree by the exchange with power political (as with a colonial or imperial establishment), power intellectual (as with reigning sciences like comparative linguistics or anatomy, or any of the modern policy sciences), power cultural (as with orthodoxies and canons of taste, texts, values), power moral (as with ideas about what "we" do and what "they" cannot do or understand as "we" do). Indeed, my real argument is that Orientalism is – and does not simply represent – a considerable dimension of modern political-intellectual culture, and as such has less to do with the Orient than it does with "our" world.

Because Orientalism is a cultural and a political fact, then, it does not exist in some archival vacuum; quite the contrary, I think it can be shown that what is thought, said, or even done about the Orient follows (perhaps occurs within) certain distinct and intellectually knowable lines. [. . .]

[. . . N]early every nineteenth-century writer (and the same is true enough of writers in earlier periods) was extraordinarily well aware of the fact of empire: this is a subject not very well studied, but it will not take a modern Victorian specialist long to admit that liberal cultural heroes like John Stuart Mill, Arnold, Carlyle, Newman, Macaulay, Ruskin, George Eliot, and even Dickens had definite views on race and imperialism, which are quite easily to be found at work in their writing. So even a specialist must deal with the knowledge that Mill, for example, made it clear in *On Liberty and Representative Government* that his views there could not be applied to India (he was an India Office functionary for a good deal of his life, after all) because the Indians were civilizationally, if not racially, inferior. The same kind of paradox is to be found in Marx[. . . . M]y whole point is to say that we can better understand the persistence and the durability of saturating hegemonic systems like culture when we realize that their internal constraints upon writers and thinkers were *productive*, not unilaterally inhibiting. [. . .]

Therefore I study Orientalism as a dynamic exchange between individual authors and the large political concerns shaped by the three great empires – British, French, American – in whose intellectual and imaginative territory the writing was produced. [. . .]

The kind of political questions raised by Orientalism, then, is [. . . *in*] *fine*, how can we treat the cultural, historical phenomenon of Orientalism as a kind of *willed human work* – not of mere unconditioned ratiocination – in all its historical complexity, detail, and worth without at the same time losing sight of the alliance between cultural work, political tendencies, the state, and the specific realities of domination? [. . .]

Yet what German Orientalism had in common with Anglo-French and later American Orientalism was a kind of intellectual *authority* over the Orient within Western culture. This authority must in large part be the subject of any description of Orientalism, and it is so in this study. Even the name *Orientalism* suggests a serious, perhaps ponderous style of expertise; when I apply it to modern American social scientists (since they do not call themselves Orientalists, my use of the word is anomalous), it is to draw attention to the way Middle East experts can still draw on the vestiges of Orientalism's intellectual position in nineteenth-century Europe.

There is nothing mysterious or natural about authority. It is formed, irradiated, disseminated; it is instrumental, it is persuasive; it has status, it establishes canons of taste and value; it is virtually indistinguishable from certain ideas it dignifies as true, and from traditions, perceptions, and judgments it forms, transmits, reproduces. Above all, authority can, indeed must, be analyzed. All these attributes of authority apply to Orientalism, and much of what I do in this study is to describe both the historical authority in and the personal authorities of Orientalism. [. . .]

It is clear, I hope, that my concern with authority does not entail analysis of what lies hidden in the Orientalist text, but analysis rather of the text's surface, its exteriority to what it describes. I do not think that this idea can be overemphasized. Orientalism is premised upon exteriority, that is, on the fact that the Orientalist, poet or scholar, makes the Orient speak, describes the Orient, renders its mysteries plain for and to the West. He is never concerned with the Orient except as the first cause of what he says. What he says and writes, by virtue of the fact that it is said or written, is meant to indicate that the Orientalist is outside the Orient, both as an existential and as a moral fact. The principal product of this exteriority is of course representation[. . . .]

Another reason for insisting upon exteriority is that I believe it needs to be made clear about cultural discourse and exchange within a culture that what is commonly circulated by it is not "truth" but representations. It hardly needs to be demonstrated again that language itself is a highly organized and encoded system, which employs many devices to express, indicate, exchange messages and information, represent, and so forth. In any instance of at least written language, there is no such thing as a delivered presence, but a *re-presence*, or a representation. The value, efficacy, strength, apparent veracity of a written statement about the Orient therefore relies very little, and cannot instrumentally depend, on the Orient as such. [. . .] Thus all of Orientalism stands forth and away from the Orient: that Orientalism makes sense at all depends more on the West than on the Orient, and this sense is directly indebted to various Western techniques of representation that make the Orient visible, clear, "there" in discourse about it. And these representations rely upon institutions, traditions, conventions, agreed-upon codes of understanding for their effects, not upon a distant and amorphous Orient. [. . .] At most, the "real" Orient provoked a writer to his vision; it very rarely guided it. Orientalism responded more to the culture that produced it than to its putative object, which was also produced by the West.

Thus the history of Orientalism has both an internal consistency and a highly articulated set of relationships to the dominant culture surrounding it. [. . .]

[. . .] Perhaps the most important task of all would be to undertake studies in contemporary alternatives to Orientalism, to ask how one can study other cultures and peoples from a libertarian, or a nonrepressive and nonmanipulative, perspective. But then one would have to rethink the whole complex problem of knowledge and power. [. . .]

[. . .] For the general reader, this study deals with matters that always compel attention, all of them connected not only with Western conceptions and treatments of the Other but also with the singularly important role played by Western culture in what Vico called the world of nations. Lastly, for readers in the so-called Third World, this study proposes itself as a step towards an understanding not so much of Western politics and of the non-Western world in those politics as of the *strength* of Western cultural discourse, a strength too often mistaken as merely decorative or "superstructural." My hope is to illustrate the formidable structure of cultural domination and, specifically for formerly colonized peoples, the dangers and temptations of employing this structure upon themselves or upon others. [. . .]

Much of the personal investment in this study derives from my awareness of being an "Oriental" as a child growing up in two British colonies. All of my education, in those colonies (Palestine and Egypt) and in the United States, has been Western, and yet that deep early awareness has persisted. In many ways my study of Orientalism has been an attempt to inventory the traces upon me, the Oriental subject, of the culture whose domination has been so powerful a factor in the life of all Orientals. [. . .]

[. . .] Three things have contributed to making even the simplest perception of the Arabs and Islam into a highly politicized, almost raucous matter: one, the history of popular anti-Arab and anti-Islamic prejudice in the West, which is immediately reflected in the history of Orientalism; two, the struggle between the Arabs and Israeli Zionism, and its effects upon American Jews as well as upon both the liberal culture and the population at large; three, the almost total absence of any cultural position making it possible either to identify with or dispassionately to discuss the Arabs or Islam. [. . .]

[. . .] The life of an Arab Palestinian in the West, particularly in America, is disheartening. There exists here an almost unanimous consensus that politically he does not exist, and when it is allowed that he does, it is either as a nuisance or as an Oriental. [. . .]

The nexus of knowledge and power creating "the Oriental" and in a sense obliterating him as a human being is therefore not for me an exclusively academic matter. Yet it is an *intellectual* matter of some very obvious importance. [. . .] In addition, and by an almost inescapable logic, I have found myself writing the history of a strange, secret sharer of Western anti-Semitism. [. . .] But what I should like also to have contributed here is a better understanding of the way cultural domination has operated. If this stimulates a new kind of dealing with the Orient, indeed if it eliminates the "Orient" and "Occident" altogether, then we shall have advanced a little in the process of what Raymond Williams has called the "unlearning" of "the inherent dominative mode."[4]

Notes

1 Thierry Desjardins, *Le Martyre du Liban* (Paris: Pion, 1976), 14.
2 K. M. Panikkar, *Asia and Western Dominance* (London: George, Allen and Unwin, 1959).
3 Denys Hay, *Europe: The Emergence of an Idea*, 2nd ed. (Edinburgh: Edinburgh University Press, 1968).
4 Raymond Williams, *Culture and Society, 1780–1950* (London: Chatto and Windus, 1958), 376.

6 The West and the Rest: Discourse and Power

Stuart Hall

[. . .]

Where and What is "the West"?

This question puzzled Christopher Columbus and remains puzzling today. Nowadays, many societies aspire to become "Western" – at least in terms of achieving Western standards of living. But in Columbus's day (the end of the fifteenth century) going West was important mainly because it was believed to be the quickest route to the fabulous wealth of the East. Indeed, even though it should have become clear to Columbus that the New World he had found was *not* the East, he never ceased to believe that it was, and even spiced his reports with outlandish claims: on his fourth voyage, he still insisted that he was close to Quinsay (the Chinese city now called Hangchow), where the Great Khan lived, and probably approaching the source of the Four Rivers of Paradise! Our ideas of "East" and "West" have never been free of myth and fantasy, and even to this day they are not primarily ideas about place and geography.

We have to use short-hand generalizations, like "West" and "Western" but we need to remember that they represent very complex ideas and have no simple or single meaning. At first sight, these words may seem to be about matters of geography and location. But even this, on inspection, is not straight-forward since we also use the same words to refer to a type of society, a level of development, and so on. It's true that what we call "the West," in this second sense, *did* first emerge in Western Europe. But "the West" is no longer only in Europe, and not all of Europe is in "the West." The historian John Roberts has

Excerpted from Stuart Hall, "The West and the Rest: Discourse and Power." In S. Hall and B. Gieben (eds.), *Formations of Modernity* (Cambridge: Polity Press, 1992), 275–331.

remarked that, "Europeans have long been unsure about where Europe 'ends' in the east. In the west and to the south, the sea provides a splendid marker ... but to the east the plains roll on and on and the horizon is awfully remote" (Roberts 1985: 149). Eastern Europe doesn't (doesn't yet? never did?) belong properly to "the West"; whereas the United States, which is not in Europe, definitely does. These days, technologically speaking, Japan, is "Western" though on our mental map it is about as far "East" as you can get. By comparison, much of Latin America, which is in the Western hemisphere, belongs economically to the Third World, which is struggling – not very successfully – to catch up with "the West." What are these different societies "east" and "west" of, exactly? Clearly, "the West" is as much an idea as a fact of geography.

The underlying premise of this chapter is that "the West" is a *historical*, not a geographical, construct. By "Western" we mean [. . .] a society that is developed, industrialized, urbanized, capitalist, secular, and modern. Such societies arose at a particular historical period – roughly, during the sixteenth century, after the Middle Ages and the break-up of feudalism. They were the result of a specific set of historical processes – economic, political, social, and cultural. Nowadays, any society, wherever it exists on a geographical map, which shares these characteristics, can be said to belong to "the West." The meaning of this term is therefore virtually identical to that of the word "modern." [. . .]

"The West" is therefore also an idea, a concept[. . . .] How did the idea, the language, of "the West" arise, and what have been its effects? What do we mean by calling it a *concept*?

The concept or idea of "the West" can be seen to function in the following ways:

First, it allows us to characterize and classify societies into different categories – i.e., "Western" "non-Western." It is a tool to think with. It sets a certain structure of thought and knowledge in motion.

Secondly, it is an image, or set of images. It condenses a number of different characteristics into one picture. It calls up in our mind's eye – it *represents* in verbal and visual language – a composite picture of what different societies, cultures, peoples, and places are like. It functions as part of a language, a "system of representation." (I say "system" because it doesn't stand on its own, but works in conjunction with other images and ideas with which it forms a set: for example, "Western" = urban = developed: or "non-Western" = non-industrial = rural = agricultural = underdeveloped.)

Thirdly, it provides a standard or model of comparison. It allows us to compare to what extent different societies resemble, or differ from, one another. Non-Western societies can accordingly be said to be "close to" or "far away from" or "catching up with" the West. It helps to explain *difference*.

Fourthly, it provides criteria of evaluation against which other societies are ranked and around which powerful positive and negative feelings cluster. (For example, "the West" = developed = *good* = desirable: or the "non-West" = underdeveloped = *bad* = undesirable.) It produces a certain kind of *knowledge* about a subject and certain attitudes towards it. In short, it functions as an *ideology*. [. . .]

We know that the West itself was produced by certain historical processes operating in a particular place in unique (and perhaps unrepeatable) historical circumstances. Clearly, we must also think of the *idea* of "the West" as having been produced in a similar way. These two aspects are in fact deeply connected, though exactly how is one of the big puzzles in sociology. We cannot attempt to resolve here the age-old sociological debate as to which came first: the idea of "the West," or Western societies. What we can say is that, as these societies emerged, so a concept and language of "the West" crystallized. And yet, we can be certain that the idea of "the West" did not simply reflect an already established Western society: rather, it was essential to the very formation of that society.

What is more, the idea of "the West," once produced, became productive in its turn. It had real effects: it enabled people to know or speak of certain things in certain ways. It produced knowledge. It became *both* the organizing factor in a system of global power relations *and* the organizing concept or term in a whole way of thinking and speaking.

The central concern [. . .] is to analyze the formation of a particular pattern of thought and language, a "system of representation" which has the concepts of "the West" and "the Rest" at its center.

The emergence of an idea of "the West" was central to the Enlightenment [. . . .] The Enlightenment was a very European affair. European society, it assumed, was the most advanced type of society on earth, European man (*sic*) the pinnacle of human achievement. It treated the West as the result of forces largely *internal* to Europe's history and formation.

However, [. . .] we argue that the rise of the West is also a *global* story. As Roberts observes, "'Modern' history can be defined as the approach march to the age dominated by the West" (Roberts 1985: 41). The West and the Rest became two sides of a single coin. What each now is, and what the terms we use to describe them mean, depend on the relations which were established between them long ago. The so-called uniqueness of the West was, in part, produced by Europe's contact and self-comparison with other, non-Western, societies (the Rest), very different in their histories, ecologies, patterns of development, and cultures from the European model. The difference of these other societies and cultures from the West was the standard against which the West's achievement was measured. It is within the context of these relationships that the idea of "the West" took on shape and meaning.

The importance of such perceived difference needs itself to be understood. Some modern theorists of language have argued that *meaning* always depends on the relations that exist between the different terms or words within a meaning system[. . . .] Accordingly, we know what "night" means because it is different from – in fact, opposite to – "day." The French linguist who most influenced this approach to meaning, Ferdinand de Saussure (1857–1912), argued that the words "night" and "day" on their own can't mean anything; it is the *difference* between "night" and "day" which enables these words to carry meaning (to signify).

Likewise, many psychologists and psychoanalysts argue that an infant first learns to think of itself as a separate and unique "self" by recognizing its separation – its difference – from others (principally, of course, its mother). By analogy, national cultures acquire their strong sense of identity by contrasting themselves with other cultures. Thus, we argue, the West's sense of itself – its identity – was formed, not only by the internal processes that gradually molded Western European countries into a distinct type of society, but also through Europe's sense of difference from other worlds – how it came to represent itself in relation to these "others." In reality, differences often shade imperceptibly into each other. (When exactly does "night" become "day"? Where exactly does "being English" end and "being Scottish" begin?) But, in order to function at all, we seem to need distinct, positive concepts many of which are sharply polarized towards each other [. . . S]uch "binary oppositions" seem to be fundamental to all linguistic and symbolic systems and to the production of meaning itself.

This [. . .] is about the role which "the Rest" played in the formation of the idea of "the West" and a "Western" sense of identity. At a certain moment, the fates of what had been, for many centuries, separate and distinct worlds became – some would say, fatally – harnessed together in the same historical time-frame. They became related elements in the same *discourse*, or way of speaking. They became different parts of one global social, economic, and cultural system, one interdependent world, one language.

A word of warning must be entered here. In order to bring out the distinctiveness of this "West and the Rest" discourse, I have been obliged to be selective and to simplify my representation of the West, and you should bear this in mind as you read. Terms like "the West" and "the Rest" are historical and linguistic constructs whose meanings change over time. More importantly, there are many different discourses, or ways in which the West came to speak of and represent other cultures. Some, like "the West and the Rest," were very Western-centered, or Eurocentric. Others, however, which I do not have space to discuss here, were much more culturally relativistic. I have elected to focus on what I call the discourse of "the West and the Rest" because it became a very common and influential discourse, helping to shape public perceptions and attitudes down to the present.

Another qualification concerns the very term "the West," which makes the West appear unified and homogeneous – essentially one place, with one view about other cultures and one way of speaking about them. Of course, this is not the case. The West has always contained many internal differences – between different nations, between Eastern and Western Europe, between the Germanic Northern and the Latin Southern cultures, between the Nordic, Iberian, and Mediterranean peoples, and so on. Attitudes towards other cultures within the West varied widely, as they still do between, for example, the British, the Spanish, the French, and the German.

It is also important to remember that, as well as treating non-European cultures as different and inferior, the West had its own *internal* "others." Jews, in particular, though close to Western religious traditions, were frequently excluded and ostracized. West Europeans often regarded Eastern Europeans as "barbaric," and, throughout the West, Western women were represented as inferior to Western men.

The same necessary simplification is true of my references to "the Rest." This term also covers enormous historical, cultural, and economic distinctions – for example, between the Middle East, the Far East, Africa, Latin America, indigenous North America and Australasia. It can equally encompass the simple societies of some North American Indians and the developed civilizations of China, Egypt, or Islam.

These extensive differences must be borne in mind as you study the analysis of the discourse of "the West and the Rest" in this chapter. However, we can actually use this simplification to make a point about discourse. For simplification is precisely what this discourse itself *does*. It represents what are in fact very differentiated (the different European cultures) as homogeneous (the West). And it asserts that these different cultures are united by one thing: the fact that *they are all different from the Rest*. Similarly, the Rest, though different among themselves, are represented as the same in the sense that *they are all different from the West*. In short, the discourse, as a "system of representation," *represents* the world as divided according to a simple dichotomy – the West/the Rest. That is what makes the discourse of "the West and the Rest" so destructive – it draws crude and simplistic distinctions and constructs an oversimplified conception of "difference." [. . .]

What is a Discourse?

In common-sense language, a discourse is simply "a coherent or rational body of speech or writing; a speech, or a sermon." But here the term is being used in a more specialized way [. . .]. By "discourse," we mean a particular way of *representing* "the West," "the Rest," and the relations between them. A discourse is a group of statements which provide a language for talking about – i.e., a way of representing – a particular kind of knowledge about a topic. When statements about a topic are made within a particular discourse, the discourse makes it possible to construct the topic in a certain way. It also limits the other ways in which the topic can be constructed.

A discourse does not consist of one statement, but of several statements working together to form what the French social theorist, Michel Foucault (1926–84), calls a "discursive formation." [. . .] The statements fit together because any one statement implies a relation to all the others: "They refer to the same object, share the same style and support 'a strategy . . . a common institutional . . . or political drift or pattern'" (Cousins and Hussain 1984: 84–5).

One important point about this notion of discourse is that it is not based on the conventional distinction between thought and action, language and practice. Discourse is about the production of knowledge through language. But it is itself produced by a practice: "discursive practice" – the practice of producing meaning. Since all social practices entail *meaning*, all practices have a discursive aspect. So discourse enters into and influences all social practices. Foucault would argue that the discourse of the West about the Rest was deeply implicated in practice – i.e., in how the West behaved towards the Rest.

To get a fuller sense of Foucault's theory of discourse, we must bear the following points in mind.

1   A discourse can be produced by many individuals in different institutional settings (like families, prisons, hospitals, and asylums). Its integrity or "coher-

ence" does not depend on whether or not it issues from one place or from a single speaker or "subject." Nevertheless, every discourse constructs positions from which alone it makes sense. Anyone deploying a discourse must position themselves as *if* they were the subject of the discourse. For example, we may not ourselves believe in the natural superiority of the West. But if we use the discourse of "the West and the Rest" we will necessarily find ourselves speaking from a position that holds that the West is a superior civilization. As Foucault puts it, "To describe a . . . statement does not consist in analysing the relations between the author and what he [*sic*] says . . . ; but in determining what position can and must be occupied by any individual if he is to be the subject of it [the statement]" (Foucault 1972: 95–6).

2   Discourses are not closed systems. A discourse draws on elements in other discourses, binding them into its own network of meanings. Thus [. . .] the discourse of "Europe" drew on the earlier discourse of "Christendom," altering or translating its meaning. Traces of past discourses remain embedded in more recent discourses of "the West."

3   The statements within a discursive formation need not all be the same. But the relationships and differences between them must be regular and systematic, not random. Foucault calls this a "system of dispersion": "Whenever one can describe, between a number of statements, such a system of dispersion, whenever . . . one can define a regularity . . . [then] we will say . . . that we are dealing with a *discursive formation*" (Foucault 1972: 38). [. . .]

Discourse and Ideology

A discourse is similar to what sociologists call an "ideology": a set of statements or beliefs which produce knowledge that serves the interests of a particular group or class. Why, then, use "discourse" rather than "ideology"?

One reason which Foucault gives is that ideology is based on a distinction between *true* statements about the world (science) and *false* statements (ideology), and the belief that the facts about the world help us to decide between true and false statements. But Foucault argues that statements about the social, political, or moral world are rarely ever simply true or false; and "the facts" do not enable us to decide definitively about their truth or falsehood, partly because "facts" can be construed in different ways. The very language we use to describe the so-called facts interferes in this process of finally deciding what is true, and what false.

For example, Palestinians fighting to regain land on the West Bank from Israel may be described either as "freedom fighters" or as "terrorists." It is a fact that they are fighting; but what does the fighting *mean*? The facts alone cannot decide. And the very language we use – "freedom fighters/terrorists" – is part of the difficulty. Moreover, certain descriptions, even if they appear false to us, can be *made* "true" because people act on them believing that they are true, and so their actions have real consequences. Whether the Palestinians are terrorists or not, if we think they are, and act on that "knowledge," they in effect become terrorists because we treat them as such. The language (discourse) has real effects in practice: the description becomes "true."

Foucault's use of "discourse," then, is an attempt to side-step what seems an unresolvable dilemma – deciding which social discourses are true or scientific, and which false or ideological. Most social scientists now accept that our values enter into all our descriptions of the social world, and therefore most of our statements, however factual, have an ideological dimension. What Foucault would say is that knowledge of the Palestinian problem is produced by competing discourses – those of "freedom fighter" and "terrorist" – and that each is linked to a contestation over power. It is the outcome of *this* struggle which will decide the "truth" of the situation.

You can see, then, that although the concept of "discourse" side-steps the problem of truth/falsehood in ideology, it does *not* evade the issue of power. Indeed, it gives considerable weight to questions of power since it is power, rather than the facts about reality, which make things "true": "We should admit that power produces knowledge. . . . That power and knowledge directly imply one another; that there is no power relation without the correlative constitution of a field of knowledge, nor any knowledge that does not presuppose and constitute . . . power relations" (Foucault 1980: 27).

Can a Discourse be "Innocent"?

Could the discourse which developed in the West for talking about the Rest operate outside power? Could it be, in that sense, purely scientific – i.e., ideologically innocent? Or was it influenced by particular class interests?

Foucault is very reluctant to *reduce* discourse to statements that simply mirror the interests of a particular class. The same discourse can be used by groups with different, even contradictory, class interests. But this does *not* mean that discourse is ideologically neutral or "innocent." Take, for example, the encounter between the West and the New World. There are several reasons why this encounter could not be innocent, and therefore why the discourse which emerged in the Old World about the Rest could not be innocent either.

First, Europe brought its own cultural categories, languages, images, and ideas to the New World in order to describe and represent it. It tried to fit the New World into existing conceptual frameworks, classifying it according to its own norms, and absorbing it into Western traditions of representation. This is hardly surprising: we often draw on what we already know about the world in order to explain and describe something novel. It was never a simple matter of the West just looking, seeing, and describing the New World/the Rest without preconceptions.

Secondly, Europe had certain definite purposes, aims, objectives, motives, interests, and strategies in setting out to discover what lay across the "Green Sea of Darkness." These motives and interests were mixed. The Spanish, for example, wanted to:

(a)   get their hands on gold and silver,
(b)   claim the land for Their Catholic Majesties, and
(c)   convert the heathen to Christianity.

These interests often contradicted one another. But we must not suppose that what Europeans said about the New World was simply a cynical mask for their own self-interest. When King Manuel of Portugal wrote to Ferdinand and Isabella of Spain that, "the principal motive of this enterprise [da Gama's voyage to India] has been ... the service of God our Lord, and our own advantage" (quoted in Hale 1966: 38) – thereby neatly and conveniently bringing God and Mammon together into the same sentence – he probably saw no obvious contradiction between them. These fervently religious Catholic rulers fully believed what they were saying. To them, serving God and pursuing "our advantage" were not necessarily at odds. They lived and fully believed their own ideology.

So, while it would be wrong to attempt to reduce their statements to naked self-interest, it is clear that their discourse was molded and influenced by the play of motives and interests across their language. Of course, motives and interests are almost never wholly conscious or rational. The desires which drove the Europeans were powerful; but their power was not always subject to rational calculation. Marco Polo's "treasures of the East" were tangible enough. But the seductive power which they exerted over generations of Europeans transformed them more and more into a myth. Similarly, the gold that Columbus kept asking the natives for very soon acquired a mystical, quasi-religious significance.

Finally, the discourse of "the West and the Rest" could not be innocent because it did not represent an encounter between equals. The Europeans had outsailed, outshot, and outwitted peoples who had no wish to be "explored," no need to be "discovered," and no desire to be "exploited." The Europeans stood *vis-à-vis* the Others in positions of dominant power. This influenced what they saw and how they saw it, as well as what they did not see.

Foucault sums up these arguments as follows. Not only is discourse always implicated in *power*; discourse is one of the "systems" through which power circulates. The knowledge which a discourse produces constitutes a kind of power, exercised over those who are "known." When that knowledge is exercised in practice, those who are "known" in a particular way will be subject (i.e., subjected) to it. This is always a power-relation. (See Foucault 1980: 201.) Those who produce the discourse also have the power to *make it true* – i.e., to enforce its validity, its scientific status.

This leaves Foucault in a highly relativistic position with respect to questions of truth because his notion of discourse undermines the distinction between true and false statements – between science and ideology – to which many sociologists have subscribed. These epistemological issues (about the status of knowledge, truth, and relativism) are too complex to take further here[. ...] However, the important idea to grasp now is the deep and intimate relationship which Foucault establishes between discourse, knowledge, and power. According to Foucault, when power operates so as to enforce the "truth" of any set of statements, then such a discursive formation produces a "regime of truth":

> Truth isn't outside power ... Truth is a thing of this world; it is produced only by virtue of multiple forms of constraint ... And it induces regular effects of power. Each society has its regime of truth, its "general politics" of truth; that is, the types

of discourse which it accepts and makes function as true; the mechanisms and instances which enable one to distinguish "true" and "false" statements; the means by which each is sanctioned; and the techniques and procedures accorded value in the acquisition of truth; the status of those who are charged with saying what counts as true. (Foucault 1980: 131)

[. . .]

References

Cousins, M. and Hussain, A. 1984: *Michel Foucault*. London: Macmillan.
Foucault, M. 1972: *The Archaeology of Knowledge*. London: Tavistock.
Foucault, M. 1980: *Power/Knowledge*. Brighton: Harvester.
Hale, J. R. et al. 1966: *Age Of Exploration*. The Netherlands: Time-Life International.
Roberts, J. M. 1985: *The Triumph of the West*. London: British Broadcasting Corporation.

7 Black Bodies, White Bodies: Toward an Iconography of Female Sexuality in the Late Nineteenth Century

Sander L. Gilman

How do we organize our perceptions of the world? Recent discussions of this age-old question have centered around the function of visual conventions as the primary means by which we perceive and transmit our understanding of the world about us.[1] Nowhere are these conventions more evident than in artistic representations, which consist more or less exclusively of icons. Rather than presenting the world, icons represent it. Even with a modest nod to supposedly mimetic portrayals it is apparent that, when individuals are shown within a work of art (no matter how broadly defined), the ideologically charged iconographic nature of the representation dominates. And it dominates in a very specific manner, for the representation of individuals implies the creation of some greater class or classes to which the individual is seen to belong. These classes in turn are characterized by the use of a model which synthesizes our perception of the uniformity of the groups into a convincingly homogeneous image. The resulting stereotypes may be overt, as in the case of caricatures, or covert, as in eighteenth-century portraiture. But they serve to focus the viewer's attention on the relationship between the portrayed individual and the general qualities ascribed to the class.

Specific individual realities are thus given mythic extension through association with the qualities of a class. These realities manifest as icons representing perceived attributes of the class into which the individual has been placed. The myths associated with the class, the myth of difference from the rest of humanity, is thus, to an extent, composed of fragments of the real world, perceived through the ideological bias of the observer. These myths are often so powerful, and the associations of their conventions so overpowering, that they are able to move from class to class without substantial alteration. In linking otherwise marginally

Excerpted from Sander L. Gilman, "Black Bodies, White Bodies: Toward an Iconography of Female Sexuality in Late Nineteenth-century Art, Medicine, and Literature." *Critical Inquiry* 12 (1985), 259–74.

or totally unrelated classes of individuals, the use of these conventions reveals perceptual patterns which themselves illuminate the inherent ideology at work. [. . .]

This essay is an attempt to plumb the conventions (and thus the ideologies) which exist at a specific historical moment in both the aesthetic and scientific spheres. [. . .] Medicine offers an especially interesting source of conventions since we do tend to give medical conventions special "scientific" status as opposed to the "subjective" status of the aesthetic conventions. But medical icons are no more "real" than "aesthetic" ones. Like aesthetic icons, medical icons may (or may not) be rooted in some observed reality. Like them, they are iconographic in that they represent these realities in a manner determined by the historical position of the observers, their relationship to their own time, and to the history of the conventions which they employ. Medicine uses its categories to structure an image of the diversity of mankind; it is as much at the mercy of the needs of any age to comprehend this infinite diversity as any other system which organizes our perception of the world. The power of medicine, at least in the nineteenth century, lies in the rise of the status of science. The conventions of medicine infiltrate other seemingly closed iconographic systems precisely because of this status. In examining the conventions of medicine employed in other areas, we must not forget this power.

One excellent example of the conventions of human diversity captured in the iconography of the nineteenth century is the linkage of two seemingly unrelated female images – the icon of the Hottentot female and the icon of the prostitute. In the course of the nineteenth century, the female Hottentot comes to represent the black female *in nuce*, and the prostitute to represent the sexualized woman. Both of these categories represent the creation of classes which correspondingly represent very specific qualities. While the number of terms describing the various categories of the prostitute expanded substantially during the nineteenth century, all were used to label the sexualized woman. Likewise, while many groups of African blacks were known to Europeans in the nineteenth century, the Hottentot remained representative of the essence of the black, especially the black female. Both concepts fulfilled an iconographic function in the perception and the representation of the world. How these two concepts were associated provides a case study for the investigation of patterns of conventions, without any limitation on the "value" of one pattern over another.

Let us begin with one of the classic works of nineteenth-century art, a work which records the idea of both the sexualized woman and the black woman. Edouard Manet's *Olympia*, painted in 1862–3, [. . .] assumes a key position in documenting the merger of these two images. The conventional wisdom concerning Manet's painting states that the model, Victorine Meurend, is "obviously naked rather than conventionally nude,"[2] and that her pose is heavily indebted to classical models[. . . .][3] Manet was also using a convention of early erotic photography in having the central figure directly confront the observer.[4] The black female attendant, based on a black model called Laura, has been seen as a reflex of both the classic black servant figure present in the visual arts of the eighteenth century as well as a representation of Baudelaire's *Vénus noire*.[5] Let us juxtapose the *Olympia*, with all its aesthetic and artistic analogies and parallels, to a work by Manet [. . .] – the *Nana* of 1877. Unlike Olympia, Nana is modern, a creature of present-day Paris[. . . .] But like Olympia, Nana was perceived as a sexualized female and is so represented. [. . . C]ertain major shifts in the iconography of the sexualized woman take place, not the least of which is the apparent disappearance of the black female.

The figure of the black servant in European art is ubiquitous. [. . . O]ne of the black servant's central functions in the visual arts of the eighteenth and nineteenth centuries was to sexualize the society in which he or she is found. [. . .] The association of the black with concupiscence reaches back into the Middle Ages. [. . .] By the eighteenth century, the sexuality of the black, both male and female, becomes an icon for deviant sexuality in general; as we have seen, the black figure appears almost always paired with a white figure of the opposite sex. By the nineteenth century, as in the *Olympia*, [. . .] the central female figure is associated with a black female in such a way as to imply their sexual similarity. The association of figures of the same sex stresses the special status of female sexuality. [. . .] The relationship between the sexuality of the black woman and that of the sexualized white woman enters a new dimension when contemporary scientific discourse concerning the nature of black female sexuality is examined.

Buffon commented on the lascivious, apelike sexual appetite of the black, introducing a commonplace of early travel literature into a "scientific" context. [. . .] The black female thus comes to serve as an icon for black sexuality in general. Buffon's view was based on a confusion of two applications of the great chain of being to the nature of the black. Such a scale was employed to indicate the innate difference between the races: in this view of mankind, the black occupied the antithetical position to the white on the scale of humanity. This polygenetic view was applied to all aspects of mankind, including sexuality and beauty. The antithesis of European sexual mores and beauty is embodied in the black, and the essential black, the lowest rung on the great chain of being, is the Hottentot. The physical appearance of the Hottentot is, indeed, the central nineteenth-century icon for sexual difference between the European and the black[. . . .]

Such labeling of the black female as more primitive, and therefore more sexually intensive, by writers like the Abbé Raynal would have been dismissed as unscientific by the radical empiricists of late eighteenth- and early nineteenth-century Europe. To meet their scientific standards, a paradigm was needed which would technically place both the sexuality and the beauty of the black in an antithetical position to that of the white. This paradigm would have to be rooted in some type of unique and observable physical difference; they found that difference in the distinction they drew between the pathological and the normal in the medical model. [. . .]

[. . .] In the nineteenth century, the black female was widely perceived as possessing not only a "primitive" sexual appetite but also the external signs of this temperament – "primitive" genitalia. Eighteenth-century travelers to southern Africa, such as François Le Vaillant and John Barrow, had described the so-called Hottentot apron, a hypertrophy of the labia and nymphae caused by the manipulation of the genitalia and serving as a sign of beauty among certain tribes, including the Hottentots and Bushmen as well as tribes in Basutoland and Dahomey.

The exhibition in 1810 of Saartjie Baartman, also called Sarah Bartmann or Saat-Jee and known as the "Hottentot Venus," caused a public scandal in a London inflamed by the issue of the abolition of slavery, since she was exhibited "to the public in a manner offensive to decency." [. . .] The state's objection was as much to her lewdness as to her status as an indentured black. [. . .] After more than five years of exhibition in Europe, Sarah Bartmann died in Paris in 1815 at the age of twenty-five. An autopsy was performed on her which was first written up by Henri de Blainville in 1816 and then, in its most famous version, by Cuvier in 1817.[6] [. . .] It is important to note that Sarah Bartmann was exhibited not to show her genitalia but rather to present another anomaly which the European audience (and pathologists such as de Blainville and Cuvier) found riveting. This was the steatopygia, or protruding buttocks, the other physical characteristic of the Hottentot female which captured the eyes of early European travelers. Thus the figure of Sarah Bartmann was reduced to her sexual parts. The audience which had paid to see her buttocks and had fantasized about the uniqueness of her genitalia when she was alive could, after her death and dissection, examine both, for Cuvier presented to "the Academy the genital organs of this woman prepared in a way so as to allow one to see the nature of the labia."[7]

Sarah Bartmann's sexual parts, her genitalia and her buttocks, serve as the central image for the black female throughout the nineteenth century. [. . .] To an extent, this reflects the general nineteenth-century understanding of female sexuality as pathological: the female genitalia were of interest partly as examples of the various pathologies which could befall them but also because the female genitalia came to define the female for the nineteenth century. [. . .]

By mid-century the image of the genitalia of the Hottentot had assumed a certain set of implications. The central view is that these anomalies are inherent, biological variations rather than adaptions. [. . .] By 1877 it was a commonplace that the Hottentot's anomalous sexual form was similar to other errors in the development of the labia. [. . .]

When the Victorians saw the female black, they saw her in terms of her buttocks and saw represented by the buttocks all the anomalies of her genitalia. In a mid-century erotic caricature of the Hottentot Venus, a white, male observer views her through a telescope, unable to see anything but her buttocks. This fascination with the uniqueness of the sexual parts of the black focuses on the buttocks over and over again. [. . .] Female sexuality is linked to the image of the buttocks, and the quintessential buttocks are those of the Hottentot.

We can see in Edwin Long's painting of 1882, *The Babylonian Marriage Market*, the centrality of this vocabulary in perceiving the sexualized woman. This painting was the most expensive work of contemporary art sold in nineteenth-century London. It also has a special place in documenting the perception of the sexualized female in terms of the great chain of aesthetic perception presented by Ellis. Long's painting is based on a specific text from Herodotus, who described the marriage auction in Babylon in which maidens were sold in order of comeliness. In the painting they are arranged in order of their attractiveness. Their physiognomies are clearly portrayed. Their features run from the most

European and white (a fact emphasized by the light reflected from the mirror onto the figure at the far left) to the Negroid features (thick lips, broad nose, dark but not black skin) of the figure furthest to the observer's right. The latter figure fulfills all of Virey's categories for the appearance of the black. This is, however, the Victorian scale of sexualized women acceptable within marriage, portrayed from the most to the least attractive, according to contemporary British standards. The only black female present is the servant-slave shown on the auction block, positioned so as to present her buttocks to the viewer. While there are black males in the audience and thus among the bidders, the only black female is associated with sexualized white women as a signifier of their sexual availability. Her position is her sign and her presence in the painting is thus analogous to the figure of the black servant, Laura, in Manet's *Olympia*. Here, the linkage between two female figures, one black and one white, represents not the perversities of human sexuality in a corrupt society, such as the black servants signify in Hogarth; rather, it represents the internalization of this perversity in one specific aspect of human society, the sexualized female, in the perception of late nineteenth-century Europe.

In the nineteenth century, the prostitute is perceived as the essential sexualized female. She is perceived as the embodiment of sexuality and of all that is associated with sexuality – disease as well as passion.[8] Within the large and detailed literature concerning prostitution written during the nineteenth century [. . .] the physiognomy and physiology of the prostitute are analyzed in detail. We can begin with the most widely read early nineteenth-century work on prostitution, that of A. J. B. Parent-Duchatelet, who provides a documentation of the anthropology of the prostitute in his study of prostitution in Paris (1836).[9] Alain Corbin has shown how Parent-Duchatelet's use of the public health model reduces the prostitute to yet another source of pollution, similar to the sewers of Paris. Likewise in Parent-Duchatelet's discussion of the physiognomy of the prostitute, he believes himself to be providing a descriptive presentation of the appearance of the prostitute. He presents his readers with a statistical description of the physical types of the prostitutes[. . . .] Prostitutes have a "peculiar plumpness" which is attributed to "the great number of hot baths which the major part of these women take" or perhaps to their lassitude, since they rise at ten or eleven in the morning, "leading an animal life." They are fat as prisoners are fat, from simple confinement. As an English commentator noted, "the grossest and stoutest of these women are to be found amongst the lowest and most disgusting classes of prostitutes."[10] These are the Hottentots on the scale of the sexualized female.

When Parent-Duchatelet considers the sexual parts of the prostitutes, he provides two sets of information which merge to become part of the myth of the physical anthropology of the prostitute. [. . .] Parent-Duchatelet's two views – first, that there is no adaption of the sexual organ and, second, that the sexual organ is especially prone to labial tumors and abscesses – merge in the image of the prostitute as developing, through illness, an altered appearance of the genitalia. From Parent-Duchatelet's description of the physical appearance of the prostitute [. . .] it is but a small step to the use of such catalogs of stigmata as a means of categorizing those women who have, as Freud states, "an aptitude for prostitution."[11] The major work of nineteenth-century physical anthropology, public health, and pathology to undertake this was written by Pauline Tarnowsky[. . . .] Her categories remain those of Parent-Duchatelet. She describes the excessive weight of prostitutes, their hair and eye color; she provides anthropometric measurements of skull size, a catalog of their family background (as with Parent-Duchatelet, most are the children of alcoholics), and their level of fecundity (extremely low) as well as the signs of their degeneration. These signs deal with the abnormalities of the face: asymmetry of features, misshapen noses, overdevelopment of the parietal region of the skull, and the appearance of the so-called Darwin's ear. All of these signs are the signs of the lower end of the scale of beauty, the end dominated by the Hottentot. All of these signs point to the "primitive" nature of the prostitute's physiognomy, for stigmata such as Darwin's ear (the simplification of the convolutes of the ear shell and the absence of a lobe) are a sign of the atavistic female. [. . .]

Change over time affects the physiognomy of the prostitute just as it does her genitalia, which become more and more diseased as she ages. For Tarnowsky, the appearance of the prostitute and her sexual identity are preestablished by heredity. What is most striking is that as the prostitute ages, she begins to appear more and more mannish. The link between the physical anomalies of the Hottentot and those of the lesbian appear in Billroth's *Handbuch der Frauenkrankheiten* [*Handbook of gynecological diseases*]; here, the link is between two further models of sexual deviancy, the prostitute and the lesbian. Both are seen as possessing the physical signs which set them apart from the normal.

The paper in which Tarnowsky undertook her documentation of the appearance of the prostitute is repeated word for word in the major late nineteenth-century study of prostitution. This study of the criminal woman, subtitled *The Prostitute and the Normal Woman*, written by Cesare Lombroso and his son-in-law, Guillaume Ferrero, was published in 1893. Lombroso accepts Tarnowsky's entire manner of seeing the prostitute and articulates one further subtext of central importance in the perception of the sexualized woman in the nineteenth century. [. . .] Lombroso accepts Parent-Duchatelet's image of the fat prostitute and sees her as similar to women living in asylums and to the Hottentot female. He regards the anomalies of the prostitute's labia as atavistic throwbacks to the Hottentot, if not the chimpanzee. Lombroso deems the prostitute to be an atavistic subclass of woman, and he applies the power of the polygenetic argument to the image of the Hottentot to support his views. [. . .]

The perception of the prostitute in the late nineteenth century thus merged with the perception of the black. Both categories are those of outsiders, but what does this amalgamation imply in terms of the perception of both groups? It is a commonplace that the primitive was associated with unbridled sexuality. [. . .] Such a loss of control was, of course, viewed as pathological and thus fell into the domain of the medical model. For the medical model, especially as articulated in the public health reforms of the mid- and late nineteenth century, had as its central preoccupation the elimination of sexually transmitted disease through the institution of social controls; this was the project which motivated writers such as Parent-Duchatelet and Tarnowsky. [. . .]

[. . .] It is not very surprising, therefore, to read in the late nineteenth century

– after social conventions surrounding the abolition of slavery in Great Britain and France, as well as the trauma of the American Civil War, forbade the public association of at least skin color with illness – that syphilis was not introduced into Europe by Christopher Columbus's sailors but rather that it was a form of leprosy which had long been present in Africa and had spread into Europe in the Middle Ages. The association of the black, especially the black female, with the syphilophobia of the late nineteenth century was thus made manifest. Black females do not merely represent the sexualized female, they also represent the female as the source of corruption and disease. It is the black female as the emblem of illness who haunts the background of Manet's *Olympia*.

For Manet's *Olympia* stands exactly midway between the glorification and the condemnation of the sexualized female. She is the antithesis of the fat prostitute. Indeed, she was perceived as thin by her contemporaries, much in the style of the actual prostitutes of the 1860s. But Laura, the black servant, is presented as plump, which can be best seen in Manet's initial oil sketch of her done in 1862–3. Her presence in both the sketch and in the final painting emphasizes her face, for it is the physiognomy of the black which points to her own sexuality and to that of the white female presented to the viewer unclothed but with her genitalia demurely covered. The association is between these hidden genitalia and the signifier of the black. Both point to potential corruption of the male viewer by the female. This is made even more evident in that work which art historians have stressed as being heavily influenced by Manet's *Olympia*, his portrait *Nana*. Here the associations would have been quite clear to the contemporary viewer. First, the model for the painting was Henriette Hauser, called Citron, the mistress of the prince of Orange. Second, Manet places in the background of the painting a Japanese crane, for which the French word (*grue*) was a slang term for prostitute. He thus labels the figure as a sexualized female. Unlike the classical pose of the *Olympia*, Nana is presented being admired by a well-dressed man-about-town (a *flâneur*). She is not naked but partially clothed. What Manet can further draw upon is the entire vocabulary of signs which, by the late nineteenth century, were associated with the sexualized female. Nana is fulsome rather than thin. Here Manet employs the stigmata of fatness to characterize the prostitute. This convention becomes part of the visualization of the sexualized female even while the reality of the idealized sexualized female is that of a thin female. Constantin Guys presents a fat, reclining prostitute in 1860, while Edgar Degas's *Madam's Birthday* (1879) presents an entire brothel of fat prostitutes. At the same time, Napoleon III's mistress, Marguerite Bellanger, set a vogue for slenderness. She was described as "below average in size, slight, thin, almost skinny." This is certainly not Nana. Manet places her in a position *vis-à-vis* the viewer (but not the male observer in the painting) which emphasizes the line of her buttocks, the steatopygia of the prostitute. Second, Nana is placed in such away that the viewer (but again not the *flâneur*) can observe her ear. It is, to no one's surprise, Darwin's ear, a sign of the atavistic female. Thus we know where the black servant is hidden in Nana – within Nana. Even Nana's seeming beauty is but a sign of the black hidden within. All her external stigmata point to the pathology within the sexualized female.

Manet's *Nana* thus provides a further reading of his *Olympia*, a reading which stresses Manet's debt to the pathological model of sexuality present during the late nineteenth century. The black hidden within *Olympia* bursts forth in Pablo Picasso's 1901 version of the painting: Olympia is presented as a sexualized black, with broad hips, revealed genitalia, gazing at the nude *flâneur* bearing her a gift of fruit, much as Laura bears a gift of flowers in Manet's original. But, unlike Manet, the artist is himself present in this work, as a sexualized observer of the sexualized female. Picasso owes part of his reading of the *Olympia* to the polar image of the primitive female as sexual object, as found in the lower-class prostitutes painted by Vincent van Gogh or the Tahitian maidens *à la* Diderot painted by Paul Gauguin. Picasso saw the sexualized female as the visual analogue of the black. Indeed, in his most radical break with the impressionist tradition, *Les Demoiselles d'Avignon* (1907), he linked the inmates of the brothel with the black by using the theme of African masks to characterize their appearance. The figure of the male represents the artist as victim. Picasso's parody points toward the importance of seeing Manet's *Nana* in the context of the medical discourse concerning the sexualized female which dominated the late nineteenth century.

The portrait of *Nana* is also embedded in a complex literary matrix which provides many of the signs needed to illustrate the function of the sexualized female as the sign of disease. The figure of Nana first appeared in Emile Zola's novel *L'Assommoir* (1877) in which she was presented as the offspring of the alcoholic couple who are the central figures of the novel. Her heredity assured the reader that she would eventually become a sexualized female – a prostitute – and, indeed, by the close of the novel she has run off with an older man, the owner of a button factory, and has begun her life as a sexualized female. Manet was captivated by the figure of Nana (as was the French reading public), and his portrait of her symbolically reflected her sexual encounters presented during the novel. Zola then decided to build the next novel in his Rougon-Macquart cycle about the figure of Nana as a sexualized female. Thus in Zola's *Nana* the reader is presented with Zola's reading of Manet's portrait of Nana. Indeed, Zola uses the portrait of the *flâneur* observing the half-dressed Nana as the centerpiece for a scene in the theater in which Nana seduces the simple Count Muffat. Immediately before this meeting, Zola presents Nana's first success in the theater (or, as the theater director calls it, his brothel). She appears in a revue, unable to sing or dance, and becomes the butt of laughter until, in the second act of the revue, she appears unclothed on stage:

> Nana was in the nude: naked with a quiet audacity, certain of the omnipotence of her flesh. She was wrapped in a simple piece of gauze: her rounded shoulders, her Amazon's breasts of which the pink tips stood up rigidly like lances, her broad buttocks which rolled in a voluptuous swaying motion, and her fair, fat hips: her whole body was in evidence, and could be seen under the light tissue with its foamy whiteness.[12]

What Zola describes are the characteristics of the sexualized woman, the "primitive" hidden beneath the surface: "all of a sudden in the comely child the woman arose, disturbing, bringing the mad surge of her sex, inviting the unknown element of desire. Nana was still smiling: but it was the smile of a man-eater."

Nana's atavistic sexuality, the sexuality of the Amazon, is destructive. The sign of this is her fleshliness. And it is this sign which reappears when she is observed by Muffat in her dressing room, the scene which Zola found in Manet's painting[. . . .]

Nana's childlike face is but a mask which conceals the hidden disease buried within, the corruption of sexuality. Thus Zola concludes the novel by revealing the horror beneath the mask: Nana dies of the pox. [. . .]

It is this uncleanliness, this disease, which forms the final link between two images of woman, the black and the prostitute. Just as the genitalia of the Hottentot were perceived as parallel to the diseased genitalia of the prostitute, so too the power of the idea of corruption links both images. Thus part of Nana's fall into corruption comes through her seduction by a lesbian, yet a further sign of her innate, physical degeneracy. She is corrupted and corrupts through sexuality. Miscegenation was a fear (and a word) from the late nineteenth-century vocabulary of sexuality. It was a fear not merely of interracial sexuality but of its results, the decline of the population. Interracial marriages were seen as exactly parallel to the barrenness of the prostitute; if they produced children at all, these children were weak and doomed. [. . .]

It is thus the inherent fear of the difference in the anatomy of the Other which lies behind the synthesis of images. The Other's pathology is revealed in anatomy. It is the similarity between the black and the prostitute – as bearers of the stigmata of sexual difference and, thus, pathology – which captured the late nineteenth century. [. . .]

The "white *man's* burden" thus becomes his sexuality and its control, and it is this which is transferred into the need to control the sexuality of the Other, the Other as sexualized female. The colonial mentality which sees "natives" as needing control is easily transferred to "woman" but woman as exemplified by the caste of the prostitute. This need for control was a projection of inner fears; thus, its articulation in visual images was in terms which described the polar opposite of the European male.

The roots of this image of the sexualized female are to be found in male observers, the progenitors of the vocabulary of images through which they believed themselves able to capture the essence of the Other. Thus when Freud, in his *Essay on Lay Analysis* (1926), discusses the ignorance of contemporary psychology concerning adult female sexuality, he refers to this lack of knowledge as the "dark continent" of psychology (*SE*, 20: 212). In using this phrase in English, Freud ties the image of female sexuality to the image of the colonial black and to the perceived relationship between the female's ascribed sexuality and the Other's exoticism and pathology. It is Freud's intent to explore this hidden "dark continent" and reveal the hidden truths about female sexuality, just as the anthropologist-explorers [. . .] were revealing the hidden truths about the nature of the black. Freud continues a discourse which relates the images of male discovery to the images of the female as object of discovery. The line from the secrets possessed by the "Hottentot Venus" to twentieth-century psychoanalysis runs reasonably straight.

Notes

1 The debate between E. H. Gombrich, *The Image and the Eye* (Ithaca, NY, 1982) and Nelson Goodman, *Ways of Worldmaking* (Hassocks, 1978) has revolved mainly around the manner by which conventions of representation create the work of art. Implicit in their debate is the broader question of the function of systems of conventions as icons within the work of art itself. On the limitation of the discussion of systems of conventions to aesthetic objects, see the extensive bibliography compiled in Ulrich Weisstein, "Bibliography of Literature and the Visual Arts, 1945–1980," *Comparative Criticism* 4 (1982), 324–34, in which the special position of the work of art as separate from other aspects of society can be seen. This is a holdover from the era of *Geistesgeschichte* in which special status was given to the interaction between aesthetic objects.

   This can be seen in the alternative case of works of aesthetic provenance which are, however, part of medical discourse. One thinks immediately of the anatomical works of Leonardo or George Stubbs or of paintings with any medical reference such as Rembrandt's *Dr. Tulp* or Théodore Géricault's paintings of the insane. When the literature on these works is examined, it is striking how most analysis remains embedded in the discourse of aesthetic objects, i.e., the anatomical drawing as a "subjective" manner of studying human form or, within medical discourse, as part of a "scientific" history of anatomical illustration. The evident fact that both of these modes of discourse exist simultaneously in the context of social history is lost on most critics. An exception is William Schupbach, *The Paradox of Rembrandt's "Anatomy of Dr. Tulp,"* Medical History, supp. 2 (London, 1982).

2 George Heard Hamilton, *Manet and His Critics* (New Haven, CT, 1954), 68. I am ignoring here George Mauner's peculiar position that "we may conclude that Manet makes no comment at all with this painting, if by comment we understand judgment or criticism" (*Manet: Peintre-Philosophe: A Study of the Painter's Themes* [University Park, PA, 1975], 99).

3 For my discussion of Manet's works, I draw especially on Theodore Reff, *Manet: "Olympia"* (London, 1976), and Werner Hofmann, *Nana: Mythos und Wirklichkeit* (Cologne, 1973); neither of these studies examines the medical analogies. See also Eunice Lipton, "Manet: A Radicalized Female Imagery," *Artforum* 13 (March 1975), 48–53.

4 See George Needham, "Manet, *Olympia,* and Pornographic Photography," in Thomas Hess and Linda Nochlin (eds.), *Woman as Sex Object* (New York, 1972), 81–9.

5 See Philippe Rebeyrol, "Baudelaire et Manet," *Les Temps modernes* 5 (October 1949), 707–25.

6 See Henri de Blainville, "Sur une femme de la race hottentote," *Bulletin des sciences par la société philomatique de Paris* (1816), 183–90. This early version of the autopsy seems to be unknown to William B. Cohen, *The French Encounter with Africans: White Response to Blacks, 1530–1880* (Bloomington, 1980), esp. 239–45. See also Stephen Jay Gould, "The Hottentot Venus," *Natural History* 91 (1982), 20–7.

7 Georges Cuvier, "Extraits d'observations faites sur le cadavre d'une femme connue à Paris et à Londres sous le nom de Vénus Hottentote," *Mémoires du Museum d'histoire naturelle* 3 (1817), 259–74; rpt. with plates in Geoffrey Saint-Hilaire and Frederic Cuvier, *Histoire naturelle des mammifères avec des figures originales,* 2 vols. (Paris, 1824), 1: 1–23. The substance of the autopsy is reprinted again by Flourens in the *Journal complémentaire du dictionnaire des science médicales* 4 (1819), 145–9, and by Jules Cloquet, *Manuel d'anatomie de l'homme descriptive du corps humaine* (Paris, 1825), pl.

278. Cuvier's presentation of the "Hottentot Venus" forms the major signifier for the image of the Hottentot as sexual primitive in the nineteenth century.

8   The best study of the age of the prostitute is Alain Corbain, *Les Filles de noce: Misère sexuelle et prostitution (dix-neuvième et vingtième siècles)* (Paris, 1978). On the black prostitute, see Khalid Kishantainy, *The Prostitute in Progressive Literature* (London, 1982), 74–84. On the iconography associated with the pictorial representation of the prostitute in nineteenth-century art, see Hess and Nochlin, *Woman as Sex Object*; Nochlin, "Lost and Found: Once More the Fallen Woman," *Art Bulletin* 60 (March 1978), 139–53; and Lynda Nead, "Seduction, Prostitution, Suicide: *On the Brink* by Alfred Elmore," *Art History* 5 (September 1982), 310–22. On the special status of medical representations of female sexuality, see the eighteenth-century wax models of female anatomy in the Museo della Specola, Florence, and reproduced in Mario Bucci, *Anatomia come arte* (Florence, 1969), esp. pl. 8.

9   See A. J. B. Parent-Duchatelet, *De la prostitution dans la ville de Paris*, 2 vols. (Paris, 1836), 1: 193–244.

10 Parent-Duchatelet, *On Prostitution in the City of Paris* (London, 1840), 38. It is exactly the passages on the physiognomy and appearance of the prostitute which this anonymous translator presents to his English audience as the essence of Parent-Duchatelet's work.

11 Sigmund Freud, *The Standard Edition of the Complete Psychological Works of Sigmund Freud*, ed. and trans. James Strachey, 24 vols. (London, 1953–74), 7: 191; all further references to this work, abbreviated *SE* and with volume and page numbers, will be included in the text. See my "Freud and the Prostitute: Male Stereotypes of Female Sexuality in *fin de siècle* Vienna," *Journal of the American Academy of Psychoanalysis* 9 (1981), 337–60.

12 Emile Zola, *Nana*, trans. Charles Duff (London, 1953), 27.

Part III

Development as Discourse

Introduction

This section begins with two readings that have applied the conceptual maps of discourse and power outlined in Part II to the contemporary knowledge practices of development. Arturo Escobar's book, *Encountering Development*, is the most extensive study of development as a discourse of power/knowledge. In this extract he summarizes his deconstruction of development through an analysis of how the Third World is constructed as poor within development discourse. He traces the ways in which Western understandings of poverty as material deprivation became the key criterion for evaluating social wellbeing.

Employing this discourse approach to development, James Ferguson looks at how World Bank reports construct Lesotho, a small, nominally independent country surrounded by the Republic of South Africa, as a "Less Developed Country." In this extract, he describes how an instrumental logic informs the ways in which the Bank's experts construct this stereotype by representing Lesotho outside its context of linkage with the South African economy.

A more personal account of the power of development discourse to categorize and stereotype is provided in Shrestha's autobiographical piece of his own experience of becoming a development category. Echoing Escobar's unpacking of the concept of poverty within development discourse, Shrestha describes his early years as a village boy in Nepal. Access to state-funded primary education and, subsequently, participation in an international development program gradually make him aware of himself and his community as "underdeveloped" and "poor" in ways he was not before.

The reading from the World Bank Report of 1999 extends this exploration of development discourse into an analysis of the role of knowledge in transforming the global economy in the twenty-first century. The continuing features of the West and the Rest embedded in the "knowledge economy" are demonstrated in the World Bank extract, which maintains a binary of a majority world that "lacks" what the minority world has. The extract argues that the technological gap between the "fortunate few" and poor countries can be closed by enlightened policies facilitating their acquisition of "knowledge." A definition of "knowledge" as that which is productive of economic gain is unapologetically allocated primary importance, and once again positions the "Rest" as those who "lack" what the West has got.

8 The Problematization of Poverty: The Tale of Three Worlds and Development

Arturo Escobar

> The word "poverty" is, no doubt, a key word of our times, extensively used and abused by everyone. Huge amounts of money are spent in the name of the poor. Thousands of books and expert advice continue to offer solutions to their problems. Strangely enough, however, nobody, including the proposed "beneficiaries" of these activities, seems to have a clear, and commonly shared, view of poverty. For one reason, almost all the definitions given to the word are woven around the concept of "lack" or "deficiency." This notion reflects only the basic relativity of the concept. What is necessary and to whom? And who is qualified to define all that?
>
> Majid Rahnema, *Global Poverty: A Pauperizing Myth*, 1991

One of the many changes that occurred in the early post-World War II period was the "discovery" of mass poverty in Asia, Africa, and Latin America. Relatively inconspicuous and seemingly logical, this discovery was to provide the anchor for an important restructuring of global culture and political economy. The discourse of war was displaced onto the social domain and to a new geographical terrain: the Third World. Left behind was the struggle against fascism. In the rapid globalization of US domination as a world power the "war on poverty" in the Third World began to occupy a prominent place. Eloquent facts were adduced to justify this new war: "Over 1,500,000 million people, something like two-thirds of the world population, are living in conditions of acute hunger, defined in terms of identifiable nutritional disease. This hunger is at the same time the cause and effect of poverty, squalor, and misery in which they live" (Wilson 1953: 11).

Statements of this nature were uttered profusely throughout the late 1940s and 1950s (Orr 1953; Shonfield 1950; United Nations 1951). The new emphasis

Excerpted from Arturo Escobar, "The Problematization of Poverty: The Tale of Three Worlds and Development." In *Encountering Development: The Making and Unmaking of the Third World* (Princeton, NJ: Princeton University Press, 1995), 21–54.

was spurred by the recognition of the chronic conditions of poverty and social unrest existing in poor countries and the threat they posed for more developed countries. The problems of the poor areas irrupted into the international arena. The United Nations estimated that per capita income in the United States was $1,453 in 1949, whereas in Indonesia it barely reached $25. This led to the realization that something had to be done before the levels of instability in the world as a whole became intolerable. The destinies of the rich and poor parts of the world were seen to be closely linked. "Genuine world prosperity is indivisible," stated a panel of experts in 1948. "It cannot last in one part of the world if the other parts live under conditions of poverty and ill health" (Milbank Memorial Fund 1948: 7; see also Lasswell 1945).

Poverty on a global scale was a discovery of the post-World War II period. As Sachs (1990) and Rahnema (1991) have maintained, the conceptions and treatment of poverty were quite different before 1940. In colonial times the concern with poverty was conditioned by the belief that even if the "natives" could be somewhat enlightened by the presence of the colonizer, not much could be done about their poverty because their economic development was pointless. The natives' capacity for science and technology, the basis for economic progress, was seen as nil (Adas 1989). As the same authors point out, however, within Asian, African, and Latin or Native American societies – as well as throughout most of European history – vernacular societies had developed ways of defining and treating poverty that accommodated visions of community, frugality, and sufficiency. Whatever these traditional ways might have been, and without idealizing them, it is true that massive poverty in the modern sense appeared only when the spread of the market economy broke down community ties and deprived millions of people from access to land, water, and other resources. With the consolidation of capitalism, systemic pauperization became inevitable.

Without attempting to undertake an archaeology of poverty, as Rahnema (1991) proposes, it is important to emphasize the break that occurred in the conceptions and management of poverty first with the emergence of capitalism in Europe and subsequently with the advent of development in the Third World. Rahnema describes the first break in terms of the advent in the nineteenth century of systems for dealing with the poor based on assistance provided by impersonal institutions. Philanthropy occupied an important place in this transition (Donzelot 1979). The transformation of the poor into the assisted had profound consequences. This "modernization" of poverty signified not only the rupture of vernacular relations but also the setting in place of new mechanisms of control. The poor increasingly appeared as a social problem requiring new ways of intervention in society. It was, indeed, in relation to poverty that the modern ways of thinking about the meaning of life, the economy, rights, and social management came into place. "Pauperism, political economy, and the discovery of society were closely interwoven" (Polanyi 1957: 84).

The treatment of poverty allowed society to conquer new domains. More perhaps than on industrial and technological might, the nascent order of capitalism and modernity relied on a politics of poverty the aim of which was not only to create consumers but to transform society by turning the poor into objects of knowledge and management. What was involved in this operation was "a techno-discursive instrument that made possible the conquest of pauperism and the invention of a politics of poverty" (Procacci 1991: 157). Pauperism, Procacci explains, was associated, rightly or wrongly, with features such as mobility, vagrancy, independence, frugality, promiscuity, ignorance, and the refusal to accept social duties, to work, and to submit to the logic of the expansion of "needs." Concomitantly, the management of poverty called for interventions in education, health, hygiene, morality, and employment and the instillment of good habits of association, savings, child rearing, and so on. The result was a panoply of interventions that accounted for the creation of a domain that several researchers have termed "the social" (Donzelot 1979, 1988, 1991; Burchell, Gordon, and Miller 1991).

As a domain of knowledge and intervention, the social became prominent in the nineteenth century, culminating in the twentieth century in the consolidation of the welfare state and the ensemble of techniques encompassed under the fabric of social work. Not only poverty but health, education, hygiene, employment, and the poor quality of life in towns and cities were constructed as social problems, requiring extensive knowledge about the population and appropriate modes of social planning (Escobar 1992). The "government of the social" took on a status that, as the conceptualization of the economy, was soon taken for granted. A "separate class of the 'poor'" (Williams 1973: 104) was created. Yet the most significant aspect of this phenomenon was the setting into place of apparatuses of knowledge and power that took it upon themselves to optimize life by producing it under modern, "scientific" conditions. The history of modernity, in this way, is not only the history of knowledge and the economy, it is also, more revealingly, the history of the social.[1]

The history of development implies the continuation in other places of this history of the social. This is the second break in the archaeology of poverty proposed by Rahnema: the globalization of poverty entailed by the construction of two-thirds of the world as poor after 1945. If within market societies the poor were defined as lacking what the rich had in terms of money and material possessions, poor countries came to be similarly defined in relation to the standards of wealth of the more economically advantaged nations. This economic conception of poverty found an ideal yardstick in the annual per capita income. The perception of poverty on a global scale "was nothing more than the result of a comparative statistical operation, the first of which was carried out only in 1940" (Sachs 1990: 9). Almost by fiat, two-thirds of the world's peoples were transformed into poor subjects in 1948 when the World Bank defined as poor those countries with an annual per capita income below $100. And if the problem was one of insufficient income, the solution was clearly economic growth.

Thus poverty became an organizing concept and the object of a new problematization. As in the case of any problematization (Foucault 1986), that of poverty brought into existence new discourses and practices that shaped the reality to which they reflected. That the essential trait of the Third World was its poverty and that the solution was economic growth and development became self-evident, necessary, and universal truths. This chapter analyzes the multiple processes that made possible this particular historical event. It accounts for the "developmentalization" of the Third World, its progressive insertion into a regime of thought and practice in which certain interventions for the eradication of poverty became central to the world order. This chapter can also be seen as an account of the production of the tale of three worlds and the contest over the development of the third. The tale of three worlds was, and continues to be despite the demise of the second, a way of bringing about a political order "that works by the negotiation of boundaries achieved through ordering differences" (Haraway 1989: 10). It was and is a narrative in which culture, race, gender, nation, and class are deeply and inextricably intertwined. The political and economic order coded by the tale of three worlds and development rests on a traffic of meanings that mapped new domains of being and understanding, the same domains that are increasingly being challenged and displaced by people in the Third World today. [. . .]

The Discourse of Development

The space of development

What does it mean to say that development started to function as a discourse, that is, that it created a space in which only certain things could be said and even imagined? If discourse is the process through which social reality comes into being – if it is the articulation of knowledge and power, of the visible and the expressible – how can the development discourse be individualized and related to ongoing technical, political, and economic events? How did development become a space for the systematic creation of concepts, theories, and practices?

An entry point for this inquiry on the nature of development as discourse is its basic premises as they were formulated in the 1940s and 1950s. The organizing premise was the belief in the role of modernization as the only force capable of destroying archaic superstitions and relations, at whatever social, cultural, and political cost. Industrialization and urbanization were seen as the inevitable and necessarily progressive routes to modernization. Only through material advancement could social, cultural, and political progress be achieved. This view determined the belief that capital investment was the most important ingredient in economic growth and development. The advance of poor countries was thus seen from the outset as depending on ample supplies of capital to provide for infrastructure, industrialization, and the overall modernization of society. Where was this capital to come from? One possible answer was domestic savings. But these countries were seen as trapped in a "vicious circle" of poverty and lack of capital, so that a good part of the "badly needed" capital would have to come from abroad[. . . .] Moreover, it was absolutely necessary that governments and international organizations take an active role in promoting and orchestrating the necessary efforts to overcome general backwardness and economic underdevelopment.

What, then, were the most important elements that went into the formulation of development theory? [. . .] There was the process of capital formation, and the various factors associated with it: technology, population and resources, monetary and fiscal policies, industrialization and agricultural development, commerce and trade. There were also a series of factors linked to cultural considerations, such as education and the need to foster modern cultural values. Finally, there was the need to create adequate institutions for carrying out the complex task ahead: international organizations (such as the World Bank and the International Monetary Fund, created in 1944, and most of the United Nations technical agencies, also a product of the mid-1940s); national planning agencies (which proliferated in Latin America, especially after the inauguration of the Alliance for Progress in the early 1960s); and technical agencies of various kinds.

Development was not merely the result of the combination, study, or gradual elaboration of these elements (some of these topics had existed for some time); nor the product of the introduction of new ideas (some of which were already appearing or perhaps were bound to appear); nor the effect of the new international organizations or financial institutions (which had some predecessors, such as the League of Nations). It was rather the result of the establishment of a set of relations among these elements, institutions, and practices and of the systematization of these relations to form a whole. The development discourse was constituted not by the array of possible objects under its domain but by the way in which, thanks to this set of relations, it was able to form systematically the objects of which it spoke, to group them and arrange them in certain ways, and to give them a unity of their own.[2]

To understand development as a discourse, one must look not at the elements themselves but at the system of relations established among them. It is this system that allows the systematic creation of objects, concepts, and strategies; it determines what can be thought and said. These relations – established between institutions, socioeconomic processes, forms of knowledge, technological factors, and so on – define the conditions under which objects, concepts, theories, and strategies can be incorporated into the discourse. In sum, the system of relations establishes a discursive practice that sets the rules of the game: who can speak, from what points of view, with what authority, and according to what criteria of expertise; it sets the rules that must be followed for this or that problem, theory, or object to emerge and be named, analyzed, and eventually transformed into a policy or a plan.

The objects with which development began to deal after 1945 were numerous and varied. Some of them stood out clearly (poverty, insufficient technology and capital, rapid population growth, inadequate public services, archaic agricultural practices, and so on), whereas others were introduced with more caution or even in surreptitious ways (such as cultural attitudes and values and the existence of racial, religious, geographic, or ethnic factors believed to be associated with backwardness). These elements emerged from a multiplicity of points: the newly formed international organizations, government offices in distant capitals, old and new institutions, universities and research centers in developed countries, and, increasingly with the passing of time, institutions in the Third World. Everything was subjected to the eye of the new experts: the poor dwellings of the rural masses, the vast agricultural fields, cities, households, factories, hospitals, schools, public offices, towns and regions, and, in the last instance, the world as a whole. The vast surface over which the discourse moved at ease practically covered the entire cultural, economic, and political geography of the Third World.

However, not all the actors distributed throughout this surface could identify objects to be studied and have their problems considered. Some clear principles of authority were in operation. They concerned the role of experts, from whom certain criteria of knowledge and competence were asked; institutions such as the United Nations, which had the moral, professional, and legal authority to name subjects and define strategies; and the international lending organizations, which carried the symbols of capital and power. These principles of authority also concerned the governments of poor countries, which commanded the legal political authority over the lives of their subjects, and the position of leadership of the rich countries, who had the power, knowledge, and experience to decide on what was to be done.

Economists, demographers, educators, and experts in agriculture, public health, and nutrition elaborated their theories, made their assessments and observations, and designed their programs from these institutional sites. Problems were continually identified, and client categories brought into existence. Development proceeded by creating "abnormalities" (such as the "illiterate," the "underdeveloped," the "malnourished," "small farmers," or "landless peasants"), which it would later treat and reform. Approaches that could have had positive effects in terms of easing material constraints became, linked to this type of rationality, instruments of power and control. As time went by, new problems were progressively and selectively incorporated; once a problem was incorporated into the discourse, it had to be categorized and further specified. Some problems were specified at a given level (such as local or regional), or at various of these levels (for instance, a nutritional deficiency identified at the level of the household could be further specified as a regional production shortage or as affecting a given population group), or in relation to a particular institution. But these refined specifications did not seek so much to illuminate possible solutions as to give "problems" a visible reality amenable to particular treatments.

This seemingly endless specification of problems required detailed observations in villages, regions, and countries in the Third World. Complete dossiers of countries were elaborated, and techniques of information were designed and constantly refined. This feature of the discourse allowed for the mapping of the economic and social life of countries, constituting a true political anatomy of the Third World.[3] The end result was the creation of a space of thought and action the expansion of which was dictated in advance by the very same rules introduced during its formative stages. The development discourse defined a perceptual field structured by grids of observation, modes of inquiry and registration of problems, and forms of intervention; in short, it brought into existence a space defined not so much by the ensemble of objects with which it dealt but by a set of relations and a discursive practice that systematically produced interrelated objects, concepts, theories, strategies, and the like.

To be sure, new objects have been included, new modes of operation introduced, and a number of variables modified (for instance, in relation to strategies to combat hunger, knowledge about nutritional requirements, the types of crops given priority, and the choices of technology have changed); yet the same set of relations among these elements continues to be established by the discursive practices of the institutions involved. Moreover, seemingly opposed options can easily coexist within the same discursive field (for instance, in development economics, the structuralist school and the monetarist school seem to be in open contradiction; yet they belong to the same discursive formation and originate in the same set of relations [. . .]; it can also be shown that agrarian reform, green revolution, and integrated rural development are strategies through which the same unity, "hunger," is constructed[. . . .] In other words, although the discourse has gone through a series of structural changes, the architecture of the discursive formation laid down in the period 1945–55 has remained unchanged, allowing the discourse to adapt to new conditions. The result has been the succession of development strategies and substrategies up to the present, always within the confines of the same discursive space.

It is also clear that other historical discourses influenced particular representations of development. The discourse of communism, for instance, influenced the promotion of those choices which emphasized the role of the individual in society and, in particular, those approaches which relied on private initiative and private property. So much emphasis on this issue in the context of development, so strong a moralizing attitude probably would not have existed without the persistent anti-Communist preaching that originated in the Cold War. Similarly, the fact that economic development relied so much on the need for foreign exchange influenced the promotion of cash crops for export, to the detriment of food crops for domestic consumption. Yet the ways in which the discourse organized these elements cannot be reduced to causal relations[. . . .]

In a similar vein, patriarchy and ethnocentrism influenced the form development took. Indigenous populations had to be "modernized," where modernization meant the adoption of the "right" values, namely, those held by the white minority or a mestizo majority and, in general, those embodied in the ideal of the cultivated European; programs for industrialization and agricultural development, however, not only have made women invisible in their role as producers but also have tended to perpetuate their subordination[. . . .] Forms of power in terms of class, gender, race, and nationality thus found their way into development theory and practice. The former do not determine the latter in a direct causal relation; rather they are the development discourse's formative elements.

The examination of any given object should be done within the context of the discourse as a whole. The emphasis on capital accumulation, for instance, emerged as part of a complex set of relations in which technology, new financial institutions, systems of classification (GNP per capita), decision-making systems (such as new mechanisms for national accounting and the allocation of public resources), modes of knowledge, and international factors all played a role. What made development economists privileged figures was their position in this complex system. Options privileged or excluded must also be seen in light of the dynamics of the entire discourse – why, for instance, the discourse privileged the promotion of cash crops (to secure foreign exchange, according to capital and technological imperatives) and not food crops; centralized planning (to satisfy economic and knowledge requirements) but not participatory and decentralized approaches; agricultural development based on large mechanized farms and the use of chemical inputs but not alternative agricultural systems, based on smaller farms, ecological considerations, and integrated cropping and pest management; rapid economic growth but not the articulation of internal markets to satisfy the needs of the majority of the people; and capital-intensive but not labor-intensive solutions. With the deepening of the crisis, some of the previously excluded choices are being considered, although most often within a development perspective[. . . .]

Finally, what is included as legitimate development issues may depend on specific relations established in the midst of the discourse; relations, for instance, between what experts say and what international politics allows as feasible (this may determine, for instance, what an international organization may prescribe out of the recommendation of a group of experts); between one power segment and another (say, industry versus agriculture); or between two or more forms of authority (for instance, the balance between nutritionists and public health specialists, on the one hand, and the medical profession, on the other, which may determine the adoption of particular approaches to rural health care). Other types of relations to be considered are those between sites from which objects appear (for instance, between rural and urban areas); between procedures of assessment of needs (such as the use of "empirical data" by World Bank missions) and the position of authority of those carrying the assessment (this may determine the proposals made and the possibility of their implementation).

Relations of this type regulate development practice. Although this practice is not static, it continues to reproduce the same relations between the elements with which it deals. It was this systematization of relations that conferred upon development its great dynamic quality: its immanent adaptability to changing conditions, which allowed it to survive, indeed to thrive, up to the present. By 1955 a discourse had emerged which was characterized not by a unified object but by the formation of a vast number of objects and strategies; not by new knowledge but by the systematic inclusion of new objects under its domain. The most important exclusion, however, was and continues to be what development was supposed to be all about: people. Development was – and continues to be for the most part – a top-down, ethnocentric, and technocratic approach, which treated people and cultures as abstract concepts, statistical figures to be moved up and down in the charts of "progress." Development was conceived not as a cultural process (culture was a residual variable, to disappear with the advance of modernization) but instead as a system of more or less universally applicable technical interventions intended to deliver some "badly needed" goods to a "target" population. It comes as no surprise that development became a force so destructive to Third World cultures, ironically in the name of people's interests.

The professionalization and institutionalization of development

Development was a response to the problematization of poverty that took place in the years following World War II and not a natural process of knowledge that gradually uncovered problems and dealt with them; as such, it must be seen as a historical construct that provides a space in which poor countries are known, specified, and intervened upon. To speak of development as a historical construct requires an analysis of the mechanisms through which it becomes an active, real force. These mechanisms are structured by forms of knowledge and power and can be studied in terms of processes of institutionalization and professionalization.

The concept of professionalization refers mainly to the process that brings the Third World into the politics of expert knowledge and Western science in general. This is accomplished through a set of techniques, strategies, and disciplinary practices that organize the generation, validation, and diffusion of development knowledge, including the academic disciplines, methods of research and teaching, criteria of expertise, and manifold professional practices; in other words, those mechanisms through which a politics of truth is created and maintained, through which certain forms of knowledge are given the status of truth. This professionalization was effected through the proliferation of development sciences and subdisciplines. It made possible the progressive incorporation of problems into the space of development, bringing problems to light in ways congruent with the established system of knowledge and power.

The professionalization of development also made it possible to remove all problems from the political and cultural realms and to recast them in terms of the apparently more neutral realm of science. It resulted in the establishment of development studies programs in most major universities in the developed world and conditioned the creation or restructuring of Third World universities to suit the needs of development. The empirical social sciences, on the rise since the late 1940s, especially in the United States and England, were instrumental in this regard. So were the area studies programs, which became fashionable after the war in academic and policy-making circles. As already mentioned, the increasingly professionalized character of development caused a radical reorganization of knowledge institutions in Latin America and other parts of the Third World. Professionalized development required the production of knowledge that could allow experts and planners "scientifically [to] ascertain social requirements," to recall Currie's words (Fuenzalida 1983: 1987).[4]

An unprecedented will to know everything about the Third World flourished unhindered, growing like a virus. [. . .] The Third World witnessed a massive landing of experts, each in charge of investigating, measuring, and theorizing about this or that little aspect of Third World societies. The policies and programs that originated from this vast field of knowledge inevitably carried with them strong normalizing components. At stake was a politics of knowledge that allowed experts to classify problems and formulate policies, to pass judgment on entire social groups and forecast their future – to produce, in short, a regime of truth and norms about them. The consequences for these groups and countries cannot be emphasized enough.

Another important consequence of the professionalization of development was the inevitable translation of Third World people and their interests into research data within Western capitalist paradigms. There is a further paradox in this situation. As an African scholar put it, "Our own history, culture and practices, good or bad, are discovered and translated in the journals of the North and come back to us re-conceptualized, couched in languages and paradigms which make it all sound new and novel" (Namuddu 1989: 28; quoted in Mueller 1991: 5). [. . .]

The invention of development necessarily involved the creation of an institutional field from which discourses are produced, recorded, stabilized, modified, and put into circulation. This field is intimately imbricated with processes of professionalization; together they constitute an apparatus that organizes the production of forms of knowledge and the deployment of forms of power, relating one to the other. The institutionalization of development took place at all levels, from the international organizations and national planning agencies in the Third World to local development agencies, community development committees, private voluntary agencies, and nongovernmental organizations. Starting in the mid-1940s with the creation of the great international organizations, this process has not ceased to spread, resulting in the consolidation of an effective network of power. It is through the action of this network that people and communities are bound to specific cycles of cultural and economic production and through which certain behaviors and rationalities are promoted. This field of intervention relies on myriad local centers of power, in turn supported by forms of knowledge that circulate at the local level.

The knowledge produced about the Third World is utilized and circulated by these institutions through applied programs, conferences, international consultant services, local extension practices, and so on. A corollary of this process is the establishment of an ever-expanding development business; as John Kenneth Galbraith wrote, referring to the climate in US universities in the early 1950s, "No economic subject more quickly captured the attention of so many as the rescue of the people of the poor countries from their poverty" (1979: 29). Poverty, illiteracy, and even hunger became the basis of a lucrative industry for planners, experts, and civil servants (Rahnema 1986). This is not to deny that the work of these institutions might have benefited people at times. It is to emphasize that the work of development institutions has not been an innocent effort on behalf of the poor. Rather, development has been successful to the extent that it has been able to integrate, manage, and control countries and populations in increasingly detailed and encompassing ways. If it has failed to solve the basic problems of underdevelopment, it can be said – perhaps with greater pertinence – that it has succeeded well in creating a type of underdevelopment that has been, for the most part, politically and technically manageable. The discord between institutionalized development and the situation of popular groups in the Third World has only grown with each development decade, as popular groups themselves are becoming apt at demonstrating.

Conclusion

The crucial threshold and transformation that took place in the early post-World War II period [. . .] were the result not of a radical epistemological or political breakthrough but of the reorganization of a number of factors that allowed the Third World to display a new visibility and to irrupt into a new realm of language. This new space was carved out of the vast and dense surface of the

Third World, placing it in a field of power. Underdevelopment became the subject of political technologies that sought to erase it from the face of the Earth but that ended up, instead, multiplying it to infinity.

Development fostered a way of conceiving of social life as a technical problem, as a matter of rational decision and management to be entrusted to that group of people – the development professionals – whose specialized knowledge allegedly qualified them for the task. Instead of seeing change as a process rooted in the interpretation of each society's history and cultural tradition – as a number of intellectuals in various parts of the Third World had attempted to do in the 1920s and 1930s (Gandhi being the best known of them) – these professionals sought to devise mechanisms and procedures to make societies fit a preexisting model that embodied the structures and functions of modernity. Like sorcerers' apprentices, the development professionals awakened once again the dream of reason that, in their hands, as in earlier instances, produced a troubling reality.

At times, development grew to be so important for Third World countries that it became acceptable for their rulers to subject their populations to an infinite variety of interventions, to more encompassing forms of power and systems of control; so important that First and Third World elites accepted the price of massive impoverishment, of selling Third World resources to the most convenient bidder, of degrading their physical and human ecologies, of killing and torturing, of condemning their indigenous populations to near extinction; so important that many in the Third World began to think of themselves as inferior, underdeveloped, and ignorant and to doubt the value of their own culture, deciding instead to pledge allegiance to the banners of reason and progress; so important, finally, that the achievement of development clouded the awareness of the impossibility of fulfilling the promises that development seemed to be making.

After four decades of this discourse, most forms of understanding and representing the Third World are still dictated by the same basic tenets. The forms of power that have appeared act not so much by repression but by normalization; not by ignorance but by controlled knowledge; not by humanitarian concern but by the bureaucratization of social action. As the conditions that gave rise to development became more pressing, it could only increase its hold, refine its methods, and extend its reach even further. That the materiality of these conditions is not conjured up by an "objective" body of knowledge but is charted out by the rational discourses of economists, politicians, and development experts of all types should already be clear. What has been achieved is a specific configuration of factors and forces in which the new language of development finds support. As a discourse, development is thus a very real historical formation, albeit articulated around an artificial construct (underdevelopment) and upon a certain materiality (the conditions baptized as underdevelopment), which must be conceptualized in different ways if the power of the development discourse is to be challenged or displaced.

To be sure, there is a situation of economic exploitation that must be recognized and dealt with. Power is too cynical at the level of exploitation and should be resisted on its own terms. There is also a certain materiality of life conditions that is extremely preoccupying and that requires great effort and attention. But those seeking to understand the Third World through development have long lost sight of this materiality by building upon it a reality that like a castle in the air has haunted us for decades. Understanding the history of the investment of the Third World by Western forms of knowledge and power is a way to shift the ground somewhat so that we can start to look at that materiality with different eyes and in different categories.

The coherence of effects that the development discourse achieved is the key to its success as a hegemonic form of representation: the construction of the poor and underdeveloped as universal, preconstituted subjects, based on the privilege of the representers; the exercise of power over the Third World made possible by this discursive homogenization (which entails the erasure of the complexity and diversity of Third World peoples, so that a squatter in Mexico City, a Nepalese peasant, and a Tuareg nomad become equivalent to each other as poor and underdeveloped); and the colonization and domination of the natural and human ecologies and economies of the Third World.[5]

Development assumes a teleology to the extent that it proposes that the "natives" will sooner or later be reformed; at the same time, however, it reproduces endlessly the separation between reformers and those to be reformed by keeping alive the premise of the Third World as different and inferior, as having a limited humanity in relation to the accomplished European. Development relies on this perpetual recognition and disavowal of difference, a feature identified by Bhabha (1990) as inherent to discrimination. The signifiers of "poverty," "illiteracy," "hunger," and so forth have already achieved a fixity as signifieds of "underdevelopment" which seems impossible to sunder. Perhaps no other factor has contributed to cementing the association of "poverty" with "underdevelopment" as the discourse of economists. [. . .]

Notes

1   Foucault (1979, 1980a, 1980b, 1991a) refers to this aspect of modernity – the appearance of forms of knowledge and regulatory controls centered on the production and optimization of life – as "biopower." Biopower entailed the "governmentalization" of social life, that is, the subjection of life to explicit mechanisms of production and administration by the state and other institutions. The analysis of biopower and governmentality should be an integral component of the anthropology of modernity (Urla 1993).

2   The methodology for the study of discourse used in this section follows Foucault's. See especially Foucault (1972, 1991b).

3   The loan agreements (Guarantee Agreements) between the World Bank and recipient countries signed in the late 1940s and 1950s invariably included a commitment on the part of the borrower to provide "the Bank," as it is called, with all the information it requested. It also stipulated the right of Bank officials to visit any part of the territory of the country in question. The "missions" that this institution periodically sent to borrowing countries were a major mechanism for extracting detailed information about those countries.

4   Although most Latin American professionals avidly gave themselves to the task of

extracting the new knowledge from their countries' economies and cultures, in time the transnationalization of knowledge resulted in a dialectic through which the call for a more autonomous social science was advanced (Fals Borda 1970). This dialectic contributed to intellectual and social efforts such as dependency theory and Liberation Theology.

5 The coherence of effects of the development discourse should not signify any sort of intentionality. As the discourses discussed by Foucault, development must be seen as a "strategy without strategists," in the sense that nobody is explicitly masterminding it; it is the result of a historical problematization and a systematized response to it.

References

Adas, M. 1989: *Machines as the Measure of Men*. Ithaca, NY: Cornell University Press.

Bhabha, H. 1990: "The Other Question: Difference, Discrimination, and the Discourse of Colonialism." In R. Ferguson et al. (eds.), *Out There: Marginalization and Contemporary Cultures*. New York: New Museum of Contemporary Art; Cambridge, MA: MIT Press.

Burchell, G., Gordon, C., and Miller, P. (eds.) 1991: *The Foucault Effect*. Chicago: University of Chicago Press.

Donzelot, J. 1979: *The Policing of Families*. New York: Pantheon Books.

Donzelot, J. 1988: "The Promotion of the Social." *Economy and Society* 17 (3), 217–34.

Donzelot, J. 1991: "Pleasure in Work." In G. Burchell, C. Gordon, and P. Miller (eds.), *The Foucault Effect*. Chicago: University of Chicago Press, 251–80.

Escobar, A. 1992: "Planning." In W. Sachs (ed.), *The Development Dictionary*. London: Zed Books, 112–45.

Fals Borda, O. 1970: *Ciencia Propia y Colonialismo Intelectual*. Mexico, DF: Editorial Nuestro Tiempo.

Foucault, M. 1972: *The Archeology of Knowledge*. New York: Harper Colophon.

Foucault, M. 1979: *Discipline and Punish*. New York: Vintage Books.

Foucault, M. 1980a: *Power/Knowledge*. New York: Pantheon Books.

Foucault, M. 1980b: *The History of Sexuality*. New York: Vintage Books.

Foucault, M. 1986: *The Use of Pleasure*. New York: Pantheon Books.

Foucault, M. 1991a: "Governmentality." In G. Burchell, C. Gordon, and P. Miller (eds.), *The Foucault Effect*. Chicago: University of Chicago Press, 87–104.

Foucault, M. 1991b: "Politics and the Study of Discourse." In G. Burchell, C. Gordon, and P. Miller (eds.), *The Foucault Effect*. Chicago: University of Chicago Press, 87–104.

Fuenzalida, E. 1983: "The Reception of 'Scientific Sociology' in Chile." *Latin American Research Review* 18 (2), 95–112.

Galbraith, J. K. 1979: *The Nature of Mass Poverty*. Cambridge, MA: Harvard University Press.

Haraway, D. 1989: *Primate Visions: Gender, Race, and Nature in the World of Modern Science*. New York: Routledge.

Lasswell, H. 1945: *World Politics Faces Economics*. New York: McGraw-Hill.

Milbank Memorial Fund 1948: *International Approaches to Problems of Underdeveloped Countries*. New York: Milbank Memorial Fund.

Mueller, A. 1991: In and Against Development: Feminists Confront Development on Its Own Ground. Photocopy.

Namuddu, K. 1989: "Problems of Communication between Northern and Southern Researchers in the Context of Africa." Paper presented at the Seventh World Congress of Comparative Education, Montreal, June 26–30.

Orr, J. B. 1953: *The White Man's Dilemma*. London: Allen and Unwin.

Polanyi, K. 1957: *The Great Transformation*. Boston: Beacon Press.

Procacci, G. 1991: "Social Economy and the Government of Poverty." In G. Burchell, C. Gordon, and P. Miller (eds.), *The Foucault Effect*. Chicago: University of Chicago Press, 151–68.

Rahnema, M. 1986: "Under the Banner of Development." *Development: Seeds of Change* 1–2, 37–46.

Rahmena, M. 1991: "Global Poverty: A Pauperizing Myth." *Interculture* 24 (2), 4–51.

Sachs, W. 1990: "The Archeology of the Development Idea." *Interculture* 23 (4), 1–37.

Shonfield, A. 1950: *The Attack on World Poverty*. New York: Random House.

United Nations, Department of Social and Economic Affairs 1951: *Measures for the Economic Development of Underdeveloped Countries*. New York: United Nations.

Urla, J. 1993: "Cultural Politics in the Age of Statistics: Numbers, Nations, and the Making of Basque Identities." *American Ethnologist* 20 (4), 818–43.

Williams, R. 1973: *The Country and the City*. New York: Oxford University Press.

Wilson, H. 1953: *The War on World Poverty*. London: Gollancz.

9 The Constitution of the Object of "Development": Lesotho as a "Less Developed Country"

James Ferguson

Lesotho is a small, land-locked country in Southern Africa, completely surrounded by South Africa. The former British protectorate of Basutoland, Lesotho became independent in 1966. It has a population of about 1.3 million, an area of about 30,000 square kilometers, and few economically significant natural resources. In 1981/2 the Gross National Product was about $586 million. The country is extremely mountainous, and only some 10 percent of the land is arable; the rest is suitable only for grazing of livestock. Some 95 percent of the population is rural, and most of that is concentrated in the "lowlands," a narrow crescent of land lying along the western perimeter of the country, conventionally contrasted with the much larger "mountain" zone to the east.[1] Fields are cropped chiefly in maize, wheat, and sorghum; livestock include cattle, sheep, and goats. The most important source of income for most households, however, is wage labor in South Africa, where perhaps as many as 200,000 Basotho are employed as migrant laborers (GOL 1983, World Bank 1981).

In the period 1975–84, this tiny country was receiving "development assistance" from the following bilateral sources:[2]

Australia	Ghana
Austria	India
Canada	Iran
Cyprus	Ireland
Denmark	Israel
Democratic Republic of Germany	Korea
Federal Republic of Germany	Kuwait
Finland	Libya

Excerpted from James Ferguson, *The Anti-Politics Machine: "Development," Depoliticization, and Bureaucratic Power in Lesotho* (Minneapolis and London: Oxford University Press, 1994), 3–7, ch. 2.

The Netherlands
Norway
Saskatchewan (Canada)
Saudi Arabia
South Africa

Sweden
Switzerland
Taiwan (ROC)
United Kingdom
United States

In the same period, Lesotho was also receiving assistance from the following international agencies and non- and quasi-governmental organizations:

AFL-CIO African-American Labor Center
Abu Dhabi Fund
Africa Inter-Mennonite Mission
African Development Bank
African Development Fund
African Graduate Training (US)
Afro-American Institute
Agency for Personnel Service Overseas (Ireland)
Anglo-American/De Beers
Anglo-Collieries Recruiting Organization of Lesotho
Arab Bank for Economic Development in Africa
Australian Development Assistance Agency
British Council
British Leprosy Mission
Brothers of the Sacred Heart
CARE
Catholic Relief Service
Christian Aid
Commonwealth Development Corporation
Commonwealth Fund for Technical Cooperation
Credit Union National Association (US)
Danish Church Aid Danish Volunteer Service
Dental Health International
Economic Commission for Africa
European Development Fund
European Economic Community
Food and Agricultural Organization of the UN
Ford Foundation Fund for Research and Investment for the Development of Africa

German Volunteer Service Goldfields (RSA)
IMAP International (US)
Institute for Development Management (Canada)
International Bank for Reconstruction and Development
International Civil Aviation Organization
International Cooperative Housing Development Association
International Development Association
International Extension College
International Labor Organization
International Monetary Fund
International Potato Production Center
International Telecommunications Union
International Trade Center
International Volunteer Service
Meals for Millions Foundation (US)
Mennonite Central Committee
Mine Labor Organization
Near East Foundation
Netherlands Organization for International Relations
OPEC
Overseas Development Institute (UK)
Oxford Committee for Famine Relief (UK)
Save the Children Fund
Seventh-Day Adventist World Service
Sisters of the Holy Names of Jesus and Mary
South African Mohair Board
South African Wool Board
United Nations Capital Development Fund

United Nations Fund for Population Activities

United Nations Human Habitat and Settlement Fund

US Peace Corps

Unitarian Service Committee of Canada

United Methodist Committee on Relief

United Nations Children's Emergency Fund

United Nations Development Program

United Nations Volunteers

Volunteer Development Corporation

World Food Program

World Health Organization

World Rehabilitation Fund

World University Service

Reading a list like this, or even walking down the streets of Lesotho's capital city of Maseru amidst the cosmopolitan swarm of expatriate "experts," one can hardly help posing the question: what is this all about? What is this massive internationalist intervention, aimed at a country that surely does not appear to be of especially great economic or strategic importance? [. . .]

Conceptual Apparatus: The Constitution of the Object of "Development" – Lesotho as "Less Developed Country"

Few developing countries faced such bleak economic prospects and were so ill-prepared as Lesotho when it gained independence in October 1966. In few countries of the world was economic independence more remote from political independence than in Lesotho. In spite of the fact that Lesotho is an enclave within highly industrialized South Africa and belongs with that country, Botswana, and Swaziland to the rand monetary area and the Southern African Customs Union, it was then virtually untouched by modern economic development. It was and still is, basically, a traditional subsistence peasant society. But rapid population growth resulting in extreme pressure on the land, deteriorating soil, and declining agricultural yields led to a situation in which the country was no longer able to produce enough food for its people. Many able-bodied men were forced from the land in search of means to support their families, but the only employment opportunities were in neighboring South Africa. At present, an estimated 60 percent of the male labor force is away as migrant workers in South Africa.

World Bank Country Report on Lesotho (1975), page 1, paragraph 1

Have you ever read any criminological texts? They are staggering. And I say this out of astonishment, not aggressiveness, because I fail to comprehend how the discourse of criminology has been able to go on at this level. One has the impression that it is of such utility, is needed so urgently and rendered so vital for the working of the system, that it does not even need to seek a theoretical justification for itself, or even simply a coherent framework. It is entirely utilitarian. I think one needs to investigate why such a "learned" discourse became so indispensable to the functioning of the nineteenth century penal system. Michel Foucault, "Prison Talk" (1980)

From the point of view of an academic scholar of Lesotho, the first paragraph of the World Bank Report will no doubt seem bizarre. The assertion that Lesotho in 1966 was "a traditional subsistence peasant society," "virtually untouched by modern economic development," along with the apparent implication that the migrant labor system originated only in recent years, will seem not only incorrect but outlandish. The scholar will feel compelled to point out that Lesotho has served as a labor reserve supplying migrant wage labor to South African mines, farms, and industry for more than a century; and will perhaps draw up in his or her mind a short list of some of the "modern economic developments" which had "touched" Lesotho prior to 1966: the introduction of a money economy and the establishment of Lesotho as a market for Western commodities; the introduction of plow agriculture and a host of new cash and subsistence crops; the introduction of merino sheep and angora goats, and the cash cropping of wool; the establishment and growth of a modern colonial/state administration; the development of a national elite; the growth of a capital town; the construction of airports, roads, schools, churches, and hospitals; and last, but not least, the establishment of the migrant labor system and the transformation of Lesotho into a labor reserve for the South African industrial economy. These "modern economic developments" had all been introduced long before 1966. [. . .]

The fact is, then, that Lesotho entered the twentieth century, not as a "subsistence" economy, but as a producer of cash crops for the South African market; not as a "traditional peasant society," but as a reservoir exporting wage laborers in about the same quantities, proportionate to total population, as it does today. Lesotho was not "untouched by modern economic development" but radically and completely transformed by it. [. . .]

One would be mistaken, however, to suppose that the paragraph cited from the World Bank Report is simply an error, the sign of gross ignorance or incompetent scholarship. It is true that this paragraph (like the remainder of the Report, and like the documents of other "development" agencies in Lesotho) does not meet the accepted norms of academic discourse; such a statement would not likely be found in an academic dissertation on Lesotho. But the authors of this statement, the authors of the World Bank Country Report on Lesotho, cannot simply be dismissed as second-rate academics. It must be recognized that what is being done here is not some sort of staggeringly bad scholarship, but something else entirely, just as Foucault recognized that criminology is not simply a backward social science but a special sort of discourse with a special job to do. What is needed is not so much a correction or setting straight of the discourse of the "development" industry in Lesotho [. . .] as a way of accounting for it, and of showing what it does. The analysis therefore begins by noting the discontinuity between the World Bank Report and academic norms [. . .] and sets itself the task of understanding the discursive framework and the institutional conditions within which statements such as the ones I have cited are no longer bizarre and unacceptable, but comprehensible, and even necessary.

[. . .] First, it will be necessary to demonstrate with care what has as yet been only asserted that "development" discourse on Lesotho is distinguishable from academic discourse, and that the difference between the two types of discourse is due to two different sets of rules of formation for discourse, or two different problematics, and not to any necessary difference in intellectual quality or individual authors' abilities. Secondly, in order to make sense of the domain of discourse that will have been thus picked out, it will be necessary to show what the "development" discourse in Lesotho does – what theoretical tasks it accomplishes, and to what effect. Finally, it will remain to show how and why this discourse maintains its own distinctive qualities, its closure. There are questions, then, of fact, function, and mechanism.

The first question will be addressed through a close textual analysis of the World Bank Country Report on Lesotho ("Lesotho: A Development Challenge," 1975). Here will be examined in detail the peculiar emphases, interpretations, constructs, and fabrications which combine to produce a unique "development" perspective on Lesotho, a perspective which must inevitably appear badly distorted from the point of view of the scholar.

In answering the second question, [. . .] what appeared, in the first section, as simple distortions of reality can be shown to be essential steps in the necessary theoretical task of constituting the complex reality of Lesotho as a "Less Developed Country," an "LDC"; and this in order to set up a target for a particular sort of intervention: the technical, apolitical, "development" intervention. The characteristics of this theoretical construct, the LDC, will be described in some detail, as will the techniques used in the theoretical work of translation of certain unmanageable sorts of facts into a more acceptable register.

In the third section, the task will be to show why it is necessary for "development" discourse to take the form it does; we must uncover the institutional and ideological constraints and imperatives that structure the formation of the "development" discourse.

Two cautionary notes may be appropriate before going further. First, the discourse with which I am concerned here is the discourse of "development" agencies working in Lesotho in the middle and late 1970s. The entity I am describing is thus bounded in time and space. Similarities no doubt can be demonstrated with "development" discourse elsewhere and at other times, but it is not my purpose to explore these similarities here.

Second, my concern here is with "development" discourse on Lesotho, not with what I am calling "academic discourse." Academic discourse on Lesotho has of course its own rules of formation and responds to its own ideological and institutional constraints, which could well be the subject of another analysis. Like "development" discourse, academic discourse deals not simply with "the facts" but with a constructed version of the object. This does not imply, of course, that the two versions are somehow equally true or equally adequate to any given purpose.[3] [. . .] I take the incompatibility of "development" discourse and academic norms as a point of departure for an exploration of the distinctly different way that "development" discourse is structured. [. . .]

"Development" as Discursive Regime: Mechanisms of Closure

If it is true that "development" discourse on Lesotho characteristically constructs a unique and – to the academic – strange and distorted picture of the country, one must inquire as to why that should be so. [. . .]

Is it the case that we have a closed system of knowledge, an episteme, in Foucault's sense? Clearly not. We can see that "development" discourse does operate within a familiar broad contemporary configuration of Western knowledge. [. . .] And it is easy to trace the lineage of many of its characteristic lines of thought – from modernization theory, for instance, or neo-classical economics. But tracing the origins of particular elements of "development" thought does not explain the observed difference. [. . .] As different as they are, "development" discourse and academic discourse draw on a common stock of ideas and traditions. They do not exist in two different epistemological worlds.

But, if the two discourses operate within virtually identical epistemic constraints, how is it that "development" discourse comes to have its distinctive regularities? [. . .] As long as one treats discursive practices as autonomous (Foucault [1979]), the answer to this question must remain mysterious. As Dreyfuss and Rabinow (1983: 79–85) have argued, discursive regularities or "rules of formation" cannot be elevated to causal principles. What is needed instead is a way of connecting observed discursive regularities to non-discursive practices and institutions. [. . .] What changes when we move from academic discourse to "development" is not the library of available thoughts, but the institutional context into which both discourse and thought are inserted. [. . .]

Colin Murray, perhaps the most respected academic social scientist to have written on Lesotho, concludes his monograph with the following words:

> The Basotho have a justifiable pride in their long tradition of national resistance. But they are faced with larger and very difficult questions in the years to come. . . . The answers to these questions will depend, in the first place, upon the evolving character of the post-colonial state. Subordinate as it is to the interests of foreign capital, and preoccupied as it is with repressing or co-opting internal opposition, the strategic possibilities for change, conceived within the confines of Lesotho's national autonomy, are very narrow. In the second place, therefore, the answers to the larger questions will depend upon the developing struggle within South Africa itself. (Murray 1981: 111)

Such a conclusion is well supported by everything we know about Lesotho, but the fact is that the guide to action that it suggests for those who are concerned to help bring about progressive change in Lesotho is of absolutely no use to an institution such as the World Bank. An academic analysis is of no use to a "development" agency unless it provides a place for the agency to plug itself in, unless it provides a charter for the sort of intervention that the agency is set up to do. An analysis which suggests that the causes of poverty in Lesotho are political and structural (not technical and geographical), that the national government is part of the problem (not a neutral instrument for its solution), and that meaningful change can only come through revolutionary social transformation in South Africa has no place in "development" discourse simply because "development" agencies are not in the business of promoting political realignments or supporting revolutionary struggles. [. . .]

Once one sees why "unhelpful" analyses like these are banished, it is easy to see why certain other sorts flourish under the "development" regime. For an analysis to meet the needs of "development" institutions, it must do what academic discourse inevitably fails to do; it must make Lesotho out to be an enormously promising candidate for the only sort of intervention a "development" agency is capable of launching: the apolitical, technical "development" intervention. The "development" intervention is a highly standardized operation. The forms of rural intervention available to "development" agencies (irrigation schemes, crop authorities, credit programs, integrated rural development programs, etc.) come, as Williams (1986: 12) has noted, as "large standardized packages," "exported from one country to another and from one continent to another." "Development" agencies are in the business of trying to "sell" these packages, trying to locate and justify potential applications for them. [. . .] Their problem is to find the right kind of problem; the kind of "problem" that requires the "solution" they are there to provide. This is the institutional context within which "development" discourse is located.

The analysis that is most helpful to a "development" agency, then – and the one that will naturally rise to the top of authoritative "development" discourse – is the one that "moves the money," the one that presents Lesotho as a likely target for the standard "development" intervention, and serves as a charter to justify and legitimate the sort of programs that the bureaucratic establishment is there to execute[. . . .] Through a kind of conceptual "natural selection," the theoretical apparatus of "development" thus always tends toward the representation of Lesotho as an entity, the LCD, which may be defined as the ideal country that, in order to become prosperous and solve all its problems, requires precisely those things which "development" agencies are set up to provide. [. . .]

To sum up: the most important theoretical premises in the construction of the "development" representation of Lesotho, together with their institutional rationales, are the following:

First, it must be *aboriginal*, not yet incorporated into the modern world, so that it can be transformed by roads and infrastructure, education, the introduction and strengthening of the cash economy (as against the "traditional subsistence sector"), and so on. A representation which failed to mask the extent of Lesotho's penetration by the "modern" capitalist regional economy of Southern Africa would be unable to provide a convincing justification for the "introduction" of roads, markets, and credit, as it would provide no grounds for believing that such innovations could bring about the "great transformation" to a "developed," "modern" economy. Indeed, such a representation would tend to suggest that such measures for "opening up" the country and exposing it to "the cash economy" would have little impact at all, since isolation from the world economy has never been Lesotho's problem.

Secondly, it must be *agricultural*, so that it can be "developed" through agricultural improvements, rural development projects, extension, and technical inputs. A representation in which Lesotho appeared as a labor reserve for South African mining and industry, and in which migrant wage labor was recognized as the basis of Basotho livelihood, would leave the "development" agencies with almost no role to play. The World Bank mission to Lesotho is in no position to formulate programs for changing or controlling the South African mining industry, and it has no disposition to involve itself in the political challenges to the South African system of labor control known as apartheid. It is in an excellent position, however, to devise agricultural improvement projects, for the agricultural resources of Lesotho lie neatly within its jurisdiction and always present themselves as waiting to be "developed." For this reason, they tend to move to center stage in "development" accounts, and Lesotho thus becomes a nation of farmers.

Thirdly, it must constitute a *national economy*, in order to support the idea of national economic planning and nation- and sector-based economic programs. In a representation in which this notion of national economy is absent, the economic center of gravity is seen as lying squarely within South Africa, and thus as inaccessible to a "development" planner in Lesotho. Without the idea that Lesotho's boundaries define a national economy, no great claims can be made for the ability of programs based in Lesotho to bring about the sort of transformation "development" agencies claim to be able to bring about. The "development" apparatus unconsciously selects for representations in which it appears possible for "development" agencies to deliver the goods they are set up to promise.

Fourthly, it must be subject to the principle of *governmentality*. That is, the main features of economy and society must be within the control of a neutral, unitary, and effective national government, and thus responsive to planners' blueprints. If a representation for any reason tends to suggest that the "problems" of a country lie beyond the reach of national government policy, then it at the same time tends to deny a role to "development" agencies in addressing those problems. Because "development" agencies operate on a national basis, and because they work through existing governments and not against them, they prize representations which exaggerate the power of national policy instruments, and have little use for representations which emphasize the role of extra-national or extra-governmental determinations. Because government is the tool for planning and implementing economic and social policy, representations which ignore the political character of the state and the bureaucracy and downplay political conflicts within the nation-state are the most useful. Representations which present the state in such a way as to bring into question its role as a neutral tool of enlightened policy must force upon the "development" agencies a political stance they are ill-equipped to take on, and for this reason must fall by the wayside.

It must be evident by now that in a country like Lesotho, where capitalism and the labor reserve economy were well established more than a century ago, where farming contributes only 6 percent of rural household income, where concepts such as national economy and governmentality are more than usually absurd, and where nearly all the major determinants of economic life lie outside of the national borders, the task of drawing up governmentalist plans for transforming a "national economy" through technical, apolitical intervention requires preliminary theoretical rearrangements of a more than usually violent or imaginative kind. Lesotho is for this reason a privileged case in which the nature of this theoretical rearrangement is particularly visible, and in which the schism with academic discourse is unusually pronounced. It is to be expected that in other countries, where the economic situation is less far removed from that of the mythical generic LDC (countries possessing greater national autonomy, greater economic cohesion, and greater governmental control over the economy), the discontinuity between "development" discourse and academic discourse will be less sharp, and less easily observed, although the same processes may be at work.

Conclusion

The effects of the theoretical work done by "development" discourse on Lesotho are far-reaching. The constitution of Lesotho as a suitable theoretical object of analysis is also, and simultaneously, its constitution as a suitable target for intervention. The image of Lesotho as "LDC," once constructed, thus shapes not only the formation of reports and documents, but the construction of organizations, institutions, and programs[. . . .]

Notes

1   This division of "mountains" from "lowlands" is sometimes expanded to a four-zone classification: lowlands, foothills, mountains, and the Senqu river valley, a strip of relatively low-lying land that winds some way up into the mountains.
2   The following lists of donors and "development" agencies have been assembled from the following documents: UNDP (1980), GOL (n.d., 1977, 1975), TAICH (1976). The list is only as accurate as these documents, and it does not pretend to be authoritative. A number of agencies have no doubt been left out. It should be noted, too, that the donors and agencies listed are involved in Lesotho on very different scales; some are major actors on the local scene, while many others are involved in only a very minor way.
3   This idea – that exploring the social construction of knowledges implies a "relativistic" or even-handed valuation of different constructions – is common, but nonsensical. When Foucault (1973) compared the configuration of Renaissance knowledge with that of the Modern era, for instance, he surely did not thereby commit to the Renaissance belief that walnuts, by virtue of their resemblance to the human brain, can be used to cure brain illnesses, or to the notion that the medicine of the sixteenth century and that of the twentieth are equally efficacious. His problem, as always, was with the "regime" of truth, with the procedures for determining what is to count as truth in a given time and place. Whether walnuts really do cure brain disease was not Foucault's problem, but he is hardly committed to the view that all answers ever given to such a question are equally good!

References

Dreyfuss, H. and Rabinow, P. 1983: *Michel Foucault: Beyond Structuralism and Hermeneutics.* 2nd ed. Chicago: University of Chicago Press.
Foucault, M. 1973: *The Order of Things.* New York: Vintage.
Foucault, M. 1979: *Discipline and Punish: The Birth of the Prison.* New York: Vintage.
Foucault, M. 1980: *Power/Knowledge: Selected Interviews and Other Writings, 1972–1977,* ed. Colin Gordon. New York: Pantheon.
GOL (Government of Lesotho) n.d.: "Third Five Year Plan Preview." Maseru: Central Planning and Development Office.
GOL 1975: *Donor Conference Report.* Maseru: Central Planning and Development Office.
GOL 1977: *Donor Conference Papers, September 1977.* Maseru: Central Planning and Development Office.

GOL 1983: *Annual Statistical Bulletin 1982*. Maseru: Bureau of Statistics.

Murray, C. 1981: *Families Divided: The Impact of Migrant Labour in Lesotho*. New York: Cambridge University Press.

TAICH (Technical Assistance Information Clearing House) 1976: "Development Assistance Programs of U.S. Non-profit Organizations: Lesotho." New York: American Council of Voluntary Agencies for Foreign Service.

UNDP (United Nations Development Program) 1980: "Development Assistance: Lesotho 1979". Maseru: UNDP.

Williams, G. 1986: "Rural Development: Partners and Adversaries." *Rural Africana* 25–6, 11–23.

World Bank (International Bank for Reconstruction and Development) 1981: *Accelerated Development in Sub-Saharan Africa: An Agenda for Action*. Washington, DC: World Bank.

10 Becoming a Development Category

Nanda Shrestha

History, despite its wrenching pain,
Cannot be unlived, and if faced
With courage, need not be lived again.
Maya Angelou, 1993

"Colonial domination," claimed Fanon, "manages to disrupt in spectacular fashion the cultural life of a conquered people ... [T]he intellectual throws himself in frenzied fashion into the frantic acquisition of the culture of the occupying power and takes every opportunity of unfavorably criticizing his own national culture" (1967: 236–7). Mesmerized by the glamorous notion of development, I was mentally slow to scale its ideological contours, to comprehend how development ideology is produced and reproduced, how it is propagated across space and through time, how it conquers the minds of native elites, and how it paves the path for a monolithic culture of materialism which stigmatizes poverty and the poor. Increasingly, it has dawned on me that my own development odyssey served as an autopsy of how the imported discourse of development had possessed the mind of a national ruling class, and how such a mindset had, in turn, played a major role in deepening the social roots of poverty – all, of course, in the name of development.

This chapter is an account of the process of my own seduction. This is a self-reflective narrative, a wrenching dialogue with myself, based on my encounter with development as a young student aspiring to join the ranks of educated elites and the well-to-do. However, my objective here is *not* to write my own personal biography; this is rather a post-mortem of the body of development by a colonized mind, designed to serve as a research method. Even though such a

Excerpted from Nanda Shrestha, "Becoming a Development Category." In J. Crush (ed.), *Power and Development* (London and New York: Routledge, 1995), 266–77.

methodology is uncommon in academic research, it is valuable in exposing the experience of most elites – whether self-made like myself or those born and raised in elite families. This personal narrative reveals how and why the discourse of development, with the help of foreign aid, solidifies the colonial mindset in the post-imperial world, crafting cultural values, thinking, behavior, and actions. This is how, under the guise of development, the culture of imperialism is methodically reproduced in order to maintain continued Western dominance over the myriad of nation-states which have emerged since the downfall of the formal colonial–imperial order. As Edward Said (1993: 25), describing the lingering legacy of imperialism, points out: "Westerners may have physically left their old colonies in Africa and Asia, but they retained them not only as markets but also as locales on the ideological map over which they continued to rule morally and intellectually."

As a *garib* (poor) boy growing up in a rustic town of Pokhara in Central Nepal more than forty years ago, I had few possessions of material value. My aspirations were limited to an occasional desire to have enough food and some nice clothes. Based on the contemporary measure of poverty, the World Bank and its agents would have labeled my family extremely poor. Indeed, the 1992 *World Development Report* shows Nepal as the fifth poorest country in the world. I grew up in a tiny house with a leaky roof. My family had about 1.5 acres of non-irrigated land. Along with some vegetables, we usually grew maize and millet. My mother sometimes brewed and sold millet liquor, known locally as *raksi*. This is how my family eked out a meager existence. Life was always hand-to-mouth, a constant struggle for survival. It was not unusual at all for me to go to school hungry, sometimes three or four days in a row.

I specifically recall one Dashain – the biggest Hindu festival which is celebrated with a great deal of fanfare for ten consecutive days. It signifies a celebration of victory of good over evil, namely the victory won by Goddess Durga. During this festival, most temples are littered with blood from sacrificed animals (uncastrated goats, roosters, ducks, and buffaloes). The smell of blood and raw meat is everywhere. Large quantities of meats are consumed during this festival. Even the poorest are expected to eat some meat, one of the very few times during the year that most poor families get to do so. Dashain is not just a religious celebration; it is equated with status. There is immense pressure on every family, rich and poor, to celebrate the festival with as much pomp and show as possible. Parents are expected to get brand new clothes and other material items for their children. As a consequence, each year countless families plunge deep into debt. Many mortgage, if not sell outright, whatever little land or other assets (e.g., gold) they have to raise money for celebration. The festival is very expensive, with many households never recovering from debt. My father used to call Dashain *dasha* (misery) or the "Festival of Sorrow."

That particular Dashain, I was eight years old. My family had no money to acquire any of the necessities for the Dashain. It was the eighth day of the Dashain, two days before its culmination. On the eighth or ninth day, families are supposed to sacrifice animals. We had not even a rooster to worship Goddess Durga. We all sat in the house the whole day, huddled around and feeling sad, not knowing what to do. My parents could not get me even one new shirt, let alone a complete outfit. Even today, the memory of that Dashain brings tears to my eyes. Because of that bitter memory, I have never been able to enjoy any festival. Finally, on the morning of the ninth day of the Dashain, I received a small sum of money from my brother-in-law, for whom I had done some work. The money saved that Dashain, and my family was just able to ward off a social embarrassment.

To my innocent mind, poverty looked natural, something that nobody could do anything about. I accepted poverty as a matter of fate, caused by bad *karma*. That is what we were repeatedly told. I had no idea that poverty was largely a social creation, not a bad karmic product. Despite all this, it never seemed threatening and dehumanizing. So, poor and hungry I certainly was. But underdeveloped? I never thought – nor did anybody else – that being poor meant being "underdeveloped" and lacking human dignity. True, there is no comfort and glory in poverty, but the whole concept of development (or underdevelopment) was totally alien to me and perhaps to most other Nepalis.

There is a word for development in the Nepali language: *bikas*. Following the overthrow of the Rana autarchy in 1951, the word began to gain currency. A status divide emerged between the *bikasi* and the *abikasi*. Those who had acquired some knowledge of so-called modern science and technology identified themselves as *bikasis* (developed), supposedly with a "modern" outlook, and the rest as *abikasis* or *pakhe* (uncivilized, underdeveloped, or backward). There was money in *bikas*, and the funding for *bikas* projects, mostly through foreign aid, was beginning to swell. Development was thus no longer just a concept. It became a practice which fortified, and even exacerbated, the existing class hierarchy. The wealthy, the powerful, the more educated embraced *bikas*, becoming *bikasis*. The *garib* (poor) were *abikasis*. As the logic went, the poor became poor because they were *abikasi*; they impeded *bikas*.

Bikas was generally associated with objects such as roads, airplanes, dams, hospitals, and fancy buildings. Education was also a key component, essential to build human capital. Education could salvage the *abikasi* mind, but only if it was "modern," emphasizing science, technology, and English, the language of *bikas*. Sanskrit, previously the language of the learned, was a deterrent to *bikas*. There was tension in the family. Educated children were viewed as future agents of *bikas*, and our parents were usually seen as *abikasis*. True, there were things our parents did that had little scientific basis or made any logical sense. But there were also many things they did that had more practical values than the theoretical "science" we were learning at school. Yet, in the eyes of *bikasis*, whatever human capital, productive forces or knowledge our parents had accumulated over the years did not count for much. Many students felt ashamed to be seen in public with their parents. The new education gave us the impression that our parents' manual labor was antithetical to *bikas*. So we sneered at manual work, thinking that it was something only an *abikasi* or intellectually "underdeveloped" mind would do. It was not for the high-minded *bikasis*. The new educational system was producing a whole new way of thinking about the value of labor. *Bikas* meant, to apply Ivan Illich's (1992) logic, denying as well as uprooting the existing labor use system, traditional bonds, and knowledge base, rather than building on them.

Before development, hard manual labor was a common way of life. The vast majority of people did it from early childhood, from the time they were seven or eight years old. Now the delusionary vision of *bikas* had made it an anathema. The new attitude toward labor created a backlash against education in general. My father opposed my education although I always did manual labor. Many children were actually pulled out of their schools by their parents before completing their elementary education. In an agrarian society like Nepal, children formed a vital source of labor or economic assets, but they had developed an aversion to manual work as a result of education. So what good was their education if it meant depriving the family of much needed family labor and potential supplementary income the children would generate when hired by others? Such a calculation was particularly important among the poor parents who did not see much prospect for their educated children's employment in the civil service – the principal source of salaried employment for the educated. To most poor parents, their children's education did not mean an investment in future prosperity; rather it entailed, at least in the short run, lost labor and potential income.

The devaluation of manual labor was hardened by our observation of Westerners whom we considered educated, developed, sophisticated, civilized. We rarely observed any of the growing contingency of Westerners in Nepal doing manual work. They all had at least one maid; some had two or three. Even meagerly paid Peace Corps Volunteers (PCVs) had personal cooks or maids. Many lived a life of luxury. They saw themselves as advisers and exhibited an aura of superiority. We thought that their lifestyle represented that of a modern, educated *bikasi*. Consequently, local educated people began to emulate them and aspire to the "good life" the Westerners enjoyed and represented. Development was the fountain of good life.

Not all parents resented "Western" education, however. For the elites, the architects of the national culture, modern education was the umbilical cord between themselves and the West. Since they cherished such linkage and wanted to be associated with *bikas*, educating their children in "modern" schools and in the West was very important for them. Within Nepal they preferred to send their children to St. Mary's School for girls and St. Xavier's School for boys, run by Christian missionaries, mostly from England. Several wealthy families in Pokhara sent their children to these two schools, both located in Kathmandu Valley. When these children, some of whom lived in my neighborhood, came back home during breaks, we could hear them speak fluent English. They would have little contact with us, and sometimes treat us like *pakhes* (uncivilized). Educationally, we felt very deficient in front of those elite children. The new education was preparing a new generation who not only controlled the rapidly expanding bureaucracy, but also dominated the development enterprise, thereby reaping the lopsided benefits of *bikas*. Education and *bikas* both not only displayed a distinct class character, but also accentuated the prevailing class biases of colonial society. Most educated people shunned hard work and looked for work in the civil service sector where they could boss their juniors around. They wore two disparate faces: one looking meek and saying *hajur, hajur* (yes sir, yes sir) to those above them and another stern and rude, treating those below them as worthless subhumans.

By the mid-1950s, the idea of *bikas* had been firmly transplanted in the Nepalese psyche. Whether *bikas* was actually occurring did not matter. It had permeated almost every Nepalese mind, from peons to the prime minister and the king. The higher the bureaucratic authority, the louder the voices of *bikas*. *Bikas* was regarded as a secret passage to material paradise. The myth of *bikas* projected materialism as human salvation, the sole source of happiness, emancipation, and redemption from hunger and poverty (Ullrich 1992: 275). Materialism appeared to have replaced a traditional Hindu conception of *bhakti* (devotion) and *dharma* (duty, good deeds) as a channel of *moksha* (salvation). Not that Hinduism is devoid of material values; it has always played hide-and-seek with materialism. *Laxmi* (the goddess of wealth) is actually highly revered. But this new form of materialism was much more pronounced and had quickly emerged as a new deity.

I believe it was 1951 when the first group of British Christian missionaries arrived in Pokhara (missionary activity had started in Nepal much earlier). Although they probably were not the first white people to come to Pokhara, they are the first ones I remember. Because of the British policy of Gorkha (Gurkha) recruitment, many recruits from the surrounding hills had already served the British. While the citizens of other colonies were exploited as slaves, indentured plantation workers, and coolies, Britain's exploitation of young and able Nepalis was somewhat unique, raw material for the war machine of the British imperial army. Although their bodies belonged to Nepal, their labor belonged to the British. In this sense, the dance of British imperialism was already in full swing across Nepal.

The missionaries' "civilizing mission" brought Christianity and modern medical facilities to the town of Pokhara as they set up a small hospital called the Shining Hospital. While the hospital seemed to have brought medical miracles as patients often responded faster to their (Western) medicines than to local medical practices, it also undermined local medical knowledge. Missionaries mocked our local medical practices, and made us feel ashamed of them. Even more important, however, their presence led to a total psychological metamorphosis in our perception of whites. Almost everybody, regardless of their socioeconomic status in the community, started addressing white missionaries, or for that matter all whites, as *sahib* or *sab* for males and *mimsab* for females (master, boss, teacher, or sir/madam depending upon the context). Although the word *sahib* is a fairly common honorific term, it clearly has connotations of dominance and subordination. Whites, called *sahib* from the very start, were thus accorded a dominant position. The *sahib* culture became engraved in the Nepalese mind, a culture in which whites were placed at the apex, with the Nepalis looking up to them in the way devotees look up to the statues of their gods, begging for blessings or waiting at the end of the table for crumbs to fall. This, in turn, accentuated whites' preexisting feeling of superiority and, in their own minds, justified their treatment of us as uncivilized and inferior or as needing salvation.

Previously, white people were often referred to as monkeys (in appearance). The Hindu caste codes regarded whites as *mlaksha*, the polluted, the untouchable, and hence relegated to the bottom of the caste hierarchy. If any high-caste individual (Brahman, Kshatriya, and Vaishay) touched a white person, that person would be considered unclean, and thus required to undergo a cleansing ritual. In fact, as late as the 1940s, all Nepalese recruits serving in the British imperial army and those who had crossed any of the oceans were, upon their return home, subjected to such ritual, for they were presumed to have come in physical contact with whites. Now whites were no longer viewed as monkeys or as *mlakshas*. Instead, they were beautiful, the *sahibs*, the masters, a super caste, even to the highest-ranking caste group: the Brahmans. Even the most sacred of the Hindu social codes was no longer sacrosanct when it came to applying them to white people. Here was a fundamental transformation of Nepalese culture, attitude, and behavior toward whites. It was hard to fathom why whites had been elevated so quickly to the top of the social hierarchy. The oppressive and archaic caste system had simply been rearranged to accommodate the emerging *sahib* culture and nascent *bikas* enterprise; caste relations had been transformed into power relations in our dealings with whites, the latter occupying the position of power and prestige.

The hospital was a sign of *bikas*, the first such symbol in Pokhara. It was brought by white people, the harbingers of *bikas*. To us, they were obviously economically superior. They spoke the language of *bikas*; they knew the modern science and technology of *bikas*. They embodied *bikas*. Being associated with them, learning their language, and imitating them became important attributes of *bikas*, attributes that all *bikasis* were expected – and wanted – to possess.

Shortly after the arrival of British missionaries came an airplane, an old DC3. When some people heard the roaring sound of an approaching airplane, it caused an incredible commotion in Pokhara and surrounding villages. The serenity of bucolic Pokhara surrounded by hills and mountains was disrupted by that noisy machine. When the airplane landed, pandemonium broke out throughout the town. Almost everybody flocked to see it. We were clamoring to touch it as if it were a divine creation, sent to us by God. Some wondered how something so big could fly. Others searched in their Hindu religious tradition to see if they could identify some divine figure resembling an airplane. They did find one: the Garuda, the eagle-looking Hindu mythical bird, the heavenly vehicle of Vishnu, who in the Hindu trinity of Brahma, Vishnu, and Shiva is the universal god of preservation, the Savior. The airplane was the talk of the town for several days. We had seen another facet of *bikas*. Not only could *bikas* cure the sick, but it could fly like the Garuda, carrying *bikasis* around the country. We adapted this *bikas* symbol to our own Hindu tradition. *Bikas* was justified.

Then came a used jeep, flown in by the mechanical Garuda. The jeep was brought in pieces, along with a foreign mechanic to assemble it. In that jeep, some saw the chariot driven by Lord Krishna during the epochal war called the *Mahabharat*, the war fought for justice between the Pandavas and the Kauravas, brothers from two different mothers. In that war, the chariot carried Arjuna, who led the five Pandavas' forces representing justice and ultimately defeated the evil forces represented by the one-hundred Kauravas. The jeep was later followed by bicycles and oxen-driven carts. Such was the order of transportation development in Pokhara and in many parts of Nepal: a retrogressive order. This was quite symptomatic of the whole process of development, everything backwards.

What we were observing was imported *bikas*, not true progress from within. We had achieved very little on our own. *Bikas* was our new religion. Various material objects represented the pantheon of *bikas* gods and goddesses. The symbolism of *bikas* and Hinduism were uncannily alike.

The first wave of *bikas* was encapsulated in the first five-year development plan launched in 1956, and almost entirely financed by foreign aid. As this plan institutionalized the development enterprise, the march of *bikas* was now official though few knew where it would lead. Following the advice of Western experts, Nepalese *bikasis* advocated industrial growth. Some actually built factories, even before embarking on the path of agricultural improvement and setting up infrastructure. Merchants in Pokhara established a match factory, but the venture collapsed because of the absence of marketing networks and transportation facilities. Such a regressive trend continued to mar the national development horizon. North Atlantic consumer culture penetrated, unchecked, every nook and corner of Nepal, rapidly generating previously non-existent wants and hence scarcities, a situation which only aggravated poverty. The local production system remained incapable of meeting the demands of this rising consumerism. So, *bikas* had arrived in Pokhara (and in Nepal in general) in many forms, represented by various objects, most of which had little use value for the general public. Excitement filled the air even though few outside the *bikas* circle climbed the ladder of progress. The jeep was symptomatic of Nepal's *bikas*: second-hand and out of reach of the masses.

In 1962 the first group of PCVs arrived in Pokhara, most of them as instructors to teach different subjects. I was in the sixth grade at that time. Before their arrival, a high school was constructed with financial aid from the United States. Our high school was chosen as one of the first multi-purpose schools in Nepal. Along with regular courses, it offered vocational education in trade and industry (carpentry and rudimentary drafting and electric wiring), home economics (cooking, sewing, and knitting), agriculture, and commerce (typing and some shorthand writing and bookkeeping). Vocational education was designed to produce a pool of skilled workers, to build human capital, needed for development, because our existing knowledge and skills were presumed worthless. So we, the vocational students, were expected to fill the knowledge and skill void and play a big role in national *bikas*. We were subsumed by this tide of *bikas*. We were its recipients, groomed as its agents.

In order to carry out the vocational training plan, fancy chairs, desks, and tables were flown in from overseas as part of the aid package. All sorts of tools and equipment for various vocational fields came from the United States, which planned and funded the whole project. The headmaster and three vocational teachers went to the United States for training. We had no idea that our school, Pokhara, Nepal were the fulfillment of President Truman's grand plan for the "poor, underdeveloped" peoples. Through the Peace Corps initiative, President Kennedy took the Truman plan to new levels, placing his own stamp on it. The Peace Corps plan was the least expensive yet most effective mechanism of intensifying American influence and countering communism. Perhaps, most PCVs were not aware of the grand plan either. There was a good mix of volunteers. There were some who had joined the Peace Corps (PC) for an idealistic purpose: the do-gooders. Some had joined the PC to avoid being drafted for the Vietnam war, and others did it because they were indulging in the hippie movement or alternative lifestyles. They were going overseas, as PC volunteers, to "exotic" countries, some in search of cheap marijuana and hashish and others in search of cultural relief from the material opulence of stale suburban life. Nepal was viewed as a mecca for such relief. How ironic that many volunteers, sent to promote American values and materialistic development, were themselves yearning for reprieve from that very same material life in a culture that was described as backward and poverty-stricken.

We sought ways to be close to Westerners, for we viewed them as the messiahs of development. Since the PC policy presented the best opportunity to be close to whites, we hailed it. PCVs were usually friendly and accessible unlike most high-flying diplomatic types and so-called development advisers. PCVs lived and socialized with local people, and rarely demonstrated the religious zeal of the missionaries. We constantly hung around the PCVs, and fantasized about going to America with them. We neither knew nor cared about the motives and hidden agenda of the Truman/Kennedy plan. The degrading specter of colonialism appeared to have vanished like a shadow. The vituperative language of colonial hegemony and racial superiority had been replaced by a new language with a neutral tone. A euphemistic lexicon of American partnership and collaboration for development emerged. It proved to be a potent seductive force in the modern diplomacy of domination. So I was sold on *bikas*.

Bikas seemed to be spreading: a brand new school with a corrugated tin roof that had nice windows and blackboards, fine furniture and tools, objects beyond our imagination, and of course an ever increasing horde of Westerners. For those who grew up going to school in an open field or in open sheds made of bamboos and thatch, who used to play football (soccer) with unripe grapefruits, the school looked like a castle in a fairy tale. I had never dreamed of such things; now they were part of our daily reality. Our school even had a generator to produce electricity and operate fancy equipment. *Bikas* looked glistening and sumptuous, at least on the outside and at school. A little bit of US educational aid had done wonders. So we thought. We felt like we were taking a giant leap to the top of the stairway. We did not even have to work, let alone work hard. *Bikas* could bring things instantly, and we did not have to work hard to acquire what we wanted. But we were all bewitched. Foreign aid had become our sole medium of material nirvana. Pride in self-achievement and self-reliance was conspicuously absent.

Bikas solidified the colonial notion that we were incapable of doing things for ourselves and by ourselves. The colonial "civilizing mission" was resurrected as the mission of development. These Western "civilizers" first undermined our relative self-sufficiency and self-reliance, and then categorized us as inferior and poverty-stricken. Closely interwoven with nature and its cyclical rhythm, our way of life was certainly different, but not inferior. True, it was not prepared to bring nature under large-scale human subjugation. But our relatively harmonious coexistence with nature was interpreted as a sign of backwardness and primitiveness. Development was measured in terms of the distance between humans and nature. The greater the distance between the two, the higher the level of development. The distance between the two definitely increased – in some cases literally, as poor Nepalese village women walked further and further every year in search of fire wood and animal fodder.

In hindsight, I see a great deal of sadness in the glitter of *bikas*. While we saw *bikas* at school, there was no change at home, at least not for most poor families. *Bikas* had done nothing to reduce our hunger. Life at school and at home were an ocean apart. Every morning we went to school excited, ready to enjoy our new chairs and work with fancy tools. After school many of us returned home to face the same old hunger. Nonetheless our expectations had been raised. Disappointment became more frequent as the gap between the promise and the reality widened. Since wants were rising, poverty had grown a new face. It had a much deeper materialistic undertone than ever before. Poverty was never so frightening and degrading in the past. We did not help ourselves either. Self-reliance and cooperation gave way to despondency and dependency. In the past, if a trail was damaged, the villagers from the surrounding villages organized a work force and repaired it. Now the villagers felt that somebody else, a foreign donor or government agency, would come and fix it. Nowadays, nothing moves without foreign aid.

Before the onslaught of *bikas*, the poor and poverty were rarely stigmatized. Despite the oppressive feudalistic social structure that existed in Nepal, the rich seemed to bear some sense of shared moral responsibility toward the poor. Patron–client relations, though onerous in many ways, offered some economic cushion for the poor (Brass 1990). Poverty in the past was padded with a modicum of security; now it meant total insecurity. The principles of *bikas* denigrated traditional behaviors. Everything was defined in stark economic terms. Those who disregarded these principles were labeled irrational. Development categories were being constantly invented and reinvented, used and reused.

The national ruling elites internalized the new civilizing mission of development. As Nandy (1992: 269) has observed elsewhere: "When, after decolonization, the indigenous elites acquired control over the state apparatus, they quickly learnt to seek legitimacy in a native version of the civilizing mission and sought to establish a similar colonial relationship between state and society." As envisioned and practiced, development legitimized the ruling elites' authority. Well-accustomed to the Western way of life, irrespective of their political ideology, they subscribed to the mistaken belief that Western-style development was the only way out of poverty. They also managed to project themselves as the champions of the poor. Prevailing modes of life were vilified by development fetishism acquired from the West.

When I reflect on my own development experience and journey, it is transparent that my mind had been colonized. I was proud of my contact with PCVs. Being able to speak a little bit of broken English was a big thing. I viewed my PCV contact and English-speaking ability as my *bikas* ladder to the summit of modernity. I acquired American values, copied their habits. In my mind, I thought like an American although I had no idea what that really meant. I believed that if a person spoke English, they were very bright, *bikas*-minded, and sophisticated. That person also gained respect from others. At school, I decided to pursue vocational education because it was an American initiative. We were told that if we passed the national high school matriculation examination in first class, we would receive a full scholarship to go overseas to study. Such a prospect had a magnetic appeal to my colonized mind. Since foreign education was deeply cherished, many students aspired to go to America and Europe to study. America was the most preferred destination, followed by England and other countries.

I passed the examination in first class. But no scholarship came my way. A sense of betrayal surrounded me. With my *bikas* hopes and dreams dashed, there seemed a big void in my life. I felt that *bikas* had failed to deliver on its promise. With nothing left to look forward to, I became a primary school teacher, attended college in the morning, and stayed active in student politics. Then, in 1971, my life suddenly took a new turn. I received a letter from a Peace Corps friend who had returned to the USA in 1968. Thanks to his efforts, I obtained a full college scholarship in Minnesota. *Bikas* had at last arrived. Such was the development odyssey of my colonized mind. In recent years though, I have come full circle. I am no longer the passionate subscriber to Western development that I once was. The more I observe what is happening in countries like Nepal, especially the social, political, and economic outcomes of their booming enterprise of development rooted in Western materialism, the more I question its value.

These days, I am frequently haunted by the many diverse images I have encountered over the years – all victims of development in one respect or another – some struggling to survive, some going hungry, and others rejoicing in their financial success and ostensive material acquisitions. In my quiet moments, many muttering voices fill my ears, with a sense of both ecstasy and deep pain. "We have been seduced by the goddess of development, by the voracity of the North Atlantic material culture," pronounce these voices. Yes, I too have been seduced; we have all been seduced. There has been a structural violence of our psyche. But who caused it and how can it be repaired?

I am not trying to suggest that whatever was old was good and desirable and that every aspect of our lost heritage should be reclaimed. Nor am I implying that the old social structure should be revived in its entirety and that we should adopt an exclusionary position and advocate "nativism." Such a fundamentalist position is neither possible nor acceptable. Nobody should be oblivious to the many tyrannical practices of our feudal–religious heritage. My contention is that the indigenous economic system and values were generally self-reliant, self-sufficient, sustainable, and far less destructive of humanity as well as nature. At least, it served as a hedge against total deprivation. But now in the name of *bikas*, the dignity and humanity of the poor were questioned, while poverty itself deepened. Yet, this seemed to matter little. We had already developed a blind faith in *bikas* and its objects. We accepted development as a *fait accompli*. We seemed to have convinced ourselves that more *bikas* meant less poverty. What a fallacy!

In this self-reflective narrative, I have recounted the development journey of my own colonized mind. In doing so, I have attempted to show how the culture of imperialism transfused Nepalese society, how the colonial mindset was created among its elites, how manual labor and indigenous economic activities were devalued. In all of this, foreign aid played a critical role, captivating minds and actions. Many still claim that foreign aid is being used to achieve economic development for all citizens. We still insist that the poor need the kind of development we have practiced since the early 1950s. Although the poor were never asked if they wanted to be helped or preferred Westernized development at all, now they too seem to have been intoxicated by the brew called foreign aid.

A cruel choice confronts us all. The underlying logic of this narrative dictates that we reframe our minds and take a hard look at the seductive power of development. Even if we can gather enough strength and determination to navigate a relatively self-reliant path, our efforts should not be guided by what Edward Said (1993) calls "nativism" – a twisted nationalistic tendency often rooted in religious fundamentalism, which is no less dangerous than the seductive power of "Westernism." The way I see it, the elites – whether self-made like myself or born and raised like those from elite families – are at the root of most social and economic problems haunting Nepal. In the name of development, we pursued our own interests, both individually and as a class. We incarnated ourselves as domestic *sahibs*, denigrating the poor and their labor. In our attempt to look and become Westernized, we have created a monster out of developmentalism, lost touch with our social consciousness and humanity, and surrendered our national dignity and culture. We trust Westerners more than ourselves, virtually in every respect. We learned how to seize the currents of international development, propelled by the World Bank, US Agency for International Development (USAID), and other prominent development agencies. We turn their fads into overriding national concerns, instantly churning out reports to corroborate our claims. When they were concerned about deforestation and other environmental problems, we suddenly discovered our deforestation, soil erosion, and many other environmental ills.

Let us get serious and have enough moral courage first to challenge our own elitism and vested interests. Let us free ourselves from the trappings of Westernized development fetishism; let us unlearn the Western values and development thinking which have infested our minds. However, unlearning is not complete without relearning. So let us relearn. All of this, of course, requires that we consciously deconstruct our colonial mindset. This is a colossal battle against the entrenched culture of imperialism. If it is to succeed, it needs to be fought on two fronts. First, the battle is waged at the personal front to decolonize individually our colonized minds. Second, the battle is fought at the societal front. This demands a collective force to deconstruct the colonial mindset that pervades Nepalese society. The outcome of the second battle will depend on the degree of success achieved at the personal front. If we muster enough moral courage to wage these battles and win them, we can then consciously demystify the seductive power of development. I am fully cognizant that this is very bitter medicine, but we have few other choices if we want to create a future of human dignity and relative economic autonomy.

References

Brass, T. 1990: "Class Struggle and the Deproletarianisation of Agricultural Labour in Haryana (India)." *Journal of Peasant Studies* 18 (1), 36–67.

Fanon, F. 1967: *Black Skin, White Masks*. New York: Grove Press.

Illich, I. 1992: "Needs." In W. Sachs (ed.), *The Development Dictionary: A Guide to Knowledge as Power*. London: Zed Books.

Nandy, A. 1992: "State." In W. Sachs (ed.), *The Development Dictionary: A Guide to Knowledge as Power*. London: Zed Books.

Said, E. 1993: *Culture and Imperialism*. New York: Knopf.

Ullrich, O. 1992: "Technology." In W. Sachs (ed.), *The Development Dictionary: A Guide to Knowledge as Power*. London: Zed Books.

11 Knowledge for Development

World Bank

Knowledge is like light. Weightless and intangible, it can easily travel the world, enlightening the lives of people everywhere. Yet billions of people still live in the darkness of poverty – unnecessarily. Knowledge about how to treat such a simple ailment as diarrhea has existed for centuries – but millions of children continue to die from it because their parents do not know how to save them.

Poor countries – and poor people – differ from rich ones not only because they have less capital but because they have less knowledge. Knowledge is often costly to create, and that is why much of it is created in industrial countries. But developing countries can acquire knowledge overseas as well as create their own at home. Forty years ago, Ghana and the Republic of Korea had virtually the same income per capita. By the early 1990s Korea's income per capita was six times higher than Ghana's. Some reckon that half of the difference is due to Korea's greater success in acquiring and using knowledge.

Knowledge also illuminates every economic transaction, revealing preferences, giving clarity to exchanges, informing markets. And it is lack of knowledge that causes markets to collapse, or never to come into being. When some producers began diluting milk in India, consumers could not determine its quality before buying it. Without that knowledge, the overall quality of milk fell. Producers who did not dilute their milk were put at a disadvantage, and consumers suffered.

Poor countries differ from rich in having fewer institutions to certify quality, enforce standards and performance, and gather and disseminate information needed for business transactions. Often this hurts the poor. For example, village moneylenders often charge interest rates as high as 80 percent, because of the difficulty in assessing the creditworthiness of poor borrowers.

Excerpted from *World Development Report 1988/99. Knowledge for Development* (Oxford: Oxford University Press, 1999), 1–6.

This *World Development Report* proposes that we look at the problems of development in a new way – from the perspective of knowledge. There are many types of knowledge. In this Report we focus on two sorts of knowledge and two types of problems that are critical for developing countries:

- *Knowledge about technology,* which we also call technical knowledge or simply know-how. Examples are nutrition, birth control, software engineering, and accountancy. Typically, developing countries have less of this know-how than industrial countries, and the poor have less than the nonpoor. We call these unequal distributions across and within countries *knowledge gaps.*
- *Knowledge about attributes,* such as the quality of a product, the diligence of a worker, or the creditworthiness of a firm – all crucial to effective markets. We call the difficulties posed by incomplete knowledge of attributes *information problems.* Mechanisms to alleviate information problems, such as product standards, training certificates, and credit reports, are fewer and weaker in developing countries. Information problems and the resulting market failures especially hurt the poor.

The relationship between knowledge gaps and information problems, their impact on development, and the ways that international institutions and developing-country governments can better address them are the central themes of this Report.

As we shall see, considering development from a knowledge perspective reinforces some well-known lessons, such as the value of an open trade regime and of universal basic education. It also focuses our attention on needs that have sometimes been overlooked: scientific and technical training, local research and development, and the critical importance of institutions to facilitate the flow of information essential for effective markets.

Approaching development from a knowledge perspective – that is, adopting policies to increase both types of knowledge, know-how and knowledge about attributes – can improve people's lives in myriad ways besides higher incomes. Better knowledge about nutrition can mean better health, even for those with little to spend on food. Knowledge about how to prevent the transmission of AIDS can save millions from debilitating illness and premature death. Public disclosure of information about industrial pollution can lead to a cleaner and more healthful environment. And microcredit programs can make it possible for poor people to invest in a better future for themselves and their children. In short, knowledge gives people greater control over their destinies.

The twin issues of knowledge gaps and information problems cannot be untangled in real life: to unleash the power of knowledge, governments must recognize and respond to both types of problems, often simultaneously. For the sake of clarity, however, we analyze these issues separately, beginning with knowledge gaps. [. . .]

The Green Revolution: A Paradigm of Knowledge for Development

Few stories better illustrate the potential of knowledge for development – or the obstacles to diffusing that knowledge – than that of the green revolution, the decades-long, worldwide movement dedicated to the creation and dissemination of new agricultural knowledge. This quest, breeding new seeds for enhanced agricultural productivity, was undertaken in the early postwar years by a vast array of agents – nonprofit organizations, governments, multilateral institutions, private firms, banks, village moneylenders, land-rich farmers, and landless laborers – all working, deliberately or not, to improve the daily bread (or rice, or maize) of people everywhere. The English economist Thomas Malthus had predicted in the eighteenth century that the population of any country would eventually outstrip its food supply. What the green revolution showed instead was that Malthus had underestimated how quickly knowledge – in agriculture, in transportation, in mechanization – would transform food production. By the second half of the twentieth century, world food supply was more than keeping up with population growth.

Since the early 1950s, Asia and South America have more than doubled yields of staple crops[. . . .] Global gains in output per hectare have been dramatic, particularly for wheat, maize, and rice[. . . .] And although the impact of the green revolution on the poor was initially a matter of controversy, time has made it clear that poor people have benefited significantly, through higher incomes, cheaper food, and increased demand for their labor.

The early steps in the green revolution mostly involved narrowing knowledge gaps. The first step was to narrow the gap between what scientists already knew about plant genetics and the widespread ignorance on this score in developing countries, reflected in the unavailability there of new crop strains based on this knowledge. This gap was narrowed largely through the research and development efforts of governments and nonprofit organizations. But why was their action necessary? Why didn't private, for profit firms make a greater effort to address food security? Why didn't they, for example, try to commercialize existing scientific knowledge about genetics by developing more productive plant varieties themselves?

The answer is that the knowledge embodied in the seed of a new plant variety is not easily appropriated by any breeder, seed company, farmer, or even country. The varieties most suitable for transfer to developing countries, once transferred, could be easily reproduced. Farmers had only to collect the seeds from the plants grown from the original seeds and replant them. That meant no repeat business for seed developers, and not enough profit to make their effort worthwhile.

Put another way, improved seeds, like many other research outputs, have many of the characteristics of a public good. A public good is one whose full benefits in the form of profits cannot be captured by its creator but instead leak out to society at large, without the creator receiving compensation. Because private entrepreneurs have diminished incentives to provide such goods, the tradition of entrusting public entities with providing them is long. (A good example is the agricultural research the US government funded in the nineteenth century.) Indeed, it is widely recognized in many fields that, without some collective action, there will be far too little research into developing new knowledge.

After the first modern seed varieties proved successful in the early 1960s, many developing countries established national agriculture research organizations, as some had already done, mainly with public funding, to develop second-generation varieties better suited to local conditions. As a result, the number of new varieties of rice and maize released by national research organizations doubled between 1966 and 1985.

To disseminate this knowledge, developing-country governments established agricultural extension services. At first the main job of the extension agents was to inform farmers about the new seeds and techniques. But the best extension agents – and the most effective extension services – quickly learned that listening was also an important part of the job. By listening to farmers and learning from them, extension agents not only gained a better understanding of the farmers' needs and concerns. They also sometimes stumbled upon seed varieties and cultivation techniques that the researchers had missed. This two-way flow of information furthered the local adoption and adaptation of green revolution technology.

At this point in the story, the focus shifts to information problems. The driving force in the early stages of the green revolution had been the creation, dissemination, and adaptation of agricultural know-how. But the potential of these innovations could not be unleashed until millions of small farmers planted the new seeds. For this to happen, a variety of information problems had to be addressed. In particular, what assurance did farmers have that the seeds would work? Why should a farmer risk his livelihood on the say-so of an extension agent? This uncertainty, coupled with the inability of the poor to obtain credit – another classic market failure closely related to information problems – had significant implications for the rate of adoption of the new seeds.

Large landholders and farmers with more education were among the first to try the new seeds, for a variety of reasons. Farmers with extensive landholdings could limit their risk by trying new seeds in test sowings on only a part of their land. They could also more quickly recover the fixed cost of their early adoption by applying what they learned across their larger farms. Educated farmers were better equipped to find out about the new varieties in the first place, and to learn the changes in cultivation practices needed to make the most of them. Perhaps most important, however, more prosperous farmers had ready access to credit and the ability to absorb risk. Poor farmers, unable to borrow and lacking insurance or the savings to fall back on in the event of failure, could only watch and wait until their wealthier neighbors proved the value of the new seeds.

Why didn't banks or village moneylenders lend small farmers the money to buy the new seeds and fertilizer? Many poor people would repay small loans at reasonable interest, if such loans were available. But the costs of identifying the good credit risks among the poor are high relative to the size of the loans they would take out. Unsure which prospective borrowers will repay, lenders charge high interest and require collateral, which the poor often lack. Even when the poor have assets (small landholdings) that could be pledged as collateral, weak legal infrastructure, including lack of land title and ineffective courts, means that enforcement of collateral pledges may be weak. Without enforcement, incentives to repay are limited, and this weakens incentives to lend. The result is that the poor often cannot borrow.

In recent years microcredit schemes have arisen to address these problems. But at the time of the green revolution, poor farmers' lack of credit, combined with their scant education (also partly attributable to lack of credit) and other factors, meant that they were often the last to adopt the new crop strains. The resulting lag between the introduction of new seeds and their widespread use can be seen in the slow expansion of areas sown with new varieties[. . . .]

The costs of these delays were significant. If all the information problems could have been addressed – that is, if farmers could have been immediately persuaded of the potential of the new seeds, and if mechanisms had existed to provide credit to poor farmers – the productivity gains from the green revolution would have been even greater. One study found that, for a farm family with 3.7 hectares, the average loss of potential income over five years from slow adoption and inefficient use of high-yielding varieties was nearly *four times* its annual farm income before the introduction of the new seeds.

Eventually the green revolution did boost the incomes of poor farmers and the landless. A survey in southern India concluded that, between 1973 and 1994, the average real income of small farmers increased by 90 percent, and that of the landless – among the poorest in the farm community – by 125 percent. The poor benefited greatly from increased demand for their labor, because the high-yielding varieties demanded labor-intensive cultivating techniques. Calorie intakes for small farmers and the landless rose 58 to 81 percent, and protein intakes rose 103 to 115 percent.

What Knowledge Gaps and Information Problems Mean for Development

The story of the green revolution shows how creating, disseminating, and using knowledge can narrow knowledge gaps. It also shows that know-how is only one part of what determines society's wellbeing. Information problems lead to market failures and impede efficiency and growth. Development thus entails the need for an institutional transformation that improves information and creates incentives for effort, innovation, saving, and investment and enables progressively complex exchanges that span increased distances and time.

The relationship between knowledge gaps and information problems is clear from the history of the green revolution, because with time it became obvious that improved varieties of plants were necessary but not sufficient to improve the lives of the rural poor. The twin challenges of knowledge for development – knowledge gaps and information problems – are also illustrated in many other examples in this Report. How they will be manifested in the next green revolution, perhaps involving gene splicing and cloning, we can only guess. We can be sure, however, that whether or not new technologies are used in ways that help the poor will depend on how well society addresses knowledge gaps and information problems.

Part IV

Development, Culture, and Human Rights

Introduction

The readings in this section take human rights as a site in which the cultural politics of development discourse are played out. Human rights is a key theme through which the old ways of thinking about development and culture have engaged with new ways of thinking in international debates. Underlying the debates over human rights are the tensions between universalism and particularism, which mesh with the dualism of modern and traditional.

In the first extract, Ernesto Laclau argues against the cultural relativism informing some positions on human rights, according to which human rights are Western constructs that are inappropriate to non-Western cultural practices and values. He points out that just because social agents that initially advocated a universal principle of rights were located in the West does not preclude their general application. Closer inspection reveals particularism and universalism to be closely connected, with universalism turning out to be the other side of the particularist coin. As Laclau points out, there is no minority group that does not build its claims for self-determination on universalist principles.

Ann-Belinda Preis's article describes the late twentieth-century debate between cultural relativism and universalism as having reached a stalemate. She highlights the irony that cultural relativism is a hotly debated issue in human rights debates at a time when the theory has lost its import within the discipline of anthropology, which had been its long-time advocate. Under the impact of decolonization and globalization, many anthropologists have gradually abandoned conceptions of culture as a homogeneous, integral, and coherent unity, now embracing notions such as creolization and hybridity to capture the fluidity of cultural experience and practice. Preis then goes on to give three examples of how in different African countries the human rights discourse is appropriated and localized. She argues that understanding human rights as social practice in everyday life situations helps us to move beyond the universal/relativist debate.

One example of such a move is anthropologist Margaret Jolly's article. She examines the ways in which the problem of domestic violence is caught locally in debates over the authenticity of indigenous social practices. Jolly traces how Vanuatu women use a discourse of universal human rights to argue against the contention that raising the issue of violence threatens Vanuatu identity.

12 Universalism, Particularism, and the Question of Identity

Ernesto Laclau

[...]

Let us start by considering the historical forms in which the relationship between universality and particularity has been thought. A first approach asserts: (a) that there is an uncontaminated dividing line between the universal and the particular; and (b) that the pole of the universal is entirely graspable by reason. In that case there is no possible mediation between universality and particularity: the particular can only *corrupt* the universal. We are in the terrain of classical ancient philosophy. Either the particular realizes in itself the universal – that is, it eliminates itself as particular and transforms itself in a transparent medium through which universality operates; or it negates the universal by asserting its particularism (but as the latter is purely irrational, it has no entity of its own and can only exist as corruption of being). The obvious question concerns the frontier dividing universality and particularity: is it universal or particular? If the latter, universality can only be a particularity which defines itself in terms of a limitless exclusion; if the former, the particular itself becomes part of the universal, then the dividing line is again blurred. But the very possibility of formulating this last question would require that the *form* of universality as such, then the actual *contents* to which it is associated, are subjected to a clear differentiation. The thought of this difference, however, is not available to ancient philosophy.

The second possibility of thinking of the relation between universality and particularity is related to Christianity. The point of view of the totality exists, but it is God's, not ours, so that it is not accessible to human reason. [...] Thus, the universal is mere event in an eschatological succession, only accessible to us through revelation. This involves an entirely different conception of the relation-

Excerpted from Ernesto Laclau, "Universalism, Particularism, and the Question of Identity." In J. Rajchman (ed.), *The Identity in Question* (London: Routledge, 1995), 93–108.

ship between particularity and universality. The dividing line cannot be, as in ancient thought, that between rationality and irrationality, between a deep and a superficial layer *within the thing*, but that between two series of events: those of a finite and contingent succession, on the one hand, and those of the eschatological series, on the other. Because the designs of God are inscrutable, the deep layer cannot be a timeless world of rational forms, but a temporal succession of essential events which are opaque to human reason; and because each of these universal moments has to realize itself in a finite reality which has no common measure with them, the relation between the two orders has to be also an opaque and incomprehensible one. This type of relation was called *incarnation*, its distinctive feature being that between the universal and the body incarnating it there is no rational connection whatsoever. God is the only and absolute mediator. A subtle logic destined to have a profound influence on our intellectual tradition was starting in this way: that of the *privileged agent of History*, the agent whose particular body was the expression of a universality transcending it. The modern idea of a "universal class" and the various forms of Eurocentrism are nothing but the distant historical effects of the logic of incarnation.

Not entirely so, however, because modernity at its highest point was, to a large extent, the attempt to interrupt the logic of incarnation. God, as the absolute source of everything existing, was replaced in its function of universal guarantor by Reason, but a *rational* ground and source has a logic of its own, which is very different from that of a divine intervention – the main difference being that the effects of a rational grounding have to be fully transparent to human reason. Now, this requirement is entirely incompatible with the logic of incarnation; if everything has to be transparent to reason, the connection between the universal and the body incarnating it has also to be so; and in that case the incommensurability between a universal to be incarnated and the incarnating body has to be eliminated. We have to postulate a body which is, in and by itself, the universal.

The full realization of these implications took several centuries. Descartes postulated a dualism by which the ideal of a full rationality still refused to become a principle of reorganization of the social and political world; but the main currents of the Enlightenment were going to establish a sharp frontier between a past, which was the realm of mistakes and follies of men, and a rational future, which had to be the result of an act of absolute institution. A last stage in the advance of this rationalistic hegemony took place when the gap between the rational and the irrational was closed through the representation of the act of its cancellation as a necessary moment in the self-development of reason: this was the task of Hegel and Marx, who asserted the total transparency, in absolute knowledge, of the real to reason. The body of the proletariat is no longer a particular body in which a universality external to it has to be incarnated: it is instead a body in which the distinction between particularity and universality is canceled, and as a result the need for any incarnation is definitely eradicated.

This was the point, however, in which social reality refused to abandon its resistance to universalistic rationalism. For an unsolved problem still remained. The universal had found its own body, but this was still the body of a certain particularity – European culture of the nineteenth century. So European culture was a particular one, and at the same time the expression – no longer the incarnation – of universal human essence (as the USSR was going to be considered later the *motherland* of socialism). The crucial issue here is that there were no intellectual means of distinguishing between European particularism and the universal functions that it was supposed to incarnate, given that European universalism had precisely constructed its identity through the cancellation of the logic of incarnation and, as a result, of the universalization of its own particularism. So, European imperialist expansion had to be presented in terms of a universal civilizing function, modernization and so forth. The resistances of other cultures were, as a result, presented not as struggles between particular identities and cultures, but as part of an all-embracing and epochal struggle between universality and particularisms – the notion of peoples without history expressing precisely their incapacity to represent the universal.

This argument could be conceived in very explicit racist terms, as in the various forms of social Darwinism, but it could also be given some more "progressive" versions – as in some sectors of the Second International – by asserting that the civilizing mission of Europe would finish with the establishment of a universally freed society of planetary dimensions. Thus the logic of incarnation was reintroduced – Europe having to represent, for a certain period, universal human interests. In the case of Marxism, a similar reintroduction of the logic of incarnation takes place. Between the universal character of the tasks of the working class and the particularity of its concrete demands, an increasing gap opened which had to be filled by the Party as representative of the historical interests of the proletariat. The gap between class itself and class for itself opened the way to a succession of substitutions: the Party replaced the class, the autocrat the Party, and so on. Now, this well-known migration of the universal through the successive bodies incarnating it differed in one crucial point from Christian incarnation. In the latter a supernatural power was responsible both for the advent of the universal event and for the body which had to incarnate the latter. Human beings were on an equal footing *vis-à-vis* a power that transcended all of them. In the case of a secular eschatology, however, as the source of the universal is not external but internal to the world, the universal can only manifest itself through the establishment of an *essential* inequality between the objective positions of the social agents. Some of them are going to be privileged agents of historical change, not as a result of a contingent relation of forces, but because they are incarnations of the universal. The same type of logic operating in Eurocentrism will establish the ontological privilege of the proletariat. [. . .]

This whole story is apparently leading to an inevitable conclusion: the chasm between the universal and the particular is unbridgeable – which is the same as saying that the universal is no more than a particular that at some moment has become dominant, that there is no way of reaching a reconciled society. And, in actual fact, the spectacle of the social and political struggles in the 1990s seems to confront us [. . .] with a proliferation of particularisms, while the point of view of universality is increasingly put aside as an old-fashioned totalitarian dream. And, however, I will argue that an appeal to pure particularism is no solution to the problems that we are facing in contemporary societies. In the first place, the assertion of pure particularism, independently of any content and of the appeal to a universality transcending it, is a self-defeating enterprise. For if it is the only accepted normative principle, it confronts us with an unsolvable paradox. I can defend the right of sexual, racial, and national minorities in the name of particularism; but if particularism is the only valid principle, I have to accept also the rights to self-determination of all kinds of reactionary groups involved in antisocial practices. Even more: as the demands of various groups will necessarily clash with each other, we have to appeal – short of postulating some kind of preestablished harmony – to some more general principles in order to regulate such clashes. In actual fact, there is no particularism which does not make appeal to such principles in the construction of its own identity. These principles can be progressive in our appreciation – such as the right of peoples to self-determination – or reactionary – such as social Darwinism or the right to *Lebensraum* – but they are always there, and for essential reasons.

There is a second and perhaps more important reason why pure particularism is self-defeating. Let us accept, for the sake of the argument, that the above-mentioned preestablished harmony is possible. In that case, the various particularisms would not be in antagonistic relation with each other, but would coexist one with the other in a coherent whole. This hypothesis shows clearly why the argument for pure particularism is ultimately inconsistent. For if each identity is in a differential, nonantagonistic relation to all other identities, then the identity in question is purely differential and relational; so it presupposes not only the presence of all the other identities but also the total ground which constitutes the differences as differences. Even worse: we know very well that the relations between groups are constituted as relations of power – that is, that each group is not only different from the others but constitutes in many cases such difference on the basis of the exclusion and subordination of other groups. Now, if the particularity asserts itself as mere particularity, in a purely differential relation with other particularities, it is sanctioning the status quo in the relation of power between the groups. This is exactly the notion of "separate developments" as formulated in apartheid: only the differential aspect is stressed, while the relations of power on which the latter is based are systematically ignored.

This last example is important because, coming from a discursive universe – South African apartheid – which is quite opposite to that of the new particularisms that we are discussing, and revealing, however, the same ambiguities in the construction of any difference, it opens the way to an understanding of a dimension of the relationship particularism/universalism which has been generally disregarded. The basic point is this: I cannot assert a differential identity without distinguishing it from a context, and, in the process of making the distinction, I am asserting the context at the same time. And the opposite is also true: I cannot destroy a context without destroying at the same time the identity of the particular subject who carries out the destruction. It is a very well-known historical fact that an oppositionist force whose identity is constructed within a certain system of power is ambiguous *vis-à-vis* that system, because the latter is what prevents the constitution of the identity and it is, at the same time, its condition of existence. And any victory against the system destabilizes also the identity of the victorious force.

Now, an important corollary of this argument is that, if a fully achieved difference eliminates the antagonistic dimension as constitutive of any identity, the possibility of maintaining this dimension depends on the very failure in the full constitution of a differential identity. It is here that the "universal" enters into the scene. Let us suppose that we are dealing with the constitution of the identity of an ethnic minority, for instance. As we said earlier, if this differential identity is fully achieved, it can only be so within a context – for instance, a nation-state – and the price to be paid for total victory *within that context* is total integration to it. If, on the contrary, total integration *does not* take place, it is because that identity is not fully achieved – there are, for instance, unsatisfied demands concerning access to education, to employment, to consumption goods, and so on. But these demands cannot be made in terms of difference, but of some universal principles that the ethnic minority shares with the rest of the community: the right of everybody to have access to good schools, or live a decent life, or participate in the public space of citizenship, and so on.

This means that the universal is part of my identity as far as I am penetrated by a constitutive lack, that is, as far as my differential identity has failed in its process of constitution. The universal emerges out of the particular not as some principle underlying and explaining the particular, but as an incomplete horizon suturing a dislocated particular identity. This points a way of conceiving the relation between the universal and the particular which is different from those that we had explored earlier. In the case of the logic of incarnation, the universal and the particular were fully constituted but totally separated identities, whose connection was the result of a divine intervention, impenetrable to human reason. In the case of secularized eschatologies the particular had to be eliminated entirely: the universal class was conceived as the cancellation of all differences. In the case of extreme particularism there is no universal body – but as the ensemble of nonantagonistic particularities purely and simply reconstructs the notion of social totality, the classical notion of the universal is not put into question in the least. (A universal conceived as a homogeneous space differentiated by its internal articulations and a *system* of differences constituting a unified ensemble are exactly the same.) Now we are pointing to a fourth alternative: the universal is the symbol of a missing fullness and the particular exists only in the contradictory movement of asserting at the same time a differential identity and canceling it through its subsumption in a nondifferential medium.

I will devote the rest of this essay to discussing three important political conclusions that one can derive from this fourth alternative. The first is that the construction of differential identities on the basis of total closure to what is outside them is not a viable or progressive political alternative. It would be a reactionary policy in Western Europe today, for instance, for immigrants from Northern Africa or Jamaica to abstain from all participation in Western European institutions, with the justification that theirs is a different cultural identity and that European institutions are not their concern. In this way all forms of subordination and exclusion would be consolidated with the excuse of maintaining pure identities. The logic of apartheid is not only a discourse of the dominant groups; as we said before, it can also permeate the identities of the oppressed. At its very limit, understood as *mere* difference, the discourse of the oppressor and the discourse of the oppressed cannot be distinguished. The reason for this we have given earlier: if the oppressed is defined by its difference from the oppressor, such a difference is an essential component of the identity of the oppressed. But in that case, the latter cannot assert its identity without asserting that of the oppressor as well. [. . .]

This shows the ambiguity which is inherent in all forms of radical opposition: the opposition, in order to be radical, has to put in a common ground both what it asserts and what it excludes, so that the exclusion becomes a particular form of assertion. But this means that a particularism really committed to change can only do so by rejecting both what denies its own identity and this identity itself. There is no clear-cut solution to the paradox of radically negating a system of power while remaining in secret dependency on it. It is well known how opposition to certain forms of power requires identification with the very places from which the opposition takes place; as the latter are, however, internal to the opposed system, there is a certain conservatism inherent in *all* opposition. The reason why this is unavoidable is that the ambiguity inherent in *all* antagonistic relation is something we can negotiate with but not actually supersede – we can play with both sides of the ambiguity and produce political results by preventing any of them prevailing in an exclusive way, but the ambiguity as such cannot be properly *resolved*. To surpass an ambiguity involves going beyond *both* its poles, but this means that there can be no simple politics of preservation of an identity. If a racial or cultural minority, for instance, has to assert its identity in new social surroundings, it will have to take into account new situations which will inevitably transform that identity. This means, of course, moving away from the idea of negation as radical reversal.[1] The main consequence that follows is that, if the politics of difference means continuity of difference by being always an *other*, the rejection of the other cannot be radical elimination either, but constant renegotiation of the forms of his presence. Aletta J. Norval asked herself recently about identities in a post-apartheid society:

> The question looming on the horizon is this: what are the implications of recognising that the identity of the other is constitutive of the self, in a situation where apartheid itself will have become something of the past? That is, how do we think of social and political identities as post-apartheid identities?

And after asserting that:

> if the other is merely rejected, externalized *in toto* in the movement in which apartheid receives its signified, we would have effected a reversal of the order, remaining in effect in the terrain in which apartheid has organised and ruled,

she points to a different possibility:

> Through a remembrance of apartheid as other, post-apartheid could become the site from which the final closure and suturing of identities is to be prevented. Paradoxically, a post-apartheid society will then only be radically beyond apartheid in so far as apartheid itself is present in it as its other. Instead of being effaced once and for all, "apartheid" itself would have to play the role of the element keeping open the relation to the other, of serving as watchword against any discourse claiming to be able to create a final unity.[2]

This argument can be generalized. Everything hinges on which of the two equally possible movements leading to the supersession of oppression is initiated. None can avoid maintaining the reference to the "other," but they do so in two completely different ways. If we simply *invert* the relation of oppression, the other (the former oppressor) is maintained as what is now oppressed and repressed, but his inversion of the *contents* leaves the form of oppression unchanged. And as the identity of the newly emancipated groups had been constituted through the rejection of the old dominant ones, the latter continue shaping the identity of the former. The operation of inversion takes place entirely within the old *formal* system of power. But this is not the only possible alternative. As we have seen, all political identity is internally split, because no particularity can be constituted except by maintaining an internal reference to universality as that which is missing. But in that case the identity of the oppressor will equally be split: on the one hand, he will represent a particular system of oppression; on the other, he will symbolize the *form* of oppression as such. This is what makes possible the second move suggested in Norval's text: instead of inverting a particular relation of oppression/closure in what it has of concrete particularity, inverting it in what it has of universality: the *form* of oppression and closure as such. The reference to the other is maintained here also, but as the inversion takes place at the level of the universal reference and not of the concrete contents of an oppressive system, the identities of *both* oppressors and oppressed are radically changed. [. . .]

These remarks allow us to throw some light on the divergent courses of action that current struggles in defense of multiculturalism can follow. One possible way is to affirm, purely and simply, the right of the various cultural and ethnic groups to assert their differences and their separate developments. This is the route to self-apartheid, and it is sometimes accompanied by the claim that Western cultural values and institutions are the preserve of white male Europeans or Anglo-Americans and have nothing to do with the identity of other groups living in the same territory. What is advocated in this way is total segregationism, the mere opposition of one particularism to another. Now, it is true that the assertion of any particular identity involves, as one of its dimensions, the affirmation of the right to a separate existence. But it is here that the difficult questions start, because the separation – or better, the right to difference – has to be asserted within a global community – that is, within a space in which that particular group has to coexist with other groups. Now, how could that coexistence be possible without some shared universal values, without a sense of belonging to a community larger than each of the particular groups in question? Here people say, sometimes, that any agreement should be reached through *negotiation*. Negotiation, however, is an ambiguous term that can mean very different things. One of these is a process of mutual pressures and concessions whose outcome depends only on the balance of power between antagonistic groups. It is obvious that no sense of community can be constructed through that type of negotiation. The relation between groups can only be one of potential war. [. . .] The dilemma of the defenders of extreme particularism is that their political action is anchored in a perpetual incoherence. On the one hand, they defend the right to difference as a *universal* right, and this defense involves their engagement in struggles for the change of legislation, for the protection of minorities in courts, against the violation of civil rights, and so forth. That is, they are engaged in a struggle for the internal reform of the present institutional setting. But as they assert, at the same time, that this setting is necessarily rooted in the cultural and political values of the traditional dominant sectors of the West, *and that they have nothing to do with that tradition*, their demands cannot be articulated into any wider hegemonic operation to reform that system. This condemns them to an ambiguous peripheral relation with the existing institutions, which can have only paralyzing political effects.

This is not, however, the only possible course of action for those engaged in particularistic struggles – and this is our second conclusion. As we have seen before, a system of oppression (that is, of closure) can be combated in two different ways – either by an operation of inversion which performs a new closure, or by negating in that system its universal dimension: the principle of closure as such. It is one thing to say that the universalistic values of the West are the preserve of its traditional dominant groups; it is very different to assert that the historical link between the two is a contingent and unacceptable fact which can be modified through political and social struggles. When Mary Wollstonecraft, in the wake of the French Revolution, defended the rights of women, she did not present the exclusion of women from the declaration of rights of man and citizen as a proof that the latter are intrinsically male rights, but tried, on the contrary, to deepen the democratic revolution by showing the incoherence of establishing universal rights which were restricted to particular sectors of the population. The democratic process in present-day societies can be considerably deepened and expanded if it is made accountable to the demands of large sections of the population – minorities, ethnic groups and so on – who traditionally have been excluded from it. Liberal democratic theory and institutions have, in this sense, to be deconstructed. As they were originally thought for societies which were far more homogeneous than the present ones, they were based on all kinds of unexpressed assumptions which no longer obtain in the present situation. Present-day social and political struggles can bring to the fore this game of decisions taken in an undecidable terrain, and help us to move in the direction of new democratic practices and a new democratic theory which is fully adapted to the present circumstances. That political participation can lead to political and social integration is certainly true, but for the reasons we gave before, political and cultural segregationism can lead to exactly the same result. Anyway, the decline of the integrationist abilities of the Western states make political conformism a rather unlikely outcome. I would argue that the unresolved tension between universalism and particularism opens the way to a movement away from Western Eurocentrism, through an operation that we could call asystematic decentering of the West. As we have seen, Eurocentrism was the result of a discourse which did not differentiate between the universal values that the West was advocating and the concrete social agents that were incarnating them. Now, however, we can proceed to a separation of these two aspects.

If social struggles of new social actors show that the concrete practices of our society restrict the universalism of our political ideals to limited sectors of the population, it becomes possible to retain the universal dimension while widening the spheres of its application – which, in turn, will define the concrete contents of such universality. Through this process, universalism as a horizon is expanded at the same time as its necessary attachment to any particular content is broken. The opposite policy – that of rejecting universalism *in toto* as the particular content of the ethnia of the West – can only lead to a political blind alley.

This leaves us, however, with an apparent paradox – and its analysis will be my last conclusion. The universal, as we have seen, does not have a concrete content of its own (which would close it in itself), but is the always receding horizon resulting from the expansion of an indefinite chain of equivalent demands. The conclusion seems to be that universality is incommensurable with any particularity and, however, cannot exist apart from the particular. In terms of our previous analysis: if only particular actors, or constellations of particular actors can actualize at any moment the universal, in that case the possibility of making visible the nonclosure inherent to a post-dominated society – that is, a society that attempts to transcend the very form of domination – depends on making permanent the asymmetry between the universal and the particular. The universal is incommensurable with the particular, but cannot, however, exist without the latter. How is this relation possible? My answer is that this paradox cannot be solved, but that its non-solution is the very precondition of democracy. The solution of the paradox would imply that a particular body would have been found, which would be the *true* body of the universal. But in that case, the universal would have found its necessary location, and democracy would be impossible. If democracy *is* possible, it is because the universal has no necessary body and no necessary content; different groups, instead, compete between themselves to temporarily give to their particularisms a function of universal representation. [. . .]

Notes

1   It is at this point that, in my recent work, I have tried to complement the idea of radical antagonism – which still involves the possibility of a radical representability – with the notion of dislocation which is previous to any kind of antagonistic representation. Some of the dimensions of this duality have been explored by Bobby Sayyid and Lilian Zac in a short written presentation to the Ph.D. seminar in Ideology and Discourse Analysis, University of Essex, December 1990.

2   Aletta J. Norval, "Letter to Ernesto," in E. Laclau, *New Reflections on the Revolution of Our Time* (London, 1990), 157.

13 Human Rights as Cultural Practice: An Anthropological Critique

Ann-Belinda S. Preis

[...]

For quite some time now, the theory [of "cultural relativism"] has [...] been nurturing a seemingly never-ending debate among human rights researchers on the question of the "universalism" or "relativism" of human rights. The "classical" conflict is well known: cultural relativists see the Universal Declaration of Human Rights as enumerating rights and freedoms which are culturally, ideologically, and politically nonuniversal. They argue that current human rights norms possess a distinctively "Western" or "Judeo-Christian" bias, and hence, are an "ethnocentric" construct with limited applicability. Conversely, universalists assert that human rights are special entitlements of all persons. They are grounded in human nature and as such, are inalienable. "To have human rights one does not have to be anything other than a human being. Neither must one do anything other than be born a human being," as a common phrase goes.[1] Despite various attempts to reject relativist propositions as a confusion of human rights and human dignity, or of rights and duties, the question of the "transferability" and "cross-cultural validity" of human rights continues to be a battlefield of fierce, heated, and passionate debate, with researchers making strong – and strongly varying – philosophical, political, or moral commitments. [...]

This essay suggests that recent anthropological reflections on the notion of culture might contribute not only to pushing the universality–relativity debate out of its present stalemate, but also to assisting in the formulation of a more promising framework for comprehending the real and symbolic dimensions of the current flows of human rights values in what we used to call "foreign cultures." In several, formerly "remote" areas of the world, different human

Excerpted from Ann-Belinda S. Preis, "Human Rights as Cultural Practice: An Anthropological Critique." *Human Rights Quarterly*, 18, 2 (1996), 286–315.

rights discourses have now become a vehicle for the articulation of a wide variety of concerns of different people at different levels of society. Human rights increasingly form part of a wider network of perspectives which are shared and exchanged between the North and South, centers and peripheries, in multiple, creative, and sometimes conflict-ridden ways. Human rights have become "universalized" as values subject to interpretation, negotiation, and accommodation. They have become "culture."

I attempt to illustrate this point through the analysis of three empirical cases from the Southern African country of Botswana: the societal position attributed to the Basarwa or San people of the Kalahari desert, a recent event known as the Unity Dow court case, and finally, the presentation of an extract of dialogue between two researchers on the issue of "freedom of expression." The complexity of these examples suggests, in different ways and at different levels of analysis, that a more dynamic approach to culture is needed in order to capture the various ways in which human rights give meaning to, and are attributed with meaning in, the on-going life experiences and dilemmas of men and women. A theoretical shift must be made from the static view of culture to the analysis of culture as practice, a practice embedded in local contexts and in the multiple realities of everyday life. [. . .]

The Impasse of Human Rights and Culture

In their well-known, and often-cited work on human rights as "A Western Construct with Limited Applicability," Adamantia Pollis and Peter Schwab engage in serious criticism of what they see as a cultural and ideological ethnocentrism in the area of human rights and human dignity. They view the Universal Declaration of Human Rights as a document with underlying democratic and libertarian values, "based on the notion of atomized individuals possessed of certain inalienable rights in nature."[2] Because of the pervasiveness of the notion of the group rather than the individual in many cultures, they conclude that "[t]he Western conception of human rights is not only inapplicable" and "of limited validity," but even "meaningless" to Third World countries.[3] In a similar vein, Asmarom Legesse argues that "[d]ifferent societies formulate their conception of human rights in diverse cultural idioms,"[4] and that in the liberal democracies of the Western world "[t]here is a perpetual, and in our view obsessive, concern with the dignity of the individual, his worth, personal autonomy, and property."[5] [. . .]

In a critical response to some of the above writers, Jack Donnelly claims that their standpoints are based on outright confusion of human rights and human dignity, and between rights and duties, a position he largely shares with Rhoda Howard.[6] In Donnelly's view, "most non-Western cultural and political traditions lack not only the practice of human rights but the very concept."[7] He illustrates this through a "political culture" analysis of human rights in Islam, traditional Africa, Confucian China, Hindu India, and in the Soviet Union.[8] This permits him to draw the conclusion that "the differences between Western and non-Western approaches to human dignity certainly are large."[9] He sees the incorporation of Third World views, such as the valuing of the group or the community over that of the individual, as a "great risk" to the essential character of human rights, which would come "dangerously close to destroying or denying human rights as they have been understood."[10] [. . .]

The point I wish to emphasize here is that at this metageneral level of analysis, almost all arguments become plausible, or equally true or false. One glosses over a multitude of cultural particularities such as those in Islam or traditional Africa, in a few pages, just for the sake of creating an argument about the presence or absence of human rights, an argument that can be contradicted the next moment with just as many convincing arguments. One might further ask at what analytical level the above "phenomena" – a religion, a continent, an epoch, a subcontinent, a regime – are at all comparable? [. . .] When the debate on the universalism or relativism of human rights is so radically removed from the cultural "realities" it alleges to speak about, it hardly creates anything but its own impasse.

A major reason behind this apparent stalemate is that the notion of culture is repeatedly launched, both by universalists and relativists, as if it were an unproblematic, everyday term about which there exists overall, common consent. However, expressions such as "cultures," "other cultures," and "non-Western cultures," do in fact carry with them a specific, underlying conceptualization of culture; namely, as an almost physically concrete, quantitatively measurable entity. Culture is implicitly defined as a homogeneous, bounded unit, almost as if it were "a thing." At best then, the debates on the universality or relativity of human rights reveal a continued preoccupation with various outmoded approaches to "culture contact" that developed within North American anthropology in the 1930s, mostly on the basis of the "melting pot" vision or on the idea of "acculturation."[11] Hence, debaters are inclined to conceptualize "culture contacts" as if they were new or at least recent. It is doubtful that this concept could be justified at the time; in any case, another half-century later, such situations have become practically nonexistent. As a result, the universality–relativity debates seem somehow unsatisfying, despite the vigor and passion with which they are launched. It is as if larger, more important questions are lurking under the surface, but they remain unexplored and somewhat blocked, precisely because of the rigid "us" and "them" dichotomy inherent in the "culture contact" perspective. [. . .]

Beyond the Universality–Relativity Debate?

[. . .] Although the classic vision of unique cultural patterns has proven merit, its limitations are seen today as serious, indeed. Most importantly, this vision emphasizes shared patterns at the expense of processes of change and internal inconsistencies, conflicts, and contradictions. In contrast with the "classic view, which posits culture as a self-contained whole made up of coherent patterns," culture, therefore, is increasingly conceived of as "a more porous array of intersections where distinct processes crisscross from within and beyond its borders."[12] One of the most well-founded rejections of the usage of culture in anthropological analysis as a sort of "sum total" of observable patterns and ideological bases was made some years ago by Frederik Barth, who convincingly demonstrated that people's realities are culturally constructed.[13] In a central passage Barth wrote that "[p]eople participate in multiple, more or less discrepant, universes of discourse; they construct different, partial and simultaneous worlds in which they move; their cultural construction of reality springs not from one source and is not of one piece."[14] A major implication of these perspectives is that ethnography is no longer defined as the interpretation of distinct, "whole" ways of life, but rather as a series of specific dialogues, impositions, and inventions. Cultural difference is no longer viewed as a stable, exotic otherness; self–other relations are increasingly considered to be matters of power and rhetoric rather than essence.[15] Modern anthropology thus attempts to overcome the rigid opposition of subjectivity and objectivity by arguing that interpretation begins from the postulate that the web of meaning constitutes human existence to such an extent that it cannot ever be reduced to constitutively prior speech, acts, didactic relations, or any predefined elements. "Culture, the shared meanings, practices, and symbols that constitute the human world, does not present itself neutrally or with one voice. It is always multivocal and overdetermined, and both the observer and the observed are always enmeshed in it. . . . There is no privileged position, no absolute perspective, no final recounting."[16]

Case One: Basarwa Complexities

Consider how the above perspectives relate in the case of the "Basarwa" – the "San," "Kung," or "Bushmen," as they have been called by anthropologists and others (along with a variety of different, local group names), of the Southern African Kalahari desert: they are considered to be some of the possibly best known, most intensely studied, if not over-researched, people of the world today. [. . .] Despite this massive amount of "knowledge" on the Basarwa, accumulated through various forms of contact between them and anthropologists, development consultants, government officials, and now also human rights experts, the Basarwa themselves have remained remarkably remote. They are still predominantly considered to belong to the "hunter-gatherer populations in Africa [who] have long endured harsh treatment from more powerful adjoining societies."[17] Additionally, they have been described as people who "preceded the settlement of black people and white people," and lived "undisturbed, together with the wildlife" until "[t]he land which they had come to know as 'theirs' was taken away from them" – an act that is viewed as fundamental in contributing to their present "alienation."[18] In a recent article, Akhil Gupta and James Ferguson correctly point out that there has been surprisingly little criticism of the eroticization implicit in such assessments.[19] They emphasize M. L. Pratt's point about the "blazing contradiction" between the portrait of primordial beings untouched by historical events and the genocidal advance of the White "Bushman conquest."[20] Yet, even in Pratt's account, the Basarwa are basically presented "as a preexisting ontological entity – 'survivors,' not products (still less producers), of history. 'They' are victims, having suffered the deadly process of 'contact' with 'us.'"[21]

What is obviously ignored in much of the work on the San-speaking people is that they "always" have been in continuous interaction with other groups; hence, the picture of the isolated "Bushman tribe" of the desert is in serious need of revision. According to the anthropologist Edwin N. Wilmsen, the Zhu (!Kung), for instance, have never been a classless society, and if they give such an impression, "it is because they are incorporated as an underclass in a wider social formation that includes Batswana, Ovaherero, and others." Furthermore, Wilmsen shows how the Bushman/San label has been produced through the "retribalization" of the colonial period, and how the "cultural conservation uniformly attributed to these people by almost all anthropologists who have worked with them until recently, is a consequence – not a cause – of the way in which they have been integrated into the modern capitalist economies of Botswana and Namibia." The conclusion is that "[t]he appearance of isolation and its reality of dispossessed poverty are recent products of a process that unfolded over two centuries and culminated in the last moments of the colonial era."[22] [. . .]

Case Two: Multivocality

The second example concerns the highly published Unity Dow court case,[23] which unfolded in Botswana in the early 1990s, and became immediately significant because it was the first time in the history of the country that a woman challenged the government in court. The case, correctly known as Dow v. State of Botswana, has its origins in changes to the Citizenship Act that were enacted in 1984 when the government amended the Act to restrict the categories of persons who could become citizens through birth or descent. Section four said that children born to Batswana women married to foreigners no longer had the right of Botswana citizenship by virtue of their birth there. Section five dealt with citizenship by descent, and it prevented Batswana women married to foreign men from passing on Botswana citizenship to their children. Only unwed Batswana women who gave birth to children of foreigners, and all Batswana men, even those with foreign wives, were accorded that right.

Unity Dow is a prominent Gaborone lawyer, a leading member of the feminist organization Emang Basadi ("Stand Up Women"), and a participant in the Women and Law in Southern Africa Research Project, who, prior to 1984, had married a US citizen, Peter Nathan Dow. They have three children, two of whom were born after 1984, and therefore are affected by the changes to the Citizenship Act. Under the amended Act, the two children are not citizens of Botswana, even though they were born in Botswana and have lived there all their lives, and even though their mother is a citizen of Botswana. In November of 1990, Unity Dow decided to challenge sections four and five of the Citizenship Act in court. She argued that her children were denied Botswana citizenship because her husband was a noncitizen. She also contended that if it were a man who married a woman from outside Botswana, his children would have been granted citizenship without any problem; hence, sections four and five of the Act stripped away women's rights guaranteed in 1966 by Botswana's Constitution. [. . .]

In June 1991, Judge Horowitz delivered his twenty-four page verdict. Writing that in matters of human rights he was compelled to take a generous interpretation of the law, the judge found for Unity Dow and declared sections four and five of the Citizenship Act "null and void." He accepted that Unity Dow had been discriminated against on the basis of her sex and had thereby been denied fundamental rights to liberty, protection from being subjected to degrading treatment, and protection from restrictions on her freedom of movement – all arguments made by Dow's lawyer. He rejected the argument of the state defense that gender discrimination is allowed, writing that "the time when women were treated as chattels or were there to obey the whims and wishes of males is long past."[24] As to the state's contention that Unity Dow and the children should just follow Mr. Dow if he decided to leave the country, the judge dismissed this as an irrelevant view, which "would have appealed to the patriarchs of Biblical times."[25]

The reaction to the verdict was swift and largely divided along gender lines. Supporters of Unity Dow hailed it as a breakthrough for women. [. . .] Government ministers, however, who seemed to speak for the vast majority of men on this issue, vehemently attacked the decision as an unacceptable affront to Tswana culture. What the government feared was the same thing that the feminists welcomed – a major overhaul of the laws of Botswana. [. . .] In December 1991, however, the appeal was heard by the full bench of the Court of Appeals, which in July 1992 upheld Justice Horowitz's judgment in the Dow case.[26] [. . .]

Unity Dow's attack on the government of Botswana [. . .] clearly and explicitly shows how "concepts such as cultural relativity . . . are happily adopted by those who control the state."[27] However, to conceive of this rich scenario solely in terms of an antagonism between the universality and cultural relativity of human rights would be to simplify what is going on in the Unity Dow court case. Much more is happening here than the legal category of constitutional sex discrimination or the "accountability" versus "empowerment" model of human rights struggles is capable of revealing.

First, the case exemplifies what has already been signaled with regard to the San Bushmen, but here at a different level of analysis: there is no Botswana culture in the sense of a unitary whole, a bounded entity, to which human rights may be said to apply. This culture is itself being vehemently contested, negotiated, and debated. This suggests that the numerous disagreements and conflicts within this debate are not simply unpleasant, external disturbances to an otherwise stable and harmonious "Botswana culture," but rather, constitutive of it. [. . .]

Furthermore, in the process of negotiating what (women's) human rights in Botswana are, or ought to be, power is far from absent. Various knowledge, or more broadly, discursive forms are manipulated by various actors in specific contexts in the pursuit of certain ends and stereotypic positions abound. Batswana feminists, assisted by their Western sisters, generalize about "patriarchal" Botswana, just like government representatives do about the assumed "subservience" of Batswana women. Had rural women joined the debate, other interpretations perhaps would have been revealed. [. . .]

In any case, human rights as culture in action in and around the Unity Dow court case is obviously multivocal and multidimensional. It is constituted by many voices from within and outside Botswana itself. This clashes conspicuously with old perceptions of the autonomy and integrity of territorially based cultures. It simultaneously suggests that the traditional relativist view of human rights as particularly "Western" can no longer be sustained; Unity Dow and her feminist supporters certainly consider human rights to be theirs as well. Human rights clearly have become part of a much wider, globalized, cultural network of perspectives. This does not mean, however, that they simply constitute an influx of alien meaning or cultural form which enters into a vacuum or inscribes itself on "a cultural tabula rasa."[28] They enter various kinds of interactions with already existing meanings and meaningful forms; in this case, particular conceptualizations of Batswana men and women, for instance. The root metaphor of "creole culture," fashionable in contemporary anthropology, captures the fact that cultural processes, such as the Unity Dow case, are not simply a matter of constant "pressure" from the center toward the periphery, but of a much more creative interplay. The periphery indeed "talks back" [. . .].

Case Three: Intersubjectivity

Indeed, the unpredictability and open-endedness of cultural processes can no longer be ignored. Consider this last example of a dialogue between an "outsider" and "insider" researcher on the issue of freedom of expression in contemporary Botswana. The dialogue should be viewed against a descriptive term that constantly reappears in the writings of scholars of contemporary Botswana: "unique."[29] A general consensus seems to exist that the history, the politics, and the socioeconomic constellations of that land-locked, sparsely populated country, two-thirds of which is covered by the Kalahari desert, occupy a remarkably unique position in the African context.[30] The uniqueness is first and foremost attributed to the fact that, placed in a broader African, Third World, or even global context, Botswana's human rights record has been surprisingly good.[31] [. . .]

While the conglomeration of these features has rightly made Botswana earn such titles as "Africa's success story" and "shining star of democracy," and has projected her as a political and economic model for many developing countries, the stability and durability of the country's liberal democracy are today being increasingly questioned by observers and scholars of different disciplinary backgrounds. The following dialogue, part of an interview with Dr. Bojosi Otlhogile at the Faculty of Law in October 1992, illustrates this essential point. The dialogue begins as Dr. Otlhogile first responds to a question of why and how Botswana is always referred to in terms of its democratic uniqueness:

> *Otlhogile*: People look at Botswana in a context of a continent which has violated all democratic norms, a continent which does not respect the basics of democracy, where one-party systems are the order of the day. The comparison is between us and all these other countries, that made us an exception.

A.B.P.: Some people say that this perception has allowed for some sort of ignorance of the different weaknesses inherent in the democratic system here?

Otlhogile: Oh, yes. If you look at the reports from Danida [the Danish International Development Agency] or from Sweden, they never talk about the right of assembly in this country. There were cases where the government did not allow the people to organize, or where they organized and there was state intervention. Until very recently – they are trying to amend the law at present – the Minister of Home Affairs could dissolve a committee and appoint his own people at any time, or even insist on having his representatives in the meetings of Trade Unions. The ILO [International Labor Organization] knows about it, but the Human Rights Bulletins from the Scandinavian countries never mention it. Not even the Americans, let alone Amnesty, look into, for example, the issue of death penalty in Botswana; it simply does not appear. Or even take, for instance, the question of freedom of expression. Look at all the reports from Article 19; they never include Botswana.

A.B.P.: But that is because your press has been free since . . . is it 1982, or . . . ?

Otlhogile: (interrupts) Well, is it free? I don't know, but that is a different matter. The impression here is that it is not. I mean, you must have heard that there is a case against a newspaper in this country at present?

A.B.P.: Yes, against the *Mmegi*, isn't it?

Otlhogile: Yes, and it is not the first case of its kind. They have been going on for many years. And there are even cases where journalists were thrown out of the country, deported. Some have been arrested and persecuted. But we never heard anything from Article 19. We never heard anything from human rights organizations throughout the world. As I say, this is because they see us as an exception to the general picture within the African continent.

A.B.P.: Isn't this because one can speak of isolated incidents in Botswana, and not a real trend?

Otlhogile: I think a real trend is developing. You are free to publish as long as it does not affect the government. If it does affect the government, it will intervene. This is a trend, one cannot call it an incident. . . .

The above conversation not only reveals that there is disagreement about Botswana's human rights performance, but that the culture of human rights (its meanings, practices, and symbols) does not present itself neutrally or with one voice. This is probably the most "universal" characteristic of human rights. [. . .] Perhaps an even more important fact revealed by the dialogue is that the "reality" of human rights is culturally constructed and that both the observer and the observed are enmeshed in this process. This suggests that one cannot determine, in any absolute sense of the term, whether there is freedom of expression in Botswana or not. There simply is no objective position from which human rights can be truly "measured." [. . .]

In legal terminology the concept of "rights" is often referred to as an "evolving paradigm."[32] The Unity Dow court case and the above dialogue suggest that they are certainly also cultural practice. Human rights are continuously in the process of reconstituting and reformulating themselves; they are always "at work." In the (post)modern, and post-Berlin Wall world, the important issue is not any longer whether human rights are universal or relative, applicable or inapplicable, transferable or nontransferable. Human rights now form part of the multiple cultural flows between centers and peripheries in a world where "cultures have lost their moorings in particular places," and "the rapidly expanding and quickening mobility of people combines with the refusal of cultural products and practices, to 'stay put.'"[33] In this culture-play of diaspora, familiar lines between "here" and "there," center and periphery, colony and metropole have become blurred; hence, the question of the relevance or irrelevance of human rights has become strictly irrelevant. [...]

From Abstract Categories to Social Actors

[...] One way forward is to seek inspiration in the theoretical and methodological advances made over the past years within the field known as "development research." Of particular relevance to human rights is the growing interest in the notion of human agency, and in the search for a more thorough-going actor-oriented approach, as recently outlined by Norman Long and others in an excellent, thought-provoking volume.[34] The immediate importance of these perspectives for human rights lies in their obvious connection to the question of practice. Human rights researchers often make statements about the relationship between the theory and practice of human rights, but rarely, if ever, on the basis of more thorough definitions of what the practice(s) might actually, and more concretely, consist of. [...]

In Norman Long's definition, the essence of an actor-oriented approach is that its concepts are grounded in everyday life experiences and understandings of men and women, be they – as in the present essay – Basarwa, feminists, government representatives, politicians, or researchers.[35] [...] In general terms, the notion of agency attributes to the individual actor the capacity to process social experience and to devise ways of coping with life, even under the most extreme forms of coercion. Within the limits of information, uncertainty, and other constraints (for example, physical, normative, or politico-economic), social actors are knowledgeable and capable. They attempt to solve problems, learn how to intervene in the flow of social events around them, and continuously monitor their own actions, observing how others react to their behavior and taking note of the various contingent circumstances: "[A]ll forms of dependence offer some resources whereby those who are subordinate can influence the activities of their superiors."[36] In these ways they actively engage in the construction of their own social worlds, although, as Long reminds us (with Marx), the circumstances they encounter are not simply of their own choosing.[37]

In his fundamental concern to reconcile structure and actor perspectives analytically, Long argues that "development and social change are all too often seen as emanating primarily from centers of power in the form of intervention by state or international interests, and following some broadly determined developmental path, signposted by 'stages of development' or by the succession of 'dominant modes of production.'"[38] The same applies [...] to the more or less hidden, progressionist assumptions of many human rights texts. However, such models are tainted by determinist, linear, and externalist views of social change. Although it might be true that certain important structural changes result from the impact of outside forces (due to encroachment by the state, for instance), it is theoretically unsatisfactory to base one's analysis on the concept of external determination. As the Unity Dow court case so brilliantly illustrates, "[a]ll forms of external determination necessarily enter the existing life-worlds of the individuals and social groups affected, and in this way are mediated and transformed by these same actors and structures."[39] [. . .]

Finally, the significance of adopting an actor perspective lies in viewing the researcher as an active agent influencing specific events and the construction of the final human rights text. Long continually stresses the central importance of treating the researcher herself as an active social agent who struggles to understand social processes by entering the life-worlds of local actors, who, in turn, actively shape the researcher's own fieldwork strategies, thus molding the contours and outcomes of the research process itself. In this sense, the dialogue with Mr. Otlhogile forces us to repudiate the existence of an objective (human rights) "reality" beyond specific people's forms of sociability, mutual understandings, and conceptual horizons. [. . .]

Introducing this methodology to human rights, thus, clearly involves much more than the simple task of "translating" the rights into different cultural idioms, as several writers on the intercultural intelligibility of human rights seem to suggest.[40] In explaining or translating human rights action, there is always the danger that we might "displace the agency or intentions of those we study by our own 'folk' notions or theoretical concepts."[41] This is indeed the case with the [. . .] "tolerance" approach to human rights, the different versions of which converge in an ethnocentric view of social behavior based upon the individualism of "utilitarian man," leaving very little space for cultural and contextual differentiation. If the question of "culture" and "cultural difference" is to be addressed in a less abstract and demystifying manner, we must attempt to see "human worlds as constructed through historical and political processes, and not as brute timeless facts of nature."[42] This seems to be all the more important in human rights research where the temptation to confuse our local culture with universal human nature has proven to be such a marvelous temptation. [. . .]

Notes

1 Jack Donnelly, "Human Rights and Human Dignity: An Analytical Critique of Non-Western Conceptions of Human Rights," 76 *Am. Pol. Sci. Rev.* 303, 306 (1982).

2 Adamantia Pollis and Peter Schwab, "Human Rights: A Western Construct with Limited Applicability," in Adamantia Pollis and Peter Schwab (eds.), *Human Rights: Cultural and Ideological Perspectives* 1, 8 (1980) [hereinafter *Cultural and Ideological Perspectives*].

3 Id. at 13.

4 Asmarom Legesse, "Human Rights in African Political Culture," in Kenneth W. Thompson (ed.), *The Moral Imperatives of Human Rights: A World Survey*, 123, 124 (1980).

5 Id.

6 Donnelly, supra note 1, at 313, 304; Rhoda E. Howard, "Dignity, Community, and Human Rights," in Abdullah Ahmed An-Na'im (ed.), *Human Rights in Cross-cultural*

Perspectives: A Quest for Consensus 81, 90–1 (1992) [hereinafter *Human Rights in Cross-cultural Perspectives*]; Rhoda E. Howard, "Cultural Absolutism and the Nostalgia for Community," 15 *Hum. Rts. Q.* 315 (1993).

7   Donnelly, supra note 1, at 303.

8   Id. at 306–11.

9   Id. at 304.

10   Id. at 312.

11   Robert Redfield et al., "Memorandum for the Study of Acculturation," 38 *Am. Anthropologist* 149 (1936); Gregory Bateson, "Culture Contact and Schismogenesis," 199 *Man: Monthly Rec. Anthropological Sci.* 178 (1935).

12   Renato Rosaldo, *Culture and Truth: The Remaking of Social Analysis* 20 (1989).

13   Frederik Barth, "The Analysis of Culture in Complex Societies," 3–4 *Ethnos* 120 (1989).

14   Id. at 130.

15   James Clifford, *The Predicament of Culture: Twentieth-century Ethnography, Literature, and Art* 14 (1988).

16   Paul Rabinow and William M. Sullivan (eds.), *Interpretive Social Science: A Reader* (1979), at 6.

17   Robert K. Hitchcock and John D. Holm, "Bureaucratic Domination of Hunter-Gatherer Societies: A Study of the San in Botswana," 24 *Dev. & Change* 305–6 (1993).

18   Botswana Christian Council, "Who Was (T)here First? An Assessment of the Human Rights Situation of Basarwa in Selected Communities in the Gantsi District," 10 Occasional Paper, 5–7 (1992).

19   Akhil Gupta and James Ferguson, "Beyond 'Culture': Space, Identity, and the Politics of Difference," 7:1 *Cultural Anthropology* 6, 15 (1992).

20   Id. at 15.

21   Id.

22   Id. at 16 (quoting Edwin N. Wilmsen).

23   The following account draws on Chris Brown, "The Unity Dow Court Case: Liberal Democracy and Patriarchy in Botswana," paper presented to the Canadian Association of African Studies, May 14, 1992, and on a number of articles, mainly from newspapers in Botswana: the *Botswana Gazette*, June 19 and July 8, 1991; *Mmegi*, June 14–20, 1991 and July 10–16, 1992; *Newslink*, June 14, 1991.

24   "Judgment." In the Appeal Court of Botswana Held at Lobatse. Court of Appeal Civil Appeal No. 4/91. High Court Misca. No. 124/90. In the matter between The Attorney General (Appellant) and Unity Dow (Respondent), reprinted in 13 *Hum. Rts. Q.* 614, 623 (1991).

25   Id. at 621.

26   See id.

27   Jack Donnelly and Rhoda E. Howard (eds.), *International Handbook of Human Rights* 20 (1987).

28   Ulf Hannerz, *Cultural Complexity: Studies in the Social Organization of Meaning* 262 (1992).

29   Louis A. Picard, *The Politics of Development in Botswana: A Model for Success?* 2 (1987); Patrick P. Molutsi and John D. Holm, "Developing Democracy When Civil Society is Weak," 89 *Afr. Aff.* 232–340 (1990); Mpho G. Molomo, "Botswana's Political Process," in Mpho G. Molomo and Brian T. Mokopakgosi (eds.), *Multi-party Democracy in Botswana* 11, 16–18 (1991).

30   Picard, supra note 29, at 2.

31   Molomo, supra note 29, at 11.

32   Virginia A. Leary, "Postliberal Strands in Western Human Rights Theory: Personalist–

Communitarian Perspectives," in *Human Rights in Cross-cultural Perspectives*, supra note 6, at 105, 128.

33   Gupta and Ferguson, supra note 19, at 7, 9.
34   Norman Long and Ann Long (eds.), *Battlefields of Knowledge: The Interlocking of Theory and Practice in Social Research and Development* (1992) [hereinafter *Battlefields*].
35   *Battlefields*, supra note 34, at 3, 5.
36   Norman Long, "From Paradigm Lost to Paradigm Regained? The Case for an Actor-oriented Sociology of Development," in *Battlefields*, supra note 34, at 16, 24 (quoting A. Giddens).
37   Id. at 24.
38   Id. at 19.
39   Id. at 20.
40   See Jack Donnelly, *Universal Human Rights in Theory and Practice* 109–10 (1989); Pollis and Schwab, supra note 2, at 15; Alison Dundes Renteln, *Relativism and the Search for Human Rights: Universalism versus Relativism* 64 (1990).
41   *Battlefields*, supra note 34, at 42 n. 16.
42   Rosaldo, supra note 12, at 39.

14 Women's Rights, Human Rights, and Domestic Violence in Vanuatu

Margaret Jolly

Introduction

Universalism and relativism in anthropology have often been seen as conflicting but complicit epistemologies, generating a tension which defies easy resolution. As a feminist and an anthropologist I aspire to sustain a creative tension between the universal and the particular, but I also desire to be aware of the positions from which the global and the local are viewed. What engages me here is a particular form of that tension – universalism and relativism – not so much as divergent epistemologies but as embodied and situated stances. Thus it is not just the difference between seeing what we share as against seeing what we do not share, but in how our very notions of identity and difference are grounded in historical, political, and moral relations.[1] This is nowhere more obvious than in contemporary debates about women and human rights.

I focus these broad questions in the context of some recent conversations with Pacific feminists – in particular my participation at a conference in Port Vila in August 1994 on Violence and the Family in Vanuatu. This essay works through three phases, a review of a recent text about women and human rights, a portrait of the conference and its situation in a regional and historical frame, and finally an exploration of whether or how, in the words of Grace Mera Molisa, quoted in my title, "women have human rights or not."

Excerpted from Margaret Jolly, "Woman Ikat Raet Long Human Raet O No? Women's Rights, Human Rights, and Domestic Violence in Vanuatu." *Feminist Review* 52 (1996), 169–90.

Women's Rights, Human Rights – Global and Local Relations

Despite the strenuous critique of the notion of the human subject as Enlighten-ment archaism, as imperialist residue, or as mere discursive effect on the part of poststructuralist theorists, the "human" is again globally vaunted in debates and political campaigns about human rights. From the huge literature generated by this process, I select as my key text Katarina Tomasevski's *Women and Human Rights* (1993) not because it is especially profound, but because it is a widely used handbook which comes with weighty credentials, being commissioned as part of the UN-NGO Women and Development Series and celebrated by none other than Professor Erica Irene-Daes, Chairperson of the Joint Inspection Unit of the United Nations System.

This book, like some others, takes for granted not only the notion of the human but that humans have natural rights. As in much of the human rights literature, the human person is modeled on notions of the individual derived from Western liberal humanist traditions. The problem then for Tomasevski is that the "human" and "rights" have been conceived from the viewpoint of a masculine subject.[2] [. . .]

[. . . I]n successive chapters of the book she documents how "he" has not included "her" in innumerable national laws and international conventions – in rights to vote and hold political office, in rights to work and join unions, in rights to hold property and pass it on, in rights in family and personal law, and in rights to education and health. A major embarrassment is revealed (1993: 11). The UN Convention on the Rights of the Child enacted in 1989 up until its final draft used "he" throughout, and the specific forms of discrimination against female children – infanticide, unequal education, vulnerability to sexual abuse or debt-bonded prostitution – were countenanced too late for inclusion.

But Tomasevski is rather happier about extending the human to woman than she is about recognizing sexual difference. Thus she tends to see maternity as a problem which impedes the full realization of women's natural rights. One chapter is entitled "From protection of motherhood to equal rights." Tomasevski is committed ultimately to the view that women should become like men[. . . .] Moreover, she has little tolerance for those who pussyfoot about human rights in the name of "cultural sensitivity" [. . .]. But what if such a reliance on law and international conventions proves unproductive or even counterproductive? And are culture and tradition only to be seen as impediments to the realization of women's natural rights?

Culture and tradition in her text appear primarily in their role as obstacles to human rights – evidence canonically in practices such as genital mutilation, child marriage, and female sequestration. And more often than not the cultures which are chosen to typify these impediments are in Africa, Asia, or Latin America rather than her native Denmark or North America. Patriarchal prac-tices such as cosmetic surgery, pornography, or sex tourism are mentioned but are not so privileged nor seen as "traditional." Moreover, tradition is rarely seen as something worth recuperating or perpetuating for women and the "human" comes dangerously close to the Western value of an individual subject with natural rights. Now of course this is precisely what various states like China have claimed, in opposing UN and US criticisms of their human rights record and attempted sanctions against human rights abuses through aid and development strategies. Ancestral values and cultural relativism may thus be a way of securing repressive political regimes. But are all ancestral values equally repressive?

One of the hazards of this kind of debate is that the human slides imperceptibly into the Western, and is too readily dismissed as a new form of colonialism (see below). This risk is even greater if there is a difference or conflict between male and female subjects, whereby tradition comes to stand for female subordination and human rights female liberation. This is nowhere more obvious than in debates about domestic violence, in the Pacific as elsewhere.

Violence and the Family in Vanuatu

I now turn to the conference. We are sitting in a large, airy room at the University of South Pacific Extension Center, Port Vila, Vanuatu. It is August 1994. At one end, a large banner proclaims the title "Violence and the Family in Vanuatu" in the canonical feminist palette of purple, green and white – it is reiterated in more indigenous form in the weave of a pandanus mat. The walls of the room are covered in posters made by schoolchildren, all of which represent the problem as one of male violence toward women – the winning entry portrays a man standing over a woman like a sadistic alien. Many of these posters, like the poetry and personal testimonials of other schoolchildren, graphically implicate alcohol – a bottle appears to be stuck in a woman's head, an adolescent boy painfully recounts the horrific consequences of his father beating up his mother in a drunken rage, killing her. On the opening night we had heard a stirring speech against domestic violence by a government minister (for Justice, Culture, Religion, Women's Affairs and Archives), Hon Sethy Regenvanu, were led by his wife Dorothy in Christian prayers that the conference might help redress the problem, and witnessed a hilarious but poignant skit by the all-female TUA theater group.[3] This depicted a young woman, the victim of sexual assault by her uncle, whose mother would not believe her story.

The conference was sponsored by the Vanuatu Women's Center, an indigenous non-governmental organization (NGO), set up in September 1992 "to provide support and counseling to the victims of violence," and to "empower our women with information and training."[4] It is a collective of volunteers – activists, researchers, and counselors – coordinated by Merilyn Tahi.[5] Those present over the four days of the conference were mainly ni-Vanuatu women, primarily well-educated women from the port towns of Vila and Santo.[6] [. . .] But a few women came from village church groups or Vanuatu National Council of Women (VNKW) chapters in the outer islands. There were a few ni-Vanuatu men – a sprinkling of policemen, bureaucrats, and custodians of ancestral traditions associated with the Cultural Center. There were several white men, mainly members of the judiciary, and a few white women from the various High Commissions and aid agencies, and myself, the sole anthropologist. Most of the locals were Christian with the exception of an Iranian man, his wife, and sister – articulate and passionate proponents of the Baha'i faith. [. . .]

The issues which circulated and recirculated were familiar and might arise at similar conferences elsewhere. What is domestic violence – is it only physical abuse or does it include psychological torture? Does it have to be intended? Who are the perpetrators and who are the victims? How does male violence compare with female violence? Are they sequentially linked? What about violence toward children? What makes violence "domestic" or private rather than public? Is domestic violence acceptable to some, even legitimate? Is domestic violence increasing? If so, why? Is the increase in rates only an increase in reporting, with greater awareness of the problem and with easier access to police, to judges, to community workers? Did the very existence of the Vanuatu Women's Center increase women's ability and propensity to report domestic violence?

All familiar stuff. But there were other questions which might seem strange to Europeans[. . .] Is sorcery violence? Has violence increased as people have moved into towns? Is the growth of the cash economy and the increased isolation of the family to blame? Moreover, throughout the several days of presentations, questions, and conversations the same trio of concepts occurred – *kastom* or tradition, Christianity, and human rights.

Kastom, Christianity, and the Human: A Historical Frame

[. . .] Vanuatu is a small group of islands, 1,700 km distant from the eastern coast of Australia, with a population now approaching 160,000, most of whom are indigenes or ni-Vanuatu. The name Vanuatu, which means "land standing up" or "independent land," was assumed in 1980, when it was proclaimed an independent republic. Its colonial title – New Hebrides/Nouvelles Hébrides – was a place name conferred by Captain Cook[. . . .] Then, from the nineteenth century on, the land and its people had been subject to the extractions of those who came to trade in sandalwood, in *bêche de mer*, and in labor for the plantations of Queensland (Australia), Fiji, and nearby New Caledonia. From the mid-nineteenth century, these were joined by foreign planters and settlers, including Christian missionaries both Protestant and Catholic. Commercial and denominational differences were entangled with the rivalry between the two colonial powers – Britain and France. [. . .] In the early twentieth century, they proclaimed joint colonial control and then a Condominium – a government chronically divided between Anglo and French interests, which was both weak and indifferent to the local population, who later dubbed it "Pandemonium" government. In contrast to most other states of the Southwest Pacific, where independence was conferred peacefully and even peremptorily by foreign powers, here there was a struggle which at points erupted into violence. The French were as keen to stay as the British were to withdraw, and promoted anti-independence movements and secessionist attempts which impeded the nationalist struggle but were ultimately defeated, by political maneuvers and by military forces brought in from Papua New Guinea. In this movement for independence, there was [. . .] a recuperation of the local, the indigenous, "traditional" values and practices of life prior to European incursion. In Vanuatu this is signaled in the concept *kastom*.

Kastom [. . .] evokes not so much the totality of ancestral practices as a particular selection of such practices for the present (see Jolly 1992). Indigenous forms of sociality were based on root crop horticulture, pig breeding, and exchange, with small settlements of people clustered according to variable relations of kinship and place. There were patterns of achieved or inherited rank, and in most places the segregation of male and female persons, who embodied differentiated, even antithetical sacred powers. The precolonial religion conse-crated origins in place and ancestral being and witnessed their power in healthy and fertile people, good crops, and pigs which were corpulent or had fine ivory tusks. Indigenous sociality was vastly transformed from the early nineteenth century[. . . .] But precolonial practices were probably most changed by the arrival from the 1840s of Christian missionaries – the London Missionary Society (LMS), Reformed Presbyterians, Melanesian Mission (Anglican), Marists, and later a congeries of more fundamentalist faiths – Church of Christ, Seventh Day Adventists, and Assemblies of God. The independent state proclaimed in 1980 avows both *kastom* and Christianity as indigenous values and at the local level, all except those traditionalists or *kastom* adherents [. . .] are effecting compromises and conjunctions between the two. But how does all this bear on domestic violence?

In some motivated caricatures of their relation, *kastom* is seen as the source of violence and Christianity as the source of peace. Indigenous narratives of conversion typically talk of the transformation from the time of darkness to the time of light. [. . .]

[. . .] The very tropes of darkness and light derive from missionary discourses, but are also appropriated and indigenized. Early European observers were inclined to see the ancestral cultures of Vanuatu as violent, not only because of the endemic practices of warfare but because of more intimate violent acts – infanticide, widow strangulation, and domestic brutality – which travelers, colonial officials, and particularly missionaries portrayed as pervasive and typical. In such accounts Europeans often emphasized the violence of ni-Vanuatu (and especially ni-Vanuatu men) for rhetorical reasons, as part of the projects of mission and state to pacify, convert, and reform. Simultaneously they deemphas-ized the violence inherent in their own countries of origin which were also arguably in a constant state of war and military preparedness and where domestic violence was hardly rare. [. . .]

The ancestral cultures of Vanuatu did manifest violence but was it any greater than the violence of the ancestral (or even the contemporary) cultures of Europe? Warfare and violence were endemic in the precolonial past but were always opposed by the countervailing values of peace and consensus (which no doubt appeared less salient to European witnesses). London Missionary Society, Cath-olic, and especially Presbyterian missionaries resident in the southern islands of Aneityum, Tanna, and Aniwa from the late 1840s represented domestic violence as rampant. But they merged infanticide, widow strangulation, and physical assault in contentious ways and probably amplified the occurrence of all three for rhetorical effect (see Jolly 1991b). Much of the conjugal violence which they reported ensued from struggles over conversion or "going to the mission." Moreover, the intimate link which they drew between warfare and domestic violence is hard to sustain (especially since warfare has ended but domestic violence has not).

Given such prior colonialist discourses I was surprised when I arrived in the *kastom* communities of South Pentecost in the early 1970s to discover that they were extremely pacific places. Domestic violence was very rare – only one case of "wife-beating" came to a village court in my two years there. Moreover there were strong contrary ideals of the inviolability of the person and the sanctity of the body. Assault on man, woman, or child, especially if it drew blood, necessitated compensation (to the maternal kin of that person). An alleged threat of sexual violence against an unmarried woman was adjudged culpable and occasioned a massive fine. In these villages in the late colonial period [. . .] there were strong pressures to keep the peace in public and domestic spaces. So, in some of Vanuatu's *kastom* villages, even where male domination is aggressively pronounced, domestic violence is not routinely condoned. [. . .]

The views of the family advanced by women at this conference as in many other Pacific contexts were derived from (but importantly not identical to) those promulgated by Christian missionaries from the nineteenth century. They deplored arranged marriages, the bride price, polygyny, and domestic violence in the name of those preeminently Christian values of freely chosen partners, the nuclear family, marital monogamy, and conjugal harmony. But as well as the blessings of Papa God and the wisdom of the *blak buk* (the Bible) women are also increasingly drawing on a new language of human rights. A brochure issued by the Vanuatu Women's Center at the conference proclaimed, "In the Name of Love Stop Violence Against Women." This summarized the local history of the Vanuatu Women's Center and the many cases it has dealt with since its inception in 1992. But it also quoted from Charlotte Bunch's speech at the Second World Conference on Human Rights held in Vienna in June 1993 and derived its title from Anita Roddick's Body Shop's book, *In the Name of Love*. It advocated educating and empowering women, concepts and strategies now shared by many United Nations Conventions and aid projects dedicated to women's equality in development. The VNKW had earlier strongly endorsed the United Nations Convention to Eliminate All Forms of Discrimination Against Women (CEDAW), in a publication written by Grace Mera Molisa called *Woman Ikat Raet Long Human Raet O No?* (1991). Successive governments stalled on that – suggesting that they had not received a copy of the CEDAW report, which in fact had been sent through several official channels and also disseminated in this book in English, French, and *bislama* with attached interpretative comments. As elsewhere in the Pacific the reservations which male politicians consistently expressed related to ancestral values or *kastom*. In the Pacific until the present, few countries have ratified the convention – the Cook Islands and Tuvalu, and most recently, after the conference, Vanuatu.[7]

But the debt to the UN and to aid agencies is in more than just the language of human rights. The Vanuatu Women's Center is an indigenous NGO[. . . .] The Center is locally supported by fundraising and donations, but also by overseas aid. [. . .] Such overseas funding sources and allies are crucial to the women involved, but also lay them open to the charges of undue foreign influence and, worse, a betrayal of *kastom*.

The dynamics of this process were graphically highlighted at the conference in the content of and responses to several speeches, delivered by the expatriate judiciary. They documented a litany of horrific crimes of violence against women.[8] In several such cases the recent behavior of male *kastom jifs* (customary chiefs) in adjudicating such crimes was severely criticized. Some *kastom jifs* on the outer islands are presently presuming to settle cases which should, by law, be referred to the courts. Thus we heard from the Chief Justice, Charles Vaudin d'Imecourt, the gruesome and complicated details of a case of rape on Ambae.[9] This is an island which is usually renowned for its powerful women. This was settled by a *kastom jif* through a series of compensations in the form of pigs and mats. In tracing the flow and value of these payments the Chief Justice revealed that those paying the heaviest fines were the man who had rescued her from her rapist and carried her back to her house after the rape, and the woman who was the victim of the rape. Another memorable case involved a woman from Tanna who was having matrimonial difficulties with her husband. He wanted to sort out their dispute in a *kastom* meeting; she refused to attend but was forced to do so. At this meeting a *kastom jif* declared that she must return to Tanna and she was kidnapped by eleven Tannese men and put on a boat for home.[10] The Chief Justice proclaimed: "*kastom* is failing ni-Vanuatu women."[11]

My discussions afterwards with a number of women revealed conflicting sentiments. They were outraged at the cavalier treatment of violent offenses against women but some also expressed disquiet about the white judges' lack of knowledge of or appreciation for *kastom*.[12] One woman thought the Chief Justice clearly had not understood the principles of compensation involved in the Ambae case, and indeed seemed to share the usual colonialist denigration of pigs. Other women were worried about their failure to influence male politicians and local men. [. . .]

Women's disquiet perhaps emanates from a political process whereby having powerful foreigners as allies risks alienating the very local men they are trying to influence and change. A spectacular instance of the charged political atmosphere around these issues of violence and the law occurred in the week prior to the conference. The President released twenty-six of Vanuatu's worst prisoners, amongst whom was the notorious Morris Ben, who was at that point due to serve forty-two years in prison for several crimes of burglary and rape against ni-Vanuatu and white women (the last of whom he bludgeoned till she was unconscious and near death). He had escaped from custody several times before but this time was released in honor of Vanuatu's celebration of fourteen years of independence on July 30, 1994. [. . .]

Now it may be that these releases were an act of political largesse. But I am inclined to interpret them in the same way as I interpret the actions of *kastom jifs* on outer islands in preempting the power of the police and the courts to arrest and try rape and other violent crimes against women. In acting against the power of Western-derived laws and the expatriate male judiciary, some men at both local and national levels are not so much reclaiming powers which they had in *kastom* as asserting new and more strenuous forms of male control over women, in contestation with outside powers and foreign values.[13] So it seems the universalizing discourse of "human rights" presents both attractions and risks for Pacific feminists.

The language of human rights exerts a powerful allure for educated elite women in Vanuatu. But is the modern female subject, the new kind of person being posited in some expressions of women's emancipation in the Pacific perforce an isolated individual apart from, even against, her collectivity? Must the modern woman set herself against the "other woman," the traditional woman as object or victim? Must she deny all the values of tradition in order to embrace the human? The answer from ni-Vanuatu women is no. This we can perceive in present debates about the relationship between domestic violence and the bride price. As Merilyn Tahi expressed it, "Women are paid for in the guise of bride price for their labor, both in bed and in the garden, they allow their bodies to be battered, to be abused and discarded and thrown away when their usefulness is deemed to be over by their men" (Vanuatu Women's Center 1994). Here Tahi condenses the two extreme negativities of women as victims and women as objects.[14] But rather than finding an individualist or a separatist solution to this problem Tahi insists rather that collective values must be changed, that social norms which legitimate violence must be transformed by women and by men acting in concert. For her, "the roots of violence are cultural" but so are the means of digging up those roots. "Attitudes to violence, like culture, [are] not static. They depend on our needs and our interpretations of what we want to be, how we want to be and how we get there. To be static is to be dead" (Vanuatu Women's Center 1994). Thus she envisages a newly created tradition and renewed collective values in accord with the values of non-violence and human rights.

Misogynist caricatures have often represented well-educated, professional, or elite Pacific women as unduly autonomous, mobile, and sexually free (see Hogan 1985). Most Pacific women by contrast stress that their form of feminism differs from that in countries such as Australia in its emphasis on the values of collectivity and on connecting women's movements to broader sociopolitical struggles for self-determination where the self is a collectivity rather than an individual (see Jolly 1991a). Ni-Vanuatu feminists have in the past successfully negotiated those invidious oppositions which equate tradition with women's oppression and modernity with women's liberation by simultaneously claiming greater powers in both. The particularly powerful sentiments generated by domestic violence threaten such past efforts insofar as they tend to situate men on the side of tradition and cultural relativism and women on the side of the human and universalism.

Such insidious dichotomies can only be challenged by women insisting that human rights are not necessarily inconsistent with *kastom*, by appropriating and indigenizing notions of the "human" to suit their local context and by insisting, as does Merilyn Tahi, that tradition is not a static burden of the past but something created for the present. There are again, one year or so after the conference, some hopeful signs that, by their stress on *kastom* as created and recreated by women and by men, ni-Vanuatu women are starting to make headway on the difficult issues of domestic violence and family law, and indeed a range of other women's rights envisioned in CEDAW.

Conclusion

In conclusion I want to situate this specific, Pacific example of claims about women's rights in the broader context of contention between universalism and relativism in contemporary human rights discourses. Universalism and relativism are not just moral or philosophical abstractions but epistemologies which are politically grounded in the global divisions which are typified as East and West, South and North – cardinal points which oddly naturalize and dehistoricize the dispositions of different nation-states in the world system.

Some perceive the language of human rights as the globalizing discourse appropriate to the latest epoch of an imperializing capitalism. They argue that the notions of the human are little more than pious projections of wealthy Western nations, stressing the values of the individual – civil and political rights and the right to own property. This is ranged against the rights allegedly preferred by the East or the South – economic and social rights, and the rights of self-determination and economic development by collectivities rather than individuals. Thus Messer (1993) has argued for Africa that it is groups and not individuals which are endowed with rights. Of course one of the problems of perceiving the debate in terms of these contending antitheses is that it is a play of reciprocal caricatures. Notions of "rights" in the West have in fact historically been claimed and fought for on behalf of collectivities, such as social classes, "women's," "minorities," as well as on behalf of "the individual." And although cultures and civilizations beyond the "West" may not value the *individuated* person, they might still sustain notions of humanity pertaining to individuals as well as collectivities. Moreover, the East and the South are not the same place. Within the richer, industrialized nations are now many countries of East and Southeast Asia, for example, which, though they are rampantly engaged in capitalist development, allegedly do not share the Western value of "freedom," and like many underdeveloped parts of Africa, Asia, and the Pacific rhetorically stress collective rather than individual rights. There have been some particularly powerful criticisms from Asian politicians and commentators of Western presumptions about the "human" (see Abdullah 1993) and the need to broaden the definition of the human to include core values from other philosophical traditions, such as those of Asia. The same might be argued for the Pacific.

Clearly this kind of relativism may be simply a justification of repression, although it is important not to summarily equate the two. And as Steiner (1994) has recently warned, it is important to discriminate between the political contexts in which the contest between universalism and relativism occurs and not to conflate the state with "culture" as some have done. He perceives a significant irony in that the very Asian states which are vaunting relativism in their foreign relations may be vaunting universalism within – trying to erase traditional cultures through modernization or to eclipse ethnic or regional differences through state rhetoric of "unity in diversity." [. . .]

How does all this bear on women's rights? In Vanuatu, [. . .] women's groups and NGOs are at the forefront of those employing the language of human rights. And the tensions between relativism and universalism, between the values of collectivity and person, are especially potently expressed in debates by and about women. But we can also witness, as in the conference at Port Vila, how the "new women" of the Pacific are skillfully negotiating the competing claims to their persons by the more parochial collectivities of villages, the languages of citizenship in new states, and the new discourses of human rights emergent within a globalizing world system.

Notes

1   See, for example, the debates about colonialism and feminism and the politics of ethnic and cultural difference in women's movements (Bulbeck 1988; Jolly 1991a; Mohanty et al. 1991).

2   It is no doubt true that female subjects have been marginalized in human rights debates, focusing as they have on male subjects suffering abuses as soldiers or prisoners. As Tomasevski (1993) notes, human rights activism emerged in response to blatant abuses of liberty and political repression – summary executions, arbitrary arrests, disappearances, and torture. But of course increasingly, women are also victims of political repression, rape, torture, and death.

3   This is a theater group attached to the Vanuatu Women's Center which performs as part of their public education programs. The Center holds workshops and meetings with young people in schools and with various groups and communities in the outer islands and Port Vila.

4   This is quoted from the brochure issued by the Vanuatu Women's Center at the conference entitled "In the Name of Love Stop Violence Against Women" (Vanuatu Women's Center 1994).

5   The conference was co-organized primarily by Merilyn Tahi, and Andonia Piau-Lynch, a Papua New Guinean woman now resident in Port Vila.

6   I was invited to attend this conference and present a paper. I do not see my particular conversations with Pacific feminists in Port Vila as representative. I am not saying that their views represent those of most ni-Vanuatu women in towns or in villages, nor those Pacific women who call themselves "feminists." I am also not suggesting that the particular predicaments which Pacific feminists face are generalizable to other parts of the so-called "Third World": this is a specific site of intersection of the local and the global.

7   By contrast, the Vanuatu government speedily ratified the UN Convention on the Child. This is curious since in many ways ancestral values are equally at odds with the terms of that convention. CEDAW was finally ratified by the Parliament of Vanuatu in March 1995.

8   The Public Prosecutor (Baxter-Wright 1994) was also keen to stress women's propensity for violence, and noted that of thirty-three intentional assault cases brought in Port Vila so far that year, 42 percent had been committed by women. This is higher than the percentage in 1993, when 36 percent of all defendants were female. Moreover in 1993 36 percent of unlawful assaults upon women were committed by other women.

9   It might be noted that the laws on rape significantly differ from those in Australia, stressing as they do violation by vaginal penetration rather than the full range of sexually violent acts as in the reformed law of Australia. This was stressed by Marin Mason in her interview with Patti Orifino on Radio Australia, Wednesday April 12, 1995, 3 a.m.

10 The men were subsequently charged but received a suspended sentence, fines, and costs of 60,000 *vatu*.
11 To be fair he said that the law was failing women too.
12 Marin Mason also noted, especially from her tours through the outer islands, that women often supported the rights of *kastom jifs* to hear such violent disputes and that many were also unaware that they had a right to press charges through the courts.
13 I am not suggesting that all men do this, and indeed some *kastom jifs* are sympathetic to women's interests. But, as Marin Mason noted, only men are chiefs.
14 Elsewhere, ni-Vanuatu and Solomon Islands women have in published poetry been more satiric and playful about the comparisons which might be made between women and other valuables – from shells to speedboats (Billy et al. 1983: 103; Mera Molisa 1992).

References

Abdullah, F. et al. 1993: *Perceiving "Human Rights."* Australian-Asian Perceptions Project, Working Paper No. 2. Sydney: University of New South Wales.

Baxter-Wright, J. 1994: "Crimes of Violence against Women in the Past Two Years." Paper presented at the Conference on Violence and the Family in Vanuatu, Port Vila, August 2–5.

Billy, A., Lulei, H., and Sipolo, J. (eds.) 1983: *Mi Mere: Poetry and Prose by Solomon Islands Women Writers*. Honiara: University of the South Pacific, Solomon Islands Centre.

Bulbeck, C. 1988: *One World Women's Movement*. London: Verso.

Hogan, E. 1985: "Controlling the Bodies of Women: Reading Gender Ideologies in Papua New Guinea." In O'Collins (ed.), *Women and Politics in Papua New Guinea*. Department of Political and Social Change, Working Paper No. 6. Canberra: Research School of Pacific Studies, Australian National University.

Jolly, M. 1991a: "The Politics of Difference: Feminism, Colonialism and Decolonialisation." In G. Bottomley, M. de Lepervanche, and J. Martin (eds.), *Intersexions: Gender, Class, Culture, Ethnicity*. North Sydney: Allen and Unwin.

Jolly, M. 1991b: "'To Save the Girls for Brighter and Better Lives': Presbyterian Missions and Women in Southern Vanuatu, 1848–1870." *Journal of Pacific History* 26 (1), 27–48.

Jolly, M. 1992: "Custom and the Way of the Land: Past and Present in Vanuatu and Fiji." In M. Jolly and N. Thomas (eds.). (Abbreviated version to be republished in R. Barowsky and D. Hanlon (eds.), *Pacific Histories*. Hawaii: University of Hawaii Press, 1996.)

Mera Molisa, G. 1992: *Woman Ikat Raet Long Human Raet O No? Konvensen Blong Stopem Evri Kaen Diskrimineisen Agensem Ol Woman*. Port Vila: Blackstone Publications/Sun Productions.

Messer, E. 1993: "Anthropology and Human Rights." *Annual Review of Anthropology* 22, 221–49.

Mohanty, C. T., Russo, A., and Torres, L. (eds.) 1991: *Third World Women and the Politics of Feminism*. Bloomington: Indiana University Press.

Steiner, H. J. 1994: "Cultural Relativism and the Attitude of Certain Asian Countries towards the Universality of Human Rights." Canberra: Senate Occasional Lecture Series, August 26.

Tomasevski, K. 1993: *Women and Human Rights*. UN-NGO Group on Women and World Development Series. London and New Jersey: Zed Press.

Part V

Global/Local

Introduction

There is an extensive literature on globalization and culture. We have chosen extracts from Arjun Appadurai and Allan Pred because they offer interesting ways to conceptualize the relationships between the global and the local. Appadurai's piece sets up the cultural dimensions of globalization. The extract outlines his influential formulation of "scapes" that are constructed out of the global flows of people, finance, ideas, technologies, and images, to form the building blocks of imagined worlds. Appadurai's model, while undoubtedly useful, has been criticized for paying insufficient attention to the ways in which capitalism structures these scapes. Pred looks at how the impact of global capitalism generates symbolic contestations with already existing local patterns of everyday life. In the excerpt, he describes how the symbolic contestations involved in the articulation of local and global occur, and how local agency reconfigures place, space, and identity. Pred's text is unusual in its visual construction. He asks, "If the worlds of symbolic discontent are polyphonous, must we restrict ourselves to univocal modes of expression?" To convey the multiplicity of contemporary capitalisms and modernities, he experiments with a non-linear sentence format that aims to disrupt the readers' taken-for-granted frameworks through which they make sense of the text.

The extracts from Jane Margold and Richard Wilk present case studies of particular locales in which the relationship between global and local is being played out. Both readings engage with the debate over the extent to which the global determines the local. In Wilk's discussion of beauty contests in Belize, he identifies the way in which hegemonic global cultural formations, such as the beauty contest, both allow and constrain the productivity of local and national agencies. However, this relationship is not deterministic; instead, the global provides the outer framework within which local agencies operate to map and remap national and local identities.

Margold's study of Filipino migrant workers in Saudi Arabia shows how globalization at times disrupts the dichotomy of the West/Rest. A combination of exploitative capitalist labor relations and Saudi racism undermines Ilokano men's masculinity, which underpins their sense of self and social identity. Upon returning to their villages, many of these men find it difficult to reintegrate into the local community and reinstate their self-esteem as men.

15 Disjuncture and Difference in the Global Cultural Economy

Arjun Appadurai

[. . .] The central problem of today's global interactions is the tension between cultural homogenization and cultural heterogenization. A vast array of empirical facts could be brought to bear on the side of the homogenization argument, and much of it has come from the left end of the spectrum of media studies (Hamelink 1983; Mattelart 1983; Schiller 1976), and some from other perspectives (Iyer 1988). Most often, the homogenization argument subspeciates into either an argument about Americanization or an argument about commoditization, and very often the two arguments are closely linked. What these arguments fail to consider is that at least as rapidly as forces from various metropolises are brought into new societies they tend to become indigenized in one or another way: this is true of music and housing styles as much as it is true of science and terrorism, spectacles and constitutions. The dynamics of such indigenization have just begun to be explored systemically (Barber 1987; Feld 1988; Hannerz 1987, 1989; Ivy 1988; Nicoll 1989; Yoshimoto 1989), and much more needs to be done. But it is worth noticing that for the people of Irian Jaya, Indonesianization may be more worrisome than Americanization, as Japanization may be for Koreans, Indianization for Sri Lankans, Vietnamization for the Cambodians, and Russianization for the people of Soviet Armenia and the Baltic republics. Such a list of alternative fears to Americanization could be greatly expanded, but it is not a shapeless inventory: for polities of smaller scale, there is always a fear of cultural absorption by polities of larger scale, especially those that are nearby. One man's imagined community is another man's political prison.

This scalar dynamic, which has widespread global manifestations, is also tied to the relationship between nations and states, to which I shall return later. For

Excerpted from Arjun Appadurai, "Disjuncture and Difference in the Global Cultural Economy." In *Modernity at Large: Cultural Dimensions of Globalization* (Minneapolis: University of Minnesota Press, 1996), 32–43.

the moment let us note that the simplification of these many forces (and fears) of homogenization can also be exploited by nation-states in relation to their own minorities, by posing global commoditization (or capitalism, or some other such external enemy) as more real than the threat of its own hegemonic strategies.

The new global cultural economy has to be seen as a complex, overlapping, disjunctive order that cannot any longer be understood in terms of existing center–periphery models (even those that might account for multiple centers and peripheries). Nor is it susceptible to simple models of push and pull (in terms of migration theory), or of surpluses and deficits (as in traditional models of balance of trade), or of consumers and producers (as in most neo-Marxist theories of development). Even the most complex Marxist tradition (Amin 1980; Mandel 1978; Wallerstein 1974; Wolf 1982) are inadequately quirky and have failed to come to terms with what Scott Lash and John Urry have called disorganized capitalism (1987). The complexity of the current global economy has to do with certain fundamental disjunctures between economy, culture, and politics that we have only begun to theorize.[1]

I propose that an elementary framework for exploring such disjunctures is to look at the relationship among five dimensions of global cultural flows that can be termed (a) *ethnoscapes*, (b) *mediascapes*, (c) *technoscapes*, (d) *financescapes*, and (e) *ideoscapes*.[2] The suffix *-scape* allows us to point to the fluid, irregular shapes of these landscapes, shapes that characterize international capital as deeply as they do international clothing styles. These terms with the common suffix *-scape* also indicate that these are not objectively given relations that look the same from every angle of vision but, rather, that they are deeply perspectival constructs, inflected by the historical, linguistic, and political situatedness of different sorts of actors: nation-states, multinationals, diasporic communities, as well as subnational groupings and movements (whether religious, political, or economic), and even intimate face-to-face groups, such as villages, neighborhoods, and families. Indeed, the individual actor is the last locus of this perspectival set of landscapes, for these landscapes are eventually navigated by agents who both experience and constitute larger formations, in part from their own sense of what these landscapes offer.

These landscapes thus are the building blocks of what (extending Benedict Anderson) I would like to call *imagined worlds*, that is, the multiple worlds that are constituted by the historically situated imaginations of persons and groups spread around the globe[. . . .] An important fact of the world we live in today is that many persons on the globe live in such imagined worlds (and not just in imagined communities) and thus are able to contest and sometimes even subvert the imagined worlds of the official mind and of the entrepreneurial mentality that surround them.

By *ethnoscape*, I mean the landscape of persons who constitute the shifting world in which we live: tourists, immigrants, refugees, exiles, guest workers, and other moving groups and individuals constitute an essential feature of the world and appear to affect the politics of (and between) nations to a hitherto unprecedented degree. This is not to say that there are no relatively stable communities and networks of kinship, friendship, work, and leisure, as well as of birth, residence, and other filial forms. But it is to say that the warp of these stabilities is everywhere shot through with the woof of human motion, as more persons and groups deal with the realities of having to move or the fantasies of wanting to move. What is more, both these realities and fantasies now function on larger scales, as men and women from villages in India think not just of moving to Poona or Madras but of moving to Dubai and Houston, and refugees from Sri Lanka find themselves in South India as well as in Switzerland, just as the Hmong are driven to London as well as to Philadelphia. And as international capital shifts its needs, as production and technology generate different needs, as nation-states shift their policies on refugee populations, these moving groups can never afford to let their imaginations rest too long, even if they wish to.

By *technoscape*, I mean the global configuration, also ever fluid, of technology and the fact that technology, both high and low, both mechanical and informational, now moves at high speeds across various kinds of previously impervious boundaries. Many countries now are the roots of multinational enterprise: a huge steel complex in Libya may involve interests from India, China, Russia, and Japan, providing different components of new technological configurations. The odd distribution of technologies, and thus the peculiarities of these technoscapes, are increasingly driven not by any obvious economies of scale, of political control, or of market rationality but by increasingly complex relationships among money flows, political possibilities, and the availability of both un- and highly skilled labor. So, while India exports waiters and chauffeurs to Dubai and Sharjah, it also exports software engineers to the United States – indentured briefly to Tata-Burroughs or the World Bank, then laundered through the State Department to become wealthy resident aliens, who are in turn objects of seductive messages to invest their money and know-how in federal and state projects in India.

The global economy can still be described in terms of traditional indicators (as the World Bank continues to do) and studied in terms of traditional comparisons (as in Project Link at the University of Pennsylvania), but the complicated technoscapes (and the shifting ethnoscapes) that underlie these indicators and comparisons are further out of the reach of the queen of social sciences than ever before. How is one to make a meaningful comparison of wages in Japan and the United States or of real-estate costs in New York and Tokyo, without taking sophisticated account of the very complex fiscal and investment flows that link the two economies through a global grid of currency speculation and capital transfer?

Thus it is useful to speak as well of *financescapes*, as the disposition of global capital is now a more mysterious, rapid, and difficult landscape to follow than ever before, as currency markets, national stock exchanges, and commodity speculations move megamonies through national turnstiles at blinding speed, with vast, absolute implications for small differences in percentage points and time units. But the critical point is that the global relationship among ethnoscapes, technoscapes, and financescapes is deeply disjunctive and profoundly unpredictable because each of these landscapes is subject to its own constraints and incentives (some political, some informational, and some techno-environmental), at the same time as each acts as a constraint and a parameter for movements in the others. Thus, even an elementary model of global political economy must take into account the deeply disjunctive relationships among human movement, technological flow, and financial transfers.

Further refracting these disjunctures (which hardly form a simple, mechanical global infrastructure in any case) are what I call *mediascapes* and *ideoscapes*, which are closely related landscapes of images. *Mediascapes* refer both to the distribution of the electronic capabilities to produce and disseminate information (newspapers, magazines, television stations, and film-production studios), which are now available to a growing number of private and public interests throughout the world, and to the images of the world created by these media. These images involve many complicated inflections, depending on their mode (documentary or entertainment), their hardware (electronic or preelectronic), their audiences (local, national, or transnational), and the interests of those who own and control them. What is most important about these mediascapes is that they provide (especially in their television, film, and cassette forms) large and complex repertoires of images, narratives, and ethnoscapes to viewers throughout the world, in which the world of commodities and the world of news and politics are profoundly mixed. What this means is that many audiences around the world experience the media themselves as a complicated and interconnected repertoire of print, celluloid, electronic screens, and billboards. The lines between the realistic and the fictional landscapes they see are blurred, so that the farther away these audiences are from the direct experiences of metropolitan life, the more likely they are to construct imagined worlds that are chimerical, aesthetic, even fantastic objects, particularly if assessed by the criteria of some other perspective, some other imagined world.

Mediascapes, whether produced by private or state interests, tend to be image-centered, narrative-based accounts of strips of reality, and what they offer to those who experience and transform them is a series of elements (such as characters, plots, and textual forms) out of which scripts can be formed of imagined lives, their own as well as those of others living in other places. These scripts can and do get disaggregated into complex sets of metaphors by which people live (Lakoff and Johnson 1980) as they help to constitute narratives of the Other and protonarratives of possible lives, fantasies that could become prolegomena to the desire for acquisition and movement.

Ideoscapes are also concatenations of images, but they are often directly political and frequently have to do with the ideologies of states and the counterideologies of movements explicitly oriented to capturing state power or a piece of it. These ideoscapes are composed of elements of the Enlightenment worldview, which consists of a chain of ideas, terms, and images, including *freedom, welfare, rights, sovereignty, representation,* and the master term *democracy.* The master narrative of the Enlightenment (and its many variants in Britain, France, and the United States) was constructed with a certain internal logic and presupposed a certain relationship between reading, representation, and the public sphere. (For the dynamics of this process in the early history of the United States, see Warner 1990.) But the diaspora of these terms and images across the world, especially since the nineteenth century, has loosened the internal coherence that held them together in a Euro-American master narrative and provided instead a loosely structured synopticon of politics, in which different nation-states, as part of their evolution, have organized their political cultures around different keywords (e.g., Williams 1976).

As a result of the differential diaspora of these keywords, the political narratives that govern communication between elites and followers in different parts of the world involve problems of both a semantic and pragmatic nature: semantic to the extent that words (and their lexical equivalents) require careful translation from context to context in their global movements, and pragmatic to the extent that the use of these words by political actors and their audiences may be subject to very different sets of contextual conventions that mediate their translation into public politics. Such conventions are not only matters of the nature of political rhetoric: for example, what does the aging Chinese leadership mean when it refers to the dangers of hooliganism? What does the South Korean leadership mean when it speaks of discipline as the key to democratic industrial growth?

These conventions also involve the far more subtle question of what sets of communicative genres are valued in what way (newspapers versus cinema, for example) and what sorts of pragmatic genre conventions govern the collective readings of different kinds of text. So, while an Indian audience may be attentive to the resonances of a political speech in terms of some keywords and phrases reminiscent of Hindi cinema, a Korean audience may respond to the subtle codings of Buddhist or neo-Confucian rhetoric encoded in a political document. The very relationship of reading to hearing and seeing may vary in important ways that determine the morphology of these different ideoscapes as they shape themselves in different national and transnational contexts. This globally variable synaesthesia has hardly even been noted, but it demands urgent analysis. Thus *democracy* has clearly become a master term, with powerful echoes from Haiti and Poland to the former Soviet Union and China, but it sits at the center of a variety of ideoscapes, composed of distinctive pragmatic configurations of rough translations of other central terms from the vocabulary of the Enlightenment. This creates ever new terminological kaleidoscopes, as states (and the groups that seek to capture them) seek to pacify populations whose own ethnoscapes are in motion and whose mediascapes may create severe problems for the ideoscapes with which they are presented. The fluidity of ideoscapes is complicated in particular by the growing diasporas (both voluntary and involuntary) of intellectuals who continuously inject new meaning-streams into the discourse of democracy in different parts of the world.

This extended terminological discussion of the five terms I have coined sets the basis for a tentative formulation about the conditions under which current global flows occur: they occur in and through the growing disjunctures among ethnoscapes, technoscapes, financescapes, mediascapes, and ideoscapes. This formulation, the core of my model of global cultural flow, needs some explanation. First, people, machinery, money, images, and ideas now follow increasingly nonisomorphic paths; of course, at all periods in human history, there have been some disjunctures in the flows of these things, but the sheer speed, scale, and volume of each of these flows are now so great that the disjunctures have become central to the politics of global culture. The Japanese are notoriously hospitable to ideas and are stereotyped as inclined to export (all) and import (some) goods, but they are also notoriously closed to immigration, like the Swiss, the Swedes, and the Saudis. Yet the Swiss and the Saudis accept populations of guest workers, thus creating labor diasporas of Turks, Italians, and other circum-Mediterranean groups. Some such guest-worker groups maintain continuous contact with their home nations, like the Turks, but others, like high-level South Asian migrants, tend to desire lives in their new homes, raising anew the problem of reproduction in a deterritorialized context.

Deterritorialization, in general, is one of the central forces of the modern world because it brings laboring populations into the lower-class sectors and spaces of relatively wealthy societies, while sometimes creating exaggerated and intensified senses of criticism or attachment to politics in the home state. Deterritorialization, whether of Hindus, Sikhs, Palestinians, or Ukrainians, is now at the core of a variety of global fundamentalisms, including Islamic and Hindu fundamentalism. In the Hindu case, for example, it is clear that the overseas movement of Indians has been exploited by a variety of interests both within and outside India to create a complicated network of finances and religious identifications, by which the problem of cultural reproduction for Hindus abroad has become tied to the politics of Hindu fundamentalism at home.

At the same time, deterritorialization creates new markets for film companies, art impresarios, and travel agencies, which thrive on the need of the deterritorialized population for contact with its homeland. Naturally, these invented homelands, which constitute the mediascapes of deterritorialized groups, can often become sufficiently fantastic and one-sided that they provide the material for new ideoscapes in which ethnic conflicts can begin to erupt. The creation of Khalistan, an invented homeland of the deterritorialized Sikh population of England, Canada, and the United States, is one example of the bloody potential in such mediascapes as they interact with the internal colonialisms of the nation-state (e.g., Hechter 1975). The West Bank, Namibia, and Eritrea are other theaters for the enactment of the bloody negotiation between existing nation-states and various deterritorialized groupings.

It is in the fertile ground of deterritorialization, in which money, commodities, and persons are involved in ceaselessly chasing each other around the world, that the mediascapes and ideoscapes of the modern world find their fractured and fragmented counterpart. For the ideas and images produced by mass media often are only partial guides to the goods and experiences that deterritorialized populations transfer to one another. In Mira Nair's brilliant film *India Cabaret*, we see the multiple loops of this fractured deterritorialization as young women, barely competent in Bombay's metropolitan glitz, come to seek their fortunes as cabaret dancers and prostitutes in Bombay, entertaining men in clubs with dance formats derived wholly from the prurient dance sequences of Hindi films. These scenes in turn cater to ideas about Western and foreign women and their looseness, while they provide tawdry career alibis for these women. Some of these women come from Kerala, where cabaret clubs and the pornographic film industry have blossomed, partly in response to the purses and tastes of Keralites returned from the Middle East, where their diasporic lives away from women distort their very sense of what the relations between men and women might be.

These tragedies of displacement could certainly be replayed in a more detailed analysis of the relations between the Japanese and German sex tours to Thailand and the tragedies of the sex trade in Bangkok, and in other similar loops that tie together fantasies about the Other, the conveniences and seductions of travel, the economics of global trade, and the brutal mobility fantasies that dominate gender politics in many parts of Asia and the world at large.

While far more could be said about the cultural politics of deterritorialization and the larger sociology of displacement that it expresses, it is appropriate at this juncture to bring in the role of the nation-state in the disjunctive global economy of culture today. The relationship between states and nations is everywhere an embattled one. It is possible to say that in many societies the nation and the state have become one another's projects. That is, while nations (or more properly groups with ideas about nationhood) seek to capture or co-opt states and state power, states simultaneously seek to capture and monopolize ideas about nationhood (Baruah 1986; Chatterjee 1986; Nandy 1989). In general, separatist transnational movements, including those that have included terror in their methods, exemplify nations in search of states. Sikhs, Tamil Sri Lankans, Basques, Moros, Quebecois – each of these represents imagined communities that seek to create states of their own or carve pieces out of existing states. States, on the other hand, are everywhere seeking to monopolize the moral resources of community, either by flatly claiming perfect coevality between nation and state, or by systematically museumizing and representing all the groups within them in a variety of heritage politics that seems remarkably uniform throughout the world (Handler 1988; Herzfeld 1982; McQueen 1988).

Here, national and international mediascapes are exploited by nation-states to pacify separatists or even the potential fissiparousness of all ideas of difference. Typically, contemporary nation-states do this by exercising taxonomic control over difference, by creating various kinds of international spectacle to domesti-cate difference, and by seducing small groups with the fantasy of self-display on some sort of global or cosmopolitan stage. One important new feature of global cultural politics, tied to the disjunctive relationships among the various land-scapes discussed earlier, is that state and nation are at each other's throats, and the hyphen that links them is now less an icon of conjuncture than an index of disjuncture. This disjunctive relationship between nation and state has two levels: at the level of any given nation-state, it means that there is a battle of the imagination, with state and nation seeking to cannibalize one another. Here is the seedbed of brutal separatisms – majoritarianisms that seem to have appeared from nowhere and microidentities that have become political projects within the nation-state. At another level, this disjunctive relationship is deeply entangled with the global disjunctures discussed throughout this chapter: ideas of nation-hood appear to be steadily increasing in scale and regularly crossing existing state boundaries, sometimes, as with the Kurds, because previous identities stretched across vast national spaces or, as with the Tamils in Sri Lanka, the dormant threads of a transnational diaspora have been activated to ignite the micropolitics of a nation-state.

In discussing the cultural politics that have subverted the hyphen that links the nation to the state, it is especially important not to forget the mooring of such politics in the irregularities that now characterize disorganized capital (Kothari 1989; Lash and Urry 1987). Because labor, finance, and technology are now so widely separated, the volatilities that underlie movements for nationhood (as large as transnational Islam on the one hand, or as small as the movement of the Gurkhas for a separate state in Northeast India) grind against the vulnerabilities that characterize the relationships between states. States find themselves pressed to stay open by the forces of media, technology, and travel that have fueled consumerism throughout the world and have increased the craving, even in the non-Western world, for new commodities and spectacles. On the other hand, these very cravings can become caught up in new ethnoscapes, mediascapes, and, eventually, ideoscapes, such as democracy in China, that the state cannot tolerate as threats to its own control over ideas of nationhood and peoplehood. States throughout the world are under siege, especially where contests over the ideoscapes of democracy are fierce and fundamental, and where there are radical disjunctures between ideoscapes and technoscapes (as in the case of very small countries that lack contemporary technologies of production and information); or between ideoscapes and financescapes (as in countries such as Mexico or Brazil, where international lending influences national politics to a very large degree); or between ideoscapes and ethnoscapes (as in Beirut, where diasporic, local, and translocal filiations are suicidally at battle); or between ideoscapes and mediascapes (as in many countries in the Middle East and Asia) where the lifestyles represented on both national and international TV and cinema completely overwhelm and undermine the rhetoric of national politics. In the Indian case, the myth of the law-breaking hero has emerged to mediate this naked struggle between the pieties and realities of Indian politics, which has grown increasingly brutalized and corrupt (Vachani 1989).

The transnational movement of the martial arts, particularly through Asia, as mediated by the Hollywood and Hong Kong film industries (Zarilli 1995) is a rich illustration of the ways in which long-standing martial arts traditions, reformulated to meet the fantasies of contemporary (sometimes lumpen) youth populations, create new cultures of masculinity and violence, which are in turn the fuel for increased violence in national and international politics. Such violence is in turn the spur to an increasingly rapid and amoral arms trade that penetrates the entire world. The worldwide spread of the AK-47 and the Uzi, in films, in corporate and state security, in terror, and in police and military activity, is a reminder that apparently simple technical uniformities often conceal an increasingly complex set of loops, linking images of violence to aspirations for community in some imagined world.

Returning then to the ethnoscapes with which I began, the central paradox of ethnic politics in today's world is that primordia (whether of language or skin color or neighborhood or kinship) have become globalized. That is, sentiments, whose greatest force is in their ability to ignite intimacy into a political state and turn locality into a staging ground for identity, have become spread over vast and irregular spaces as groups move yet stay linked to one another through sophisticated media capabilities. This is not to deny that such primordia are often the product of invented traditions (Hobsbawm and Ranger 1983) or retrospective affiliations, but to emphasize that because of the disjunctive and

unstable interplay of commerce, media, national policies, and consumer fantasies,
ethnicity, once a genie contained in the bottle of some sort of locality (however
large), has now become a global force, forever slipping in and through the cracks
between states and borders.

But the relationship between the cultural and economic levels of this new set
of global disjunctures is not a simple one-way street in which the terms of global
cultural politics are set wholly by, or confined wholly within, the vicissitudes of
international flows of technology, labor, and finance, demanding only a modest
modification of existing neo-Marxist models of uneven development and state
formation. There is a deeper change, itself driven by the disjunctures among all
the landscapes I have discussed and constituted by their continuously fluid and
uncertain interplay, that concerns the relationship between production and
consumption in today's global economy. Here, I begin with Marx's famous (and
often mined) view of the fetishism of the commodity and suggest that this
fetishism has been replaced in the world at large (now seeing the world as one
large, interactive system, composed of many complex subsystems) by two
mutually supportive descendants, the first of which I call production fetishism
and the second, the fetishism of the consumer.

By *production fetishism* I mean an illusion created by contemporary transnational production loci that masks translocal capital, transnational earning flows,
global management, and often faraway workers (engaged in various kinds of
high-tech putting-out operations) in the idiom and spectacle of local (sometimes
even worker) control, national productivity, and territorial sovereignty. To the
extent that various kinds of free-trade zones have become the models for
production at large, especially of high-tech commodities, production has itself
become a fetish, obscuring not social relations as such but the relations of
production, which are increasingly transnational. The locality (both in the sense
of the local factory or site of production and in the extended sense of the nation-
state) becomes a fetish that disguises the globally dispersed forces that actually
drive the production process. This generates alienation (in Marx's sense) twice
intensified, for its social sense is now compounded by a complicated spatial
dynamic that is increasingly global.

As for the *fetishism of the consumer*, I mean to indicate here that the consumer
has been transformed through commodity flows (and the mediascapes, especially
of advertising, that accompany them) into a sign, both in Baudrillard's sense of
a simulacrum that only asymptotically approaches the form of a real social agent,
and in the sense of a mask for the real seat of agency, which is not the consumer
but the producer and the many forces that constitute production. Global advertising is the key technology for the worldwide dissemination of a plethora of
creative and culturally well-chosen ideas of consumer agency. These images of
agency are increasingly distortions of a world of merchandising so subtle that
the consumer is consistently helped to believe that he or she is an actor, where
in fact he or she is at best a chooser.

The globalization of culture is not the same as its homogenization, but globalization involves the use of a variety of instruments of homogenization (arma-
ments, advertising techniques, language hegemonies, and clothing styles) that are
absorbed into local political and cultural economies, only to be repatriated as

heterogeneous dialogues of national sovereignty, free enterprise, and fundamentalism in which the state plays an increasingly delicate role: too much openness to global flows, and the nation-state is threatened by revolt, as in the China syndrome; too little, and the state exits the international stage, as Burma, Albania, and North Korea in various ways have done. In general, the state has become the arbitrageur of this *repatriation of difference* (in the form of goods, signs, slogans, and styles). But this repatriation or export of the designs and commodities of difference continuously exacerbates the internal politics of majoritarianism and homogenization, which is most frequently played out in debates over heritage.

Thus the central feature of global culture today is the politics of the mutual effort of sameness and difference to cannibalize one another and thereby proclaim their successful hijacking of the twin Enlightenment ideas of the triumphantly universal and the resiliently particular. This mutual cannibalization shows its ugly face in riots, refugee flows, state-sponsored torture, and ethnocide (with or without state support). Its brighter side is in the expansion of many individual horizons of hope and fantasy, in the global spread of oral rehydration therapy and other low-tech instruments of wellbeing, in the susceptibility even of South Africa to the force of global opinion, in the inability of the Polish state to repress its own working classes, and in the growth of a wide range of progressive, transnational alliances. Examples of both sorts could be multiplied. The critical point is that both sides of the coin of global cultural process today are products of the infinitely varied mutual contest of sameness and difference on a stage characterized by radical disjunctures between different sorts of global flows and the uncertain landscapes created in and through these disjunctures.

Notes

1 One major exception is Fredric Jameson, whose work on the relationship between postmodernism and late capitalism has in many ways inspired this essay. The debate between Jameson and Aijaz Ahmad in *Social Text*, however, shows that the creation of a globalizing Marxist narrative in cultural matters is difficult territory indeed (Jameson 1986; Ahmad 1987). My own effort in this context is to begin a restructuring of the Marxist narrative (by stressing lags and disjunctures) that many Marxists might find abhorrent. Such a restructuring has to avoid the dangers of obliterating difference within the Third World, eliding the social referent (as some French postmodernists seem inclined to do), and retaining the narrative authority of the Marxist tradition, in favor of greater attention to global fragmentation, uncertainty, and difference.
2 The idea of *ethnoscape* is more fully engaged in Arjun Appadurai, *Modernity at Large: Cultural Dimensions of Globalization* (Minneapolis, 1996), ch. 3.

References

Ahmad, A. 1987: "Jameson's Rhetoric of Otherness and the 'National Allegory.'" *Social Text* 17, 3–25.
Amin, S. 1980: *Class and Nation: Historically and in the Current Crisis*. New York and London: Monthly Review Press.
Barber, K. 1987: "Popular Arts in Africa." *African Studies Review* 30 (3), 1–78.

Baruah, S. 1986: "Immigration, Ethnic Conflict and Political Turmoil, Assam 1979–1985."*Asian Survey* 26 (11), 1184–1206.

Chatterjee, P. 1986: *Nationalist Thought and the Colonial World: A Derivative Discourse?* London: Zed Books.

Feld, S. 1988: "Notes on World Beat." *Public Culture* 1 (1), 31–7.

Hamelink, C. 1983: *Cultural Autonomy in Global Communications.* New York: Longman.

Handler, R. 1988: *Nationalism and the Politics of Culture in Quebec.* Madison: University of Wisconsin Press.

Hannerz, U. 1987: "The World in Creolization." *Africa* 57 (4), 546–59.

Hannerz, U. 1989: "Notes on the Global Ecumene." *Public Culture* 1 (2), 66–75.

Hechter, M. 1975: *Internal Colonialism: The Celtic Fringe in British National Development, 1536–1966.* Berkeley: University of California Press.

Herzfeld, M. 1982: *Ours Once More: Folklore, Ideology and the Making of Modern Greece.* Austin: University of Texas Press.

Hobsbawm, E. and Ranger, T. (eds.) 1983: *The Invention of Tradition.* New York: Columbia University Press.

Ivy, M. 1988: "Tradition and Difference in the Japanese Mass Media." *Public Culture* 1 (1), 21–9.

Iyer, P. 1988: *Video Night in Kathmandu.* New York: Knopf.

Jameson, F. 1986: "Third World Literature in the Era of Multi-National Capitalism." *Social Text* 15 (Fall), 65–88.

Kothari, R. 1989: *State against Democracy: In Search of Humane Governance.* New York: New Horizons.

Lakoff, G. and Johnson, M. 1980: *Metaphors We Live By.* Chicago and London: University of Chicago Press.

Lash, S. and Urry, J. 1987: *The End of Organized Capitalism.* Madison: University of Wisconsin Press.

McQueen, H. 1988: "The Australian Stamp: Image, Design and Ideology." *Arena* 84 (Spring), 78–96.

Mandel, E. 1978: *Late Capitalism.* London: Verso.

Mattelart, A. 1983: *Transnationals and the Third World: The Struggle for Culture.* South Hadley, MA: Bergin and Garvey.

Nandy, A. 1989: "The Political Culture of the Indian State." *Daedalus* 118 (4), 1–26.

Nicoll, F. 1989: "My Trip to Alice." *Criticism, Heresy and Interpretation* 3, 21–32.

Schiller, H. 1976: *Communication and Cultural Domination.* White Plains, NY: International Arts and Sciences.

Vachani, L. 1989: "Narrative, Pleasure and Ideology in the Hindi Film: An Analysis of the Outsider Formula." M.A. thesis, Annenberg School of Communication, University of Pennsylvania.

Wallerstein, I. 1974: *The Modern World System.* 2 vols. New York and London: Academic Press.

Warner, M. 1990: *The Letters of the Republic: Publication and the Public Sphere in Eighteenth Century America.* Cambridge, MA: Harvard University Press.

Williams, R. 1976: *Keywords.* New York: Oxford University Press.

Wolf, E. 1982: *Europe and the People without History.* Berkeley: University of California Press.

Yoshimoto, M. 1989: "The Postmodern and Mass Images in Japan." *Public Culture* 1 (2), 8–25.

Zarilli, P. 1995: "Repositioning the Body: An Indian Martial Art and its Pan-Asian Publics." In C. A. Breckenridge (ed.), *Consuming Modernity: Public Culture in a South Asian World.* Minneapolis: University of Minnesota Press.

16 Capitalisms, Crises, and Cultures II: Notes on Local Transformation and Everyday Cultural Struggles

Allan Pred

Society is a battlefield of representations, on which the limits and coherence of any given set are constantly fought for and regularly spoilt.
T. J. Clark, *The Painting of Modern Life*

For the victims as well as the beneficiaries of the large abstraction we choose to call capitalism ... the *experience* itself arrives in quite personal, concrete, localized, mediated forms.   James C. Scott, *Weapons of the Weak* (emphasis added)

[Raymond Williams gave Gramsci's notion of hegemony] a characteristic twist by emphasizing the continual processes of adjustment needed to secure any political or cultural hegemony above, and *its perpetual failure* – as an inherently selective definition of reality – *to exhaust the meanings of popular experience below*.
Perry Anderson, "A Culture in Contraflow" (emphasis added)

Not only is the cultural construction of meaning and symbols inherently a matter of political and economic interests, but the reverse also holds – the concerns of political economy are inherently about conflicts over meanings and symbols.
George E. Marcus and Michael J. Fischer, *Anthropology as Cultural Critique*

Prelude

Once again the question: From what vantage points are we to understand the various guises, metamorphoses, and reconfigurations of historical and contemporary capitalisms? The partial answers to be offered here build upon a recognition that the reconfiguration of historical or contemporary capitalisms always

Excerpted from Allan Pred, "Capitalisms, Crises, and Cultures II: Notes on Local Transformation and Everyday Cultural Struggles." In A. Pred and M. J. Watts, *Reworking Modernity: Capitalisms and Symbolic Discontent* (New Brunswick, NJ: Rutgers University Press, 1992), 107–17.

encompasses processes of local transformation, processes that cannot be divorced from the concrete experiences of act-ual women and men, processes that involve a "trialectical" tension between meanings, situated practices, and power relations.

As the agents of different forms of early and modern industrial capitalism
have constantly attempted to reach into new markets,
to develop new products,
to restructure existing economic activities,
to move their resources from activities with falling rates of return,
    to activities which promise higher rates of return,
as the agents of capitalism have exercised their creative energies,
    while restlessly divesting and investing,
while repeatedly coping with crises of overinvestment,
as they time and again have abandoned existing technologies,
                                        labor processes,
    and their associated working conditions,
as they thereby have engaged in "creative destruction,"
they constantly have constructed new geographies
    and eradicated old geographies,
they constantly have affected some locations, some places and regions
but not others.
Thereby,
as the ever more globally extensive processes of capitalism have unfolded
    during various phases of mutation dating back to the nineteenth
    century,[1]
they have yielded particular local transformations,
they have become integrated
    into locally sedimented forms of everyday life
    in singular ways,
they have led to the place-specific introduction
of new production- (and consumption-) related practices
                                    and power relations,
they have resulted in place-specific experiences of modernity,
    in place-specific experiences of disjuncture,
    in place-specific cultural (re)form(ation)s,
    in localized meaning-centered everyday struggles
    that are at once political and cultural.

Put more tersely, the intersection of economic restructurings – of historically and geographically specific forms of capitalism – with already existing local-ized patterns of everyday life almost inevitably elicits some form of cultural response or negotiation, some overt or covert form of symbolic contestation.[2] The repeated but varied cultural responses that emerge as a part of local transformation, as a part of the local introduction (or removal) of specific forms of capital, as a part of the articulation of the local and the global, are central to all four of the empirical stories of everyday struggle recounted in [*Reworking Modernity*]. The research underlying the two (geographical-hi)stories that I will narrate has been self-consciously informed by a particular conceptualization of culture, by a particular view of the cultural content of concrete everyday practices and their associated power relations, by a particular perspective regarding the meaning-filled qualities of culture, language, and everyday life. This fundamental conceptualization is here spelled out in a somewhat unconventional manner – in a montage of aphorisms and propositions – so as to influence your author-ized reading of these tales, so as to add a final word to the intertextual screen through which your reading is filtered.[3]

Culture, Language, and Everyday Struggles

Culture does not stand   isolated
    on its own, immutable and uncontested.
It is neither fixed, nor confined to the traditional,
    neither completely stable, nor a unified monolith of coherence.
It is not an autonomous entity,
    existing in a territory of its own,
    beyond the realms of materiality and social reality.
Culture is embodied and lived,
        actively produced and expressed,
through all social practices,
through all that is concrete and everyday,
through all that is enmeshed in power relations
    and their associated discourses,[4]
        their associated representations and rhetorics.
Culture is one with "the *meanings* and values which arise amongst distinctive social groups and classes on the basis of their given historical [and geographically specific] conditions and relations,"
one with the meanings through which women and men "handle and respond to the conditions of [everyday practical] existence,"[5]
one with the mean(ing)s through which "a social order is communicated, reproduced, experienced, and explored"[6] in the flow of everyday life.
Culture is one with the meanings both through which distinctive social groups and classes are constructed by others and through which those groups and classes (re)make themselves.
Hence,
cultural dynamics,
the birthing and rebirthing of meanings,
are embedded in social process and the unfolding of human biographies,
    In the corpo-real execution of act-ivity,
    in the exercise of agency,
    in the sit(e)-uated reproduction of the ordinary and the extra-ordinary,
    in the intricate dialectic between conditions and consciousness,
    in the simultaneous making of histories
        and construction of human geographies.[7]
Or,
in the actual course of localized everyday life,
the cultural,
the intertwining of meaning and practice,
    of meaning and event,
    of meaning and object,

the production of local and more widely spread meanings and values,
cannot be   uncoupled
    from the social,
    from the historical,
    from the human geographical,
just as the social, the historical, and the human geographical
cannot be   severed
    either from each other
      or from the cultural.[8]

As people move through their lives,
as thinking, feeling subjects
    bodily engage
      in an unbroken succession of time-space specific activities,
the meaning-filled dynamics of culture are played out
at the intersection of that which is locally sedimented,
      that which is locally ongoing, and
      or that which locally penetrates from a distance,
at the junction either where different elements
      of local interest and discourse collide in new ways,
    or where the locally distinctive and the global,
      the locally originating and the nonlocally originating,
      the microprocessual and the macroprocessual,
    meet head on.
Or,
the meaning-filled dynamics of culture are played out
at those various crossroads of practical and relational tension,
      of practical and relational con-front-ation,
where responses of active resistance or covert opposition are called for
        almost unavoidably.[9]

". . . cultural situations [are] *always* in flux, in a perpetual historically sensitive state of resistance and accommodation to broader processes of influence that are as much inside as outside the local context."[10]

"Language is . . . primarily a practical tool that gains in *meaning* from doing as doing gains its *meaning* from language. Language is therefore always in a state of becoming. . . . It is a semantic field that shifts as the practices and projects of the material world alter, setting new limits as old ones are overtaken, inventing new [local or wider] *meanings* for old words, or bringing new words and *meanings* into existence."[11]

Languages are not things in themselves.
Languages are lived and situated.
Languages do not exist outside of people and places.
They cannot be   detached
    from the human practices of the areas in which they occur,
    from the human activities in which they are learned
        and employed,
    from the human activities out of which they emerge
        and to which they give rise.
They cannot be rent   asunder
    from the social conditions in which they are produced,

reproduced, and utilized.
Especially in the form of the *meaning*-filled spoken word,
situated languages are inextricably bound up
with the practices of everyday life,
with quotidian activities of production or employment,
          of consumption and social interaction,
with the execution of recurrent routines and rituals
     in private and public spaces.
This being practic(e)ally the case, the words and meanings associated with
language usage are not only geographically and historically specific, not only
always in a state of becoming, but always entangled – at some level
with power relations
     that ultimately are a matter of who may or may not do what,
          where and when,
          under what conditions of control (if any),
with power relations
     that en-gender and class-ify,
     that otherwise simultaneously open up and restrict
          the times and spaces of human action,
               of human engagement in the world.
It is within the realm of everyday practices,
     within the flow of thought, conduct, and experience
          passing through them,
     within the field of power relations bearing upon them,
     within their attendant meanings,
     within the arena of meaning(s) in action,
that cultures and languages   lcaunlgtuarges
     overlap and disappear into one another,
     become inseparable from one another,
          except by academic legerdemain.
Or,
no matter what the scholarly sleight of hand,
in the act-ual world,
on the ground,
in place,
locally or more widely shared elements of culture and language—
     shared symbolic knowledge and meanings—
arise out of
and merge into
the experience of shared practices,
               shared asymmetrical power relations,
               shared situations.

In any historical-geographical setting,
the experiencing of shared practices and unequal power relations
     by those who are subordinate,
     by those who are subject to the practical rule(s) of others,
          to rules that are not of their own making,
     by those subject to "the social experience of
          indignities, control, submission, humiliation,
          forced deference, and punishment,"[12]

by those whose use of time and space
      is in some measure subject to the command of others,
is apt to be given some cultural or linguistic expression,
is apt to result in some form of everyday cultural struggle,
            some form of open or clandestine word warfare,
            some form of symbolic discontent.

The content of locally occurring language usages and symbolic forms is
not fixed,[13]
for among other reasons,
because they are so often an outlet for discontent
      with the content of everyday practices and power relations,
because they are so often a means of contention,
      a medium for sign-aling dissatisfaction,
            for staking out the shifting grounds of practical struggle,
because they are so frequently the scene of ideological contestation,
because they are not only the means by which local struggles
      are described and communicated,
but also themselves frequently a site of struggle and resistance,
                  an arena of conflict.

The circumstances are legion where
the spoken word, body language, or any other symbolic mode,
may serve the weak as a weapon
      for opposition, protest, or struggle,
      for rejecting reigning discourses,
      for rejecting the class-ification and categories
            of those above,
            of those who exercise power
                  over the conduct of everyday practices.

The weak may deepen their opposition or resistance
      to the conditions of everyday practice and power relations,
by using the uttered word,
      the meaning-filled symbol,
      the cultural weapon,
as an instrument of social distinction,
an indicator of difference,
an underliner of division from others,
a boundary marker of exclusion and inclusion,
a cementer of collective identity,
a reinforcer of solidarity,[14]
a commitment to community.

The weak may express symbolic discontent
through opposing visions of the same social wor(l)d,
through opposing categorical divisions of the same social
                              (and material) world,
through opposing representations of group identity
      and characterizations of collective self,
through opposing taxonomies and images of social position,
through opposing classificatory systems of class,
through opposing verbal constructions of reality.[15]

Or,
symbolic discontent may be expressed through struggles
over what is to be construed as common sense,
over which categories are allowed to make sense,
over which words are to make a difference,
        are to construct a difference,
over which names and meanings are to be taken as legitimate,[16]
over the symbolic import of past "facts" and present everyday realities
        and thereby over the future making of local (or wider) histories.

The circumstances are legion where language and other symbolic forms
may serve the subordinate as a vehicle
    for spurning the "appropriate" meanings
        of those who appropriate,
    for scorning the "propriety" of meanings
        proclaimed by those who control property,
    for casting aside the governing meanings
        pronounced by those who politically govern,
    for giving shape to grievances,
        for turning the social world upside down.[17]
But, it is especially in conjunction with the local introduction of new practices and
their associated power relations that the spoken word (or some other
representational form) is apt to become an instrument of opposition and struggle –
even if only uttered at offstage sites where one may speak freely, where one may
fearlessly offer rejoinders to those who practically control and ideologically
dominate.
New practices frequently involve a juxtapositioning of unconventional,
unprecedented contexts of action with conventional, established contexts of action.
It is also so that "new meanings [generally] emerge from the interface
between one context and another."[18]
Therefore,
participation in new local everyday practices,
        in new social interactions and social relations,
may bring about an experience of opposed meanings or symbols,
may create a threat to existing accepted-as-natural meanings or symbols,
may evoke a defense of existing meanings
        and their unexamined idea-logics,
may trigger a struggle over meanings or symbols
    that is at once political and cultural.[19]

If the locally spoken word and other symbolic forms are embedded in local
practices and their associated power relations, and if conflict over locally occurring
practices and power relations almost always involves some linguistic or symbolic
expression, then there will be some (repeated) impact on local representation, some
active cultural response, some (re)making or (re)invention of culture, wherever the
workings of modern industrial capitalism extend, wherever the actions of
entrepreneurs, corporations, investors, and other profit-seeking, accumulation-
oriented agents are implemented.
In each of its successive periods of mutation,
        of accumulation crisis and self-reinvention,
        of modernization anew and accelerated,
industrial capitalism has been characterized

by a furthering of "time-space compression,"[20]
by a temporal and spatial shrinking of the world,
by advances in transportation and communications technology
    that have increased the mobility of goods and capital,
        the spatial reach of investments,
        the ease with which everyday practices and
            power relations are transformed at a distance,
and thereby by a tendency
    for the articulations between nonlocal capital
        and local cultural contestation
    to be more geographically extensive,
by a tendency
    for the truth of experience to no longer coincide with the place
        in which it takes place.[21]

As globally extensive processes of capitalism make their distinctive local
        appearances,
        exits, and
        reappearances,
as they generate particular local transformations of practice,
those processes inevitably contribute
to some transformation of locally encountered symbols,
        of the locally spoken word,
        of locally shared meanings,
to the introduction of new terms, expressions and meanings
    regarding newly erected built facilities
        and newly modified local landscapes,
    regarding new types of machinery, equipment, and production inputs,
    regarding the organization, details and moments
        of new labor processes,
    regarding the new social relations of those processes,
    regarding who is to interact with whom under what circumstances,
    regarding who is to supervise whom under what conditions of control,
    regarding new relations between employers and wage earners.

The local appearance of new forms of capitalism is not only about the
physical deployment of new technologies or about the implementation of
new labor-process moments and their associated social relations.
The local appearance of new forms of capitalism
is also about the *experience*
of its new everyday practices and power relations,
about newly experienced oppositions,
about political and cultural opposition
    to the new material circumstances and rules of the game
        those forms force into everyday life,
about the (re)shaping of subordinate cultures
    in the face of new conditions of domination,
    in the face of newly shaped hegemonic discourses.
It is about the mediation of new experiences by past experiences,
about the previous and the ongoing forming new experimental
        and perceptual constellations,
about the conflicts and struggles that thereby emerge.

It is about the experience of,
and open or covert resistance to, that which was not before.
It is about experiencing
disjuncture and discontinuity,
incongruity and rupture,
the shocking newness of the new.
It is about experiencing
what appears extraordinary in light of the established ordinary,
what does not make sense in light of preexisting sensibilities,
what appears illogical in light of a long-acted-upon idea-logic,
what seems immoral in light of a long-practiced moral economy,
what seems unethical in the light of a long-held ideal-ogic.
It is also, thereby, about the experience of modernity,
about everyday opposition to initial modernization,
            to further instances of (re)modernization,
            to episodes of "post"-modernization,
about efforts—
    sometimes isolated and subterranean, sometimes organized and above
    ground—
on the part of women and men to cope with, or even change,
    the world that is changing them,
about the local simultaneity of modernization, modernity,
                            and modernisms.
Or, it is also about the experiences and off-stage or on-stage resistances that result
when locally sedimented ways of doing things and forms of consciousness, or
locally sedimented patterns of action and thought, are confronted by practices and
power relations that have been locally (super)imposed.

Whether occurring in connection with early appearances of industrial capitalism,[22]
or in connection with its late-twentieth-century manifestations, such localized
confrontations between some form of "tradition" and some form of "modernity"
are not likely to involve an automatic, unproblematic capitulation of the former to
the latter, an effortless absorption of the former by the latter—
even if, sooner or later, those who are subordinate
"consent" in practice to their new conditions,
accommodate themselves to new power relations.
Instead, such confrontations between the traditional and the modern are almost
certain to generate cultural tension between classes, groups, institutions, or
gendered
women and men with different interests,
almost certain to bring the cultural modalities of different classes, groups,
institutions, or
gendered women and men into new forms of opposition.
Instead, such localized confrontations are
almost certain to call into question the appropriateness of some names and
classifications that until then had been pivotal to navigating the
    everyday world,
almost certain to require some re-cognition of difference,
            and the representations thereof,
almost certain to open to contestation the fact-uality of the present moment
and its antecedents,

and,
by striking at the heart of collective memory
     and taken-for-granted differences,
thereby threaten personal or collective identity.[23]
Instead, such localized confrontations are
almost certain to demand some translation,
            some rewording,
            some reworking of the new into the old
                  or the old into the new,
almost certain to animate cultural struggles and representational contests that are
given voice in the private- or public-space languages and symbolic tactics of
everyday life,
almost certain to redefine the everyday interplay of the hegemonic and the
counterhegemonic.[24]

It is not only through terms that label new tactics of everyday resistance or in some
way refer to the execution of those tactics that the local appearance of new forms of
capitalism further impacts
upon local linguistic and symbolic expression,
upon the representational register,
    linguistic repertoire and
    multiple daily discourses of specific women and men.

In the wake of new forms of capitalism,
in the wake of new polarizations between capital and labor,
the locally spoken word and other symbolic forms
are also very likely to be altered in central ways
by cultural struggles,
by ideological battles,
by everyday power contests,
over the appropriateness of meanings,
over the legitimacy of namings,
over the preservation of identity.

Yet again,
where new forms of capitalism make their entrance,
where the custom-ary is consequently suspended,
where experiences of modernity
    are consequently in-corpo-rated into everyday life,
some precipitation of symbolic discontent is almost certain to occur.

However, the symbolic discontent following in the train of new forms of capitalism
is far from always synonymous with politically effective, protracted, and organized
forms of local resistance.

Especially when it is confined to off-stage or subterranean expression, symbolic
discontent may serve much more as an adaptive safety-valve than as an effective
form of resistance.

Admittedly, symbolic discontent may merely serve as a haven of critical
acquiescence,
as a resort to safe subversion,
for those who seek to survive,
for those who are somewhat resigned to accommodation,

for those who consciously or subconsciously recognize the futility, danger, or
impracticality
    of direct confrontation,
    of more active forms of struggle or open rebellion.
And yet,
through the recognition and penetration of power relations
    that is necessarily a part of it,
through the unveiling or underlining of everyday injustices
    that comes with it,
symbolic discontent may serve as a latent foundation for more organized
forms of resistance or pressured negotiation—
if it is not actually a prerequisite tinderbox for such collective agency.
For,
in symbolically challenging their domination and control,
in (re)constructing or (re)inventing their culture,
in (re)forming elements of their collective consciousness,
in making common sense of their situation,
locally subordinate groups
may revive their sense of community or their sense of place,
may (re)awake some sense of collective dignity, of solidarity,
and, in so doing,
may sow the seeds of future political action.

[. . .]

Notes

1   [. . .] Important discussions of capitalist mutations are provided in Davis (1978),
    Aglietta (1979), Soja (1989), and Harvey (1982).
2   Since the late 1970s, a number of pivotal anthropological and related works have
    appeared, which address the cultural conflicts and resistances resulting from the
    introduction of new forms of capitalism into specific non-Western settings. In addition
    to the works of Ong (1987) and Wolf (1990) [. . .], see, for example, Nash (1979),
    Taussig (1980), Comaroff (1985), and Scott (1985). Also see Holmes (1989) on the
    cultural struggles deriving from the insertion of urban industrial activities into the
    everyday life of peasants in the Friuli region of northeast Italy. Cf. note 22.
3   [. . .] Complementary and overlapping aphorisms and propositions are to be found in
    Pred (1989, 1990a, 1990b, 1990c). The bibliographies contained therein include numer-
    ous additional references to the literatures of critical human geography, social theory,
    anthropology, and sociolinguistics, from which this section is complexly derived.
4   Here *discourse* is employed in Foucault's (1972, 1973, 1979) sense, to refer to a set of
    interrelated concepts and values.
5   Hall (1981: 26), emphasis added. This insistence on the inseparability of culture and
    social practice is in keeping with Hall's "Birmingham school" as well as some of the
    central writings of E. P. Thompson (1968) and Raymond Williams (1973, 1977). Cf.
    Brenkman (1987: vii, 8). Also note Ryan's (1989: 8–24) constructive critique of Hall
    and Williams; and contrast with Archer (1988), who rightfully debunks the "image of
    culture as a coherent pattern, a uniform ethos or a symbolically consistent universe"
    (xv, 1–21), but insists upon the "relative autonomy of structure and culture" while at
    the same time conceptualizing some important ways in which they interplay.

6   Williams (1982: 13).

7   The construction of human geographies, or the production of space and place, at one and the same time refers to the production of an unevenly developed built environment; the shaping of landscape and land use patterns; the appropriation and transformation of nature; the organization and use of specialized locations for the conduct of economic, social, and religious or ritual practices; the generation of patterns of movement and interdependence between such localized activities; and the formation of symbolically laden, ideology-projecting sites and areas (Pred 1990c).

8   Thus, as the *Passagen-Werk* and other writings of Benjamin so richly suggest (Buck-Morss 1989), any critical understanding or interpretation of historically and geographically specific forms of society requires a simultaneous interpretation of their culture(s).

9   Compare Williams (1977: 121–7) on the interactions and conflicts occurring among "residual," "dominant," and "emergent" forms of culture.

10 Marcus and Fischer (1986: 78).

11 Thrift (1983: 46), emphasis added.

12 Scott (1990).

13 Obviously, locally occurring language usages and symbolic forms are not likely to be confined to those of local origin – especially under modern circumstances. Many, if not most, usages and forms – and their meanings – will be more or less similar over widespread areas as a result of migration, diffusion, or dissemination and reinforcement via the printed and electronic media.

14 Compare Fantasia (1988) on the cultural interplay of solidarity and acts of opposition.

15 Cf. Bourdieu (1985, 1987, 1989, 1990); Stedman Jones (1983).

16 Bourdieu (1987, 1990).

17 Compare the argumentation developed by Scott (1990) and the observations on symbolic social inversion in Babcock (1978), Bakhtin (1984), and Stallybrass and White (1986).

18 Olsson (1991).

19 Cf. Marcus and Fischer (1986: 85, 153). Much of the literature on the cultural and ideological terrains of struggle embedded in everyday life is directly or indirectly rooted in Gramsci (1971).

20 See the argumentation developed by Harvey (1989).

21 Paraphrased from Jameson (1988: 351).

22 The classic works of Thompson (1963) and Tilly (1986) in different ways attach central importance to the context-dependent, place-specific, every-day-practice-embedded cultural struggles and symbolic discontents that emerged in parts of England and France in conjunction with the factory system and early forms of industrial capitalism. Thompson's work in particular has inspired a vast literature of related studies regarding class struggle in the realm of cultural production and the production of symbolic meanings, several of which (for example, Sewell [1980], Smail [1987], and Stedman Jones [1983]) focus on language and discourse.

23 This observation is consistent with the body of theory that insists that "all identity is constructed across difference" (Hall 1987: 45), that rejects any notion of a truly autonomously arrived-at identity, and that conceptualizes ethnic or group "identity as a dynamic process of construction and reproduction over time, in direct relation or opposition to specific other groups and interests" (Löfgren 1989: 9).

24 Hegemony should not be conceptualized as something uncontested, as something definitionally strangling resistance, as something existing without a counterhegemony. "Gramsci's notion of hegemony, ... which names domination by consensus rather than by coercion, through culture rather than through the exercise of force," is

– as Hall and others point out – "never stable but instead . . . constantly negotiated through struggle" (Ryan 1989: 17–18). Furthermore, Ryan (1989: 18) adds: "One could argue . . . that hegemony is in fact itself a kind of [cultural-political] resistance, a means of securing the identities of property and of political power against very real internal threats that are always potentially active in a system of economic subordination founded on a radical difference or inequality."

References

Aglietta, M. 1979: *A Theory of Capitalist Regulation*. London: Verso.

Archer, M. S. 1988: *Culture and Agency: The Place of Culture in Social Theory*. Cambridge: Cambridge University Press.

Babcock, B. 1978: *The Reversible World: Symbolic Inversion in Art and Society*. Ithaca, NY: Cornell University Press.

Bakhtin, M. 1984: *Rabelais and His World*. Bloomington: Indiana University Press.

Bourdieu, P. 1985: "Social Space and the Genesis of Groups." *Theory and Society* 14, 723–44.

Bourdieu, P. 1987: "What Makes a Social Class? On the Theoretical and Practical Existence of Groups." *Berkeley Journal of Sociology* 22, 1–17.

Bourdieu, P. 1989: "Social Space and Symbolic Power." *Sociological Theory* 14, 14–25.

Bourdieu, P. 1990: *In Other Words: Essays towards a Reflexive Sociology*. Stanford, CA: Stanford University Press.

Brenkman, J. 1987: *Culture and Domination*. Ithaca, NY: Cornell University Press.

Buck-Morss, S. 1989: *The Dialectic of Seeing: Walter Benjamin and the Arcades Project*. Cambridge, MA: MIT Press.

Comaroff, J. 1985: *Body of Power, Spirit of Resistance: The Culture and History of a South African People*. Chicago: University of Chicago Press.

Davis, M. 1978: "Fordism in Crisis." *Review* 2 (2), 207–67.

Fantasia, R. 1988: *Cultures of Solidarity: Consciousness, Action and Contemporary American Workers*. Berkeley: University of California Press.

Foucault, M. 1972: *The Archeology of Knowledge*. New York: Harper Colophon.

Foucault, M. 1973: *The Order of Things: An Archeology of the Human Sciences*. New York: Vintage/Random House.

Foucault, M. 1979: *Discipline and Punish: The Birth of the Prison*. New York: Vintage.

Geertz, C. 1983: *Local Knowledge: Further Essays in Interpretive Anthropology*. New York: Basic Books.

Gramsci, A. 1971: *Selections from the Prison Notebooks*. New York: International Publishers.

Hall, S. 1981: "Notes on Deconstructing the Popular." In R. Samuel (ed.), *People's History and Socialist Theory*. London: Routledge, 256–83.

Hall, S. 1987: "Minimal Selves." In L. Appignanesi (ed.), *Post-Modernism and the Question of Identity*. ICA Documents No. 6. London: Institute of Contemporary Arts, 44–6.

Harvey, D. 1982: *The Limits to Capital*. Oxford: Blackwell.

Harvey, D. 1989: *The Condition of Postmodernity: An Enquiry into the Origins of Cultural Change*. Oxford: Blackwell.

Holmes, D. R. 1989: *Cultural Disenchantments: Worker Peasantries in Northeastern Italy*. Princeton, NJ: Princeton University Press.

Jameson, F. 1988: "Cognitive Mapping." In C. Nelson and L. Grossberg (eds.), *Marxism and the Interpretation of Culture*. Urbana: University of Illinois Press, 347–60.

Löfgren, O. 1989: "The Nationalization of Culture." *Ethnologia Europaea* 19, 5–24.

Marcus, G. E. and Fischer, M. J. 1986: *Anthropology as Cultural Critique: An Experimental Moment in the Human Sciences*. Chicago: University of Chicago Press.

Nash, J. 1979: *We Eat the Mines and the Mines Eat Us: Dependency and Exploitation in Bolivian Tin Mines*. New York: Columbia University Press.

Olsson, G. 1991: *Lines of Power, Limits of Language*. Minneapolis: University of Minnesota Press.

Ong, A. 1987: *Spirits of Resistance and Capitalist Discipline: Factory Women in Malaysia*. Albany: State University of New York Press.

Pred, A. 1989: "The Locally Spoken Word and Local Struggle." *Society and Space* 7, 211–33.

Pred, A. 1990a: "In Other Worlds: Fragmented and Integrated Observations on Gendered Languages, Gendered Spaces and Local Transformation." *Antipode* 22, 33–52.

Pred, A. 1990b: *Lost Words and Lost Worlds: Modernity and the Language of Everyday Life in Late Nineteenth-century Stockholm*. Cambridge: Cambridge University Press.

Pred, A. 1990c: *Making Histories and Constructing Human Geographies: The Local Transformation of Practice, Power Relations, and Consciousness*. Boulder, CO: Westview.

Ryan, M. 1989: *Politics and Culture: Working Hypotheses for a Post-revolutionary Society*. Baltimore: Johns Hopkins University Press.

Scott, J. C. 1985: *Weapons of the Weak: Everyday Forms of Peasant Resistance*. New Haven, CT: Yale University Press.

Scott, J. C. 1990: *Domination and the Arts of Resistance: The Hidden Transcript*. New Haven, CT: Yale University Press.

Sewell, W. H., Jr. 1980: *Work and Revolution in France: The Language of Labor from the Old Regime to 1848*. Cambridge: Cambridge University Press.

Smail, J. 1987: "New Languages for Labour and Capital: The Transformation of Discourse in the Early Years of the Industrial Revolution." *Social History* 12, 49–71.

Soja, E. 1989: *Postmodern Geographies: The Reassertion of Space in Critical Social Theory*. London: Verso.

Stallybrass, P. and White, A. 1986: *The Politics and Poetics of Transgression*. Ithaca, NY: Cornell University Press.

Stedman Jones, J. G. 1983: *Languages of Class: Studies in English Working Class History, 1832–1982*. Cambridge: Cambridge University Press.

Taussig, M. 1980: *The Devil and Commodity Fetishism in South America*. Chapel Hill: University of North Carolina Press.

Thompson, E. P. 1963: *The Making of the English Working Class*. London: Gollancz.

Thompson, E. P. 1968: *The Making of the English Working Class*. New edition. Harmondsworth: Penguin.

Thrift, N. J. 1983: "On the Determination of Social Action in Time and Space." *Society and Space* 1, 23–57.

Tilly, C. 1986: *The Contentious French: Four Centuries of Popular Struggle*. Cambridge, MA: Harvard University Press.

Williams, R. 1973: *The Country and the City*. New York: Oxford University Press.

Williams, R. 1977: *Marxism and Literature*. Oxford: Oxford University Press.

Williams, R. 1982: *The Sociology of Culture*. New York: Schocken Books.

Wolf, D. 1990: *Gender, Households and Rural Industrialisation: Factory Daughters and their Families in Java*. Berkeley: University of California Press.

17 Narratives of Masculinity and Transnational Migration: Filipino Workers in the Middle East

Jane A. Margold

[. . .]

In a performance piece entitled "1991," the Mexican-American protagonist identifies himself as a migrant poet, a "high-tech Aztec" who wanders through the borderlands of pastiche cultures and multiple epochs. The male subjectivity he enacts is fragmented and self-parodic. Standing astride an imaginary line on stage, the poet reflects that his "manhood" is "perfectly bisected" by the border between Mexico and the United States. No bodily integrity or unitary consciousness is possible for this liminal male self. The poet exits stage as he entered, the perplexed child of *desmodernidad*: chaos, motherlessness, and late modernity.[1]

Fractured Identities and Flexible Labor Regimes

The migrant poet's performance of his splintered, uncertain masculinity raises questions about the effects of international migration on the gender identities of subaltern men. For Mexican migrants, the prospect of betraying their own culture while "trespassing" in the society of the other is the paramount source of tension (Anzaldua 1987). Although the Filipino labor migrants whose narratives are analyzed here are not viewed by their communities as "cultural traitors," their quest for international employment still exposes them to analogous psychic risks. Like their Mexican counterparts, they are cast as transgressors in the countries that buy their labor. Their migration stories are threaded through with a similar

Excerpted from Jane A. Margold, "Narratives of Masculinity and Transnational Migration: Filipino Workers in the Middle East." In A. Ong and M. G. Peletz (eds.), *Bewitching Women, Pious Men: Gender and Body Politics in Southeast Asia* (Berkeley, Los Angeles, and London: University of California Press, 1995), 274–94.

sense of bodily sacrifice, psychic disintegration, and startled outrage at the negative images ("dogs," "tools," "slaves") that assault them in the international workplace.

Scholars investigating the incorporation of Third World women into the fluid global labor markets of the last two decades have rejected the more static, unicausal approaches to gender-role formation, insisting instead on analyzing the interplay of culture, class, nationality, and power with engenderment (Ong 1987, 1990, 1991; Enloe 1989). In applying their insights to the ethnographic case of peasant men who migrate from the Philippines' Ilocos region to the wealthy Arab Gulf states, I argue that geopolitics and geoeconomics can crucially transfigure masculine identities. Drawing on anthropological fieldwork conducted in 1987 and 1989–90 in a heavily migratory village in the northern Philippines, I seek to show that the sense of manhood that develops locally may be partially disassembled when the migrant is incorporated into the lowest ranks of the global labor force. There, he is ghettoized, ordered to work at top speed, and quickly repatriated, often before his economic gains outweigh his feelings of shock.

As we will see, the Ilokano men attempt to retain an observing eye and a critical voice while encountering an industrial work environment they experience as emotionally and bodily threatening. These perceptions become apparent in the excerpts below. I then consider the applicability of several Western theories of masculinity to peasant-migrants who straddle often contradictory worlds of subsistence production and deeply commodified relations.

Biographies of Male Upheaval

If a Muslim is caught stealing, they will cut off his hand. For the [nonMuslim] Filipino, they will parade him around the city for hours, chained to whatever he stole. With a police escort. Until he gets on the airplane [to be deported], he is chained so every one can see he is a thief. A fellow Filipino! Of course we feel pity and shame.
Ruben, a carpenter in his twenties who worked in Saudi Arabia

The Filipino is used to his independent ways. . . . Here, in the Philippines, you can do what you want, make trouble, work, sleep, you are free to move. You can bring your body anywhere you like. . . . We carry that freeness in our body, so when there is something we cannot accept, it is hard to keep silent.
Rogelio, a tricycle (small transport vehicle) driver and small farmer who worked in Iraq

Embedded in the narratives of Ilokano male returnees from the Gulf is a pattern of personal crisis experienced abroad, of work and public incidents the men perceived as assaults to their sense of manhood. Tales of unusual punishments overseas (whippings, amputations, beheadings) alternate with some migrants' confessions of their fears of homosexual rape by employers – a worry unimaginable in the Philippines, where attitudes toward gay men (*bakla*) are tolerant.

Overtly hostile local youths are a further bitter surprise to men from a country

in which invidious racial distinctions are made, but not openly or confronta-
tively. Disquieting, too, to the peasant-migrants are power clashes with labor
recruiters, employers, and impatient supervisors, who treat workers like robots
or tools. A story volunteered by a returned migrant named Avelino reveals his
disorientation at the techniques of intimidation he encountered overseas:

> My first day there, I almost got into trouble. Our foreman, an Italian . . . asked me
> to give him a hammer. Hammer is called in Arabic, *jacus*. . . . During my first day,
> how do I know he means hammer when he said *jacus*? So I don't know what to
> hand him. He's getting angry. But still I don't get what he means, so how could I
> give him? Then he got the hammer [*here, Avelino mimed coming so close and shaking
> the tool in my face that I could not help but rear back in alarm*] and told me [*gritting his
> teeth in imitation*]: *jacus, jacus, jacus.*

Workers of several nationalities witnessed the angry gesture:

> There are Egyptian, Pakistani, Eritrean, Indian [workers] watching. And we are five
> Filipinos in that group . . . at that point, I was in a place of humiliation. I decided, it
> was our first day. I grabbed the hammer from him. . . . Then I throw it, almost
> hitting his feet. I tell him, this is *martillo* [*gritting his teeth*]. *Martillo, martillo*. Then I
> again got the hammer and almost hit him with it.

The critical qualifier "almost," repeated several times, points to the cautious self-
control that orchestrated this performance. If the foreman's shaking of the
hammer in Avelino's face is an impulsive aggressive display, Avelino's response
is much more choreographed. He tosses the hammer so as to miss the boss's feet,
thereby de-escalating the conflict. And Avelino "almost" hits the foreman, but
only in fantasy, judging from the foreman's reaction:

> You know what happened? He was very much surprised, not afraid. Not angry. He
> said: "what, *martillo*?" It is also *martillo* in Italy. We have the common name! [*laughs
> delightedly.*] Yes, Philippines, *martillo*. Italy, *martillo*. [*He grins and nods, repeating the
> word, first enunciating it sharply in Ilokano, then with a lingering, Italian accent.*] So right
> after that, when he saw my response, that Filipinos are not cowardly, ready to fight,
> management conducted a meeting. They said in the meeting: these are the charac-
> teristics of the Filipino. They are sensitive, but they have brains. . . . They respect us
> because if we hear insults, we will make trouble instantly. Particularly the Europe-
> ans, they underestimate us. But then they find out that we have a brain . . . after
> that, no more trouble.

Avelino's and other migrants' accounts of such experiences are a potentially
instructive means for exploring the impact of a sharply patriarchal industrial
culture on men from a Southeast Asian country where androcentrism is more
subtle. Yet, current approaches to the study of masculinity focus heavily on
childhood, neglecting both adult psychological plasticity and the capacity of
more powerful men to resocialize the subordinate male, divesting him of public
voice and rendering him ineffectual except as raw energy. [. . .]

Colonial and Ilokano Perspectives on Ilokano Manhood

Turning to indigenous accounts of Ilokano life, which provide a clearer portrait of masculinity and male–female relations, the Ilokano journalist and historian Isabelo de los Reyes emphasized a gentle, sweet character as a manly ideal, combined with industriousness, common sense, and a profound respect for elders (1888: 153). The socially respected Ilokano thought before he spoke; verbal insults were punished more severely than bodily assaults and the slanderer was not forgiven (Zialcita 1989; Foronda and Foronda 1972).

To win an Ilokana, whom de los Reyes described (perhaps teasingly) as "surly, churlish" (*arisca*) compared to Tagalog women, the suitor had to display his capacity to provide well, his freedom from vices (1888: 141–2), and his sincerity and loyalty. Graceful rhetoric was essential in wooing a potential bride; the chosen woman had to be approached with an attitude of entreaty, a moving voice and clear, concise yet emotionally convincing phrasing (1888: 142).

Ilokano masculinity, then, blended social sensitivity with an emphasis on verbality that would make labor migration throughout [the twentieth] century particularly painful. Racial slights hounded the agricultural laborers who worked in the US during the 1920s and 1930s (Bulosan n.d.; Wood ca. 1931). Compounding the debasement of Ilokano masculinity was the men's expectation that prestige should be accorded the traveler who had experienced life widely. Male honor in the Ilocos had long been predicated upon heroic quests, as the Ilokanos' epic poem *Lam-ang* indicates. The acquisition of male prestige through travel was still a motivating force for men in the early part of the twentieth century. As a future migrant wrote, after watching a crowd excitedly greet a man who had just returned from the US: "I was thrilled and inspired ... In my fancy, I made the trip to America and I, too, returned a hero ... in the style of our ... old legends [in which] a ... man had gone forth to slay the winged giants and flying devils in the days before history" (Buaken 1948: 41, 40).

In the contemporary rural Ilocos, dreams of male distinction coexist with daily practices that reinforce mutuality and interdependence in domestic and subsistence tasks. While boys compete with each other,[2] they are not allowed to act aggressively toward little girls. Child-rearing practices train boys as well as girls in obedience and social nurturance (Lagmay 1983). Small girls (aged seven and older) play managerial games, reflecting women's entry into professional and business domains (albeit at lower levels than men). Men often cook, sweep, and do some child care, while women perform many agricultural chores.

Contemporary Ilokanos initially say that the ideal husband attends to his household and familial duties, including, most importantly, securing their economic stability. However, "the good provider is not such an exciting topic: he's mostly praised when he's dead," women commented. Ilokanas, of all classes, have "sidelines" or multiple small businesses utilized not merely to supplement a spouse's income but often to support the household. The widow of a town mayor, a woman considered rich by rural standards, revealed that she had never known her husband's income, nor received money from him. Her extensive entrepreneurial activities had not only sustained six children, but covered the costs of feeding the mayor's frequent guests. Reliance on the wife for household support was common. In one town, women pointed to at least fifteen "house-bands" – "domesticated husbands" – who stayed home and performed most domestic tasks, while their wives brought in cash.

Intrigued by the theme of defining good and bad husbands, women specified tenderness (*managayat*), good character (*nasingpet*), and, with some embarrass-ment, attractive looks.[3] In jokes about courting, men are scrutinized for "funny" physical characteristics, just as the young bride in the Ilokano epic *Lam-ang* insists on watching her husband walk in front of her so that she can study his movements and body, even after he has demonstrated his heroism and super-natural powers.[4] Male bodily comportment becomes a metonymic predictor of male sexual and generative capacity, another sine qua non of powerful masculinity.

In the Ilocos, where kinship is reckoned bilaterally, fathering children and thereby founding a line of descent has been an important means of asserting political claims (Rafael 1988). Hence, the "Saudi Syndrome,"[5] as the Philippine media termed the overseas worker's "haunting" fear of his wife's infidelity (Arcinas et al. 1986: 67), had a double edge: male absence not only endangered the worker's control over his wife's and daughters' sexuality, but limited the number of children that could be produced.

Married men who were childless before going to "Saudi" pressured their wives into pregnancy when they returned (or cut short women's employment abroad). Daughters were as desired as sons. Ilokanos view the marriage of daughters as an opportunity to extend familial networks of assistance and influence, not as a financial burden. There is thus no preference for sons. Indeed, male children are more costly: ideally, fathers help sons by contributing to the male dowry (*sab-ong*) that Ilokanas historically expected.[6]

Parent–son bonds also tend to be close, so that a son who fails to marry may remain comfortably in his parents' household all his adult life. As an extreme example of Ilokano filial devotion, Ferdinand Marcos never stopped calling his mother "Mommy" and refused to have her buried if he could not be present at her funeral (Ellison 1988: 86). [. . .]

The Political Economy of Foreign Debt and Poverty

[. . .] In the Ilocos, a mountainous area far from the FTZs, underemployed young men had become a fixture in the late 1980s, as a result of huge price fluctuations in the region's cash crops (garlic, tobacco), long-standing overpopulation, and the failure of urban areas to absorb more than a few of the available workers. The Ilokano word *standby* (unemployed) captured the reality of men lingering in village rest houses, joking uncomfortably about becoming mail-order bride-grooms for Filipinas in the US.

Labor Migration and the Debt Crisis

Seeking employment overseas became an increasingly attractive household option when news of the oil-fueled construction boom in the Arab Gulf reached the Ilocos. The government actively encouraged the labor outflow; remittances earned dollars. [. . .]

In a buyers' market, reports were abundant of gross overcharges by recruiters, contract substitutions, sudden layoffs, and other abuses. Attempts at work stoppage, sick-outs, and other conventional expressions of discontent were received with impatience and contempt in the highly systematized industrial work place. "Work or go home," the men were told if they attempted to negotiate with management. The migrants had no labor rights: union activity was banned throughout the Gulf.[7] Islamic courts were reputedly protective of workers, but access to them was logistically difficult for the Ilokano migrants and little help could be offered by understaffed Philippine consulates and embassies. The peasant migrants were thus left unprotected in an industrial environment bent on extracting their bodily energy while containing and immobilizing its human source. [. . .]

The Import of Foreign Labor to the Middle East

The oil boom of the 1970s drew a massive tide of foreign labor to thinly populated countries; by the 1980s, foreigners accounted for an overwhelming 70 to 80 percent of the workforce in most of the Gulf states (Owen 1985: 4). For complex reasons of nationalist, religious, class, and gender politics, Asian workers came to be preferred over foreign Arab laborers at the lower levels of the workforce. Non-Muslim Asians were unlikely to espouse pan-Arabist, pan-Islamic ideals, staking moral claims to citizenship, and potentially exacerbating religious tensions by allying with local Shiite communities at a time when Gulf rulers had to deal delicately with the Islamic radicalism of their younger, more educated citizens (Eickelman 1989). While the Gulf state governments hired (through agencies) only a small percentage of the migrants, as street sweepers, gardeners, and other menial workers, TNCs and other Gulf employers synchronized their interests with those of the dominant families. TNCs could not operate locally without Gulf citizens as partners and agents.

The Gulf political elite, in turn, when their other interests did not conflict, acceded to the TNCs' restless worldwide search for the most cost-effective labor. Asian workers, rather than foreign Arabs from the countries that earlier in the century had supplied less-skilled laborers (e.g., Tunisia and Egypt), were recruited into the lowest rungs of the workforce. Wages could be keyed to deteriorating conditions in the countries of origin, resulting in a meticulously stratified labor force, with Euro-American technocrats on top, foreign Arabs in the middle, and Asians on the lowest tier (Owen 1985).

Asians were also easier to regulate socially: racial distinctiveness made it easier to enforce policies that segregated foreigners' housing. The Filipinos, like many other migrant groups, preferred to live with each other, socially insulating themselves from their unwelcoming surroundings. Yet, problematically, their self- and externally imposed ghettoization exposed them to public notice, and to constant monitoring aimed at preventing them from transgressing the boundaries of the narrow social space allotted them.

A watchful environment closed in around them at city construction sites and desert work camps, which were set up to maximize productivity by tightly controlling individuals' time, space, and movements. The typical project operated at high efficiency, with an intensification of working hours, militarization of discipline, and rapid expulsion of the workforce, often every eighteen months (Guzman 1985: 13). The lightning speed of these industrial arrangements, which orbited men away from their homelands, instantly set them to work, and ejected them out of the Gulf before they could regain their equilibrium, instilled new forms of alienation. The migrants rarely saw a finished project and often were propelled home before their profits matched their expenses. Some expressed a visceral sense of disintegration, as sponsors and agents pocketed percentages of their earnings. "Drop by drop," the men said, "it is as if these people melt you away" (*Isu nga i-dribol-dribol da ti tattao*).

The emotional tone in the Gulf seemed assaultive to the Ilokano men. "You have to dance to their music," the migrants said with dismay, indicating the difficulty of stepping fast enough to the orders of officials, police, and employers.

"Dancing" was also the trope men invoked when they were able, in some cases, to make friends with their employers. "He could dance with us," an Ilokano truck driver said approvingly of his Saudi Arabian boss. "He invited us to his house to eat. He treated me respectfully, as a man older than he."

Mutual "dancing," with neither permanently in the lead, stood as a metonymy for the close emotional relationships the Ilokano men expected to have with one another. The expectation was rarely met, however, within the industrial culture.

At work sites, "strict," "irritable" job superiors chipped away at the cheerful demeanor the Ilokanos maintained as an emotional amulet against adversity. Preoccupied with construction schedules, these bosses offered few of the token indulgences that reduced class frictions in the Philippines. Contractual relations unsettled men accustomed to an easy camaraderie.

Returnees from the Gulf thus reacted strongly to the tensions of the foreign work site and to transnational strains on their affective ties. These collisions, in which culture, class, gender, and familial ideologies intermingled, struck the men as experiences of "agony," "sacrifice," and "torment":

> There is only one thing we talk about at night in the barracks. [*emphatically*] Our agony. How we want to go home to our families, after earning big money. Nobody goes to Saudi out of choice. You sacrifice for the [economic improvement] of your family. . . . So if some employers take advantage of your weakness and do not pay full wages, you are tormented. You cannot say anything because they speak Arabic. You have no way to explain.

Uncertain Passages

The entire trajectory of industrial work relations seemed off-kilter to the peasant-migrants. Human immediacies and needs were ignored in the circulation of bodies through time and space. A mechanic, who considered himself "lucky" to have worked at his own trade in the Gulf, described the dislocation of workers who arrived overseas to find that they had been recruited for jobs they knew little about:

> The people . . . cannot read Arabic, so they don't know what is on the visa. A poor man reaches his destination . . . [*high, outraged voice*] "Why? This is not my position that I applied for." [*Voice turns severe.*] "You are here. [*The words are pounded out, one by one, emphatically.*] You . . . must . . . work."

Deskilling was as common as fraudulent contracts that forced men to learn jobs on the spot or be deported, with no means of paying off their usurious creditors in the Philippines. In countries with a long history of industrialization, deskilling has been linked with class and political impotence. Over time, English workers developed a discursive means of externalizing the source of their misery, blaming it on "the despots of capital" who destroyed the nostalgic dream of organizing labor so that work and domestic life were a smoothly flowing unity (Alexander 1990: 38). For migrants from a rural area in a largely agricultural country, no systematic articulation of capital's tendency to select only certain elements of workers and discard others had gained widespread usage.

Without an effective means of exteriorization, the men found that the slurs they heard on the job or in the street eroded their masculine self-confidence, already chastened by the lack of demand for male labor in the Philippines. "You tell them you are a degree-holder," said one man disconsolately. "You say you teach in the high school, farming skills. 'A teacher?' they say. 'Okay, you – you will be good at cleaning the streets.'"

National and racial sensitivities, submerged in the homogeneity of the rural Ilocos, resurfaced. A hierarchy of difference positioned Asians as a lower Other than the expatriate Arabs, then distinguished among the Asians, endowing them with imagined cultural attributes that sought to explain their differing pay. Filipinos were said to be "cleaner" and hence deserving of higher wages than Bangladeshis and Sri Lankans. But the Ilokanos did not miss the implication of contamination and of a treacherous, unruly carnality that police reaffirmed by waylaying them and asking them to display marriage licenses even when their companions were not Arab but Asian women.

The notion that they were "cleaner" than certain other migrants was relative to an absolute standard that was set beyond their reach. Orientalism proceeded eastward, from the Arab to the Asian world, in search of new terrain to penetrate. Petrodollars facilitated the repositioning of the wealthiest Gulf citizens far away from the poorer, darker, Asian Others and closer to the Occidental nations. In the void, those from economically dispossessed countries, such as the Philippines, were represented as bestialized or as apparatuses, stripped of human voice.

"The Arabs say that Filipinos are like dogs," men lamented, indicating their awareness that Arabs considered dogs the most loathsome of creatures: homeless and scavenging. "On the streets, they yell at us that we *are* dogs," said a migrant who was particularly embittered after being jailed overseas. "Filipinos are treated like slaves, made to work in the sun even when it is too hot to touch a piece of metal," he added. [. . .]

The net impact for the Ilokano men was to render them structurally invisible, while paradoxically their physical visibility continued to draw unwanted attention. "In the street, when the Arab teenagers are driving their cars, they throw Pepsi cans. You can't go to the authorities, because they don't believe the Filipino's complaints," men said. [. . .]

Affirmations of Nonexistence

[. . .] The distinctiveness of the regimes of power that rotated the migrants from the unemployment of the Ilocos to the intensive production zones of the Gulf lay in an elusive yet forceful agency. The matrices of power were obscure, yet the terrain they bounded was tightly patrolled. Particular skills and the bodies that housed them could be summoned at a moment's notice from anywhere in the world. As the bodies cycled rapidly in and out of the Gulf, individual rights were suspended; persons segregated; sexuality frozen by multiple, interlocking regulations; color stigmatized and intelligence discounted. Yet who or what was in command had no name to the workers. One man recalled his work in Libya:

> Many people, many Filipinos, were afraid . . . especially if [they] were assigned in the desert places. . . . In the city, it's somewhat . . . civilized. But . . . in the desert . . . it's full of thieves, full of wicked people. They are hungry . . . There's no law in the desert. If . . . they catch you doing not nice in their eyes . . . [*matter-of-fact voice*] they will just shoot you and leave you there. [*nervous laugh*] That's it. So I risked my life going to such places. Just to [*savors the word*] EARN. Just to save [*slow, drawn-out*] MONEY. [*Laughs.*]

[. . .] Such chronicles of disjuncture and loss reveal the Ilokano workers' sense of being caught up in an overwhelmingly intrusive industrial environment. Their narrations of their experience overseas recouped a male identity that was highly contingent. To an appreciative audience, their masculinity could be presented as adventuresome, striving, and imbued with a moral aim: securing their family's future. Yet, for men who felt that their earnings had been shamefully small, the family was no longer a warm, enfolding community.

As an extreme example of disturbed social functioning, a returned migrant installed his Filipina mistress from "Saudi" in his household, explaining publicly that she would be his newly pregnant wife's helper. Other men exerted an aggressive control over wives and children, commenting that their wives had been "too soft," "indecisive," or "weak-minded": depictions that surprised the Ilokanas, although most remained silent.

With female migration increasing, men no longer had an exclusive hold on the prestige once associated with male travel. In the Ilocos (and elsewhere in

Southeast Asia [Siegel 1969]), male status had long derived not from the sexual division of labor but from the cosmopolitan knowledge that men gleaned from their regional and international journeys. Remarkably, male migrants to the Middle East had hardly spoken publicly of their trips. Even wives were often surprised to hear the details that emerged during my interviews with the men. In a society where verbal prowess is an important aspect of male social esteem, the returned migrants were caught in a contradictory, ironic situation. By remaining silent about the humiliations they had endured overseas, the men could trade upon the cultural notion that foreign travel had imbued them with new social and political skills. Yet, without a display of those skills, the returnees could not be sure that their trip to Saudi had conveyed a higher status upon them in the eyes of their village and town mates.

Ethnographic inquiry over time indicated that even for those who profited financially from their migration, the experience of desexualization and dehumanization had led to a psychological withdrawal from their local community. Returned male migrants tended to remain at home when not actively working. The world outside the domestic household failed to affirm the peasant-migrant as an integral whole. Quite the opposite, as I have argued: the international political economy that interpenetrated with individual lives had splintering effects, selecting muscles and energy and denying human totalities. The Ilokano migrant caught up in the labor markets of the late twentieth century did surround himself with a protective margin of reason, critiquing the inequities he perceived. But his cultural commentary was a fragile insulation against the stigmatizing gaze of states and the expropriations of a newly fluid form of transnational capital, which no longer "advanced," "marched," "penetrated," or "thrusted" as the old Marxian metaphors would have it – but was now "delocalized," "footloose," "deterritorialized," "dispersed" (Lipietz 1986; Coronil and Skurski 1991) and especially difficult to rally against.

Identity is always precarious and provisional, never fixed. But until the global political economy opens new spaces for the self-assertion of the subaltern male, the Ilokano migrant is likely to remain liminal, unable to resuture himself into a seamless whole.

Notes

1   The word is an amalgam of *desmadre* (motherlessness/chaos) and *modernidad* (modernity), according to the program notes for Guillermo Gomez-Pena's "1991." It is likely that it comes from Roger Bartra's *Cage of Melancholy* (1992), as Matt Gutmann kindly pointed out.
2   Mothers note their sons' habit of lining up to urinate together to see who can propel a stream the highest and furthest. Boys also take pride at being "big enough" to be the first in the age group to be circumcised (an operation performed on eleven- to thirteen-year-olds).
3   A typical comment discounted the importance of looks, but pointed out that women's susceptibility to rogues could be explained by the Ilokanas' taste for good looks and charm. Thus, a variety of cads were capable of attracting women: the *malaki* or *maingel a lalaki*, like wine that is highly intoxicating, but referring to courage in fighting; the

sabongero, who spends all his time at cockfights; the *mannakiringor* and *napudot ti panagul-ulona* (violent noisemakers, hotheads), the *bartekero* (a hard drinker, which is not limited to men), the *sugalero* (gambler), the *babaero* (playboy, womanizer), and the *mananggundaway* (exploiter of women). Of this nightmarish but tolerated bunch, only the *mammalit* or *reypis* (rapist) could not compensate for his deviance with looks or magnetism.

4   She is merciless in her critique, complaining about his clumsiness, messy hair, the size and prominence of his backside, the way his hips sway, while he tries jokingly to convince her to accept him the way he is. He criticizes her physically as well, but much more gently.

5   "Saudi" in Ilokano and Tagalog refers not only to Saudi Arabia but generically to the Middle East.

6   In a situation of widespread poverty, the *sab-ong* is now expected only from *Hawaiianos*, the relatively affluent retirees who marry young brides in the Philippines after spending their work lives as agricultural laborers in the US. Their social security pensions are a key attraction for the young brides. Even where the groom's resources preclude a dowry, his family pays for the wedding. If the man's side is unable to provide a feast, there may be quiet negotiations in which the bride's family provide some cash. But the more face-saving solution is to have the couple elope.

7   Kuwait was an exception, but residence requirements precluded foreigners' entry into labor unions.

References

Alexander, S. 1990: "Women, Class and Sexual Differences in the 1830s and 1840s: Some Reflections on the Writing of a Feminist History." In T. Lovell (ed.), *British Feminist Thought*. Oxford: Blackwell, 28–50.

Anzaldua, G. 1987: *Borderlands: The New Mestiza = La Frontera*. San Francisco: Spinsters/ Aunt Lute.

Arcinas, F. R. n.d. (ca. 1983): *Asian Migrant Workers to the Gulf Region: The Philippine Case*. Quezon City: University of the Philippines, Department of Social Sciences.

Arcinas, F. R., Banzon-Bautista, C., and David, R. S. 1986: *The Odyssey of the Filipino Migrant Workers to the Gulf Region*. Quezon City: University of the Philippines, Department of Social Sciences.

Buaken, M. 1948: *I Have Lived with the American People*. Caldwell, ID: Caxton Printers.

Bulosan, C. n.d.: *America is in the Heart*. New York: Harcourt, Brace and Co.

Coronil, F. and Skurski, J. 1991: "Dismembering and Remembering the Nation: The Semantics of Political Violence in Venezuela." *Comparative Studies in Society and History* 33 (2), 288–337.

De los Reyes y Florentino, I. 1888: *Articulos Varios Sobre Etnografia, Historia y Costumbres de Filipinas*. Manila: J. A. Ramos.

Eickelman, D. F. 1989: *The Middle East: An Anthropological Approach*. Englewood Cliffs, NJ: Prentice Hall.

Ellison, K. 1988: *Imelda*. New York: McGraw Hill.

Enloe, C. 1989: *Bananas, Beaches and Bases: Making Feminist Sense of International Politics*. Berkeley: University of California Press.

Foronda, M. and Foronda, J. A. 1972: "The Establishment of the First Missionary Centers in Ilocos, 1572–1612." In M. Foronda and J. A. Foronda (eds.), *Samtoy: Essays on Iloko History and Culture*. Manila: United Publishing, 1–65.

Gomez-Pena, G. 1991: *"1991," a Performance Piece*. University of California, Berkeley, November 8.

Guzman, A. de 1985: "Filipino Labour Outmigration: A Preliminary Analysis." *Kasarinlan* 1 (1), 11–20.

Lagmay, L. A. 1983: *Cruz-na-Ligas: Early Socialisation in an Urbanising Community*. Quezon City: University of the Philippine Press.

Lipietz, A. 1986: "New Tendencies in the International Division of Labor: Regimes of Accumulation and Modes of Regulation." In A. Scott and M. Storper (eds.), *Production, Work and Territory*. Boston: Allen and Unwin, 16–39.

Ong, A. 1987: *Spirits of Resistance and Capitalist Discipline: Factory Women in Malaysia*. Albany: State University of New York Press.

Ong, A. 1990: "Japanese Factories, Malay Workers: Class and Sexual Metaphors in West Malaysia." In J. M. Atkinson and S. Errington (eds.), *Power and Difference: Gender in Island Southeast Asia*. Stanford, CA: Stanford University Press, 385–422.

Ong, A. 1991: "The Gender and Labor Politics of Postmodernity." *Annual Review of Anthropology* 20, 279–309.

Owen, R. 1985: *Migrant Workers in the Gulf*. London: Minority Rights Groups.

Rafael, V. 1988: *Contracting Colonialism*. Ithaca, NY: Cornell University Press.

Siegel, J. T. 1969: *The Rope of God*. Berkeley: University of California Press.

Unamuno, M. de 1959: *Andanzas y Visiones Espanolas*. Madrid: Espana-Calpe.

Wood, J. E. ca. 1929–31: *James Earl Wood Papers*. Berkeley: Bancroft Library, University of California.

Zialcita, F. N. 1989: *Nations of Justice*. Quezon City: Atenio de Manila University Press.

18 Learning to be Local in Belize: Global Systems of Common Difference

Richard Wilk

[. . .]

This essay could be read as another account of commodification, of the production of national culture, and the progressive penetration of global commodities into every crevice of daily life, turning even the beauty of the human body into an image to be bought and sold. But this is far from my intention; in fact my ultimate goal is to subvert this now traditional narrative and challenge some of the basic oppositions that it depends upon: indigenous and imported, authentic and false, local and global.

The intent is to suggest some ways to move beyond the polarities of global hegemony and local appropriation. I argue that in the process of absorbing the beauty pageants into a local context, Belizeans have also been absorbed into global *contest*. By asserting their distinctiveness and difference through this medium, they have entered what I call a "structure of common difference," creating one of Appadurai's "global localities" (1990). [This essay deals] with the complex interplay *between* local context and global content, rather than arguing for the primacy of one over the other.

As I define it, the global stage does not consist of common content, a lexicon of goods or knowledge. Instead it is a common set of formats and structures that mediate between cultures; something more than a flow of things, or of the meanings attached to things, or even the channels along which those things and meanings flow. As in Friedman's concept of "hard globalization," the connections between localities are created by widespread and common forms of contest for the exercise of power over *what* to produce, consume, watch, read, and write.

Excerpted from Richard Wilk, "Learning to be Local in Belize: Global Systems of Difference." In D. Miller (ed.), *Worlds Apart: Modernity through the Prism of the Local* (London: Routledge, 1995), 110–33.

These contests follow channels that put diversity in a common frame, and scale it along a limited number of dimensions, celebrating some kinds of difference and submerging others.

The Local in the Global in Belize

Belize, independent from Britain since 1981, has a tiny but diverse population – fewer than 200,000 people who speak more than six languages. Today the country is increasingly cosmopolitan. The economy is open to foreign capital, the stores full of imports. Belizeans themselves are transnational – their families scattered across the United States and the Caribbean, with most of the young expecting to spend parts of their lives abroad. Those at home are bombarded by foreign media – there are nine stations broadcasting a steady diet of American and Mexican satellite TV, and one can hook up to full-service cable systems in every town with more than a thousand people. When Belizeans turn off the TV they can look out the window at a parade of foreign tourists, resident expatriates, and students in search of authentic local experience, traditional medicine, untouched rainforests, and ancient ruins.

The paradox is that amidst all this transnational influence, Belize's national and ethnic cultures have never been so strong or so distinct. In fact, until foreign cultural influence became so pervasive, most people denied that such a thing as "Belizean culture" existed at all. When I began to work in Belize in the early 1970s, people carefully explained to me that the numerically dominant African-European group, the descendants of slaves and their masters collectively labeled "Creoles," had no culture of their own. They were "really" British or Caribbean. The predominantly Spanish-speaking rural communities were "just Mestizos," the same people as neighboring Guatemalans or Mexicans. The only people in the country who were generally acknowledged to have culture were marginalized minority immigrants – Mayans, Hindus, Lebanese, Chinese, Garifuna, and Mennonites.

When I asked about "Belizean food," I was met with blank stares or nervous laughter, or a patient explanation that there was no such thing. "Creole food" was a term of embarrassment; like the local English-Creole dialect, it was considered a "broken" and imperfect version of the metropolitan English standard. By definition, cooking was the preparation of European and American dishes with imported ingredients, a skill that required sophistication and training. As an honored guest from the north, I was usually treated to something from a can (Wilk 1992).

In those days when I looked for Belizean gifts for my friends in the US, there were simply no distinctive or emblematic objects one could take home to prove that one had been to a place called "Belize." Only stamps, coins, and bottles of "local" Belikin beer (brewed next to the Belize City airport by an American, in a Canadian brewery using Dutch malt concentrate and English bottles). Belize was an ethnographic blank. While *I* found something there quite special and distinctive, there were no public symbols, no public discussions about that distinction.

About the only other people who seemed to believe in something called

"Belizean culture" were politicians, especially in the nationalist Peoples United Party, which had engaged in some fitful cultural decolonization projects after achieving internal self-government in 1964. Black woolen coats and ties were banned as official garb, and a plain Guayabera dubbed a "Belize Jack," or a neutral safari suit were briefly in vogue. The party leader and first Prime Minister George Price gave speeches about the need to develop a Belizean culture that would bring together the country's diverse ethnic groups, sometimes hinting at American-style syncretism, but more recently favoring the pluralist metaphor of the stewpot over the blender (Judd 1989).

But the content of this national culture was never specified, beyond that it was to be a unique blend of the best of the Caribbean and Latin American.[1] Starting in 1975, local intellectuals and public servants tried to fill the void by staging an annual cultural festival, modeled explicitly on the Jamaican "Carifesta." But through the 1970s and early 1980s, "Belizean culture" was still the project of a small minority – in the countryside it was still an oxymoron.

Today all of this has dramatically changed. Belize is awash with emblematic local goods – woodcrafts, hot pepper sauces, dolls, and dresses. There is a literally booming local music industry, boasting its own "Punta Rock," now internationally marketed. A Belizean cuisine has appeared, first in expatriate Belizean restaurants in New York and Los Angeles, then in the form of a "Belizean Dish of the Day" at tourist hotels. Belizean cookbooks were produced by the Peace Corps, and today almost every eatery which isn't Chinese is advertising "authentic Belizean food." There is a touring national dance troupe, a national theater movement, a new historical society that is designating landmarks and choosing national heroes. Art galleries feature oils of village life by Belizean artists, Belizean poetry flourishes.

This furious rate of cultural production is not just a preoccupation of an educated or economic elite. When I conducted a large-scale survey in 1990, reproducing the format of Bourdieu's *Distinction*, I found that a majority in all ethnic, occupational, and income groups believe there is a national culture, and are proud of it. In ranking their favorite music, food, home decorations, and entertainment, they consistently placed local products above foreign imports. Even as actual consumption of imports of all kinds has increased dramatically, as frozen and packaged foods from the United States have entered every home, pride in emblematic local products has risen too (Wilk 1990, 1991).

This is not to say that Belizeans in any way agree about the content or meaning of their national culture. Controversy and political contest over the cultural content and effects of local and foreign television, sports, music, arts, dance, food, money, drugs, and migration are intense. But "culture" has emerged as a legitimate topic, as an objectified matter of debate and dispute in everything from political campaigns to the wildly popular radio call-in programs.[2] There is now a daily program of "cultural music" on Radio Belize, "cultural dance" graces most public events, and shops feature cabinets of "cultural goods." [. . .]

The emergence of an objectified national culture in Belize is a clear example of what Friedman calls "the production of local difference on a global scale" and his description raises important questions about the status of the local within the global. First is the issue of whether or not this production of local culture is something new, radical, and transforming; the symptom, sign, or substance of a new cultural world order, creolized, commodified, and transnational. A second and related question asks how these objectified and politicized phenomena relate to everyday social practice in a place like Belize – do they merely overlay other, more immediate forms of lived identity that preserve the local in the form of habitus? Do the public and objectified forms parasitize practice, sucking away its power and substance to leave only a shell? Or is it the everyday world of lived practice that absorbs, organizes, and co-opts the public rhetoric of group identity, domesticating the national into a stable and continuous regime of localized meaning and small-scale social groups? [. . .]

While anthropology has long surpassed an equation of objects or customs with culture, this conception is still at the core of the popular imagination in most modern states. The emerging "folk model" of national culture in Belize identifies foreign words, ideas, and goods as evidence of cultural intrusion, threatening a parallel loss of authentic local culture. People in every social category accept and lament the Belizean taste for imported goods (even as they raise their voice over the sound of country and western music on their stereos), and only disagree over the degree to which resistance is possible or desirable. They interpret consumption in a context of foreign domination and local resistance, as external modernizing forces standing against long-standing local practice, the major cause of recent cultural changes. Like the French (on both left and right) who resisted the importation of Coca-Cola in the 1950s, Belizeans thereby implicitly accept a concept of culture as a limited taxonomic corpus which can change through substitution (Coke replaces wine), not through expansion (adding new categories of beverages alongside wine) (Kuisel 1993). The most benign possibility is dilution of the national essence.

Anthropologists also often implicitly accept this model of culture, when we try to make the opposite point; that global media or goods are effectively localized and incorporated into local cultural lexicons. (The literature on the different ways that the TV program *Dallas* has been locally interpreted is a good example of this tendency [Liebes and Katz 1990].) If we follow this logic far enough, we can lull ourselves into thinking that the global spread of goods and culture is nothing new, that each culture will just absorb global culture and recontextualize it. And there have been a number of excellent recent anthropological studies of how foreign and international ideas and objects are effectively localized – incorporated into local systems of meaning and value, in the contexts of long-standing local structures of power. This is what James Carrier has called the "It's All Right, They've Appropriated It" school of thought (personal communication, 1993).

In this way a focus on commodities and goods, on the specific content of consumption, can lead us right back to the time-worn theme of domination and resistance, of hegemony and the localized struggle for autonomy.[3] Historical evidence shows on the contrary that the content of Caribbean culture has been thoroughly globalized for hundreds of years, that the foreign and the local have long been deployed in a stable regime of competition (for thorough discussion see Olwig 1993). They are part of a semiotic landscape in which people have pursued a variety of strategies, without challenging the underlying order. Below

I will sketch something of this order, and then go on to suggest some of the ways in which it is changing, as the local drama is increasingly played out on a truly global stage, constituted through *structures of common difference*. [. . .]

What integrates the constant flow of imports and permits something Belizean to continue to emerge? Surely it is not the meanings or valences of the objects themselves; I have seen dreadlocks change from a generally recognized symptom of the lowest outcast street-life, to an emblem of the educated and politically conscious pan-Caribbean, and then into a sign of middle-class teenage rebellion, all in less than five years. The coherence lies in the circuits, in the connections forged not by common agreement, but by a common system for communicating difference, a shared political and moral contest, in which all Belizeans take part (elsewhere I have likened this to a common *drama* [Wilk 1991]). A central problem of interpreting the role of imported and local goods in this drama is confusing contest (agreement on the terms of conflict, on what is at stake) with consensus (agreement on substance, on what goods mean). Belizeans themselves rarely make this mistake – they are quite aware that goods and styles are deployed strategically, and that public display is a persuasive assertion, not a fact (and there are pertinent local proverbs that make this point).

I now want to move on to suggest some ways in which the arena of cultural contest in Belize is undergoing structural change. Until the last decade Belize could be seen as a relatively stable arena; while goods, language, fashion, and capital flowed in and out quite freely, they were effectively naturalized and localized in the context of structures of common difference, of which the drama of respectability and reputation is only one. The props, sets, and costumes changed, but the players and the dramatic themes did not. What is happening now, however, is that the boundaries that previously defined the local Belizean stage are breaking down. The Belizean arena is losing its autonomy, as it is incorporated into *global* structures of common difference.

Global Structures of Common Difference

In several important papers, Jonathan Friedman has discussed a variety of ways that local cultural systems have interacted with hegemonic Western modernism in a "global arena of potential identity formation" (1992: 837). He equates hegemony and homogeneity, and sees the recent increase in the number and vitality of local cultural phenomena as a product of the breakdown of that pervasively powerful modernism. The master narrative is passing, and so are the subaltern dialogues with which it was engaged.

I would argue, instead, that the nature of cultural hegemony may be changing, but it is hardly disappearing, and the consequence is not dehomogenization or global fragmentation. The new global cultural system *promotes difference* instead of suppressing it, but difference of a particular kind. Its hegemony is not of content, but of form. Global structures organize diversity, rather than replicating uniformity (to paraphrase Hannerz 1990 and Appadurai 1990). [. . .]

In other words, we are not all becoming the same, but we are portraying, dramatizing, and communicating our differences to each other in ways that are more widely intelligible. The globalizing hegemony is to be found in *structures of common difference*, which celebrate particular kinds of diversity while submerging, deflating, or suppressing others. The global system is a common code, but its purpose is not common identification; it is the expression of distinctions, boundaries, and disjunctures. The "local," "ethnic," and the "national" cannot therefore be seen as opposed to or resisting global culture, but instead, insofar as they can be domesticated and categorized, they are essential constitutive *parts* of global culture. [. . .]

I want to emphasize that my argument for the expression of locality through a system of common difference is not an attack on the *authenticity* of those differences. The typical postmodern critique of commoditization of culture on the global stage argues that all local cultures are becoming equally inauthentic, distanced, and incoherent, as images become disconnected from experience (see Featherstone 1991: 122–8). In sharp contrast, I see a world where very real and "authentic" differences in experience and culture continue to exist, but are being expressed and communicated in a limited and narrow range of images, channels, and contests. Furthermore, people have very good reasons to want to express themselves in this way.

Structures of common difference are built through processes of commoditization and objectification that do produce an appearance of artificiality and homogeneity. They are especially powerful because they often act directly on the human body, promoting particular kinds of uniformity and regimentation. But people still infuse commodities, goods, and their own refashioned bodies with meaning grounded in local practice, to their own ends, and the result cannot be pushed to extremes of global hegemony and/or arbitrary artificiality. [. . .]

Beauty Pageants in Belize

In the 1930s and 1940s the "variety show" was a popular entertainment in Belize, with singing, dancing, monologues, skits, and comedy from local amateurs and visiting professionals. This was a middle- and working-class entertainment, distinct from the sacred and classical concerts, poetry recitals, and Shakespearean dramas staged by the elite to "enlighten" the populace. Beauty pageants took on the format of the variety show, but also blended elements of the street display of the annual September festivities, which are the local equivalent of the *carnival* celebrated elsewhere in the Caribbean. The pageant also amalgamated some elements of the poetry, essay, and cooking contests promoted by schools and churches throughout the 1920s and 1930s. Pageants therefore blended elements of rituals of respectability and reputation, of high and street cultures, though there was no question that respectability remained dominant. A sexual gaze is focused on the bodies of young women in a way that speaks directly to the values of reputation, but the stage performance stresses talents, education, patriotism, and other respectable values.[4]

The emergence of beauty pageants as a popular entertainment has deep roots in local politics, particularly the local responses to the economic stagnation of the British empire in the late 1930s and 1940s. When nationalist, labor-union, populist, and anti-British movements began to grow, members of the urban middle class, who dominated the civil service, reacted by forming the "Loyal and Patriotic Order of the Baymen" (LPOB) in 1945. Organized by neighborhoods into "lodges" modeled on existing fraternal and Masonic organizations, the LPOB's main public activity revolved around the annual celebration of the battle of St. George's Cay on September 10. While the nationalists and trade unionists argued that the British were dominating and exploiting the country, the LPOB stressed their pride in being British subjects. The battle of St. George's Cay dramatized the unity of British Hondurans with the British, for this heavily mythologized eighteenth-century event was supposedly a time when Baymen (as the local white inhabitants were then known), slaves, and British troops stood "shoulder to shoulder" to drive back a Spanish fleet. [. . .]

The Queen of the Bay was added to the celebration in 1946 at the instigation of several older women in the LPOB. They conceived of the contest as something which would bring the lodges together, and add respectability and a reminder of royal leadership to the celebrations. [. . .]

Each lodge selected a candidate at a meeting of its membership. A week before the celebrations, the pageant was held as part of a dance to an orchestra. The girls would march on stage to patriotic music. One organizer told me that the contest was judged "not much for beauty, light skin or curly hair, it was just for dignity." Three judges would ask them questions about colonial history and the battle, and they would recite patriotic verse. "It was to try to enlighten them. The queen must be dignified! The answer would have to be intelligent. Not like today with bath suit!" Nevertheless, the first queen of the Bay *was* white skinned with straight hair. [. . .]

The LPOB strategy was to fight the *political* issue of independence and self-government, within the *cultural* arena of respectability, education, and "taste." Their strategy equated the foreign with the upper-class British and thereby with respectability; the local could not be a source of culture in these terms. For some participants there was an underlying and unspoken goal of continuing the privileged position of a small, educated middle class in a stagnant and marginal local economy. But for many the issue was one of "uplifting" the masses with a respectable spectacle.

The need for public affirmation of respectability grew from the increasing popularity of the populist and anti-British "People's Committee," which held unruly mass street demonstrations in favor of independence and against West Indian union and the devaluation of the Belize dollar (Shoman 1987). [. . .]

The People's Committee, prevented from direct economic or political action through harsh libel and labor laws, was forced to attack the colonial order in its symbolic heart. In 1950 their supporters attended the tenth celebration, but wore the Committee's colors of blue and white instead of the Union Jack. They refused to participate in the celebration of the Battle of St. George's Cay, and publicly questioned whether the battle had ever really occurred. They popularized the use of the term "Belizean" (instead of British Honduran) and objected to the symbolic merging of the local to the British in such practices as marching under the Union Jack and singing "God Save the King." Early meetings of the People's Committee were held under the flag of the United States (meant to signal independence from the British) and were accompanied by singing "God Bless America." The political party that emerged from this movement quickly created its own flag and song, and never gave up its opposition to the celebration of the battle (Judd 1989).

Division and Replication of Pageants

Under the loyalist LPOB, the extension of Queen of the Bay pageants into the countryside began to play a role in nation building. In 1946 all of the contestants came from Belize City, but in 1949 some contestants came from LPOB chapters in the districts, and the winner was from the mostly Hispanic Cayo district. In 1949 most district capitals, and some small villages elected their own queens, who served in local festivities, but in 1950 a hierarchical structure was built. The district queens went to Belize City for a final competition called "The National Beauty Pageant." The complexities of ethnicity, class, and politics were now partly submerged under a theme of competition between districts.

The pageants were an important method of fund-raising and publicity for the loyalists, who contested their first city council elections as the National Party in 1950. In the same year the People's Committee became the People's United Party (PUP), and the colonial governor responded to their demonstrations by declaring a state of emergency, and eventually jailed most of its leaders for sedition. Amidst this turmoil, as the British rewrote the colonial constitution, with its leaders in jail, the People's United Party plotted not a revolution, but a beauty pageant – "Miss British Honduras." The PUP committees in each district selected contestants, who were presented in local meetings that were notable more for their lack of British trappings than for the presence of anything local (American styles and popular songs were prominent). Significantly, the winner's prize was a trip to Guatemala, a strong statement of the PUP's policy of seeking closer ties with its Hispanic neighbors.[5] The National Party's Queen of the Bay went to Miami (no winner ever took the more expensive trip to England, where few Belizeans live).

This dual structure of Belizean pageantry is still very much alive. The two major political parties each conduct their own annual pageant, organized as a contest between representatives of the six districts and Belize City. The final contest is held in the city, and the winner becomes a focus of each party's separate September festivities. The content of the pageants symbolically mirrors the political programs of the two parties. The rightist United Democratic Party (the descendant of the National Party) stresses high culture, deportment, marching, grace, and "refined beauty," accompanied by more respectable forms of European band music. The populist and now mutedly leftist PUP pageant emphasizes talent, sexually nuanced speech and dancing, and ethnic culture, to the tunes of the latest popular American and Caribbean music.

Changes in national politics have affected the pageants. In 1964 the PUP changed their winner's title to "Miss Independence." The National Party then took control of the Queen of the Bay pageant out of the hands of the LPOB lodges and made it more overtly political. Both pageants began to accept contestants nominated by interest groups within the political parties (unions, youth groups, women's associations). And when the PUP began its long electoral dominance in the 1954 elections (they were not defeated until 1984), their party pageant became the official "national" event, while the Queen of the Bay was often ignored by the government's publications and radio.

When an Africanist "black power" movement, inspired by US models, began in the late 1960s, their group held a "Miss Afro Honduras" pageant. The front page of the *Belize Times* in 1969 had pictures of Miss Independence in a miniskirt, the Queen of the Bay in a formal gown, and Miss Afro Honduras in African-style cloth. There was also an ethnic proliferation of pageantry. The Garifuna, historically discriminated against in the colony, have a long history of forming associations based on ethnicity which celebrate "Settlement Day" each November 19 in Belize. As early as 1946 they held a coronation of the "Queen of the Settlement," and by the 1970s had a national "Miss Garifuna" contest with contestants from each Garifuna town and village. The Hispanic northern districts have "Miss Panamericana" crowned on Columbus Day, who travels to Yucatan on the Mexican pageant circuit.

Pageants of an explicitly nonpolitical and non-ethnic nature have also proliferated in splendid abundance. Secondary schools, church associations, and youth groups around the country hold "popularity contests" to raise money, and their winners often enter other pageants. Industrial associations sponsor the "Sugar Queen," "Citrus Queen," and "Miss Agriculture" competitions at district and national agricultural shows and fairs. The annual Easter bicycle races are graced by "Miss Cycling." Larger merchants and corporations sponsor contestants in most of these pageants, blending political and commercial patronage.

The most recent trend is to broaden the appeal of pageants through age segmentation. In 1985 the Minister of Youth and Culture promoted a Miss Youth pageant, which drew contestants from five other countries in the Caribbean. During 1989 there were local and national Miss Teen and Miss Preteen Belize competitions, and a variety of Ms Elegant, Ms Middle Age, and Ms Maturity pageants for older women. All were staged by private promoters as money-making ventures. One organizer told me she planned a "Miss Big and Beautiful" pageant for "larger" women.

On one level this proliferation of pageants may appear divisive; each interest group selects its own symbol to represent separate aspirations. But while the winners differ in complexion, ethnicity, party affiliation, class, employment, and region, the common format of the pageant is an underlying unifying structure. The pageants try to domesticate (in the sense of tame and control) and encapsulate the many differences between citizens within a single dramatic theme.

The International Connection

The international development of pageantry in the years after World War II was a global phenomenon, which quickly took a hierarchical form (see Deford 1971). The first moves were for regional pageants: in 1947 a representative of the "Miss Caribbean" pageant was soliciting a "Miss British Honduras" entry (*Billboard*,

September 15, 1946). The local groups did not have the money to send a contestant, however. As a poor and isolated colony, Belize was not equipped to enter the "pageant of nations" in the immediate postwar years.

Instead the international connections that emerged were a product of the rapid upswing in migration from Belize to the United States in the early 1950s. Belizean migrants, a tiny minority within the polyglot of Caribbean immigrants in New York, Los Angeles, and Chicago, began to organize national associations with an interest in politics and education back at home, tending to favor the loyalist National Party. One way they maintained their distinctiveness in the United States, *and* maintained cultural ties with the home country, was to hold concerts, dances, parades, and festivities which were modeled on those of Belize. They also held beauty pageants, and the winner's prize was usually a trip back to Belize to appear in the September festivities (ironically, in Belize the winners usually got tickets to the United States!). As early as 1957 the Queen of the Bay pageant in Belize City was attended by the "Queen of the Belize Honduran Association of New York."

It was not until the early 1970s (when British Honduras was renamed Belize by the PUP) that Belize had the resources to send entries to the major international pageants. Both political parties, at times, have put resources into local franchises for Miss World or Miss Universe, and some of the wealthiest foreign companies involved in the Belize economy have been patrons. By 1988 Miss Belize or another local contestant were going to both pageants, as well as to regional events (La Reina del Costa, Miss Caribbean USA) and smaller global competitions like Miss All Nations and Miss Wonderland.

The professionalization of the international pageants now requires coaches, consultants, and accouterments which are so costly that Belizean contestants find it hard to compete. Many Belizeans still remember the name of the only Miss Belize to survive into the final group of twelve in the Miss Universe pageant, in 1979. Despite these handicaps, attending the international competition is both an incentive for the local contestants and an assertion of sovereignty at the same level as other countries. The local organizer of the Miss Universe pageant said it concisely: "To show we *can* compete with the rest of the world." But that competition also highlights the subordinate position of Belize in a global hierarchy. [. . .]

In many interviews with organizers and contestants, I heard the same explanation of why Belizean contestants cannot win an international competition. They say that Belizeans have different standards of beauty from those of the global pageants. As one organizer said,

> The [international] judges like tall, thin and beautiful girls. In Belize they like girls who are shorter – here 5 feet 6 inches is tall – and stockier. To qualify for Belizean men, you must have some shape, you must have bust and hips. It's something completely different. If you choose a girl for the international competition the Belizean men will say "E too maaga" [she's too thin]. Bones alone, not enough *flesh*. But them [foreign] judges will look at the Belizean girl and say "E too fat."

Part of the drama of the contest, then, is the collision between local standards of beauty, deeply embedded in cultural constructs of gender and sexuality, and international standards which are widely believed to be those of the dominant white nations of the north.

The widespread awareness of this difference is the crucial link between the local scene and the global drama. While Belizean pageants are full of local, contextualized meaning, they are performed and observed with an intimate awareness of the global gaze. Foreigners do not even have to be present to watch the local competition (though they are often included on the panel of judges), because the global standard has become an ever present (and perhaps internalized) "significant other" by which the local is defined and judged.

The Local Pageant of Difference

The organizers and sponsors of the pageants see them as events that unite the nation in diversity – following the official pluralist line of the state that each ethnic group contributes something to a unique mix. As Miss Teen Belmopan 1990 put it: "Even though we all a different race, Belize da one place." The pageants attempt to organize and domesticate differences between Belizeans, by an appeal to objective standards of beauty and talent, and they provide a common code for the expression of differences.

Contestants often dress in fancied regional or ethnic costumes, perform "ethnic" dances or sing "ethnic" songs, and may themselves be considered official representatives of particular groups (though this is by no means universal). But as each pageant progresses towards the semi-finals, the ethnic themes are dropped and national unification takes over. Speeches, songs, and discussion focus on Belizean culture and nationalism. In the semi-final interviews, contestants are usually asked questions about the country, and how they will represent the whole nation.

In 1990 the aspiring Miss Belize candidates were asked "What would you as a Belizean, selling your country to tourists, tell them about Belize?" The responses mentioned the democratic government, the harmony among diverse people, and the natural environment's touristic attractions. "Belize is rich in natural beauty and we should be proud of it." "Belize is peaceful and democratic." "Belize is truly a paradise." "Belize is a curious colorful mixture of cultures such as the Maya, the Mestizo, Garifuna, Creole, Lebanese and East Indians. I am proud to be part of this mixture." These questions, and the answers they elicit, are meant to place Belize publicly in the foreigner's gaze; they project Belize outwards as a unique place, in the common descriptive terms of all the unique places that make up a global pageant.

This presentation of ethnic diversity in the context of the pageant cordons off a potentially dangerous and divisive issue by placing it in the "safe zone" of expressive culture – music, art, dance, and "customs" (see Wilk and Chapin 1990; Wilk 1986). Ethnicity is officially sanctioned and is even supported by a government "Director of Culture," as long as it remains focused on self-consciously artistic performance. Safe ethnic culture is ornamental, attractive to tourists, part of an international genre of "our nation's wonderful diversity"; it is mostly disengaged from the concerns with land, labor, and rights which predominate in ethnic discourse at the community level. It almost goes without saying that such performances are recent products of cultural professionals, and have only a mimetic (or parasitic) relationship to the everyday practice of music and dance.

Recent history shows the Belizean government is unsupportive or hostile towards ethnic expressions of a political, economic, or territorial nature. Ethnic organizations which assert legal rights, or which try to organize labor or economic cooperation are gently or violently repressed, or are co-opted with offers of support for "safe" projects. When the Maya in the southern districts formed an organization to press for land rights in 1984, the government response was to offer them money and equipment for videotaping their ritual dances (Wilk and Chapin 1990). Keeping ethnic diversity a safe and nonviolent issue is certainly a laudable goal; but in the long run it does not address the underlying disparities and discrimination that feed ethnic politics. This is not to say that the safe zone of ethnic culture is superfluous or cosmetic, merely that it is a limited arena that organizes political discourse into fairly narrow and common terms. [. . .]

[. . .] Like other global competitions, beauty pageantry is hierarchical; it moves upwards towards standards that are defined at the center, not the periphery. On the global stage the fact remains that most winners of national pageants who will go on to international competition are indeed light skinned and tall – they appear to conform more to the New York standard of beauty than that of Belize City. Can we see this as another form of colonialism, as the percolation downwards of a more powerful and superordinate set of standards and ideals, the cutting edge of cultural hegemony? Will this pressure, in the long term, lead Belizeans to change their own ideas and values and accept the subordination of their local standards to the global and foreign?[6]

But Belizeans have been under exactly the same kind of pressure for hundreds of years; their whole conception of the local has emerged, first under slavery, then in stark class stratification, in the context of a superordinate global empire. For 350 years the people of Belize have been confronted with standards of beauty and value that purport to be superior. These standards *have* percolated downwards and all Belizeans are aware of them – they believe that light skin and straight hair are prettier; and they often disparage each other as "black pots" and "bushy." But this does not mean that other conceptions of beauty do not flourish as well, that a person cannot be both ugly by one standard and beautiful by another at the same time, to the same person. Many Belizean men and women say that a woman with a full head of brightly colored hair curlers is sexy and attractive – an aesthetic that certainly does not come from American television. Many other examples abound, and these are not vestiges of some isolated past system, the remnants of an earlier autonomous aesthetic. They have grown and developed in concert with, in close relationship to the externalized, powerful, and global white images in newspaper advertisements, Bibles, television shows, and children's dolls (cf. Lundgren 1988).

A key point here is not that the pageants and competitions eliminate differences between the local and the global. They are not hegemonic tools that create homogeneity. All they do is provide a common channel and a point of focus for the debate and expression of differences. They take the full universe of possible contrasts between nations, groups, locales, factions, families, political parties, and economic classes, and they systematically narrow our gaze to *particular kinds* of difference. They organize and focus debate, and in the process of foregrounding particular kinds of difference, they submerge and obscure others by pushing them into the background. They standardize a vocabulary for describing difference, and provide a syntax for its expression, to produce a common frame of organized distinction, in the process making wildly disparate groups of people intelligible to each other. They essentialize some kinds of differences as ethnic, physical and immutable, and portray them as measurable and scalable characteristics, washing them with the legitimacy of objectivity. And they use these distinctions to draw systemic connections between disparate parts of the world system.

I would argue that in accomplishing these tasks, competitions serve political and polemic purposes for many different and contending interests. They are not hegemonic in the sense that they allow one group to simply extend and exercise its power over others. They never manage to purvey true "false consciousness" and conceal underlying differences in power and resources. (Belizeans remain quite aware that their country is tiny, poor, and dominated.) The competitions are hegemonic only in the way they involve disparate groups in a common contest, and thereby limit their ranges of possible action.

And a place like Belize has *never* had very much range for autonomous action; not under British colonialism and not under Cold War discipline. But the growth of a global order of communication and of systems of common difference forces us to think about autonomy and dependency in very different ways. The same processes that destroy autonomy are now creating new sorts of communities, new kinds of locality and identity. The kinds of hierarchical, linked structures that I describe in this essay create communities of fans and contestants that are very real, and are no more imaginary than the lineages and tribes that anthropologists have traditionally studied.

Notes

1   The question of how much would be Latin has continued to be controversial and politically charged, especially in recent years as immigration and emigration have made the once-dominant Creoles into a numerical minority.
2   Following Friedman's recent discussion of Ainu and Hawaiian identities (1990), we have to be careful not to portray this new Belizean culture as a kind of inauthentic pretense. It demonstrates instead that identity requires a significant "other" (Friedman 1990: 321), in this case provided mostly by the United States, and that it emerges in particular historical forms and circumstances.
3   Austin (1983) points out, in a perceptive review of Caribbean ethnography, a number of reasons why foreign domination and local resistance are inadequate terms for the historical analysis of cultural complexity in this region.
4   The crowds who attend Belizean pageants (both men and women in about equal proportions) judge the contestants on a variety of counts. They tend to appreciate women who "have spirit" – who are outgoing, well spoken, and engage the crowd in

some direct way. Women focus on the contestants' costume, grooming, and manners, on how current their fashion and where it was obtained, while men's comments revolve around the woman's reputations and performances as well as their physiques. As at many of the Caribbean public performances described by Abrahams (1983), when the stage projects respectability, the audience subverts and challenges their message. The crowd delights in gossip about contestants already being pregnant, having highly placed lovers or sponsors who expect more than a good stage performance.

5 The PUP sought an alliance of working-class Creoles with Hispanics, but were constantly accused by the Nationalist Party of "trying to turn Belize into a Hispanic republic." One frequent charge against the PUP leader, George Price, repeated to this day, was that he sought to "sell out" the country with a secret plan to become part of Guatemala.

6 It is clear that one of the things that makes beauty pageants so attractive to Belizean audiences is the way they allow a familiar play of reputation and respectability, of the overt and covert, of political power and faction. Does this mean that the foreign form has simply been localized and appropriated into long-standing patterns? I think not; it may have started as a relatively simple tool of local political conflict, but in the long run it has played a role in transforming the local scene (I do not mean to imply that it is the only, or even the major source of such transformations [see Wilk 1993]).

References

Abrahams, R. 1983: *The Man-of-Words in the West Indies*. Baltimore: Johns Hopkins University Press.

Appadurai, A. 1990: "Disjuncture and Difference in the Global Cultural Economy." *Theory and Society* 7, 295–310.

Austin, D. 1983: "Culture and Ideology in the English-speaking Caribbean: A View from Jamaica." *American Ethnologist* 10 (2), 223–40.

Deford, F. 1971: *There She Is: The Life and Times of Miss America*. New York: Viking.

Featherstone, M. 1991: *Consumer Culture and Postmodernism*. London: Sage Publications.

Friedman, J. 1990: "Being in the World: Globalisation and Localisation." *Theory, Culture and Society* 7, 311–28.

Friedman, J. 1992: "The Past in the Future: History and the Politics of Identity." *American Anthropologist* 94 (4), 837–59.

Hannerz, U. 1990: "Cosmopolitans and Locals in World Culture." *Theory, Culture and Society* 7, 237–51.

Judd, K. 1989: "Who Will Define Us? Creole History and Identity in Belize." Paper presented at the Annual Meeting of the American Anthropological Association, Washington DC.

Kuisel, R. 1993: *Seducing the French: The Dilemma of Americanisation*. Berkeley, CA: University of California Press.

Liebes, T. and Katz, E. 1990: *The Export of Meaning: Cross-cultural Reading of Dallas*. New York: Oxford University Press.

Lundgren, N. 1988: "'When I Grow Up I Want to be a TransAm': Children in Belize Talk about Themselves and the Impact of the World Capitalist System." *Dialectical Anthropology* 13, 269–76.

Olwig, K. F. 1993: *Global Culture, Island Identity*. Chur, Switzerland: Harwood.

Shoman, A. 1987: *Party Politics in Belize, 1950–1986*. Benque Viejo, Belize: Cubola Press.

Wilk, R. 1986: "Mayan Ethnicity in Belize." *Cultural Survival Quarterly* 10 (2), 73–8.

Wilk, R. 1990: "Consumer Goods as Dialogue about Development: Research in Progress in Belize." *Culture and History* 7, 79–100.

Wilk, R. 1991: "Consumer Goods, Cultural Imperialism and Underdevelopment in Belize." In *Spear Report* No. 6. Third Annual Studies on Belize Conference, Belize City.

Wilk, R. 1992: "I Would be Proud to be a Belizean – if I Could Figure Out What Belizean Is." Paper presented at Conference "Defining the National," Lund, April.

Wilk, R. 1993: "'It is Destroying a Whole Generation': Television and Moral Discourse in Belize." *Visual Anthropology* 5, 229–44.

Wilk, R. and Chapin, M. 1990: *Ethnic Minorities in Belize: Mopan, Kekchi and Garifuna.* Monograph No. 1, Society for the Promotion of Education and Research, Belize City.

Part VI

Place and Space

Introduction

In debates about the local and the global, place and place-based practices have been marginalized, despite the fact that place is essential for thinking about alternative constructions of politics, knowledge, and identity (Dirlik 1998). The readings selected for this section reflect on this in a variety of ways. Kevin McIntyre looks at how the development policies implemented by the Khmer Rouge under Pol Pot in Cambodia were based on an inversion of the ideas of Western thinkers studied by the Khmer leadership in their youth in France. Disenchanted with the effects of urbanization generated by French colonialism, Pol Pot inverted the economic development models of Marxism, in a desire to recreate a "pure" rural society based on collective peasant forms. This also reverses the Orientalist discourse of the city as symbol of modernity and the countryside as repository of the past. Year Zero was a radical attempt at a new beginning, not only ideologically, but in terms of the spatial organization of Cambodia.

Space and place works somewhat differently in Uma Narayan's account of how she came to a feminist sensibility. She recounts her upbringing in India, to refute the accusations made by Indian nationalists and many Western feminists that Third World feminists are simply copies of their Western counterparts. Narayan uses her own story to describe how Indian feminism is homegrown.

The three readings from Arturo Escobar, Mamoun Fandy, and Diane Nelson take up place and space within the context of the information technology revolution, globalization, and the cultural politics of identity and resistance. Escobar considers the extent to which global technologies of communication enable local knowledges to redefine and reconstruct the world. He sees the possibilities of networking offered by the Internet as such an opportunity. However, he argues that global networking is only effective if it is combined with place-based practices.

Fandy's analysis of the opposition movement in Saudi Arabia presents an unusual and interesting case of the impact of globalization on a country which is regarded by many outsiders as traditional, and which sees itself "as a country at the forefront of the global struggle against Western corruption." Fandy describes how groups that oppose the Saudi government have utilized the new information technologies to air their grievances, disseminate information, and propagate their own perspectives. The Internet has not only provided a virtual space for groups which the state can contest but finds impossible to control, it has also shifted the Saudi political struggle to London, where the resistance leaders are exiled, and from where both pro- and anti-government newspapers and magazines are published. In this sense, the world opens up for some Saudis who are part of the Internet and globalization. At the same time, the resistance movement employs cassette tapes and fax machines so that radical Islamic messages from neighboring countries are heard even by the poor, illiterate sections of Saudi society. In this way, a new global/local relationship is established through which oppositional groups can influence agenda setting in the news media.

The study by Nelson is an example not so much of political resistance, but of how the power of identity in the global informational society can be mobilized even by those groups who are marginalized from the centers of power. She looks at how Mayan intellectuals have extended the definition of Mayan identity to include "modern Mayans" who speak Spanish, are educated and live in cities. This challenges the dominant Mestizo definition, which cast Mayan identity as traditional, backward, rural, and illiterate in Spanish.

Reference

Dirlik, A. 1998: "Globalism and the Politics of Place." *Development* 41 (2), 7–13.

19 Geography as Destiny: Cities, Villages, and Khmer Rouge Orientalism

Kevin McIntyre

[. . .] Upon taking power in April 1975, the Khmer Rouge emptied the cities and towns of Cambodia, initiating a three-year regime of terror that leveled the country economically, culturally, and physically. In this typhoon of tragedy, nearly two million people died, swept aside in a whirlwind of social upheaval.[1]

The evacuation of the cities and towns was neither accidental nor hastily construed. It was a critical link in a moral campaign whose imperative, in the words of Radio Phnom Penh, was "cleaning up and eliminating the filth of the rotten old society."[2] It fit a pattern of prior Khmer Rouge behavior and had antecedents in the student days of the leaders of the party. In short, it was intrinsic to the Khmer Rouge's strategy for transforming Cambodian society; and it came to reflect in numerous, overlapping ways the Khmer Rouge belief that a person's status was determined by where they lived, that geography was destiny. [. . .]

Emptying the Cities and Towns

The decision by the Khmer Rouge to evacuate the cities and towns was a far-reaching one. Begun almost immediately after the fall of Phnom Penh, the regime's campaign had sent between two and three million people to the countryside by the time it was completed.[3] The Khmer Rouge offered several tactical reasons. Cadre who entered the city first told Phnom Penh residents that they feared possible American bombings. On the surface, this was plausible. Toward the end of the Vietnam War, the United States had engaged in an extensive campaign of carpet bombing in Cambodia. The bombings had wide

Excerpted from Kevin McIntyre, "Geography as Destiny: Cities, Villages, and Khmer Rouge Orientalism." *Comparative Studies in Society and History*, 38, 4 (1996), 730–58.

effects, destroying villages, killing peasants, and damaging the countryside.[4] The Khmer Rouge may have genuinely believed the United States would bomb larger areas of Cambodia after the fall of the Lon Nol government. Another reason offered was the fear of food shortages. In an interview with *Newsweek* magazine, Ieng Sary, deputy prime minister for Foreign Affairs in Democratic Kampuchea (DK), argued that his nation did not have the means to transport sufficient food to the number of people living in the capital, many of whom had fled there as refugees from the civil war.[5] The Khmer Rouge had a strong aversion toward accepting humanitarian assistance because the country, Sary claimed, might lose its dignity and independence. Combined, these propelled the Khmer Rouge to push the people into the countryside as a means of finding their own food. This was also a plausible explanation. The country's agricultural production had been seriously affected by the war, and reports of starvation in Phnom Penh had surfaced by the time that the city fell to the Khmer Rouge. A third reason suggested by Sary (and later by Pol Pot) concerned security: The new Cambodian leaders expected the US Central Intelligence Agency (CIA) and remnants of the Lon Nol army to engage in subversive and counter-revolutionary activities against the new regime. Lon Nol's army was not only planning to attack the Khmer Rouge with weapons that they had hidden in the cities but also to attempt to corrupt the Khmer Rouge soldiers and destroy their fighting spirit with three "evils" of the city: women, alcohol, and money.[6]

Analysts of the Khmer Rouge years have offered further explanations. According to David Chandler, the Khmer Rouge lacked experience in administering cities during the war. When they came to power, the Khmer Rouge found that running large urban areas such as Phnom Penh was a daunting exercise.[7] [. . .]

Yet several aspects of the Cambodian civil war and Khmer Rouge practice confound this image of rational decisions to emergency conditions. Despite the much-expressed concern about the need to feed the populace, Phnom Penh had enough rice to last at least thirty to sixty days.[8] DK's actions during its first two years did not match its public statements. The government did not use the harvests of 1975 and 1976 to feed Cambodians. Instead, it exported large amounts of rice to China as repayment for Chinese aid, thus contributing to widespread starvation in Cambodia after 1976. Although the potential for subversion by the CIA and Lon Nol's former soldiers may have been true for Phnom Penh, it was not valid in other areas.[9]

Evacuating Phnom Penh and the remaining provincial towns under Republican rule, such as Battambang, was not a snap decision. It was formally made at a February 1975 meeting of the central committee of the Communist Party of Kampuchea (CPK).[10] But the party had planned the capital's evacuation even before this official sanctioning. [. . .]

In September 1973, the Khmer Rouge overtook a large section of the town of Kompong Cham. Upon withdrawing, they took with them 15,000 townspeople.[11] In March 1974, Khmer Rouge soldiers captured Oudong, formerly the royal capital. They evacuated the population of 20,000, executed the schoolteachers and government officials, and demolished the town, burning and tearing down buildings.[12] Other towns evacuated by the Khmer Rouge in 1973–4 included Kratie, Kompong Trach, Ang Tasom, and Kompong Kdei.[13]

Overcoming Contradictions

[. . .] Understanding these actions requires a look at important theoretical and ideological influences on the party. The Communist Party of Kampuchea developed out of the Khmer People's Revolutionary Party (KPRP), allegedly founded on September 30, 1951. The KPRP's initial membership was drawn largely from the ranks of the Indochinese Communist Party (ICP). Founding members of the KPRP had shared in the anticolonial struggle against the French through their involvement in the nationalist Issarak movement. At a secret party congress in Phnom Penh in September 1960, attendees reorganized the party, changed its name to the Workers' Party of Kampuchea (WPK), and elected Tou Samouth as secretary-general. Elected as deputy secretary-general was Saloth Sar, later to be known as Pol Pot.[14]

Saloth Sar became secretary-general of the WPK in February 1963, following the disappearance of Tou Samouth the previous July. In July 1963, Saloth Sar and most of the party central committee left Phnom Penh to establish headquarters in the province of Kompong Cham. Two years later, Saloth Sar visited Hanoi and Beijing for an extended period. While in Beijing, he is believed to have undergone formal training. Following his return, in September 1966 the WPK renamed itself the Communist Party of Kampuchea[. . . .] As a political doctrine, Maoism synthesized nationalism and Marxism, creating a syncretic mix that posed a major alternative to the Marxism–Leninism of the day. Fundamental to each of these theories, however, was an ongoing, historical tension between town and countryside.

Marx believed that human consciousness was formed out of people's producing their material means of subsistence. A division of labor developed and progressively extended, separating mental from material labor and people from the products of their work. As this division of labor progressed, it led "to the separation of industrial and commercial from agricultural labor, and hence to the separation of town and country and to the conflict of their interests."[15] The division of labor varied under different modes of production, but the cleavage between town and country represented the penultimate separation: "The foundation of every division of labor which has attained a certain degree of development, and has been brought about by the exchange of commodities, is the separation of town from country. *One might well say that the whole economic history of society is summed up in the movement of this antithesis.*"[16] The capitalist mode of production emerged through the rise of commercial towns, concentration of capital, specialization of industries, and growth of a laboring class from the surplus rural population. For Marx, capitalism necessarily represented the triumph of the town over the countryside. [. . .]

That the first socialist revolution succeeded in Russia, a country largely rural and not capitalist, did not erase the importance of the town winning out over the countryside. Lenin, then Stalin each shared a strong belief that Russia's countryside was backward and that the town was crucial to achieving socialism. Lenin argued that the town's exploitation of the countryside followed social laws of development. This domination "(economically, politically, intellectually, and in all other respects) is a universal and inevitable thing in all countries where there is commodity production and capitalism, including Russia: only sentimental romanticists can bewail this."[17] Lenin's approach on the issue, combined with Stalin's industrialization policies, cemented the conception that cities represented modernizing forces in contrast to the stagnating and regressive countryside. For decades, the Soviet Union implemented an industrial policy bent on using the state to extract, through agricultural production in the countryside, the capital necessary for urban development. In a turnabout of socialist development, the Soviet approach exacerbated rather than eliminated the distinction between town and country.[18]

Significantly different conditions in China led to a major rethinking of several of these notions. Unlike Marxist parties in countries with strong, indigenous industrial bases, the Chinese Communist Party (CCP) saw capitalist industry as alien, brought to China by foreign powers and primarily situated in treaty ports where there was significant colonial influence. The Chinese revolution became a struggle not only against capitalism but imperialism. Maoism departed from Marxism–Leninism in fundamental ways. Modern capitalist industry was neither historically necessary nor socialism's prerequisite. Industrial proletarians were not necessarily the progressive force for a socialist future. Historical laws of development no longer applied. In their place stood a firm conviction in the "consciousness and the moral potentialities of men as the decisive factor in sociohistorical development," a moralism that would be brought to bear through the party's economic and cultural campaigns over the years.[19] For the CCP, which came to power in 1949, the primary conflicts were not between the bourgeois and feudal classes or between the bourgeoisie and proletariat in the urban areas but between landlords and peasants.[20]

The focus on peasant struggle and the emphasis on the foreign element of capitalism provided new dimensions to the town–countryside dichotomy. Urban areas were no longer the modern, revolutionary influence that Marx had imagined but sites of foreign domination. The city was equated with alien influences, the countryside with the true nation. Marx's maxim of urban dominance was inverted. Now the countryside needed to overcome the city. These themes were exemplified in the Great Leap Forward of the late 1950s, a campaign the Khmer Rouge would emulate after 1975.

The Great Leap Forward has been described by David Bachman as the CCP's attempt, over a two-year period, "to implement a communist utopia in China . . . energized by the belief that through one titanic effort everything could be transformed at once."[21] Initiated in the Fall of 1957, the Great Leap Forward was publicly announced in May 1958. It paired economic with cultural transformation. The government created communes of thousands of peasant households in order to mobilize their labor. The communes "were not just agricultural units but also industrial, governmental, educational, cultural, and military organizations."[22] People were encouraged to write poetry. The communes undertook efforts to promote literacy. The government implemented communal living and eating for peasants. Peasants were assigned to work in production brigades organized by age and sex rather than family or kinship ties. Millions of city people were sent to the countryside to work. Agricultural programs emphasized the building of canals and dams. Indigenous technologies were favored instead of imported ones.[23] The country was called upon to manufacture steel in small backyard steel mills. The government established huge increases in production quotas while continually increasing the targets. The communes were expected to eliminate the dichotomies of mental and manual labor, urban and rural living. A patchwork of policies, the Great Leap Forward lasted through 1959 and resulted in numerous agricultural and industrial disasters. Never officially discontinued, the campaign caused the death of between 14 and 43 million people due to starvation or disease.[24]

The Paris Context

Six thousand miles away, a Khmer student attending the University of Paris was preparing his doctoral dissertation. Khieu Samphan had arrived in Paris in 1955 to work on his doctorate in economics in the University's Department of Law. There he met several other Khmer students who would later become instrumental in the Khmer Rouge. These included Saloth Sar, Ieng Sary, Son Sen, Hou Yuon, Hu Nim, Khieu Thirith, Khieu Ponnary, Thiouun Prasith, and Mey Man. While studying, Samphan joined the Union of Khmer Students in France, becoming its leader after Son Sen and Ieng Sary returned to Cambodia, in 1956 and 1957, respectively.[25]

In 1950, a few of the Cambodian students had formed the Marxist Circle, a study group affiliated with the French Communist Party (PCF) as the Khmer-language section.[26] [. . .] The French intellectual and political milieu into which Khieu Samphan stepped was marked by significant developments, especially for the left. Postwar communist politics were highly turbulent and often profoundly confusing. [. . .] The PCF, strongly Stalinist under the leadership of Maurice Thorez, yanked itself between widely varying positions. The Cold War set in during 1947; and, with the establishment of the Cominform, the PCF (which had previously been following a policy of a parliamentary road to socialism) was called upon to take a hard line against the Atlantic alliance between the United States and Western Europe. [. . .]

French colonial relations during the period reflected much of the decade's turmoil. The country was defeated by the Viet Minh at Dien Bien Phu in May 1954. [. . .] And by 1958, the Algerian War, which broke out in 1954, brought the PCF's longtime wavering on the question of Algerian independence to a head. A committee of public safety composed of French army officers and settlers seized power in Algeria in May, threatening to take control in Paris through civil war. The crisis was averted when de Gaulle offered to lead the nation and was elected Prime Minister by the Parliament. In August the Algerian National Liberation Front (FLN) launched military operations in France. The next month, French voters overwhelmingly approved a new constitution in a popular referendum, ending the Fourth Republic.[27] Thorez sought to distance the PCF from the independence movement. He declared to the PCF Central Committee in October 1958 that the electoral needs of the PCF came before a military struggle for Algerian independence. By so doing, according to

François Fejtö, Thorez enunciated clearly the view that "in their struggle for national emancipation, Communists or national movements of the countries of the old Empire had to subordinate their tactics to the requirements of domestic politics at home."[28]

The Chinese Communist Party opposed this position. It viewed the communist parties in capitalist countries as having a primary responsibility to support the independence movements and socialist revolutions of Third World countries. This was one of several differences that emerged between the CCP, the CPSU, the PCF, and other national parties in the last half of the 1950s.

Remaking Cambodia

In this heady Parisian atmosphere, Khieu Samphan wrote his dissertation, "Cambodia's Economy and Industrial Development," presenting it to a faculty jury in 1959.[29] Samphan delineated four theses. First, Cambodia's economy was backward, locked into feudal and precapitalist modes of production. Second, this resulted from its integration with the more advanced French economy and the unequal and unfair free trade that characterized the relationship between the two. Third, Cambodia could escape its stasis only through autonomous development and withdrawal from the international market. Finally, structural reform must confront the dichotomy between the "productive" countryside and the "unproductive" city.

Cambodia's economy, Samphan argued, was predominantly precapitalist. The agricultural sector consisted mainly of peasant family production in rice paddy and on chamcar. Production on the rice paddies served mainly the subsistence needs of peasants. It was small-scale and feudal, resembling "the family agriculture practiced in medieval Europe."[30] Chamcar production, in which fruits and other foodstuffs were grown in areas often close to riverbeds, was geared toward selling on the local market. It had the capacity to develop into genuine capitalist business. Rubber plantations were the only true capitalist agriculture in Cambodia, since they were capital intensive and hired salaried labor.

Cambodian industry was a collection of family workshops and local factories that also harked back to an early, precapitalist Europe. This indigenous industry included handicraft workshops that made jewelry, housewares, blankets, noodles, soy sauce, and the like; factories that manufactured brick, fish sauce, cigarettes, and pottery, wove silk or refined sugar; a few water and electricity plants, some forges and foundries, and ricemills and rice alcohol distilleries. The country's industry did not meet the needs of the people nor of Khmer society's development. It was therefore "weak and unstable."[31]

The Cambodian economy was not an autonomous, integrated, national whole. It depended on foreign companies in advanced capitalist countries. Multinational companies owned the few capitalist firms that operated in the country. Indigenous Cambodian industry and crafts relied completely on foreign companies for their supply of raw and semi-processed materials. Cambodia's backwardness derived from its integration into the international (and especially the French) economy. To make this case, Samphan relied on two fundamental ideas: that

Europe was the model against which to analyze the Cambodian economy and that essential differences existed in how two relatively equal countries integrated in the market versus how unequal countries integrated. [. . .]

Samphan posited that Cambodia's integration into the international market through French colonialism perpetuated its precapitalist structures. The local market was overwhelmed with cheaper, imported goods. The crafts industries could not compete, and the sector declined. The development of light industry dramatically slowed. Instead of accentuating the social division of labor – creating more artisans who would eventually be transformed into salaried workers as Cambodian capitalism developed – French colonialism forced a "retreat to a subsistence economy."[32] Peasants came to rely on crafts industries as secondary activities, which cemented the bonds between crafts and agriculture and reinforced feudal modes of production.[33] [. . .]

This state of affairs caused Samphan to declare that "the Khmer economy is still just as it was at the time of Angkor."[34] The solution, he asserted, was to reorient Cambodia's economy from export production to internal development. Cambodia should withdraw from integration in the international market and emphasize autonomy.[35] Samphan proposed significant changes in three areas: foreign relations and trade, the financial system, and the structure of production in the city and the countryside.

Foreign relations figured prominently in Samphan's analysis. He rejected the advice of United Nations analysts who urged Third World countries to promote autonomous development and structural reform while strengthening international integration. He recommended instead that Cambodia end free trade with all countries. The state would establish a monopoly over major export commodities, including rice, rubber, and corn. Foreign aid would be accepted only if it did not result in political and economic subjugation. Foreign capital investment would be allowed only when the state could redirect demand from purchasing imports to local goods and when the value of profits exported could be significantly limited. Cambodia would seek ways to increase its exports to other countries but only after stabilizing its balance of trade and building up its internal production capacity.[36]

Samphan saw great potential for the financial system to serve Cambodia's development. Money and credit were "levers [that could] establish and guide development of the national economy."[37] Samphan advocated changes in both monetary and fiscal policy. On the monetary side, he called for severe restrictions on the activities of foreign banks, strict control of exchange by the state, and the creation of a national credit system that would hold the assets of Cambodian businesses.[38] These actions would stop the movement of private capital, eliminate usury and speculative investment, direct investment from unproductive to productive activities, and permit the state a powerful tool in "effecting needed structural reforms in the city and countryside."[39] On the fiscal side, Samphan argued for price controls, the elimination or reduction of taxes on small producers, the use of in-kind taxes on peasants, and deep cuts in unnecessary and unproductive state expenditures (especially bureaucratic civil administration and defense).[40]

The structural reform of Cambodia underpinned all other recommendations

Samphan made. He predicated this reform on several important assumptions. First, it was necessary to destroy the "ancient precapitalist economic relationships," integrate the country's economy into a national capitalist system, and create an "internal dynamic" that would push reliance on national resources.[41] Second, it was imperative to make rapid changes; allowing them to occur slowly after withdrawal from the international market would amount to "leaping into bankruptcy."[42] Third, throughout this transformation agriculture was to serve industry. Last, obtaining structural reform was not just a technical matter but a political one, too. The state needed to arouse peasants to action through peasant associations and political education because "the effort cannot succeed unless it has the support of the victims of the present situation who are most inclined to stand up for their own interests." [. . .]

Samphan's image of the city undergirded these final proposals. Early in the work, he distinguished between productive and unproductive work. Agriculture, crafts manufacture, and small industry were productive. Commerce, banking, defense, and civilian administration were not; they merely added value to products transferred in the economy.[43] Another type of unproductive work was the tertiary service sector. This included cafés, bars, restaurants, and hotels; housing construction for government officials, foreign business people, diplomats, and local *compradore* capitalists; wholesale-retail trading, boutiques, street peddling and vending; and personal services (such as those provided by household servants, pedicab drivers, and cart-pullers). These were "menial" types of work, "disguised unemployment."[44] Productive work was found primarily in the countryside; unproductive work, in the cities. [. . .]

Ordering Disorder: The Urban Archetype

We can thus draw a strong connection, if not a direct line, between the ideas in the dissertation and the later policies of Democratic Kampuchea. As a text, the dissertation informed the world of the Khmer Rouge. How is it then that we should consider the subtext of Khieu Samphan's thought? Edward Said has argued that Orientalism is a way of seeing and knowing the world such that the West comes to dominate, restructure, and have authority over the East.[45] One characteristic of Orientalism is its totalizing nature. It creates essentialized images of the Orient by taking a detail or fact and generalizing it to cover an entire people, country, region, or culture. A fundamental aspect of Orientalism is its view of the modern, historic West set against the ancient, timeless East. Flowing from this, the Occident has an historic mission to update the Orient.

An important yet often overlooked Orientalist discourse centers on the nature of the city and the village. Commenting on nineteenth- and twentieth-century social theory, Ira Katznelson has suggested that major theorists saw the city "as a central arena and symbol of modernity; as the product and locale of such fundamental social processes as state-making and capitalist development; and as the generative locale for the formation of collective identities and collective action."[46] [. . .]

The dichotomy of the city and village formed a web of thought about rational and traditional, modern and primitive, superior and inferior. In so doing, it contributed to and shaped the larger dialogue on the history and role of empire. In theory and practice, at multiple levels, Orientalism exerted itself into geographic space. Western cities displayed the features of the modern Occident against the stagnant Orient. The city came to be an archetype by which the village-based colonies could be remade to join the modern world.

Yet ideas so powerful were not easily contained. Frantz Fanon detected the thread of this Orientalist argument and spiritedly used it in his analyses of colonial relations and decolonization. *Black Skin, White Masks* was widely available and read in the intellectual environment of Paris in the 1950s, where Khieu Samphan wrote his dissertation. In it, Fanon framed a critique of the essential Manicheism in European colonization that made black – and by extension, all colonized – peoples into symbols of evil.[47] He continued the analysis through his writings over the next decade, culminating in the publication in 1961 of *The Wretched of the Earth*, a work that found colonialism's dichotomies extended to a logical conclusion. The native was not only dehumanized but transformed into the negation and enemy of European values and in this sense an "absolute evil."[48] This quintessential representation of the native was preeminently exemplified in the physical and social compartmentalization of colonial towns which separated white settlers from native peoples into reciprocally exclusive areas. The only way to overturn this Manicheism was through a struggle that would eliminate the separation within towns, even towns themselves. Decolonization was "no more and no less . . . the abolition of one zone, its burial in the depths of the earth or its expulsion from the country."[49] And the struggle was best carried out through the cleansing and purifying violence that "evokes for us the searing bullets and bloodstained knives which emanate from it. For if the last shall be first, this will only come to pass after a murderous and decisive struggle between the two protagonists."[50]

Blurring the Lines, Graying the Picture

From the core of Samphan's analysis, several themes finally emerged. Binary opposites all, they laid mental groundwork for what was to come later under Democratic Kampuchea. The dichotomies of modernity–backwardness, rational ordering–irrational confusion, and productive village–unproductive city filled Samphan's dissertation. These same binaries would later come to authorize, in different terms, the four-year plans,[51] broadcasts, teachings, and pronouncements of the Khmer Rouge.

It is ironic that Khieu Samphan wrote in Paris about Cambodia so he could talk about France in order to discuss Cambodia again; yet that is the nature of his internal discourse: Samphan wrote backward in circles. He wrote against his nation, whose recent past showed its failure to live up to his modern ideal. From this etching of Cambodia, he wrote against the colonial power that had failed to bring his backward country into its full flower. Writing in reverse one step further, he wrote against his compatriots who had allowed themselves to be seduced and tarnished by the rapacious power of France.

Khieu Samphan's doctoral dissertation was a great swirling attempt to recapture a past: one of abstract peasants, lifted from the details of their own existence, removed from any semblance of humanity as they might construct it, carved out and placed in a discourse that would fill his ideal; a past of cities, unspoiled by the French presence that had rendered them unproductive and that would have to be rationally reordered. In his renderings, he created mythical peasants, villages, traders, cities: Romantic emblems of a past he would capture in order to destroy it.

Abstract, feudal, backward, stagnant, unproductive: These were the images of Cambodia that formed in Khieu Samphan's mind as he wrote about his homeland halfway across the world. A thorough exploration of the economic challenges facing Cambodia in the late 1950s might have looked at the complexity within villages in the country's encounter with colonialism. It might have considered more fully the change that Cambodian culture had exhibited over time. It might have placed the cities of Cambodia in the context of an interwoven history of interaction with peoples from around Southeast Asia and beyond. For him, the issues were not about the richness of life. The interpolations within Cambodian society would only cloud the picture. [. . .]

Given that Cambodia has not been a well-studied country, we could allow the need for Samphan to generalize to a degree. Yet we could also suppose he would have been chastened by his few findings. That was not the case. Instead of being sobered, Samphan developed a black-and-white image of Cambodia which fit his binary opposites. Two ethnographies, done close to the time Khieu Samphan was writing, blur the lines and make gray the picture of Cambodia that escaped from his dissertation.

May Ebihara is one of the few anthropologists to do field work in Cambodia during the past forty years. She spent a year in 1959–60 in the Khmer village Sobay, thirty kilometers southwest of Phnom Penh.[52] Rather than the image of peasants as abstract beings under the tyranny of village mandarins, Ebihara found that Sobay had no socioeconomic classes. There were differences of wealth between villagers, but these were not significant and did not result in great inequalities of power or lifestyle. Most of the villagers in Sobay owned and cultivated their land. Sobay had no absentee landlords. Tenancy did exist, but the "arrangements were regarded as mutually beneficial, not as exploitative rent extracted by the rich from the poor."[53] Nuclear and extended families were the primary social unit in the village, and bilateral descent was practiced. Bilateral kinship groups had no definite boundaries and, varying in definition between people, appear to have been relatively fluid. Bilateral kinship had a profound effect on rice production: Ebihara discovered that "generations of bilateral inheritance have fragmented the rice paddies into increasingly small parcels."[54] As a result of this fragmentation of the rice paddies, production was generally subsistence-oriented. Sobay was virtually self-sufficient but not self-contained. Villagers, she found, engaged as producers and consumers in national and international trade. Ebihara studied interaction patterns between people in Sobay and other villages, towns, and cities in the region. She found that villagers traveled extensively between all of these, often to visit kin, purchase goods, and attend Buddhist ceremonies. The strict boundaries that might be expected in social interaction between village and city thus became blurred in Ebihara's research.[55]

In 1965 and 1966, Milada Kalab spent ten months in the village, Khum,[56] in Kompong Cham province northeast of Phnom Penh. She discovered several things. First, determining landholding was more complicated than might appear initially. Eighty-three percent of the land in Khum was privately owned. But when she tried to determine the size of plots people owned, Kalab ran into difficulties. People in Khum often owned land outside their village, district, or province. Peasants from other villages frequently had purchased land in Khum. Examining records was made more difficult because of the phonetic Khmer script. Sounds could be written in different ways, and the romanization of the alphabet added to her problems. Yet another factor potentially complicated the task of determining ownership: Kalab found that "half the children of the same parents use their grandfather's name and the others use their father's name as surname."[57] Second, villagers did not need someone guiding their political education (as Khieu Samphan proposed). Elections in Khum were hotly con-tested, and "everybody [read] election manifestoes of parliamentary candi-dates."[58] Third, villagers in Khum were highly mobile and migrated at significant rates. Kalab found that in "Phum [one of the hamlets] between 1961 and 1966 five houses vanished and seventeen new houses appeared. During the same period 46 inhabitants or 20 percent of the population left the village and 94 new persons or 41 percent more appeared."[59] Villagers also were socially mobile. Though most villagers were engaged in agriculture, they often pursued other jobs: teaching, smithing, tailoring, jewelry making, construction, hairdressing, trading, working in the saw mill. People "shift between agriculture and other employment as easily as they move from place to place," Kalab concluded.[60]

Ebihara and Kalab's work point toward a Cambodia resisting the image as Khieu Samphan would frame it. [. . .]

Geography as Destiny

Khieu Samphan and the Khmer Rouge engaged the Orientalist dialogue on city and village but did not shatter the dichotomy. Rather, they accepted its premise while reversing its terms. Creating a counter-image, they constructed a fiction as powerful as the one which came before them. Perhaps if they had refused the Orientalism of French colonialism, the evacuations of cities would have been avoided.

"Enemies fight the cooperatives," an article stated in *Revolutionary Flags*, the Khmer Rouge magazine, in the fall of 1976. But, "if there were no cooperatives, the true revolutionary traits would be gone. The true imperialist traits would come back. Revisionism would come back. There would be markets, there would be cities, confusion. Slavery."[61] If the urban–rural dichotomy grew out of French colonial practice, it found its glory as expressed under Democratic Kampuchea. In the swidden politics of the Khmer Rouge, Phnom Penh – the "great prostitute on the Mekong"[62] – and other cities and towns were slashed and sometimes burned to clear the brush for the new growth of Cambodian society. The urban–

rural opposition was a vital element in the Khmer Rouge pursuit of a permanent war against its internal and external enemies. The social leveling sought by the party took as one of its pillars that geography was indeed destiny, that where one lived determined one's enemy status.

Notes

1   David P. Chandler, "Preface," in May M. Ebihara, Carol A. Mortland, and Judy Ledgerwood (eds.), *Cambodian Culture Since 1975: Homeland and Exile*. (Ithaca, NY: Cornell University Press, 1994), xi. The typhoon metaphor is Chandler's.
2   Radio Phnom Penh, May 14, 1975, quoted in Karl D. Jackson, "The Ideology of Total Revolution," in Karl D. Jackson (ed.), *Cambodia 1975–1978: Rendezvous with Death* (Princeton, NJ: Princeton University Press, 1989), 66.
3   David P. Chandler, *The Tragedy of Cambodian History: Politics, War, and Revolution since 1945* (New Haven, CT: Yale University Press, 1991), 246–7.
4   Ben Kiernan has suggested the bombings, especially from 1973 on, played a major role in radicalizing parts of the Cambodian peasantry during the war, contributing to the brutality that devolved on the "new people" under DK. (Ben Kiernan, *How Pol Pot Came to Power: A History of Communism in Kampuchea, 1930–75* (London: Verso, 1985), 390–1.
5   Ieng Sary, quoted in R. A, Burgler, *The Eyes of the Pineapple: Revolutionary Intellectuals and Terror in Democratic Kampuchea* (Fort Lauderdale, FL: Verlag Beitenbach Publishers, 1990), 70–1.
6   Ibid. Pol Pot's comments on the evacuation of the cities were contained in the press release of a press conference that he conducted in October 1977. Pol Pot acknowledged that the decision to evacuate Phnom Penh was made at a party meeting in February 1975.
7   Chandler, *Tragedy of Cambodian History*, 247.
8   Charles H. Twining, "The Economy," in *Cambodia 1975–1978*, 115.
9   Chandler, *Tragedy of Cambodian History*, 247, 260.
10 Ibid., 247.
11 Kiernan, *How Pol Pot Came to Power*, 371.
12 Ibid., 384–5.
13 Ibid., 390. Kiernan implies the evacuations were related to the potential threat from American aerial bombing. He also notes, however, that they provided further experience for the Khmer Rouge following their ascension to power in Cambodia.
14 Serge Thion, "Chronology of Khmer Communism," in David P. Chandler and Ben Kiernan (eds.), *Revolution and Its Aftermath in Kampuchea: Eight Essays*, Monograph Series, no. 25 (New Haven, CT: Yale University Southeast Asia Studies, 1983), 291–5.
15 Karl Marx and Friedrich Engels, "The German Ideology," in *Karl Marx: Selected Writings*, ed. David McLellan (Oxford: Oxford University Press, 1977), 161.
16 Karl Marx *Capital*, vol.1, trans. Ben Fowkes (New York: Vintage Books, 1977, emphasis added, 472).
17 V. I. Lenin, "A Characteristic of Economic Romanticism," quoted in Maurice Meisner, *Marxism, Maoism and Utopianism: Eight Essays* (Madison: University of Wisconsin Press, 1982), 49.
18 Ibid., 48–52.
19 Ibid., 61.
20 The Chinese Communist Party did not always hold such views. From its formation

in 1921, the party focused on organizing the urban proletariat. For several years it aligned with the Kuomintang whose success, says Barrington Moore, "had been mainly due to its ability to harness and ride the tides of discontent among the peasants and the workers" (Barrington Moore, Jr., *Social Origins of Dictatorship and Democracy: Lord and Peasant in the Making of the Modern World* [Boston: Beacon Press, 1966], 188).

21 David Bachman, *Bureaucracy, Economy, and Leadership in China: The Institutional Origins of the Great Leap Forward* (Cambridge: Cambridge University Press, 1991), 2.

22 Ibid., 4.

23 Roderick MacFarquhar, "The Secret Speeches of Chairman Mao," in Roderick Mac-Farquhar et al. (eds.), *The Secret Speeches of Chairman Mao* (Cambridge, MA: Harvard University Council on East Asian Studies, 1989), 3–18. Kenneth Quinn, "Explaining the Terror," in *Cambodia 1975–1978*, 225.

24 Bachman, *Bureaucracy, Economy, and Leadership in China*, 2.

25 Chandler, *Tragedy of Cambodian History*, 52; Kiernan, *How Pol Pot Came to Power*, 172.

26 Ibid., 119.

27 M. Adereth, *The French Communist Party: A Critical History (1920–84): From Comintern to "The Colours of France"* (Manchester: Manchester University Press, 1984), 166.

28 François Fejtö, *The French Communist Party and the Crisis of International Communism* (Cambridge, MA: MIT Press, 1967), 103. Fejtö's book (especially pages 74–115) and Ronald Tiersky's *French Communism, 1920–1972* (New York: Columbia University Press, 1974), 112–225 provide the basis for much of the preceding discussion on developments in France.

29 His translator, Laura Summers, suggests that Samphan restrained his political analysis. As a Khmer student abroad he was closely watched by the royal government of Cambodia. Also, French intellectuals were deeply divided over events in Europe and Algeria, and the fall of the Fourth Republic. His jury consisted of faculty members from the right and the left. Given this, he was judicious (Laura Summers, "Translator's Introduction," in Khieu Samphan, *Cambodia's Economy and Industrial Development*, trans. Laura Summers. Data Paper, no. 111 [Ithaca, NY: Cornell University Southeast Asia Program, March 1979], 2).

30 Samphan, *Cambodia's Economy and Industrial Development*, 23. Samphan never precisely defined the terms feudal, capitalist, or precapitalist. He often used an inferential approach instead, matching various Cambodian economic forms and behaviors with what he believed were the European equivalents.

31 Ibid., 25, 28.

32 Ibid., 37.

33 Ibid., 30–7.

34 Ibid., 37–41. The Angkorean period in Cambodia lasted from AD 802 to 1431 (David Chandler, *A History of Cambodia*, 2nd ed. [Boulder, CO: Westview Press, 1992], 29).

35 Sampan, *Cambodia's Economy and Industrial Development*, 58, 68.

36 Ibid., 69–82. Samphan was not *per se* against exports but how exporting had developed under French colonialism. He was careful to note that he was not proposing autarky, a complete withdrawal from the international market. In fact, he suggested that Southeast Asian countries coordinate their efforts at industrialization.

37 Ibid., 83.

38 Ibid., 90–3. He defined strict control of exchange as "control which disregards short-term gains that might come along from any sort of foreign capital influx" (ibid., 90).

39 Ibid., 93. The movement of private capital should be stopped since it was impossible for the state to distinguish capital that came into the country for productive investment from that which was used to bolster the liquidity of foreign banks.

40 Ibid., 95–8. Samphan believed that collecting monetary taxes from peasants could "indirectly strengthen ancient structure" by making peasants more reliant for cash on usurers and traders "at a time when overall rural structure remains fundamentally precapitalist" (ibid., 97ff.).

41 Ibid., 75.

42 Ibid., 77.

43 Ibid., 29–30.

44 Ibid., 52–3, 56.

45 Edward Said, *Orientalism* (New York: Vintage Books, 1979), 3.

46 Ira Katznelson, *Marxism and the City* (Oxford: Clarendon Press, 1992), 11.

47 Frantz Fanon, *Black Skin, White Masks*, trans. Charles Lam Markmann (New York: Grove Press, 1967), 183–91.

48 Frantz Fanon, *The Wretched of the Earth*, trans. Constance Farrington (New York: Grove Press, 1963), 34. The precise influence of Fanon on Khieu Samphan and the Khmer Rouge generally is open to some speculation.

49 Ibid., 33.

50 Ibid., 30.

51 The Khmer Rouge prepared at least two four-year plans, one each in 1976 and 1977.

52 May Ebihara, "Intervillage, Intertown, and Village–City Relations in Cambodia," *Annals of the New York Academy of Sciences* 220, 6 (1974), 359. Sobay is a pseudonym for the village where she studied.

53 May Ebihara, "Revolution and Reformulation in Kampuchean Village Culture," in David A. Ablin and Marlowe Hood (eds.), *The Cambodian Agony* (Armonk, NY: M. E. Sharpe, 1987), 17.

54 Ebihara, "Intervillage, Intertown, and Village–City Relations in Cambodia," 359.

55 Ibid., 374–5.

56 Milada Kalab, "Study of a Cambodian Village," *Geographical Journal* 134, 4 (1968), 521. Khum is a pseudonym for the village where she studied.

57 Ibid. If replicated in other areas, this could have important implications for any analysis of landownership in Cambodian society, a key part of Khieu Samphan's dissertation.

58 Ibid., 533.

59 Ibid., 525.

60 Ibid., 527.

61 "Sharpen the Consciousness of the Proletarian Class to be Keen and Strong as Possible," reprinted from *Revolutionary Flags* (September–October 1976), trans. Kem Sos and Timothy Carney, in *Cambodia 1975–1978*, 283.

62 Chandler, *Tragedy of Cambodian History*, 247.

20 Contesting Cultures: Westernization, Respect for Cultures, and Third World Feminists

Uma Narayan

To try to define oneself intellectually and politically as a Third World feminist is not an easy task. It is an unsettled and unsettling identity (as identities in general often are), but it is also an identity that often feels forced to give an account of itself. There is nothing inherently wrong about the project of giving an account of oneself – of one's specific location as speaker and thinker; of the complex experiences and perceptions and sense of life that fuel one's concerns; of the reasons, feelings, and anxieties that texture one's position on an issue; of the values that inform one's considered judgment of things.

Giving such an account of oneself has much to recommend it, for all of us. It enables one to see, with humility, and gratitude, and pain, how much one has been shaped by one's contexts, to sense both the extent and the boundaries of one's vision, to see how circumstances can circumscribe as well as inspire, and to become self-aware to some extent of one's perspectives on things. What is strange, I believe, for many Third World feminists, is the sense that, in our case, such an account is especially called for, *demanded* even, by the sense that others have that we occupy a suspect location, and that our perspectives are suspiciously tainted and problematic products of our "Westernization." Many Third World feminists confront the attitude that our criticisms of our cultures are merely one more incarnation of a colonized consciousness, the views of "privileged native women in whiteface," seeking to attack their "non-Western culture" on the basis of "Western" values. This essay attempts to reveal some of the problems and paradoxes that are embedded in these charges of "Westernization" as well as to understand what provokes them.

I should admit at the outset the peculiarities of my own location. I have grown

Excerpted from Uma Narayan, "Contesting Cultures: Westernization, Respect for Cultures, and Third World Feminists." In *Dislocating Cultures: Identities, Traditions and Third World Feminism* (New York: Routledge, 1997).

up and lived in a variety of places. I was born in India and lived in Bombay until I was eight, when I moved with my family to Uganda. I returned to India when I was fourteen and lived there until I was twenty-five. As is the case with many middle-class Indian children, my formal education was in the English language. For the last dozen years I have lived in the United States, which makes my currently calling myself a Third World feminist problematic, in contrast, say, to feminists who live and function as feminists *entirely* within Third World *national* contexts. Calling myself a "Third World feminist" is problematic only if the term is understood narrowly, to refer exclusively to feminists living and functioning within Third World countries, as it sometimes is. But, like many terms, "Third World feminist" has a number of current usages. Some feminists from communities of color in Western contexts have also applied the term "Third World" to themselves, their communities, and their politics, to call political attention to similarities in the locations of, and problems faced by, their communities and communities in Third World countries. As a feminist of color living in the United States, I continue to be a "Third World feminist" in this broader sense of the term.

In writing this essay, I was caught in a struggle between my political desire to endorse this broader use of the term, and aspects of my project that seemed to indicate the narrower usage. For the most part, I have decided to use the term "Third World feminist" more narrowly in this essay, to refer to feminists who acquired feminist views and engaged in feminist politics in Third World countries, and those who continue to do so, since it is my project to argue that feminist perspectives are not "foreign" to these Third World *national* contexts. Another reason for this choice is that the charge of being "Westernized" or having a "Westernized politics" that concerns me in this essay, is more commonly leveled at feminists within Third World national contexts. While feminists from *some* communities of color in Western contexts, such as feminists from Indian diasporic communities, are sometimes charged with "Westernization," the charges of "inauthenticity" leveled at many Black or Chicana feminists often take the form of asserting that they are embracing a "White" rather than a "Westernized" politics.[1] When confronted with such difficulties about terminology, perhaps the best one can do is to clarify one's use of the terms and give an account of the reasons for one's choices.

I wish to speak as a Third World feminist in this essay for three important reasons. First, having lived the first quarter-century of my life in Third World countries, and having come of age politically in such contexts, a significant part of my sensibilities and political horizons are indelibly shaped by Third World national realities. Second, this essay is an attempt to explicate the ways in which the concerns and analyses of Third World feminists are rooted in and responsive to the problems women face within their national contexts, and to argue that they are not simple-minded emulations of Western feminist political concerns. I need to speak "as an insider" to make my point, even as I attempt to complicate the sense of what it is to inhabit a culture. Finally, though calling myself a Third World feminist is subject to qualification and mediation, it is no more so than many labels one might attach to oneself – no more so than calling myself an Indian, a feminist, or a woman, for that matter, since all these identities are not simple givens but open to complex ways of being inhabited, and do not guarantee many specific experiences or concerns, even as they shape one's life in powerful ways.

I do not "locate myself" or specify who I am because I "*assume* who I am *determines* what and how I know"[2] (italics mine), but rather to point to the complications of saying who I am, and of assuming specific identities as a speaker. I do, however, wish to suggest some *linkages* between the complexities of who I am and what I claim to know. By "linkages," I wish to suggest *weaker* forms of influence or connection than is suggested by the term "determined." I do not simply *assume* such linkages, but attempt to give open account of them, a gesture that both "authoritizes" my speech and opens the nature of this "author-ity" to evaluation and interrogation. To surrender the possibility of any connec-tions between who I am and what I know is, for the purposes of this essay, to surrender my standing to speak as an "insider" to Third World contexts, a standing that many Third World feminists are often denied simply by virtue of their feminism. This is a denial whose legitimacy is precisely that which I wish to question. [. . .]

Many feminists from Third World contexts confront voices that are eager to convert any feminist criticism they make of their culture into a mere symptom of their "lack of respect for their culture," rooted in the "Westernization" that they seem to have caught like a disease. These voices emanate from disparate sources, from family members, and, ironically enough, from other intellectuals whose own political perspectives are indebted to political theories such as Marxism and liberalism that have "Western" origins. This tendency to cast feminism as an aping of "Westernized" political agendas seems commonplace in a number of Third World contexts.[3] For instance, Mary Fainsod Katzenstein points out that while Indian feminist activism has "been of critical importance in eliciting media attention and in shaping a new consciousness around gender violence," it has also provoked criticism that "portrays feminist activism as originating out of a Western, bourgeois, modernist perspective."[4] I shall try to reveal the problematic assumptions that underlie these rhetorical dismissals of Third World feminist voices as rooted in elitist and "Westernized" views, and argue that, for many Third World feminists, our feminist consciousness is not a hot-house bloom grown in the alien atmosphere of "foreign" ideas, but has its roots much closer to home.

My sense of entitlement to contest "my culture" is threaded through with both confidence and doubt. I grew up in a fairly traditional, middle-class, South Indian family, in the urban milieu of Bombay. Besides my parents, both my paternal grandparents also lived in the household, making us what in India is called a "joint family." As the eldest grandchild, and for several years the only child, I was raised with considerable indulgence. And I also remember the boundaries and limits to this indulgence. I remember my mother saying, "What sort of a girl are you to talk back like that to your father?" and my thinking, "But his reprimand was not deserved, and he will not listen to me, and she will not even let me speak."

I remember minding particularly that the injunction to be silent came from my mother, who told me so early, because she had no one else to tell, about her sufferings in her conjugal home. I remember my mother's anger and grief at my father's resort to a silencing "neutrality" that refused to "interfere" in the domestic tyrannies that his mother inflicted on my mother. The same mother who complained about her silencing enjoined me to silence, doing what she had to do, since my failures to conform would translate as her failures to rear me well.

I also remember my mother years later saying, "When I came to Bombay right after I was married, I was so innocent I did not know how to even begin to argue or protest when my mother-in-law harassed me" with a pride and satisfaction that were difficult for me to understand. That "innocence," that silence, indicated she was a good wife, a good daughter-in-law, well brought up, a "good Indian woman," a matter of pride, even to her whose "innocence" had not prevented her from recognizing that what she was being subjected to was wrong, but which had prevented her from explicitly contesting it. And for once choosing to hold my tongue, I did not say, "But mother, you were not entirely silent. You laid it all on me. My earliest memory (you were the one who dated it after I described it to you, and were amazed that I remembered it) is of seeing you cry. I heard all your stories of your misery. The shape your 'silence' took is in part what has incited me to speech."

I am arguing that my eventual feminist contestations of my culture have something to do with the cultural dynamics of the family life that surrounded me as a child, something to do with my early sense of the "politics of home." My grandmother, whom I loved and who was indulgent to me in her own way, tormented my mother, whom I also loved, in several petty and some not so petty ways, using her inventiveness to add color and detail to the stock repertoire of domestic tyrannies available to Indian mothers-in-law. My father, clever and able and knowledgeable in so many other ways, would not "interfere." After all, "our" cultural traditions did not deem it appropriate for a son to reprimand his parents, providing a convenient cultural excuse for my father, despite his having had a "Westernized education" not very different from that which would later be blamed for the intransigence of his daughter! How could my loyalty and respect for "my culture" fail to be tainted by the fact that there was little justice or happiness for my mother in our house?[5]

So it is strange, and perhaps not strange at all, that my mother adds her voice to so many others that blame my being "Westernized" for my feminist contestations of my culture. And I want to remind her, though I cannot bring myself to it, of her pain that surrounded me when I was young, a pain that was earlier than school and "Westernization," a call to rebellion that has a different and more primary root, that was not conceptual or English, but in the mother-tongue. One thing I want to say to all who would dismiss my feminist criticisms of my culture, using my "Westernization" as a lash, is that my mother's pain too has rustled among the pages of all those books I have read that partly constitute my "Westernization," and has crept into all the suitcases I have ever packed for my several exiles.

I would argue that, for many of us, women in different parts of the world, our relationships to our mothers resemble our relationships to the motherlands of the cultures in which we were raised. Both our mothers and our mother-cultures give us all sorts of contradictory messages, encouraging their daughters to be confident, impudent, and self-assertive even as they attempt to instill conformity, decorum, and silence, seemingly oblivious to these contradictions. Thus, both my mother and many others in the specific caste and middle-class Indian context in which I was raised saw education as a good thing for daughters, encouraged us to do well at our studies, saw it as prudent that daughters have the qualifications necessary to support themselves economically, saw it as a good thing that we learned to master tasks in areas of life that had been closed to women of my mother's generation. At the same time, they were critical of the effects of the very things they encouraged. They were nervous about our intoxication with ideas and our insistence on using ideas acquired from books to question social rules and norms of life. They were alarmed at our inclination to see our careers not as something merely instrumentally valuable in the event that our marriages failed but as essential elements of fulfilling lives. They were anxious about the fact that our independence and self-assertiveness seemed to be making us into women who lacked the compliance, deference, and submissiveness deemed essential in good "Indian" wives. [. . .]

[. . . M]y mother insists on seeing my rejection of an arranged marriage, and my general lack of enthusiasm for the institution of marriage as a whole, as a "Westernized" rejection of Indian cultural values. But, in doing so, she forgets how regularly since my childhood she and many other women have complained about the oppressiveness of their marriages in my presence; she forgets how widespread and commonplace the cultural recognition is in India that marriage subjects daughters to difficult life-situations, forgets that my childish misbehaviors were often met with the reprimand, "Wait till you get to your mother-in-law's house. Then you will learn how to behave."

I would thus argue that my sense that marriage is an oppressive institution for many women is something that predates my explicit acquisition of a feminist politics, and is something I initially learned not from books but from Indian women in general, and my female relatives in particular. [. . .] I would argue that seeing the perspectives of feminist daughters simply as symptoms of our "Westernization" and as "rejections of our cultures" fails to perceive how capacious and suffused with contestation cultural contexts are. It fails to see how often the inhabitants of a culture criticize the very institutions they endorse. It fails to acknowledge that Third World feminist critiques are often just one prevailing form of *intracultural* criticism of social institutions.

Many Third World women who do not consider themselves feminists know and acknowledge that women face mistreatment within their social contexts and cultural institutions. [. . .] What may set feminist daughters apart is the ways in which they insist that these differences require us to rethink notions of what it is to "be at home" in a "culture," and to redefine notions of "cultural loyalty, betrayal, and respect" in ways that do not privilege the experiences of men.

[. . .] Re-telling the story of a mother-culture in feminist terms [. . .] is a *political* enterprise. It is an attempt to, publicly and in concert with others, challenge and revise an account that is neither the account of an individual nor an account "of the culture as a whole," but an account of *some* who have power within the culture. It is a political challenge to other political accounts that distort, misrepresent, and often intentionally fail to account for the problems and contributions of many inhabitants of the context. It is a political attempt to tell a counter-story that contests dominant narratives that would claim the entire edifice of "our Culture" and "our Nation" for themselves, converting them into a peculiar form of property, and excluding the voices, concerns, and contributions of many who are members of the national and political community. [. . .]

[. . .] While I wish to make connections between women's experiences in their families and their feminist politics, I do not wish to make these connections simplistic. An awareness of the gender dynamics within one's family and one's "culture," even a critical awareness, does not suffice to make women feminists. Women may be aware of such dynamics but may consider them to be *personal* problems to be dealt with personally, without seeing them as a *systematic* part of the ways in which their family, their "culture," and changing material and social conditions script gender roles and women's lives, or without feeling that they must contest them in more formal, public, and political ways. It takes *political connections* to other women and their experiences, political analyses of women's problems, and attempts to construct political solutions for them, to make women into feminists in any full-blooded sense, as the history of women's movements in various parts of the world shows us.

Many Third World feminist criticisms – say, of the position and treatment of women within their families or of institutions such as dowry – are both influenced by, and bear some resemblance to, criticisms voiced by many nonfeminist women within the culture reflecting upon their life experiences as affected by these institutions. In this respect, many Third World feminist issues are hardly "foreign imports" or "Westernized agendas" imposed by feminists onto contexts where "culturally authentic" nonfeminist women would entirely fail to see what the feminist fuss was about. However, the fact that feminist critical analyses are *political* analyses also works to make them different in important ways from criticisms of the same institutions voiced by women like my mother. Feminist criticisms of problems such as dowry deaths and dowry-related harassment seek to make these issues matters of *general concern and public debate,* while the criticisms voiced by my mother are articulated in more private contexts. Feminist criticisms also differ in their *terms of analysis.*[6] [. . .]

Feminist movements in various parts of the world develop when historical and political circumstances encourage public recognition that many of the norms, institutions, and traditions that structure women's personal and social lives, as well as the impact of new developments and social change, are detrimental to women's wellbeing, and enable political contestations in which the status quo is criticized and alternatives envisioned. Those in Third World contexts who dismiss the politics of feminists in their midst as a symptom of "Westernization" not only fail to consider how these feminists' experiences within their Third World contexts have shaped and informed their politics, but also fail to acknowledge that their feminist analyses are results of political organizing and political mobilization, initiated and sustained by women *within* these Third World contexts.

[. . .] Such activities clearly make feminists and feminism part of the *national political landscape* of many Third World countries.[7] I am arguing that Third World feminism is not a mindless mimicking of "Western agendas" in one clear and simple sense – that, for instance, Indian feminism is clearly a response to issues specifically confronting many *Indian* women.

[. . . I]f there seems to be considerable resemblance [. . .] between the issues addressed by Third World feminists and those addressed by Western feminists, it is a result not of faddish mimicry but of the fact that women's inequality and mistreatment are, unfortunately, ubiquitous features of many "Western" and "non-Western" cultural contexts, even as their manifestations in specific contexts display important differences of detail. Thus, while women in Western contexts might be unfamiliar with the violence against women connected to the contemporary functioning of the institutions of dowry and arranged marriages, they are no strangers to battery and violence prevalent within their own various forms of marriage and family arrangements. [. . .]

Selective Labeling and the Myth of "Continuity"

> The starting-point of critical elaboration is the consciousness of what one really is, and is "knowing thyself" as a product of the historical process to date which has deposited in you an infinity of traces, without leaving an inventory.
>
> Antonio Gramsci[8]

In this section, I would like to shift to exploring some ways in which the sense of "cultural distinctiveness" from "Western culture" that developed in colonial contexts affects the ways in which the term "Westernization" is deployed in contemporary Third World national contexts. [. . .] "Westernization" is often used to define "national culture" in ways that imagine more "cultural continuity" than is in fact the case. National cultures in many parts of the world seem susceptible to seeing themselves as *unchanging continuities* stretching back into a distant past. This picture tends to reinforce powerfully what I think of as the "Idea of Venerability," making people susceptible to the suggestion that practices and institutions are valuable *merely* by virtue of the fact that they are of long-standing. It is a picture of Nation and Culture that stresses continuities of tradition, (often imagined continuities) over assimilation, adaptation, and change.

[. . .] A frequent and noticeable peculiarity in these portrayals of unchanging "national culture, traditions, and values" in Third World contexts is the degree to which there is an *extremely selective* rejection of "Westernization." What interests me is that while *some* incorporations of "Western" artifacts and practices are perceived and castigated as "Westernization," not all are, making some of these borrowings and changes contested and problematic in ways that other changes are not. [. . .]

This "selective labeling" of certain changes and not others as symptoms of "Westernization" enables the portrayal of unwelcome changes as unforgivable betrayals of deep-rooted and constitutive traditions, while welcome changes are seen as merely pragmatic adaptations that are utterly consonant with the "preservation of our culture and values." [. . .]

Both my grandmothers were married at the age of thirteen. This was quite typical for the women of this particular community in that generation. I try not to think about what this meant to them, and above all what it could have meant to me if that particular "tradition" had continued. Like many other women of her generation and class and caste background, my mother was not married until she was twenty-one. How would my grandmothers have explained so significant a change in the space of one generation, a change that, however else it is to be explained, cannot be explained in terms of their daughters' rebellion against the practice of marriage following on the heels of the first indications of puberty?

It is not clear to me how illuminating or intelligible it is to attribute such a change to "Westernization," given *the complex interaction of local and colonial structures* that operated to produce this change. [. . .]

There are difficulties in attempting to characterize changes such as education for Indian women as "Westernization." For one thing, education for *Western* women, especially college and professional education, was a deeply contested issue in the nineteenth century, and bitter struggles around higher education continued to be a part of Western feminist suffrage struggles of the early twentieth century. Thus education for women could hardly be seen as an uncontroversial and longstanding aspect of "Western culture." For another, while Westerners, especially missionaries, were initially crucial causal components in setting up educational institutions for women, the success of these projects also depended on their being embraced and endorsed by segments of the Indian elites. Such endorsements were often couched in nationalist terms that specifically *resisted* seeing educating Indian women as "Westernization," seeing it variously as "making Indian women better wives and mothers," as helping to fulfill the urgent need for women doctors, and even as restoring to women the freedom, equality, and access to education they were believed to have enjoyed in the remote "golden age" of Hinduism. In many colonial and postcolonial contexts, it is difficult to clearly distinguish between the facts of change over time and "changes due to Western influence" since many of these changes involve complex "complicities and resistances" between aspects of "Western culture" and Third World institutions, agents, and political agendas.

I wish to call attention to the fact that these undeniably significant changes in women's access to education and in the age of marriage were not, by my mother's lifetime, seen by my mother's family as a "surrender of our traditions" or as a problematic symptom of "Westernization." The traces of cultural conflict and negotiation that gave rise to them had vanished from view. For large segments of this particular Indian community, college education for its daughters and the correspondingly older age of marriage had, within a generation, become matter-of-fact elements of its "way of life."

[. . .] The forces of "modernization" that prevented my mother from being married at thirteen are, paradoxically, also responsible for the marriages of some contemporary thirteen-year-olds. Take the publicized recent case of Ameena, found sobbing in an Air India plane by an alert flight-attendant, in the company of a sixty-three-year-old Saudi man, who was taking her out of the country as his "wife."[9] Today, there are businesses, paradigms of efficiency, organization, and modern entrepreneurial spirit, where skillful middle-men mediate, for a price, between poor Indian families anxious to marry off their barely teenage daughters and those with the foreign currency to purchase them as "wives": a complex interplay of "tradition" and "modernity," poverty and perversity, that has hundreds of Ameenas sobbing on their way to foreign fates that make my grandmothers' fates seem enviable. [. . .]

Third World feminists, whose political agendas are constantly confronted with charges that they constitute betrayals of "our traditional ways of life," need to be particularly alert to how much relatively *uncontested change* in "ways of life" has taken place. We need to redescribe and challenge this picture of "unchanging traditions" that supposedly are only now in danger of "betrayal" as a result of feminist instigation. Some of these changes, while historically pretty recent, have become *so* "taken for granted" in our lifetimes that I am often amazed to confront the details and the extent of these changes. [. . .]

Not surprisingly, the gender of the actors seems to be one factor that determines whether a particular change is regarded as an example of "Westernization that is disrespectful of our traditions." My paternal grandfather and my father, for example, wore trousers and shirts to work, not "Indian" clothes.[10] I have no idea how this particular transition was initially conceptualized or categorized. Even if it was considered "Westernization" at the start, I do not think that the millions of Indian men who wear shirts and trousers today think of themselves as putting on "Western clothes" as they get dressed. However, the women in my family of my grandmothers' and mother's generations have worn traditional "Indian" dress all their lives, and I am sure that any attempt at a similar "transition" on their part would have been a matter of cultural consternation. [. . .]

[. . .] My point is not that the adoption of "Western" dress functions in similar ways in *all* Third World contexts. Rather, I merely want to use the dress-related examples I give to underscore the fact that, in many instances, men seem to be permitted a greater degree of cultural latitude in making changes than are women, and are less frequently accused of "Westernization." [. . .]

Partha Chatterjee helps make sense of many of the examples I have given when he argues that the project of nineteenth-century Indian nationalism was not a total rejection of the West but rather comprised an "ideological justification for the selective appropriation of Western modernity."[11] This project, he argues, disproportionately conferred on women the task of preserving the "spiritual distinctiveness" of Indian culture, a distinctiveness that was located within the home. Changes that affected women and the domestic realm were thereby rendered more contentious than changes with respect to men in the "outside world." I suspect that the allocation to women of a "special role" in preserving national culture and traditions was fairly commonplace in a number of other Third World nationalist movements, making changes that affect women and family life matters of greater consternation.

I agree with Chatterjee that such selective appropriations of modernity *continue* to be pervasive in many postcolonial Third World contexts, and that women continue to be disproportionately assigned the tasks of "preserving national culture and traditions." I also wish to point out that appropriate "public" roles for women also continue to be reinterpreted, to make some changes, but not others, consonant with "preservation of tradition" at particular times. [. . .]

I do not wish to deny that "cultures" in general are always being contested, and not only by feminists; nor to imply that Third World feminists always have "*the* right take" on their cultures. Feminist critiques in any context, like other intellectual endeavors, might be mistaken in their assumptions, insensitive to context, inadequately attentive to the interests of those who are marginalized and powerless, and so forth. Such flaws, when present, should elicit serious critical dialogue instead of attempts to *dismiss* the views put forward by questioning the "authenticity" of the speaker or by characterizing feminism as a purely "Western" political agenda.

These strategies of dismissal, where political positions are characterized as "alien," as "foreign," as "representing the views of Others," and whereby individuals who endorse these positions are categorized as "betrayers" of their nation or "traitors to their communities," seem fairly ubiquitous and are not only directed at feminists.[12] These strategies of dismissal have also been used against feminists of color in Western contexts, where their perspectives are often dismissed as an espousal of a political agenda that is "white." As Cherrie Moraga points out:

> Over and over again, Chicanas trivialize the women's movement as being merely a white middle-class thing, having little to offer women of color. . . . Interestingly, it is perfectly acceptable among Chicano males to use white theoreticians, e.g. Marx and Engels, to develop a theory of Chicana oppression. It is unacceptable, however, for the Chicana to use white sources by women to develop a theory of Chicana oppression.[13]

I would argue that attempts to dismiss Third World feminist views and politics as "Westernization" should be combated, in part by calling attention to the selective and self-serving deployments of the term, and in part by insisting that our contestations are no less rooted in our experiences within "our cultures," no less "representative" of our complex and changing realities, than the views of our compatriots who do not share our perspectives. Third World feminists urgently need to call attention to the facts of change within their contexts, so that our agendas are not delegitimized by appeals to "unchanging traditions." We need to point to how demands that we be deferential to "our" Culture, Traditions, and Nation have often amounted to demands that we continually defer the articulation of issues affecting women. [. . .]

[. . .] I am not advocating that Third World feminists simplistically invert traditionalist, nationalist, or fundamentalist attempts to convey the message "Change is Bad, Traditions are Good" by insisting that "Traditions are Bad, Change is Good." While some of the changes that have taken place in Third World contexts have arguably improved the lives of women, others have clearly made things worse. In Third World contexts, as elsewhere, changes that improve the lives of *some* women may do little for others, or might affect them adversely. Feminists need to be alert and attentive to all these various possibilities and to encourage widespread and critical dialogue on various aspects of social change. [. . .]

My intention has been to point to a number of assumptions that impede Third World feminist criticisms of their cultures, and to challenge a number of assumptions about "Westernization" that are used to delegitimize such criticisms. However, problematic pictures of "national identity" and "cultural authenticity" do not pose challenges exclusively for Third World feminists. Dangerous visions of "Nation" and "national culture" seem ubiquitous across a range of nation-states in various parts of the world. I would like to end by examining the import of such views of "Nation" and "national culture" for feminist political contestations within Western as well as Third World national contexts.

[. . . I]nstead of locating ourselves as "outsiders within" Third World national contexts, Third World feminists need to challenge the notion that access to "Westernized educations," or our espousal of feminist perspectives, positions us "outside" of our national and cultural contexts. We need to problematize aspects of pictures of "our Culture and Traditions" that are deployed to delegitimize our politics, and to insist that our views be accorded the privilege of substantive criticism rather than be subject to such dismissal. [. . .]

Given the interpenetration of "Western" values and institutions with the national political and cultural landscapes of "home" and the way that "Western" and "local" elements mesh in the geography of our lives, as well as in the lives of those in the Third World who do not share our cultural critiques, I believe many Third World feminists would do better to insist that our voices are neither more or less "representative" of "our cultures" than the voices of many others who speak within our national contexts. [. . .]

We all need to recognize that critical postures do not necessarily render one an "outsider" to what one criticizes, and that it is often precisely one's status as "inside" the nation and culture one criticizes that gives one's criticisms their motivation and urgency. [. . .]

We need to move away from a picture of national and cultural contexts as sealed rooms, impervious to change, with a homogeneous space "inside" them, inhabited by "authentic insiders" who all share a uniform and consistent account of their institutions and values. Third World national and cultural contexts are as pervaded by plurality, dissension, and change, as are their "Western" counterparts. Both are often replete with unreflective and self-congratulatory views of their "culture" and "values" that disempower and marginalize the interests and concerns of many members of the national community, including women. We need to be wary about all ideals of "cultural authenticity" that portray "authenticity" as constituted by lack of criticism and lack of change. [. . .]

Feminists all over the world need to be suspicious of locally prevalent pictures of "national identity" and "national traditions," both because they are used to privilege the views and values of certain parts of the heterogeneous national population, and because they are almost invariably detrimental to the interests and political standing of those who are relatively powerless within the national community. [. . .] If nations are "imagined communities"[14] then bigoted and distorted nationalisms must be fought with feminist attempts to *reinvent* and *reimagine* the national community as more genuinely inclusive and democratic.

Feminists need to insist that *all* visions of "Nation" are constructs of political imagination, even though many of these visions see themselves as describing the "Truth" of some "National Essence." This does not, however, render all competing visions of "Nation" in any particular context morally equivalent, or leave us without ethical and political reasons for supporting some visions over others. We need to recognize that many seeming conflicts over the definition of "National Culture" are in effect political struggles over visions of the national community and over the justice of various national policies. Finally, even as we struggle to invent and endorse more inclusive and equitable visions of our national communities, national boundaries should not define the bounds of feminist imaginations that care about a more equitable and just global and international order. Justice within nations and saner forms of nationalism seem closely connected to our hopes for justice across nations at an international level. [. . .]

Visions of one's nation, one's national history and community, are deeply tied to one's sense of place, to one's sense of belonging to a larger community, to one's sense of heritage and loyalties. [. . .]

[. . .] It is not difficult to understand the seductiveness of conservatism and fundamentalism, and the political nostalgia for mythic national and cultural pasts, in a global period where the shapes and structures of life are changing rapidly all across the world, with attendant dislocations and profound uncertainties. I believe we need to reckon with the fact that, in such periods, critical social theories, including feminisms, that seem to call for even more change will face a difficult and uphill battle. [. . .]

Neither Western feminists nor Third World feminists can simply side-step their complex insertions into national political contexts, but rather they need to be alert to the fact that "the nation cannot be taken for granted."[15] I believe it is time to rethink Virginia Woolf's antinationalist assertion when she wrote in 1936 in *Three Guineas* that, "As a woman I have no country. As a woman I want no country. As a woman my country is the whole world."[16] I would argue to the contrary that, as feminists, we indeed have many countries where the fates of a great many women and men call out for critical political perspectives and action for change. At this historical juncture, I believe that any feminism that simply dismisses the idea of "Nation" and the discourses of Nationalisms as "patriarchal constructs" will only contribute to their remaining dangerously so, marginalizing progressive and feminist voices whose critical political interventions into the discourses of nationalism seems increasingly crucial. [. . .]

To accept that, as feminists, we need to intervene critically in discourses of Nation and Nationalism is not, I would argue, to surrender "the whole world" that Woolf hopes to claim by repudiating nationalism. National contexts, although important sites for feminist struggles, are increasingly just one among others that require our intervention. Increasingly, transnational economic structures adversely affect the lives of many different groups of people scattered over a multiplicity of nation-states, reinforcing structurally asymmetrical linkages between nations, as well as radical inequalities within and across nation-states. [. . .]

[. . .] In short, as feminists we need to attend both to issues within particular nations and to urgent transnational or international issues if we are to achieve greater justice within particular nations, and greater global justice in an increasingly interdependent world.

Notes

1 See, for instance, Barbara Smith, *Home Girls: A Black Feminist Anthology* (New York: Kitchen Table/Women of Color Press, 1983).
2. Christina Crosby further criticizes this assumption for being an assumption that "ontology is the ground of epistemology," "Dealing with Differences," in Judith Butler and Joan W. Scott (eds.), *Feminists Theorize the Political* (New York: Routledge, 1992), 137.
3 See the essays in Valentine M. Moghadam (ed.), *Identity Politics and Women: Cultural Reassertions and Feminisms in International Perspectives* (Boulder, CO: Westview Press, 1994).
4 Mary Fainsod Katzenstein, "Organizing Against Violence: Strategies of the Indian Feminist Movement," *Pacific Affairs* 62, 1 (1989), 69.
5 I have no desire to portray my mother as a perennially passive "victim." I was born within a year of my parents' marriage, so the mother I knew when I was young was a relatively "new" wife. A few years into her marriage, my mother did in fact both implicitly and explicitly contest her mother-in-law's treatment of her, a fairly common pattern. It is interesting to me, however, that the articulate and formidable woman my mother became continued to be "proud" of her earlier "innocence."
6 Uma Narayan, "'Male-Order' Brides: Immigrant Women, Domestic Violence and Immigration Law," *Hypatia* 10, 1 (Winter 1995).
7 As Charlotte Bunch puts it, "Feminism has been ridiculed and stereotyped worldwide, and the issues we have raised have usually not been taken seriously by the media. But, remarkably, despite this bad press, feminism has continued to grow. Women's groups all over the world, but especially in the Third World, are taking up issues ranging from housing, nutrition, and poverty to militarism, sexual and reproductive freedom, and violence against women." See her "Global Feminisms: Going Beyond the Boundaries," speech given in 1985, reprinted in *Frontline Feminism 1975–1995: Essays from Sojourner's First 20 Years* (San Francisco: Aunt Lute Books, 1995), 456.
8 Antonio Gramsci, *Selections from the Prison Notebooks*, trans. Quintin Hoare (London: Lawrence and Wishart, 1971), 324.
9 This case received a lot of attention in the Indian press, and was also the subject of a segment on *60 Minutes* that aired on January 3, 1993.
10 I remember my maternal grandfather in "traditional" South Indian dress. The explanation of this difference might have to do with my paternal grandfather working in Bombay while my maternal grandfather worked in a smaller South Indian town.
11 Partha Chatterjee, "Colonialism, Nationalism, and Colonised Women: The Contest In India," *American Ethnologist* (1989), 624. Also see his *Nationalist Thought and the Colonial World: A Derivative Discourse?* (London: Zed Books, 1986).
12 For example, Aijaz Ahmed points out that "there is a powerful political movement in India which says ... that Indian socialists are not true Indians because Marxism *originated* in Europe; that the Indian state should not be a secular state because secularism is a Western construct," Aijaz Ahmed, "The Politics of Literary Postcoloniality," *Race and Class* 36 (January–March 1995), 5.
13 Cherrie Moraga, "From a Long Line of Vendidas: Chicanas and Feminism," in Anne C. Herman and Abigail J. Stewart (eds.), *Theorizing Feminism: Parallel Trends in the*

Humanities and Social Sciences (Boulder, CO: Westview Press, 1994), 38. Moraga goes on to point out how this strategy is used to equate "lesbians" with "feminists," reinforcing the idea that lesbianism is "a white thing," a strategy that is used to depict Chicana lesbian feminists as doubly "alien" (42). For a discussion of the dismissal of feminism as "white" in the context of the African American community, see Barbara Smith's "Introduction" to *Home Girls*.

14 Benedict Anderson, *Imagined Communities: Reflections on the Origin and Spread of Nationalism*, rev. ed. (London: Verso, 1991).

15 Gayatri Chakravarti Spivak, "French Feminism Revisited," in Butler and Scott (eds.), *Feminists Theorize the Political*, 71.

16 Virginia Woolf, *Three Guineas* (New York: Harcourt, Brace and Company, 1938).

21 Gender, Place, and Networks: A Political Ecology of Cyberculture

Arturo Escobar

Networks, Gender, and the Environment

There is no doubt that "networks" are "in" today in our descriptions of the present and our image of the future. Networks – particularly electronic networks – have become central to the rise of a new type of society (the "network society"), the coproduction of technoscience and society (actor–network theory), and the politics of social transformation ("global networking for change"). Networks are essential to a new type of "virtual-imagined transnational community"; to new political actors, such as Women on the Net (WoN), [. . .] and to the utopia of a democratic, allegedly globalized world. In all of these conceptions, networks are facilitated by electronic and information technologies, particularly the Internet. A good deal of our lives and our hopes now resides in the networks linked to cyberspace.

Networks, however, are only as good as the ensemble of human, natural, and nonhuman elements they bring together and organize. Similarly, they are part of a larger world that might be inimical to their aims. Does the enlargement of opportunities for cultural resistance afforded by some technological networks, for instance, balance out with the narrowing down of real spaces by the forces of a transnational capitalism fueled by the same technologies? Is cyberspace a source of new identities and knowledge of self and the world, as some propose, or rather the medium where a "terminal-citizen," increasingly isolated from the rest of the world and mired in consumption, is being produced at a world scale, as others argue? Is the activism at a distance made possible by cyberspace not

Excerpted from Arturo Escobar, "Gender, Place, and Networks: A Political Ecology of Cyberculture." In W. Harcourt, *Women@Internet: Creating New Cultures in Cyberspace* (London and New York: Zed Books, 1999), 31–55.

counteracted and vastly surpassed by the repressive powers of global technocapitalism?

There are no clear answers to these questions yet. As in earlier periods, our ability to conceptualize the worlds coming into place and to articulate a corresponding politics of transformation leaves much to be desired. Yet there have been significant changes in how we go about it. In some fields, we now seek to derive theory from practical experience, look at everyday life as a source of theoretical insights, and enlist the company of local actors and social movements in their efforts to understand both the world and how we fit into it.

I am invoking here a loose "we" – the we, let us say for now, of gender-aware academics and intellectuals struggling to develop a new politics of expert knowledge in conjunction with the political projects of subaltern groups. I also write this as I think about the activists of the social movement of the Pacific rainforest region of Colombia, with whom I have been working for some years, and who – I believe, and they increasingly know – would benefit greatly from having access to environmental and ethnic resources in Internet and biodiversity networks. I also think about the excitement of a small and progressive NGO for popular communications in Cali, Colombia which has just inaugurated its first Web page, despite the fact that most of its members can hardly follow a discussion in English. And I think about the vast networks of environmentalist and indigenous rights activists whose voices and concerns I encounter daily on the Internet as I research the rapidly changing debates about biodiversity conservation. I have in mind, finally, the growing groups of women traveling in the nets cast by women networkers, or netweavers, particularly in the pre- and post-Beijing climate.

[. . .] I want to make the following argument. Networks – such as women's, environmental, ethnic, and other social movements networks – are the location of new political actors and the source of promising cultural practices and possibilities. It is thus possible to speak of a cultural politics of cyberspace and the production of cybercultures that resist, transform, or present alternatives to the dominant virtual and real worlds. This cybercultural politics can be most effective if it fulfills two conditions: awareness of the dominant worlds that are being created by the same technologies on which the progressive networks rely (including awareness of how power works in the world of transnational networks and flows); and an ongoing tacking back and forth between cyberpolitics (political activism on the Internet) and what I will call place politics, or political activism in the physical locations at which the networker sits and lives.

Women, environmentalists, and social movement activists on the Net are thrown into this double type of activism, with its contrasting demands: over the character of the Internet and new information and communications technologies (ICTs) in general, on one hand; and over the character of the restructuring of the world being effected by new ICTs-led transnational capitalism, on the other. From the corridors of cyberspace can thus be launched a defense of place and place-based ecological and cultural practices which might, in turn, transform the worlds that the dominant networks help to create. Because of their historical attachment to places and the cultural and ecological differences they constitute, women, environmentalists, and social movements in the Third World are particularly suited to this double task. In the end, it might become possible to think about a political ecology of cyberspace that weaves the real and the virtual, gender, environment, and development into a complex political and cultural practice. [. . .]

Flows, Networks, and Real-time Technologies

Networks of various kinds have existed for centuries. What is special about today's networks is not only that they seem to have become the backbone of society and the economy, but that they take on novel features and modes of operation. For some, we are faced with a new type of society – a global network society for Castells (1996); a modern society of long networks and hybrids for Latour (1993); a society under the tyranny of real-time technologies for Virilio (1997); a "virtual-imagined" transnational community for Ribeiro (1998) – precisely because of the novel features networks adopt. The new ICTs are the pivotal element in this profound transformation.[1] It is the rise of a new technological paradigm, and not social, economic, or political changes *per se*, that are driving it. This paradigm began gestation with the development of integrated circuits in the 1950s and microprocessors in the 1970s and has seen a progressive expansion into ever more powerful interacting networks at a global scale. [. . .]

[. . .] As interactive networks continue to expand, there is a growing divorce between spatial proximity and everyday life functions, such as work, entertainment, education, and so forth. Networks foster a new kind of space, the space of flows. Cities become "globally connected and locally disconnected, physically and socially" (Castells 1996: 404). Organized increasingly around flows – of capital, information, technology, images, symbols, etc. – this creates a new type of spatial reality that redefines places. For Castells,

> in this network, no place exists by itself, since the positions are defined by flows. Thus, the network of communication is the fundamental spatial configuration: places do not disappear, but their logic and their meaning become absorbed in the network . . . In some instances, some places may be switched off the network, their disconnection resulting in instant decline, and thus in economic, social and physical deterioration. (Castells 1996: 412–13)

Network or perish, seems to be the motto emerging from this view. [. . .]

To the networked elites belongs the world, culturally connected by new lifestyles and spatially secluded in expensive enclave communities. The impact of this networked space of flows on the space of places is noticeable: segmented from each other, places are less and less able to maintain a shared culture. Real (timeless) time rules in the space of flows, while linear, biological, or socially determined time continues to determine places.

[. . .] Castells's view is questionable precisely because it is derived from a globalocentric perspective, that is, one that finds agency only at the levels at which so-called global actors operate. Yet there is a real novelty to the network society, which arises in great part from the salience of real time. This aspect has been best analyzed recently by Paul Virilio. For this author, the essence of the current transformation is the effect that the new ICTs – operating at the speed of light and under the principle of real time – are having on the regime of time and space that has governed the world until now. Real-time technologies of communication kill the present by "isolating it from its here and now, in favour of a communicative elsewhere that no longer has anything to do with 'our concrete presence' in the world" (Virilio 1997: 10). [. . .]

[. . .] The split between place and time [. . .] is consummated as real-time events detach themselves from the place where they happen. The borders of the near and the distant become blurred, transforming our sense of our experience of the here and now. Embodied, grounded, rooted action loses a great deal of its social importance. Teletopia induces a generalized atopia. Places become newly precarious. Global dimensions are redefined as a consequence. There is an even more radical divide between those who live in the virtual community of real time of the global city, and the "have-nots" who survive in the margins of the real space of local cities, "the great planetary wasteland that in the future brings together the only too real community of those who no longer have a job or a place to live that are likely to promote harmonious and lasting socialization" (Virilio 1997: 71).

Responding to Cyberspatial Technologies

How are we to gauge these visions from the perspective of those who want to use the same technologies for different social and ecological aims? Is it possible for women, social movements, and others to deploy cyberspatial technologies in ways that do not marginalize place? The aims can be contradictory: a feminist goal of creating bonds among women through cyberspace might contribute to the erosion of place by detaching women from their locations. The question then becomes: how can women (1) defend place against the delocalization of globalization that erodes local cultures; (2) transform place(s) away from their patriarchal/domineering practices (since places, like the family and the body, have also operated to incarcerate women and control them; since places have their own forms of domination and even terror); (3) venture into the realm of real-time technologies and worldwide coalitions in search of allies and insights for gender struggles? [. . .]

Said differently, this entails conflicting demands: (1) to maintain the value of rootedness and place; the importance of face-to-face interaction for the creation of cultures; the viability of local times; the organicity of certain relations to the natural; and yet (2) to affirm the transformative potential of places and the need to transform them; finally, (3) to advance both processes through a critical engagement with cyberculture (among other means). To articulate the density of place with the density of information; real-time and local-time activism; tele-elsewheres with embodied and embedded places; hybrid cultures created in cyberspace and local hybrid cultures; etc. – these are other ways of expressing the needs confronting those who want to appropriate critically and creatively the set of new computer, communications, and biological technologies. What kinds of worlds are we in a position to weave?

For Castells and Virilio, places will become delocalized and radically trans-formed under the pressures of real-time networks. But what is really the nature of the networks in question? If it is true that networks redefine places, are not places nevertheless essential to their working? These are some of the questions Bruno Latour tries to answer in a provocative work on networks and modern culture. In Latour's view, what separates modern cultures from the rest is that they are based on a "double divide," between nature and society, and between "us" and "them." These divides, however, are largely spurious, since in reality there are always links between nature and culture, and between us and them. No matter how hard moderns have tried to keep them separate, the same divides have fostered a proliferation of hybrids of the seemingly opposed pairs. Open a newspaper and you will realize that this is the case: the ozone layer (nature) is linked up with corporations, consumers, scientists, government policies (culture); biodiversity is at once biological, social, political, cultural; cloning involves real creatures, new technologies, ethics, regulations, economics. What most defines the moderns is that they have been able to mobilize nature for the creation of culture through networks of hybrids as never before. There is, of course, one factor essential to the success of this process: science.

[. . .] Technological networks enlist the aid of machines like computers, tools like laboratories, inventions like the engine, discoveries like Pasteur's – plus, of course, a collection of diverse subjects. In these networks lies the modern specificity:

> the moderns have simply invented longer networks by enlisting a certain type of nonhumans [machines, science and technology, etc.]. . . . This enlistment of new beings had enormous scaling effects by causing relations to vary from local to global. . . . Thus, in the case of technological networks, we have no difficulty reconciling their local aspect and their global dimension. They are composed of particular places, aligned by a series of branchings that cross to other places. (Latour 1993: 117)

And what about those other societies that have failed to invent such "long networks"? These societies, which Latour refers to as "premodern," have an advantage over the moderns in that they do not deceive themselves by thinking that nature and culture are separate. This advantage, however, is also their weakness, since by insisting that every transformation of nature be in harmony with a social transformation – by insisting on being ecological, one could say – they gave up their ability to make hybrids proliferate, that is, to build longer and more powerful networks. This feature made "experimentation on a large scale impossible" (Latour 1993: 140), so that premodern societies remained "forever imprisoned within the narrow confines of their regional peculiarities and their local knowledge" (Latour 1993: 118). While the premoderns built territories (and places, I assume), the moderns built networks that were ever longer and more connected. The universality of modern networks, however, is an ideological effect of rationalism-backed science. In the long run, moderns and premoderns differ only in the size and scale of the networks they invent. For what we all produce – moderns and premoderns alike – is communities of natures and societies: "all natures-cultures are similar in that they simultaneously construct humans, divinities and nonhumans" (Latour 1993: 106). Moderns only add more and more hybrids to their networks in order to reconstitute social systems and extend their scale. "Science and technologies are remarkable not because they are true or efficient . . . but because they multiply the nonhumans enrolled in the manufacturing of collectives and because they make the community that we form with these beings a more intimate one" (Latour 1993: 108).

A Nonmodern Constitution

This view is seductive for the so-called premoderns. To accept it would mean that the future, and "catching up," would become just a matter of building longer and more connected networks. But networks of what kind? And for what purposes? To evaluate this possibility, it is necessary to examine briefly Latour's proposal for what he calls "a nonmodern constitution," a sort of synthesis of the best the moderns and the premoderns have to offer. This constitution, or agreement, is based on the following features: it retains from the premoderns their recognition of the links between nature and culture, while rejecting their imperative to always link the social and natural worlds (their organicity, let us say). It retains from the moderns their ability to construct long networks through experimentation. The nonmodern constitution must also reject the limits the premoderns "impose on the scaling of collectives, localization by territory, the scapegoating process, ethnocentrism, and finally the lasting nondifferentiation of natures and societies" (Latour 1993: 133). Latour adds a paradoxical step for the nonmodern constitution, and this is that it must reintroduce the separation of nature and culture, but allowing consciously for the proliferation of hybrids and the coproduction of technoscience and society – in other words, to make the idea of a separation between objective nature and free society work once and for all. This amounts to accepting that "the production of hybrids, by becoming explicit and collective, becomes the object of an enlarged democracy that regulates or slows down its cadence" (Latour 1993: 141).

[. . .] His proposal [. . .] is problematic on many grounds; to reduce the difference between moderns and premoderns to a question of network size and scale not only conveniently overlooks the conditions of unequal exchange between networks, it avoids looking into hybridity's contradictions, their links to power and their denigration of places. It is also questionable if Latour's nonmodern constitution solves the contradiction between nature and culture, and between moderns and others, and whether its call for a new democracy will assuage modernity's appetite for conquest and accumulation (Dirlik 1997). Even more, it says nothing about how living nonmoderns (including many of those he labels premodern) can both deal with modern networks and build different networks of their own.

From Latour, however, we have important lessons to learn about the nature of modern networks. Modern networks (1) include human and nonhuman elements; they are made of, and produce, hybrids; (2) enact connections and translations between the local and the global, the human and the nonhuman; (3) produce large effects (due to scale, size, and scope) without being out of the ordinary; (4) do not rely on essential identities (unchanging humans or nature) but on process, movement, and passages without fixed meaning. Humans and nonhumans, technoscience and society, are coproduced through these networks. [. . .]

Networks and the Defense of Place and Nature

In the last two months of 1997, Internet list serves on Amazon indigenous issues included reports on the following, among many other topics: denunciation of government concessions for forest exploitation by foreign companies in Brazil and Guyana; a successful claim to lands by the Guarani Kaiowa in Mato Grosso do Sul, Brazil; a passionate speech by Davi Kopenawa, Yanomami chief, against gold miners on their lands, proclaiming their desire for progress without destruction and the right to defend their land; assassination of, or threats to, environmental and indigenous activists in Brazil, Colombia, and other countries; opposition to a large waterways project (the *hidriovía* Paraguay–Paraná) in Uruguay, Brazil, and Bolivia by a coalition of US and South American NGOs; accusations of biopiracy against a Swiss-based organization (Selva Viva) in Acre, Brazil, also involving a London-based NGO and indigenous, Catholic, and local organizations; denunciations by a French NGO of the firm Chanel for endangering the existence of a rare Brazilian tree used in its products; the formation of regional indigenous councils in Brazil to oppose mining and for the titling of indigenous territories; a meeting of rural women leaders of the Americas against neoliberalism; approval of the claims to land and identity by descendants of escaped slaves in Brazil; updates on the class-action suit against Texaco on behalf of a coalition of indigenous peoples in Ecuador for years of devastation of their lands; a statement by indigenous women of the Ecuadorian Amazon against the presence of oil companies in their territories; a massive march by Ecuadorian indigenous organizations on Quito to demand the inclusion of unprecedented indigenous rights in the new national constitution; a report on alarming deforestation in Venezuela (600,000 hectares a year during the 1980s, continuing into the 1990s).

Similarly, during 1997 the biodiversity conference of the network EcoNet, run by the San Francisco-based Institute for Global Communications, carried (among other items) detailed and sustained information and debates on the follow-up meetings to the Convention on Biological Diversity; biodiversity programs in various countries; opposition to intellectual property rights regimes by national and international NGOs; meetings on biodiversity in various parts of the world and with sets of disparate actors; information on patenting of cell lines; opposition to mega-development projects in the name of biodiversity; new forms of grassroots activism throughout the world linked to the defense of nature; innovations by women in biodiversity conservation; and warning of a pending agreement for bioprospecting between the government of Colombia and a transnational pharmaceutical company.

Internet, Locality, and Networking

There is no doubt that the Internet has fostered a ferment of activity on a vast set of issues that is yet to be understood in terms of its contents, scope, politics, and modes of operation. What does this ferment of activity suggest in terms of networks? Who are the actors involved, what demands do they articulate, and which practices do they create? What views of nature and culture do they espouse or defend? If they do in fact constitute networks, what is the effect of these networks in terms of redefining social power, and at what levels? Conversely, what risks, if any, does the participation of, say, indigenous and grassroots groups in biodiversity networks entail for local meanings and practices of nature and culture?

A sporadic but symbolically important posting provides some clues for exploring these questions. In August and September 1997, various Internet sites sparked with an unprecedented message: an indigenous group in Eastern Colombia numbering 5,000, the U'wa, had threatened to commit [mass] suicide by jumping off a sacred cliff if the US corporation Occidental Petroleum carried out their planned oil exploration in any part of the 100,000 hectares remaining of their ancestral lands. Before its debut on the Internet, the U'wa struggle had seen the formation of a solidarity committee of environmentalists and indigenous rights activists in Colombia, failed negotiations with the government and the oil company, debates on the militarization and violence that the proposed oil exploration would entail, and mobilization by the U'wa themselves. As a result of the Internet postings, the U'wa struggle branched out in many directions – from lengthy newspaper articles in the world press that highlighted the U'wa's alleged traditional nonviolence and ecological knowledge, to the establishment of international support groups. Adopted by several international NGOs, the U'wa's struggle spread spatially and socially in unexpected directions. This included international travel by U'wa leaders themselves to disseminate knowledge of their struggle and gather support for it. They arrived with their concerns even at the door of Occidental's headquarters in Los Angeles, with the support of a transnational U'wa Defense Project.[2]

The U'wa and similar cases suggest a number of emergent grassroots practices enabled by the Internet, particularly the following: the interrelated involvement of a multiplicity of actors in various parts of the world – from grassroots groups themselves to local, national, and transnational NGOs in both "North" and "South"; coalitions among these actors with various aims, intensities, and degrees of trust; conjunctural responses to ongoing or particularly acute threats to local natures-cultures; expressions of cultural and ecological resistance; ongoing opposition to destructive development projects, neoliberal reforms, and destructive technologies (such as mining, logging, and dam construction); opposition to the apparatuses of death set in motion to put down protest or opposition; translation of local cultures into the language of global environmentalism (from which unfortunately they often emerge as another version of the noble savage); and the irruption of collective identities claiming a place in the world theater of environment, culture, gender, and development.

The processes behind all of these elements and events are very complex – ranging from the remaking of local and national identities to globalization, environmental destruction, gender and ethnic struggles. In biodiversity discussions, which constitute to some extent an exemplary case in the politics of networks, it is possible to see several processes at work: (1) the discourse of biodiversity itself constitutes a network of its own, linking humans and nonhumans in particular ways; (2) in this network, the stake for local actors can be seen in terms of the defense of culturally specific practices of constructing natures and cultures; (3) these practices can be said to be embedded in what I referred to above as the defense of place.

Let us say, then, that biodiversity is a discourse that articulates a new relation between nature and society in global contexts of science, cultures, and economies. The biodiversity discourse has resulted in an increasingly vast network – from the United Nations, the World Bank's Global Environment Facility (GEF), and the Northern environmental NGOs to Third World governments, Southern NGOs and social movements – which systematically organizes the production of forms of knowledge and types of power, linking one to the other through concrete strategies and programs. This network is composed of heterogeneous actors and sites, each with its own culturally specific interpretive system, and with dominant and subaltern sites and knowledges. As they circulate through the network, truths are transformed, reinscribed into other knowledge–power constellations, resisted, subverted, or recreated to serve other ends, for instance, by social movements, which become, themselves, the sites of important counter-discourses. Technoscientifically oriented networks such as biodiversity are continuously being transformed in the light of translations, travel, transfers, and mediations among and across sites. In fact, several contrasting conceptualizations of biodiversity have emerged in recent years from distinct network sites and processes.[3]

It can thus be said that "biodiversity," far from being the neutral conservation arena of science and management that is often assumed, underlies one of the most important networks for the production of nature in the late twentieth century. As places become entangled with the network, contestation over conceptions of nature-culture follow. [. . .]

Local models of nature exist in transnational contexts of power yet cannot be accounted for without some reference to groundedness, boundaries, and local cultures. They are based on historical, linguistic, and cultural processes that retain a certain place specificity despite their engagement with translocal processes. From this perspective, a theoretical and utopian question suggests itself: *Can the world be redefined and reconstructed from the perspective of the multiple cultural ecological and social practices embedded in local models and places?* This is perhaps the most profound question that can be posed from a radical networks perspective. What types of networks would be most conducive to this reconstruction? The question requires, however, that we look a bit closer into places and their defense.

Place-based Practices

As Arif Dirlik has pointed out (1998), place and place-based practices have been marginalized in debates on the local and the global. This is regrettable because place is essential for thinking about alternative construction of politics, knowledge, and identity. The erasure of place is a reflection of the asymmetry that exists between the global and the local in much of contemporary literature on globalization, in which the global is associated with space, capital, history, and agency while the local, conversely, is linked to place, labor, tradition, women, minorities, the poor, and, one might add, local cultures.[4] Some feminist geographers have attempted to correct this asymmetry by arguing that place can also lead to articulations across space – for instance through networks of various kinds (Massey 1994; Chernaik 1996). In resisting the marginalization of place, other authors focus on place as a form of lived and grounded space, the reappropriation of which must be part of any radical political agenda against capitalism and spaceless, timeless globalization. Politics is also located in place, not only in the supra-levels of capital and space.[5] A parallel step entails recognizing that place – as the ecological conceptions discussed above make patently clear – continues to be a grounded experience with some sort of boundaries, however porous and intersected with the global.[6]

Contemporary theories of globalization tend to assume the existence of a global power to which the local is necessarily subordinated. Under these conditions, is it possible to launch a defense of place in which place and the local do not derive their meaning only from their juxtaposition to the global? [. . .] For this to happen, we need a new language. To return to Dirlik, "glocal" is a first approximation that suggests equal attention to the localization of the global and the globalization of the local. The concrete forms in which this two-way traffic takes place are not so easily conceptualized. As Massey puts it well, "the global is in the local in the very process of the formation of the local . . . the understanding of any locality must precisely draw on the links beyond its boundaries" (1994: 120). Conversely, many forms of the local are offered for global consumption, from crafts to ecotourism. The point here would be to identify those forms of globalization of the local that can become effective political forces in defense of place and place-based identities, as well as those forms of localization of the global that locals can use to their own ends.

To be sure, "place" and "local knowledge" are no panaceas that will solve the world's problems. Local knowledge is not "pure" or free of domination; places might have their own forms of oppression and even terror; they are historical and connected to the wider world through relations of power. They as easily originate reactionary and regressive changes as they might progressive politics. Women have often been subordinated through restrictions linked to place and home (Massey 1994), and of course native groups have been spatially incarcerated and segregated. These factors have to be taken seriously. But against those who think that the defense of place and local knowledge is undeniably "romantic," one could say, with Jacobs (1996: 161), that "it is a form of imperial nostalgia, a desire for the 'untouched Native,' which presumes that such encounters [between local and global] only ever mark yet another phase of imperialism." [. . .]

The defense of place is an increasingly felt need on the part of those working at the intersection of environment and development, precisely because the development experience has meant for most people a sundering of local life from place of greater depth than ever before. Not only are scholars and activists in environmental studies confronted with social movements that maintain a strong reference to place – veritable movements of ecological and cultural attachment to places and territories – but faced also with the growing realization that any alternative course of action must take into account place-based models of nature with their accompanying cultural, ecological, and economic practices. [. . .]

Interactivity and Positionality: A Feminist Political Ecology of Cyberculture

It seems paradoxical to build a link between place and cyberculture. But if it is true that we are witnessing the emergence of a virtual-imagined transnational community which alters the conditions for activism in a shrinking world (Ribeiro 1998), then we must recognize the necessity of building just such a link. Activism at a distance makes perfect political sense in cyberculture. But this activism, as Ribeiro also points out, must be based on a further link, between cyberactivism and face-to-face activism in physical space – what I called here place-based political practice. [. . .]

[. . . D]espite the importance of cybertools and cultures, a lot of what needs to be changed depends on power relations in the real world. We might give each woman of the world or each ecology group a computer and an Internet account, and the world might remain the same. This means that the relationship between cyberculture and political change – and between cyberactivism and place-based practice – is to be politically constructed. It does not follow from the technologies themselves even if [. . .] the technology fosters certain novel modes of knowing, being, and doing. We might learn more about this political construction by drawing from the field of feminist political ecology, which focuses on the relation between gender, environment, and development (Rocheleau, Thomas-Slayter, and Wangari, 1996; Harcourt 1994).

Feminist political ecology starts by treating gender as a critical variable in shaping access to, and the knowledge and organization of, natural resources. Gendered experiences of the environment are explained in terms of women's situated knowledges, also shaped by class, culture, and ethnicity. Feminist political ecology unveils the many kinds and importance of women's local environmental knowledge; further, it attempts to link it to social movements and the defense of local cultural and biophysical ecologies. Similarly, feminist political ecology looks at gendered rights and responsibilities, often skewed against women. It finds that "women are beginning to redefine their identities, and the meaning of gender, through expressions of human agency and collective action emphasizing struggle, resistance, and cooperation. In doing so, they have also begun to redefine environmental issues to include women's knowledge, experience, and interests" (Rocheleau, Thomas-Slayter, and Wangari 1996: 15). Women's ecological activism weaves together issues of environmental policy, resource access and distribution, knowledge and gender, while fostering an alternative view of sustainability[. . . .]

The relevance of this view for the analysis of women and cyberculture is apparent, particularly the following: providing a framework for examining women's experience worldwide; linking theory and practice in women's organizations and movements for social change (the gendered roots of activism); highlighting the importance and gendered character of local knowledge; questioning the presumption of economic development and the domination of nature and women; addressing the different structural positions occupied by women and men; using feminist insights to inform policy debates; and imagining global perspectives from local experience. In feminist political ecology, women struggle simultaneously against the destruction of nature and against the conventional (gender- and culture-blind) policies to restructure nature through sustainable development and management; in feminist cybercultural politics, women struggle simultaneously against the control of cyberculture by male-dominant groups and against the restructuring of the world by the same technologies they seek to appropriate. To the extent that women's cybercultural politics is linked to the defense of place, it is possible to suggest that it becomes a manifestation of feminist political ecology. This political ecology would similarly look at gendered knowledge; gendered rights and responsibilities concerning information and technology; and gendered organizations. It would examine, in short, the gendering of technoscience and cyberspace.

Politics of Networks

[. . . T]here are two aspects that must be discussed. The first is the political character of networks. The progressive character of networks cannot be assured beforehand. As I have suggested, progressive organizations and social movements in the biodiversity conservation arena do not form an autonomous network of their own, but one that is enmeshed in a larger one, with dominant and subaltern sites that are not independent of one another. That it would be hard to construct "a network of one's own" is also attested by the experience of the pre- and post-Beijing women's movement, as lucidly analyzed by Sonia Alvarez. For Alvarez (1997, 1998), the transnationalization of Latin American feminist advocacy made possible by the proliferation of women's networks has had significant, and not always felicitous, local consequences. To be sure, the growing transnationalization of the women's movement has had many positive effects, such as the incorporation of ethnic and sexual diversity, the strengthening of alliances with transnational NGOs and movements, and the transformation of state policy at many levels. These achievements, however, have had their downside, as Alvarez explains, in terms of the growing professionalization, discursive accommodation, and compromise that women's NGOs have made with male-dominant and often market-driven policies. This accommodation has at times constrained more radical feminist cultural politics. Veronica Schild's analysis (1998) of the professionalization of the Chilean women's movement also suggests that this process has contributed to demobilizing popular women's movements and introducing neoliberal cultural discourses of market and individuality among poor working women.

This is to say that the politics of networks does not necessarily follow from who does the networking. Yet networks have important political effects. Networks elicit a way of looking at the world not so much in terms of fragmentation – as many Marxists tend to do[7] – but of possibilities for coalitions. For some feminist geographers, coalition politics is a feature of networks based on a positive notion of difference. Place-based social practices can lead to articulations across space; "the form that this global articulation takes, though, is often more a network than a system: a coalition of specific, different groups rather than a universalization of any one political identity" (Chernaik 1996: 257). This thinking about networks resonates with the feminist position of conceptualizing space, place, and identity in terms of relations rather than the imposition of boundaries (Massey 1994).[8] It is clear, in addition, that place-based social movements create spatial effects that go beyond locality. They produce forms of "glocality" that are not negligible. Witness, for instance, the social movements networks of indigenous peoples in the Americas, and of women and environmentalists in various parts of the world, despite the caveats already mentioned. The indigenous networks of the Americas are perhaps the best example of the effectivity (and limitations) of transnational networks of organizing and identity.

But can these parallel forms of glocality lead to alternative social orders? This last aspect of "the question of alternatives" remains largely intractable. For Dirlik, the survival of place-based cultures will be ensured when the globalization of the local compensates for the localization of the global – that is, when symmetry between the local and the global is reintroduced in social and conceptual terms. [. . .] For this to happen, places must "project themselves into the spaces that are presently the domains of capital and modernity" (Dirlik 1997: 40). To the extent that new ICTs are central to the remaking of the domains of capital and modernity, cybercultural politics has an essential role to play in this political project. Cybercultural politics might provide a prime mechanism for "scaling-up" – in Latour's terms – the networks through which subaltern groups seek to redefine power and defend and construct their identities.

The issue of glocality and scaling-up of place-based coalitions must nevertheless be approached with caution. As Gustavo Esteva and Madhu Suri Prakash say in criticizing the slogan "think globally, act locally," we have to be wary of all global ways of thinking. In fact, "what is needed is exactly the opposite: people thinking and acting locally, while forging solidarity with other local forces that share this opposition to the 'global thinking' and 'global forces' threatening local spaces" (Esteva and Prakash 1997: 282). It is clear that places linking together create supralocal realities. Perhaps the language of networks and glocality is only a provisional way to refer to these realities that are still poorly understood from non-globalist perspectives, while respecting the vitality, size, and scale of places. Place-based initiatives offer forms of radical pluralism that oppose globalism; engaging with supralocal forces, as Estava and Prakash say, does not make local people into globalists.

This in no way entails reifying places as "untouched" or outside of history. [. . .] To speak about activating local places, cultures, natures, and knowledge against the imperializing tendencies of capitalism and modernity is not a *deus ex machina* operation, but a way to move beyond the chronic realism fostered by established modes of analysis. Alternative ecological public spheres, for instance, might be opened up against the imperial ecologies of nature and identity of capitalist modernity. Can we think of cyberculture in similar terms? What types of public cyberspheres can be brought into existence through the networks envisioned by women, ecologists, and others? And will they foster different ways of interacting and relating, of thinking about life, gender, justice, and diversity?

New Technologies Fostering New Knowledge

This brings us to the second, and last, aspect I want to discuss. Is it possible to think that new technologies, by their very character and in the hands of subaltern groups, would foster novel practices of being, knowing, and doing? This is a complex question to which I can only give a very partial answer by invoking briefly the work of Katherine Hayles and Donna Haraway. For both authors, the critiques of objectivism made possible by feminism and technoscience point to novel practices of knowing. For Hayles, knowledge can now be thought in terms of interactivity and positionality:

> Interactivity points toward our connection with the world: everything we know about the world we know because we interact with it. Positionality refers to our location as humans living in certain times, cultures and historical traditions: we interact with the world not from a disembodied, generalized framework but from positions marked by the particularities of our circumstances as embodied human creatures. Together, interactivity and positionality pose a strong challenge to traditional objectivity, which for our purposes can be defined as the belief that we know reality because we are separated from it. What happens if we begin from the opposite premise, that we know the world because we are connected to it? (Hayles 1995: 48)

Surely, many "premodern" or nonmodern groups have always lived with and from "the opposite premise" of nonseparability of self and other, body and world, nature and society. The cultural models of nature referred to before attest to that. Interactivity and positionality are thus "natural attributes" of many people; as Hayles is quick to add, to live by these principles entails not only different epistemologies but different values. New technologies are hailed for their interactivity, but in modern contexts this interactivity is often disembodied and disembedded. Third World social groups might be more prepared culturally to embrace the interactivity and positionality that is facilitated by new information technologies. As Austerlic (1997) says, the periphery's advantage in this arena lies not in the design of hardware but in the contents, and these are culturally defined. [. . .]

New technologies summon a third principle, that of connectivity. Haraway retakes this notion, depoliticized in much techno-celebratory literature, through the image of the hypertext (perhaps more apt for our age than the network metaphor). Hypertexts are about making connections, only that today we are compelled by technoscience to make unprecedented connections – between humans and nonhumans, the organic and the artificial, and with bodies, narratives, and machines alike; in Haraway's words, we have to accept becoming "ontologically dirty" (Haraway 1997: 127). Which connections matter, why, and for whom become crucial questions. [. . .] Coalitions need to be built for more livable technoscience. "My purpose is to argue for a practice of situated knowledges in the worlds of technoscience, worlds whose fibers infiltrate deep and wide throughout the tissues of the planet, including the flesh of our personal bodies" (Haraway 1997: 130).

To be sure, we have to be mindful, as Virilio and Castells warned us, of the misery being brought to billions by transnational capitalism and technoscience. But we must also bear witness, Haraway insists, to the myriad ways in which situated knowledges extract freedoms from those regimes. We have to pay attention to how various groups appropriate the universes of knowledge, practice, and power mapped by technoscience, often through unprecedented condensations, fusions, and implosions of subjects and objects, the natural and the artificial. Perhaps then we can reweave that net called the global by fostering the production of other forms of life. Today Haraway's call can only be ignored at a high cost. It has to be approached, of course, from culture and place-specific perspectives. Biodiversity advocates of rainforest regions, for instance, are having to engage with technoscientific discourses of biotechnology bent on utilizing diversity for commercial purposes (Escobar 1998b). Indigenous activists similarly build networks to defend their cultures and ecologies against neoliberalism and depoliticized policies of diversity. The Women on the Net is another reflection of the fact that this challenge is being taken up in many quarters of Asia, Africa, Latin America, and elsewhere.

Constructing Cyberpolitics

New computer, communication, and information technologies offer unprecedented possibilities for alternative social and political practices, actors, and identities. Whether these possibilities are realized will depend on many factors, beyond the identity of the networkers themselves, particularly the relationship maintained between activism in cyberspace and place-based social change. Progressive groups wishing to appropriate and utilize these technologies for social transformation must build bridges between place and cyberspace – between activity and interactivity, presence and telepresence, existence and tele-existence, as Virilio would have it. These bridges have to be constructed politically. The experience of those working at the intersection of gender, environment, and development offers lessons for such a political construction in the field of cybercultural politics.

For historical and cultural reasons, women, environmentalists, and Third World social movements might be more attuned to the principles of interactivity, positionality, and connectivity than the feminist critique of science, and the new technologies themselves, seem to foster. These principles are conducive to new modes of knowing, being, and doing; they may ground a cultural politics of technoscience capable of transforming technoscience's current impact on the world. This requires that the interfaces we build among ourselves as users of the new technologies, the new ICTs themselves, and the task of social transformation be grounded in concrete bodies and places. "Rooting women's communication experiences and ways of communicating in their social and cultural concerns and backgrounds" is a principle of feminist communications (APC 1997: 9). The transformation of gender and ecological relations calls for actions that link together place and cyberspace. It is not impossible to think that the same networks that so many fear will erase places once and for all could enable a defense of places out of which a gender and ecological relations might emerge transformed.

Notes

1 More specifically, Castells speaks of the convergence of microelectronics, computer optoelectronics, and biological technology such as genetic engineering.
2 The U'wa Defense Project International is a collaborative effort between Amazon coalition, Amazon Watch, Cabildo Mayor U'wa, Centre for Justice and International Law, Colombian Human Rights Commission, Earth Trust Foundation, FIAN Germany, National Indigenous Organization of Colombia, Project Under Ground, Rainforest Action Network (RAN), and SOL Communications. For further information contact: http://www.solcommunications.com/uwa.html; uwaproject@aol.com
3 This is a very inadequate explanation of the biodiversity network. See Escobar (1997, 1998a) for a lengthy analysis. It is possible to differentiate among four major positions in the uneven topology of the biodiversity network: resource management (globalocen-tric perspective); sovereignty (Third World national perspectives); biodemocracy (pro-gressive Southern NGO perspective); and cultural autonomy (social movements perspective).
4 This is very clearly the case in environmental discourses, for instance, of biodiversity conservation, where women and indigenous people are credited with having the knowledge of "saving nature." Massey (1994) has already denounced the feminization of place and the local in theories of space. [. . .]
5 The June 1998 issue of *Development* (41, 2) is devoted to the question of place and alternative development, with a lead article by Arif Dirlik. See also Massey (1994); Lefebvre (1991); Soja (1996).
6 It is not the point to recapture here the complex debate on space and place of recent years. This debate – which initially brought together Marxist geographers and feminist political economists, and to which anthropologists, philosophers, and ecologists have contributed more recently – started with the growing concern of globalization and its impact on space and time (the "space-time compression" theorized by Harvey 1989). The debate on place and space also has a source in explanations of modernity, particularly Giddens's analysis of the separation of time and space that makes possible the disembedding of social systems and the differentiation of space from place: "the advent of modernity" – says Giddens – "increasingly tears space away from place by fostering relations between absent others, locationally distant from any given situation

of face-to-face interaction" (1990: 18). Virilio's "telepresence" of real-time technologies is a new step in this genealogy of the sundering of place from space.

7   For Marxist critics, networks are actually a manifestation of the fragmentation that the world economy imposes on most localities today. Networks, in this view, are incapable of anchoring a significant struggle against capitalism and globalization. Against this capitalocentric view, some feminist Marxists have reacted by insisting on the need to visualize the multiple forms of economic, cultural, and ecological difference that still exist in the world today, and the extent to which these differences can anchor alternative economies and ecologies (Gibson-Graham 1996; Escobar 1998b).

8   Chernaik also takes on the notion that home and place are ambiguous categories for women. She advocates a dialectic of place and street – of place and cyberspace, we could say – in women's "construction of a house of difference."

References

Alvarez, S. E. 1997: "Latin American Feminism 'Go Global': Trends of the 1990s and Challenges for the New Millennium." In S. E. Alvarez, E. Dagnino, and A. Escobar (eds.), *Cultures of Politics/Politics of Cultures: Re-visioning Latin American Social Movements*. Boulder, CO: Westview, 293–324.

Alvarez, S. E. 1998: "'. . . and Even Castro Can't Change That': Trans/national Feminist Advocacy Strategies and Cultural Politics in Latin America." Paper presented at the Department of Anthropology, Mellon Lecture Series on "Public Culture and Transnationalism," Duke University, NC, October 27.

APC (Association for Progressive Communication) 1997: *Global Networking for Change, Experience from the APC Women's Programme. Survey Findings.* London: APC.

Austerlic, S. 1997: "New Tendencies in Design in Latin America." *Organization* 4 (4), 620–7.

Castells, M. 1996: *The Rise of the Network Society.* Oxford: Blackwell.

Chernaik, L. 1996: "Spatial Displacements: Transnationalism and the New Social Movements." *Gender, Place and Culture* 3 (3), 251–75.

Dirlik, A. 1997: "Placed-based Imagination: Globalism and the Politics of Place." Unpublished manuscript.

Dirlik, A. 1998: "Globalism and the Politics of Place." *Development* 41 (2), 7–13.

Escobar, A. 1997: "Cultural Politics and Biological Diversity: State, Capital and Social Movements in the Pacific Coast of Colombia." In R. Fox and O. Starn (eds.), *Between Resistance and Revolution.* New Brunswick, NJ: Rutgers University Press, 40–64.

Escobar, A. 1998a: "Whose Knowledge, Whose Nature? Biodiversity, Conservation, and Social Movements' Political Ecology." Paper prepared for the IV Ajusco Forum on "Whose Nature? Biodiversity, Globalization, and Sustainability in Latin America and the Caribbean." Mexico, DF, November 19–21, 1997.

Escobar, A. 1998b: "The Place of Nature and the Nature of Place: Globalisation or Postdevelopment?" Under review, *Social Text.*

Esteva, G. and Prakash, M. S. 1997: "From Global Thinking to Local Thinking." In M. Rahnema with V. Bawtree (eds.), *The Postdevelopment Reader.* London: Zed Books, 277–89.

Gibson-Graham, J. K. 1996: *The End of Capitalism (As We Know It).* Oxford: Blackwell.

Giddens, A. 1990: *The Consequences of Modernity,* Stanford, CA: Stanford University Press.

Haraway, D. 1997: *Modest_Witness@Second_Millennium.Female_Man_Meets_OncoMouseTM.* New York: Routledge.

Harcourt, W. (ed.) 1994: *Feminist Perspectives on Sustainable Development*. London: Zed Books.

Harvey, D. 1989: *The Conditions of Postmodernity*. Oxford: Blackwell.

Hayles, K. 1995: "Searching for Common Ground." In M. Soule and G. Lease (eds.), *Reinventing Nature?* Washington: Island Press, 47–64.

Jacobs, J. 1996: *Edge of Empire: Postcolonialism and the City*. London: Routledge.

Latour, B. 1993: *We Have Never Been Modern*. Cambridge, MA: Harvard University Press.

Lefebvre, H. 1991: *The Production of Space*. Oxford: Blackwell.

Massey, D. 1994: *Space, Place and Gender*. Minneapolis: University of Minnesota Press.

Ribeiro, G. L. 1998: "Cybercultural Politics: Political Activism at a Distance in a Transnational World." In S. E. Alvarez, E. Dagnino, and A. Escobar (eds.), *Cultures of Politics/Politics of Cultures: Re-visioning Latin American Social Movements*, Boulder, CO: Westview, 325–52.

Rocheleau, D., Thomas-Slayter, B., and Wangari, E. (eds.) 1996: "Gender and Development: A Feminist Political Ecology Perspective." In D. Rocheleau, B. Thomas-Slayter, and E. Wangari (eds.), *Feminist Political Ecology*. New York: Routledge, 3–23.

Schild, V. 1998: "New Subjects of Rights? Women's Movements and the Construction of Citizenship in the 'New Democracies.'" In S. E. Alvarez, E. Dagnino, and A. Escobar (eds.), *Cultures of Politics/Politics of Cultures: Re-visioning Latin American Social Movements*, Boulder, CO: Westview, 93–117.

Soja, E. 1996: *Thirdspace*. Oxford: Blackwell.

Virilio, P. 1997: *Open Sky*. London: Verso.

22 Maya Hackers and the Cyberspatialized Nation-state: Modernity, Ethnostalgia, and a Lizard Queen in Guatemala

Diane M. Nelson

Science fiction is generically concerned with the interpenetration of boundaries between problematic selves and unexpected others and with the exploration of possible worlds in a context structured by transnational technoscience.

Haraway (1992)

I'm going to jack you into this piece with a Third World arrival scene. It is 1985 in Nebaj, Guatemala, under a military government. I am on my first research trip investigating the effects of civil war on highland indigenous communities. Guatemala's population is about one-half indigenous, and Nebaj is famous for its traditionalism. Most women and many men wear the handwoven clothing distinctive to the town; the civil-religious cargo system functions; and the yearly titular festival is intensely colorful, with saints' processions, fireworks, the Dance of the Conquest, and all-night revelry. Day keepers still practice their craft, giving readings of the present based on the Mayan calendar (Colby and Colby 1981). In other words, the town offered all the exoticism my recently conferred BA in anthropology had incited me to desire. Nebaj, however, had also been one of the towns hardest hit by the government's high- and low-tech counterinsurgency campaign, which leveled all twenty-six surrounding villages (and had killed some 70,000 Guatemalans in the preceding seven years). In addition to the dancers, weavers, and shamans, Nebaj was a town of refugees, survivors, and soldiers when I arrived.

In 1985 the journey to Nebaj took twelve hours in an extremely cramped Bluebird schoolbus (there were twelve people in my row), groaning its way over the spine of the Cuchumatanes mountains to finally drop down into the remote valley, centered on its colonial-era church. After that ride, while I was walking

Excerpted from Diane M. Nelson, "Maya Hackers and the Cyberspatialized Nation-state: Modernity, Ethnostalgia, and a Lizard Queen in Guatemala." *Cultural Anthropology* 11, 3 (1996), 287–308.

around the garrison town to stretch my legs a bit, a group of children surrounded me, inquiring if I would buy stuff or wanted my shoes shined. They asked me my name, and when I said "Diana," they all start yelling, "Queen of the lizards! Queen of the lizards!"

I was confounded. I knew this town had been strongly proguerrilla and I wondered if the kids, in calling the gringa a lizard, were displaying the effects of anti-imperialist education imbibed while the town was "liberated." On the contrary. It turns out they had been sneaking into the cantina housing the town's one television in order to watch a US science fiction series called *V*. The show dealt with the arrival on earth of an advanced and apparently benevolent group of aliens who promise all sorts of techie wonders as well as world peace. Most humans willingly accept their offerings and presence. Only a small group of hearty souls realize they are actually lizards disguised as humans, on earth to rape and pillage her natural resources – including harvesting humans for snacks back home. Those who are not duped fight a valiant guerrilla struggle against both their own kind, who refuse to see the exploitative relationship they have entered, and the lizard aliens, led by their queen, Diana. [. . .] Encountering kids who were sophisticated in the ways of lizard queens in a backwater town *was* something of a shock.

This shock seems to come from the sense that science fiction is about the future, while Guatemala's indigenous highlands tend to represent the past. This colonial binary of the modern cosmopolitan West opposed to the archaic indigenous, which Johannes Fabian (1983) has explored, is precisely the predicament faced by the growing Mayan cultural rights movement. The assimilationist discourse of Guatemalan nationalism has proposed that the majority indigenous population is inappropriate for modern nationalism. The glorious Mayan past of Tikal and traditional practices of clothing and ritual are appropriated to represent the nation, be it in tourist literature or, to note a more specific example, in a float in the 1993 Pasadena Rose Bowl Parade. However, for full representation *in* the nation, the Maya have been expected to put aside their indigenousness: to learn Spanish, to dress in Western clothes, and so forth. In fact, the binary semiotics of identity in Guatemala mean you cannot be both Indian and modern. Ladino (nonindigenous) identity is *defined* as modern in terms of technology, lifeways, and so on. Because centuries of *mestizaje* have made it difficult to tell an indigenous person from a non-Indian, the categories are marked culturally. Thus, any indigenous person who speaks Spanish, has earned an academic degree, or holds a desk job has historically been redefined as ladino. I want to argue that the newly organizing Mayan cultural rights activists are refusing ladinization and instead are "Maya hackers." Like computer hackers, who deploy intimate understandings of technologies and codes while working within a system they do not control, the Maya are appropriating so-called modern technology and knowledges while refusing to be appropriated *into* the ladino nation. They are thereby becoming what Trinh Minh-ha has termed the "Inappropriate/d Other" (Trinh 1986).

The incongruity of the term *Maya hacker* also tends to occasion chuckles, which I think highlights the continuing power of the primitive–modern divide. So, I deploy it as a caution against what I call ethnostalgia[1] – as in my sense of exoticism so rudely disrupted when my cover as concerned gringa anthropologist was blown by a positive ID as a lizard queen.[2] Ethnostalgia is a powerful contradiction for Mayan activists. It empowers their own work and wins them allies among ladino elites and foreigners, but it also limits them to the past side of the binary. I will argue that as Maya hackers, by contrast, they are decoding and reprogramming such familiar binary oppositions as those between past and future, between being rooted in geography and being mobile, between being traditional and being modern, between manual labor and white-collar technology/information manipulation, between mountain shrines and mini malls, and between unpaved roads and the information superhighway. Thinking of the site of this reprogramming work as the cyberspatialized nation-state foregrounds the importance of information and representation in the work of the Mayan activists and in the production of an imagined community like the Guatemalan nation. [. . .]

The Mayan Cultural Rights Movement

It is 1993, and I am on my sixth sojourn in Guatemala. I am sitting in an upscale Guatemala City steak house with Dr. Demetrio Cojti, a well-known Mayan professional. Between my first trip to Nebaj and 1988, when I first met Dr. Cojti, I had lived for fifteen months in highland Guatemala researching the impact of the civil war on indigenous identity. In those years, I had grudgingly come to agree with some of the doomsayers who foretold the end of Guatemala's Indians. In 1988, however, I began to interview men and women like Dr. Cojti, who were forging something new, an identity they called Mayan.

[. . . I]ndigenous identification in Guatemala is very local, taking the form of twenty-two different ethnolinguistic identity groups, including K'iche, Tzutujil, Chuj, and Mam. As Carol Smith (1990) and others have noted, these local identities are marked sartorially by distinct dress and by kin relations, dialect, and economic, civil, and religious organization. While nonladinos have been called *indios*, *naturales*, or *autoctónas*, there had been little effective organizing around a larger, pan-indigenous identity. To my surprise, in the denouement of the violence of the early 1980s, indigenous identification and organizing has exploded (Nelson 1991; Smith 1991). Some of this has involved what Eric Hobsbawm and Terence Ranger call "invented tradition" (1983). For example, activists have taken the term Maya – formerly reserved for the ancient temple builders and Guatemalan tourism campaigns – and reprogrammed it to represent an incipient pan-indigenous identity at the national level.

[. . .] So in the steak house in Guatemala City in 1993, Dr. Cojti and I are talking about the politics of creating a pan-Mayan identity, as people had begun to self-identify as Maya-Ixil, Maya-K'iche', Maya-K'ekchi, and so on. Many were also reversing the standard appropriation of indigenous people to ladinization by calling the Mestizo population "Maya-ladino" – another reprogramming of the premodern/modern that has shocked many ladinos. Planning for our next meeting, Dr. Cojti pulled out one of those amazing computerized datebooks that hold thousands of names, addresses, dates, world time zones, telephone numbers, and even maps. I said, joking, that they should invent a new identity term, the "Maya hacker."

We both laughed, but I came to think this *could* describe Dr. Cojti – a man who holds a Ph.D. in communications, who is very technologically literate and serves as a node for various information networks, including the burgeoning Mayan cultural rights movement as well as various government, NGO, and international webs, in part through his job at UNICEF. He is also connected to the rural–urban matrix through contact with his small-town home and many rural-based Mayan organizations, and he frequently contributes to the national press and indigenous publications. In its short history, the Guatemalan indigenous rights movement has been split between what are known as the popular indigenous organizations – like Rigoberta Menchú's Campesino Unity Committee (CUC) and other human rights groups that identify with class issues – and the more culturally active "Mayan" movement, which insists that racism is not reducible to capitalist exploitation (Bastos and Camus 1993; Smith 1991).[3] Dr. Cojti, however, is becoming a vital node in the attempted conciliation of these two positions, a process energized by such national and international events as the Columbus Quincentennial, the ongoing peace talks, and Rigoberta Menchú's Nobel Peace Prize and the international summits she convened during 1993, the UN Year of Indigenous Peoples. [. . .]

But in Guatemala, as elsewhere, indigenous people did not experience this process of being rendered fit as simple, passive conduits of knowledge. These translating roles offered assimilation, allowing entry into the cash economy and promising that with a generation or two of speaking Spanish and dressing "up," their children might escape the stigma of indigenous identity. However, it is precisely these middle men and women who have begun to appropriate these information technologies and to deploy them for alternative aims. The role of "vehicle for conveying knowledge" is no longer so desirable: as indigenous members of the Academia de Lenguas Mayas de Guatemala (ALMG, the Guatemalan Mayan Language Academy) have said, "Many activists come from the education field: they often find in their students the best mirror to reflect their own frustrations . . . [F]rom the inside schools are revealed to be great prisons for mental castration, true advance troops for colonial domination" (ALMG 1990: 60). Instead, they are using literacy, desktop publishing, linguistic theories, radio, and computers to promote cultural survival. [. . . T]hey say that the "decolonization of the Maya begins with knowing how to use technology and not being used by it" (ALMG 1990: 42).

Although public indigenous organizing around such cultural issues as the survival of Mayan languages began in the 1950s, by the 1970s there was a critical mass of indigenous men and women working throughout the highlands in churches, schools, agricultural cooperatives, nongovernmental development agencies, and medical services who began to meet and discuss issues of indigenous empowerment. Critics of the Mayan movement have called these people an elite. Yet many of them have only a sixth-grade education, and while they may receive a salary for their work, they are often still part-time farmers or traders, commuting, as Dr. Cojti does, between the urban and rural scenes.

Mayan leaders say that in the 1970s they began to understand the importance of language – of the indigenous languages as both a symbol and ongoing practice of indigenous identity, *and* of language and information as a way to contest racial, economic, and political oppression. They began to discuss how ladino control of the representation of indigenous peoples in history, education, and the media determined how the Maya saw themselves, in turn making them unwitting allies in this process. As one activist who had worked as a Catholic catechist with his father said in an interview: "I spoke against the traditional religion. We were the worst destroyers of our own culture. Now that I am more involved, I understand the barbarity I've committed and the need to support our traditions."

Guatemala, with a primarily agrarian economy, suffers one of the most skewed land distributions in Latin America, with much of the fertile land devoted to plantation production, while Indians are relegated to increasingly smaller (and steeper) plots. In the 1970s, with Guatemala's growing poverty, many of those who are now Mayan activists were influenced by liberation theology and other social movements (and began working closely for the first time with different ethnic-linguistic groups and ladinos) and were then radicalized by the military government's violent suppression. Rigoberta Menchú's testimonial vividly recounts the journey from nonviolent social activism to armed resistance (1987). While some indigenous activists took this route, thousands of educators, catechists, and development workers were killed for their middle(wo)man roles alone. As one Mayan leader remembers: "There was so much violence because the army was not in control of the situation. That is why the thing was so brutal, so bestial, totally excessive. It was meant to scare people. We continue to fight, but we have learned from the mistakes of the past. We are working differently now."

The catastrophic violence of the civil war and continuing human rights violations limit political organizing around taboo subjects such as land reform, but the 1986 inauguration of civilian rule has created a space for survivors and for a new generation to undertake different kinds of political work. The massive violence has convinced many of the need for new strategies and careful organizing. Unfortunately, many indigenous people were disillusioned by their experiences of racism within the popular and revolutionary movements. This has also convinced them that alternative, indigene-controlled organizing is necessary. As one activist said to me: "[our work] looks like it's just 'cultural,' but inside we are very political. We are defining different models of development. We are struggling to regain our culture, the languages, but it is the organization that is difficult to regain. Many of us have lost our identity."

Thus, contrary to fears that thirty years of ethnocidal civil war would destroy the Maya, in the past ten years hundreds of groups identified as indigenous have emerged. These Maya hackers are not challenging state and ladino power directly but instead are sharing information and creating networks. They are concentrating on education, on rural development, on research and support for languages and other cultural expressions (such as religious, sartorial, and artistic expression), on the creation of libraries and literatures devoted to indigenous issues, and on publishing, radio broadcasting, and lobbying the Guatemalan Congress (often in collaboration with international organizations that remain in contact through e-mail and faxes). These modes of "working differently" are tactical responses to violence, but they also reflect a global historical shift. While many indigenous people are small farmers, agricultural peons, textile producers, or workers in Guatemala's industries and *maquila* production, increasing numbers have service and information management jobs, such as teachers, lawyers, bureaucrats, and merchants. Thus the conditions of possibility for the Maya hacker include the emergence of a critical mass of educated indigenous people, shifts in the transnational economy that increasingly emphasize the information economy,[4] and technological changes that have made relevant hard- and software increasingly available.[5]

One expression of this "working differently" is the Guatemalan Mayan Language Academy. Organized in 1984, the ALMG is an umbrella organization for Mayan groups, including the Guatemalan Academy of Mayan Writers, the Center for Mayan Research and Documentation, the Permanent Seminar for Mayan Studies, the Coordinator of Indigenous Integral Development, and the Mayan Education and Cultural Center Cholsamaj (a publishing house). Member organizations work in Maya-controlled grassroots development projects, as well as in research, documentation, and education. They sponsor conferences and seminars and publish economically and intellectually accessible materials – what I would call "shareware."

[. . .] The ALMG's first hacking project was to create a unified alphabet for the different Mayan languages, through linguistic research and painstaking negotiations, and then to lobby the national Congress to make this alphabet official for use in school texts and government publications. In pursuing this goal, they have deployed the 1984 Constitution, which, although it enshrines Spanish as the official national language, does recognize the existence of indigenous languages. Strategically deploying the embedded code of this national operating system, the ALMG won official recognition for its new alphabet, thereby joining in the struggle for representation, in its double sense (Spivak 1988: 276). First, in the sense of a portrayal: monitoring and shaping how the Maya are portrayed in the national media is a central activity of the ALMG. Second, these efforts are directly linked to their struggle to win representation – in the sense of speaking for themselves – in the state. Through tenacious lobbying and strategic use of ladino internal divisions and ladino allies, in 1991 the ALMG itself won recognition as a government-funded, but autonomous, organization in charge of linguistic and educational research, the development of curriculum materials, and the training of teachers, among other things. Like hackers who work in the interstices of computer networks, the Maya hackers are creating spaces for themselves inside the state.

Thus, rather than the state being a "thing" to be smashed, the Maya seem to see the post-1985 Guatemalan government as a *site* for their work. [. . .]

The academy plays a major role in Mayan organizing, and it is a nodal point for the many Mayan organizations based in the countryside. [. . .] The building was filled with a procession of indigenous people from all over the country, coming in for training sessions, to turn in vocabulary lists from their linguistic areas, to confer about curricula for their Mayan schools, or to gather people to take a request to Congress or to the press. [. . .]

While Mayan groups make political and economic demands, they are keenly

aware of the power of discourse and representation – that is, that the production and deployment of information and knowledge is a potent form of
power. [. . .]

[. . . U]sing the tools at their disposal, and without large financial reserves,
Mayan activists are insisting on the appropriateness of their presence in the
postmodern world by appropriating such technology for their own ends. One
Mayan leader told me, "the Maya give thanks for food, for air, for the tools that
serve us, the office machines, and the computers." Generations of indigenous
struggle and the tools of the information revolution, combined with the historic
reconfiguration of the Guatemalan state, have opened up a new arena where
Mayan activists can hack the ladino power structure. By "hack" I mean they are
overcoming system limitations, decoding and reprogramming postcoloniality,
and pressing "enter" on the keyboard of the Guatemalan nation.

A second meaning of the term *hacker* is the sense of a romantic outlaw. [. . .] I
argue that the Guatemalan state may think of the Maya as hackers in this sense.
Decades of antiracism work in Guatemala have driven most overtly anti-
indigenous remarks out of public discourse. Most ladino state functionaries are
publicly very pro-Maya – some are most sincere, while others are clearly
attempting to appropriate this vibrant new social movement to their own ends.
However, there are suggestions that ladinos feel the Maya are invading a space
that is inappropriate for them: the urban, literate, mediatized state. I think this
space of the nation-state, the hackers' topos, and the ground of contention in
Guatemala can be visualized as cyberspace.

The Cyberspatialized Nation-state

Cyberspace is a utopia in two senses. Many proponents excitedly proclaim that
you can be anything you want to be there; it promises unlimited information
and communication – the ultimate public sphere. In this way, cyberspace offers
similar hopes to those surrounding democratization and the peace process in
Guatemala. However, it is a utopia as well in the etymological sense of a no-
place. In this sense it is also similar to the state – a notoriously difficult entity to
pin down, as Timothy Mitchell (1991) reminds us. [. . .]

[. . .] Economically, the nation-state and cyberspace both are ways of organizing material production. Also, in the nation, liberal discourses of universal
citizenship offer the ideological fantasy of total inclusion, and the proponents of
cyberspace offer a similar dream: that you can be whoever you want to be, that
all the limitations of gendered, racialized, or otherwise "disabled" physicality
will fall away.[6]

If the nation is understood as the space in which "state sovereignty is fully,
flatly, and evenly operative over each square centimetre" (Anderson 1990 [1983]:
26), cyberspace is described by "silicon positivists" (Ross 1991: 94) in similar
terms, only better. It is "a world in which the global traffic of knowledge, secrets,
measurements, indicators, entertainments . . . take on form, can be . . . accessed
from anywhere. . . . Suddenly cultural knowledge, collective memory, technological advances [become] the object of interactive democracy" (Benedikt 1991: 7).

[. . .] Both the nation and cyberspace are founded on exclusions marked by race, gender, sexuality, and so forth – the nation-state through historically embedded racism, sexism, and homophobia and cyberspace through educational and financial limits on who has access to the Internet. However, I would suggest that the metaphor works in a positive way as well, as both the democratizing Guatemalan nation-state and the technologically emerging cyberspace are spaces for active negotiations about their future configurations.

In addition, I deploy the science-fiction-like cyberspace metaphor to unsettle certain ethnostalgic tendencies, such as the New Age search for modernity's antidote in archaism[7] as well as the hopes of those who want the Maya to form the ethnicity-for-itself that will end Guatemala's long calvary. The science fiction of the cyberspatialized nation-state may also be useful for thinking about a democratizing Guatemala with both a booming stock market and 80 percent of the population in extreme poverty. The Maya are hacking a world deeply structured by transnational technoscience – whether it is the Israeli computers that allow Guatemalan army intelligence (known as the "Archive") to track guerrilla safe houses through tiny increments in electricity use or the faxes and e-mail that regulate the flows of just-in-time production that determine the daily lives of young Mayan *maquila* factory workers.

The nation-state and cyberspace as environments are also both the monstrous spawn of the military-industrial matrix: gridded and programmed in accordance with the demands of command-control-communication-intelligence, or C3I. Both the nation-state and cyberspace are concerned with mapping territories, constituting boundaries, and charting population movements, as well as constituting identities and determining potential risks. [. . .]

Guatemala's virtual nation-state seems deeply ambivalent about its Indians and their supposed embeddedness in premodernity. Ladino state officials, in interviews and other public statements, espouse the politically correct vision of an inclusive Guatemala in which unity is strengthened by diversity and everyone partakes equally in rights and responsibilities. In unguarded moments, however, they suggest that the Maya are obsolete – that the Maya express themselves through handwoven cloth in the age of the microchip and satellite transmission. In this stereotype, the Maya show up as *defined* by their commitment to tradition, that is, by their lack of modernity. [. . .] A newspaper editorial argued that Mayan languages should not be taught at the elementary level because they are "stuck in the middle of the sixteenth century" (*La Hora* 1990). In one of my interviews, a former Finance Ministry official asked: "How is a modern nation possible if we have people speaking twenty-three different languages? How can you translate Shakespeare into K'iche'? How will they have access to universal culture if they are isolated in their different languages?"

This very resistance to modernity is often lauded by these same people, however. The vice minister of labor spoke approvingly of "the amazing valor of these people – they have almost been genocided, but they maintain their culture, they do not forget their origins. Even when they migrate to other places to work, they do not change. And the women especially, they are the most resistant to foreign values. They reproduce their culture." The head of a government development agency expressed awe at the Indians' different sense of time: "This is a distinct advantage. They do not think about progress in one year or five years. They think in terms of hundreds of years! They are in no hurry."

This sense of the Maya as outside history informs the popular notion of the indigenous community as naturally equal, inherently resistant to such army counterinsurgency measures as the Civil Defense Patrols (the imposed military service for rural men), and representing a wholeness that national culture has lost. [...]

[...] Most Maya hackers, however, are quite explicit about their appropriateness in the modern world. For ALMG founder Guillermo Rodriguez Guajan, "Mayan Nationalism means combining 'modern' science and technology with traditional Mayan knowledge of language, medicine, farming know-how and community life in order to develop new forms of Mayan knowledge." This is precisely what many ladinos try to delete from their screens.

In interviews, most ladinos do not deny that the Maya have a right to inclusion, but they insist that the access code is in Spanish and English, not Kaqchikel or K'iche'. To log on to the modern, the Maya must ladinoize. Literacy, technical expertise, Spanish, Western clothes – these are by definition ladino. The colonial binary that consigns the Indians to the premodern while defining ladino as those with access to the "modern" has worked historically in Guatemala by redefining any indigenous person who spoke Spanish or wore Western clothes as ladino – in the census and in popular understanding. For example, a government development official said: "The leaders of the Indian movement are not Maya. They do not come from the communities and they all have a book under their arm." In short, if they read, they are not Maya. [...]

Those Maya who choose to jack into national and transnational information networks, to read, live in cities, do intellectual work, or carry computerized datebooks – those who snarf, or appropriate, anything "modern" – will themselves be appropriated, automatically becoming ladinos.[8] Those who remain in the premodern countryside and maintain "real" indigenous lifeways will be appropriated as well – as tourist commodities for the postmodern world eagerly seeking an "island in the net" (Sterling 1986) for a quick vacation getaway.

To many ladinos, the Maya hacker is inappropriate to the cyberspatialized nation-state. The Maya hackers themselves, however, are staking out an alternative position as "inappropriate/d others," which Trinh Minh-ha describes as the "historic positioning of those who cannot adopt the mask of either 'self' or 'other' offered by modern Western narratives of identity and politics. To be an 'Inappropriate/d Other' means to be in a critical, deconstructive relationality" (cited in Haraway 1992: 299).

In this critical relationality, the Maya hacker is always already inside the machine. As the Mayan congressman Claudio Coxaj said: "We are inside the State. We have adopted the modern." Similarly, Demetrio Cojti said: "Modernity is not the property of anyone. It is universal; no one can lay claim to it.... Everyone is always trying to say that we are inauthentic. But their ideas of indigenous people are very stereotypic, very rural. We are trying to mix things up." In fact, this might be the Maya hacker ethos. [...]

In addition to the networking I have described, the Maya are intervening in these contests through their publications, which act as shareware[....] These documents are tools for reprogramming work, manuals for writing a new operating system that will read commands in indigenous languages and lay out a menu of demands for cultural, educational, health, territorial, and human rights for the Maya.

[. . .] Through the work of the Maya hackers, the cyberspatialized nation-state is shown to be itself divided and unsure, forced to question its own hold on modernity.[9] As the Maya begin not only to appropriate the markers of "modern" ladino identity (such as technological expertise and international networking skills) but also to hack the identity itself, as they rename the nonindigenous as Maya-ladinos, many binary codes begin to misfire. [. . .]

Thankfully, there has so far been no crackdown on the Maya hackers, who have been extremely careful in their dealings with the cold embrace of the spiral arms of military systems. However, ambivalence and creeping paranoia about their border crossings are beginning to come on-line. A staff member of the presidential secretary for political affairs told me: "The government thinks the Indians are not capable of anything. They are ignorant and dependent. But they also say that the Maya are our competition for the future." Despite the vocal rejection by Mayan nationalists of much of the Guatemalan National Revolutionary Unity (URNG) movement's revolutionary politics and methods, official discourse attempts to link Mayan nationalists and the URNG, a strategy that has had bloody consequences in the past. Even powerful ladino state officials say they have been accused of being guerrillas because they express sympathy for the Mayan position.[10] [. . .]

This fear of the "interested use of the issues of the Pueblos Indigenas" colors other reactions to the Maya hacker as well. Leftist ladinos and US academics[11] have suggested that they are co-opted by the state, or even by the very technologies they are appropriating. Such concerns, well intentioned I know, reify either-or categories imbued with an ethnostalgia that posits some pure, authentic space of indigenousness that is outside of "the state," technological degradation, and history itself. Again, these imaginaries are powerful for both the Maya and those who seek to support their goals, but (besides the way they echo ladino state functionary discourse) they also refuse the "mixing up" that Maya hackers feel is so necessary.

[. . .] Despite past and present attempts to exclude them, Guatemala's indigenous peoples have always been deeply imbricated in the "modern" nation-state: as laborers, as symbolic markers for national identity, and as tourist commodities – in short, as the necessary other of the binary code.

Notes

1   Mario Loarca shared this term with me.
2   Abigail Adams (1996) is theorizing the fascinating repercussions of the term gringa. I thank her for making me think about it. Many papers could be written on the role of the gringa's virtuousness in her pursuit of virtuosity in the field of anthropology, that is, the fictions too often left out of our science concerning sexuality and the multiple "interpenetrations of boundaries" that occur when white women go to the field.
3   In long-running debates over the origins and effects of racial or ethnic identities, an

orthodox Marxist position has held that race is an ideological cover justifying class inequalities. The Guatemalan historian Severo Martinez-Pelaez (1990 [1970]), in a book that is the standard text at the National University of Guatemala, has argued that the category of Indian was created during the colonial era to designate those most exploited by the hacienda system. The result of this class reductionism has been a tendency to downplay issues of racism, insisting that once the class structure is overturned such discrimination would melt away. Partly in response to the Mayan cultural rights movement, both the armed revolutionary movement and popular organizations are becoming much more sophisticated in their analysis of the imbrications of class and ethnic identifications. Gender, unfortunately, remains relatively undertheorized.

4 There is a growing literature attempting to name and analyze these "New Times" (Hall and Jacques 1990 [1989]), which are variously characterized as post-Fordist, postindustrial, disorganized capital, the new international division of labor, and so on. I have found Castells's notion of the informational mode of development to be very useful (1989). See Amin (1994) for an overview of these discussions.

5 By this I mean the computer, but also low-cost publishing and reproduction technologies, radio equipment, and even simple telecommunications grids, including phone lines, short-wave radio, and so forth – through which to keep in touch. For example, it was not until 1993 that Nebaj received telephone service. Given Guatemala's high levels of illiteracy, radio has traditionally been an important medium and message: both in the sort of ideological work on passive listeners that some media critics have warned of (e.g., Adorno and Horkheimer 1993; Bukatman 1994; Debord 1983 [1967]) and as a carrier of other messages – in Mayan languages, for example (Adams 1996) – or of official messages that can be decoded (Cojti 1990; Hall 1993). I am arguing not that the Mayan cultural rights activists have complete control over this or other technologies but that the hacker mode is an appropriate tactical response to what Rob Latham calls "the real ambiguities of information society whose promise of technological empowerment bears with it the threat of increasing politico-economic surveillance and control" (1995: 10).

6 "Conscience of a Hacker," appearing in the hacker manifesto *Phrack*, claims: "We seek after knowledge ... and you call us criminals. We exist without skin color, without nationality, without religious bias ... and you call us criminals. You build atomic bombs, you wage war ... yet we're the criminals. Yes, I am a criminal. My crime is that of curiosity. My crime is that of judging people by what they say and think, not what they look like. My crime is that of outsmarting you, something that you will never forgive me for" (cited in Sterling 1992: 83). Stone (1991) and Haraway (1991), among others, address this trick of erasure.

7 The obsessive interest in this supposed beginning of a new age, termed the "Harmonic Convergence" and based on the Mayan long-count calendar, gripped many in North America in 1987. Thousands of people flocked to "spiritual" sites – many in Guatemala and Mexico – to experience it. The effect was lampooned by Gary Trudeau as the "Moronic Convergence."

8 To snarf is to "grab, especially to grab a large document or file for the purpose of using it with or without the author's permission. ... To acquire, with little concern for legal forms or policies (but not quite by stealing) ... with the connotation of absorbing, processing, or understanding" (Raymond 1991: 326).

9 For example, an essay by Dr. Cojti is entitled "Problems of Guatemalan 'National Identity'" (in Rodriguez Guajan 1992 [1989]).

10 URNG is the umbrella guerrilla organization that has fought Guatemala's military governments since 1963.

11   I am thinking of questions raised very passionately during presentations of this work
     at University of California-Davis and Yale University. Thanks to those colleagues for
     helping me think through this issue.

References

Academia de Lenguas Mayas de Guatemala (ALMG) 1990: *Documentos del seminario:
    Situacion actual y futuro de la ALMG.* Guatemala City: Patrocinio del Ministerio de
    Cultura y Deportes.
Adams, A. 1996: "The Word, Work, and Worship: Engendering Transnational Evangelical
    Culture between Highland Guatemala and the US." Ph.D. dissertation, University of
    Virginia.
Adorno, T. and Horkheimer, M. 1993: "The Culture Industry: Enlightenment as Mass
    Deception." In Simon During (ed.), *The Cultural Studies Reader.* London: Routledge,
    29–43.
Amin, A. 1994: *Post-Fordism: A Reader.* Oxford: Blackwell.
Anderson, B. 1990 [1983]: *Imagined Communities: Reflections on the Origin and Spread of
    Nationalism.* London: Verso.
Bastos, S. and Camus, M. 1993: *Quebrando el silencio: Organizaciones del Pueblo Maya y sus
    demandas (1986–1992).* Guatemala City: FLACSO.
Benedikt, M. (ed.) 1991: *Cyberspace: First Steps.* Cambridge, MA: MIT Press.
Bukatman, S. 1994: *Terminal Identity: The Virtual Subject in Postmodern Science Fiction.*
    Durham, NC: Duke University Press.
Castells, M. 1989: *The Informational City: Information Technology, Economic Restructuring, and
    the Urban–Regional Process.* Oxford: Blackwell.
Cojti Cuxil, D. 1990: *Configuración del pensamiento político del Pueblo Maya.* Quetzaltenango,
    Guatemala: AEMG.
Colby, B. N. and Colby, L. M. 1981: *The Daykeeper: The Life and Discourse of an Ixil Diviner.*
    Cambridge, MA: Harvard University Press.
Debord, G. 1983 [1967]: *The Society of the Spectacle.* Detroit: Black and Red.
Fabian, J. 1983: *Time and the Other: How Anthropology Makes Its Object.* New York: Columbia
    University Press.
Hall, S. 1993: "Encoding, Decoding." In Simon During (ed.), *The Cultural Studies Reader.*
    London: Routledge, 90–103.
Hall, S. and Jacques, M. (eds.) 1990 [1989]: *New Times: The Changing Face of Politics in the
    1990s.* London: Verso.
Haraway, D. 1991: *Simians, Cyborgs, and Women: The Reinvention of Nature.* New York:
    Routledge.
Haraway, D. 1992: "The Promises of Monsters: A Regenerative Politics for Inappropriate/
    d Others." In Lawrence Grossberg, Cary Nelson, and Paula A. Treichler (eds.), *Cultural
    Studies.* New York: Routledge.
Hobsbawm, E. and Ranger, T. (eds.) 1983: *The Invention of Tradition.* Cambridge: Cam-
    bridge University Press.
La Hora 1990: "Editorial." August 11, p. 2.
Latham, R. 1995: "Review of *Terminal Identity: The Virtual Subject in Postmodern Science
    Fiction.*" *New York Review of Science Fiction*, April, pp. 1–13.
Martinez-Pelaez, S. 1990 [1970]: *La patria del criollo: Ensayo de interpretación del la realidad
    colonial Guatemalteca.* Mexico City: Ediciones en Marcha.
Menchú Tum, R. 1987: *I, Rigoberta Menchú: An Indian Woman in Guatemala*, ed. Elisabeth
    Burgos-Debray, trans. Ann Wright. London: Verso.

Mitchell, T. 1991: "The Limits of the State: Beyond Statist Approaches and Their Critics." *American Political Science Review* (March), 76–95.

Nelson, D. M. 1991: "The Reconstruction of Mayan Identity." *Report on Guatemala* 12 (2), 6–14.

Raymond, E. (ed.) 1991: *The New Hacker's Dictionary.* Cambridge, MA: MIT Press.

Rodriguez Guajan, D. 1992 [1989]: *Cultura Maya y políticas de desarrollo.* Guatemala City: COCADI.

Ross, A. 1991: *Strange Weather: Culture, Science and Technology in the Age of Limits.* London: Verso.

Smith, C. A. (ed.) 1990: *Guatemalan Indians and the State, 1540–1988.* Austin: University of Texas Press.

Smith, C. A. 1991: *Maya Nationalism.* NACLA Report on the Americas. December.

Spivak, G. C. 1988: "Can the Subaltern Speak?" In Cary Nelson and Lawrence Grossberg (eds.), *Marxism and the Interpretation of Culture.* Urbana: University of Illinois Press.

Sterling, B. 1986: *Islands in the Net.* Berkeley: Berkeley Press.

Sterling, B. 1992: *The Hacker Crackdown: Law and Disorder on the Electronic Frontier.* New York: Bantam.

Stone, A. R. 1991: "Will the Real Body Please Stand Up? Boundary Stories about Virtual Cultures." In Michael Benedikt (ed.), *Cyberspace: First Steps.* Cambridge, MA: MIT Press, 83–114.

Trinh Minh-ha 1986: "She, The Inappropriate/d Other." *Discourse* 8.

23 CyberResistance: Saudi Opposition Between Globalization and Localization

Mamoun Fandy

[...]

[...] The Saudi opposition and the Saudi state have their own peculiarities, at least in the imagination of Western social scientists. Saudi Arabia appears in most Western writings as a traditional society, a misconception that must be dispelled before we can examine the highly complex and sophisticated structure of Saudi resistance. Saudi Arabia is a very complex mixture of the traditional, the modern, and the postmodern, depending on the region and the sociocultural formation.[1] For example, the eastern province is dominated by a Shi'a population, an oil industry, and an obvious American influence. Highways, shopping malls, and expatriate communities give the impression that one is in an American city, especially when one sees the number of American soldiers and civilians in Dhahran, Damam, and Khobar. Except for scattered and sometimes diffuse native cultural practices of closing shops for prayers and veiling women, these cities are a microcosm of global creolization. Even when one examines the local, one discovers that hijabs and abayahs (local dress) are made in Taiwan and Hong Kong, as well as designer abayahs prepared in Paris and London. Prayer rugs with a compass indicating the direction of Mecca are made in Japan. Moreover, the local Shi'ism transcends Saudi territories to reach Bahrain, Lebanon, and Iran. Even the holy places in Mecca and Madina are not immune to the global effect. Almost all religious icons sold outside the Prophet's mosque in Madina are made outside the country and sold to foreigners as if they were Saudi. Foreign workers, estimated to equal the population of natives, add to the peculiarity of the Saudi state. Saudi children are raised by Asian and European nannies and are frequently bilingual. Saudi culture also varies from one region

Excerpted from Mamoun Fandy, "CyberResistance: Saudi Opposition Between Globalization and Localization." *Comparative Studies in Society and History* 41 (1999), 124–47.

to the other, a few examples being the liberal Sunni cosmopolitan in the Western Region, Shi'i liberal and Western in the East, conservative but Westernized in the center. Moreover, like Kuwait, Saudi Arabia is not concentrated only in its physical and geographical space but, rather, diffused financially and information-ally in the various global scapes.

Saudi Arabia is peculiar in that the state usually presents itself as the defender of the faith in the face of a cultural and religious onslaught from the West. Thus, in macropolitical or global terms, the state presents itself as an opposition group. The state's allocation of resources to take care of the holy places and its insistence on being an Islamic state that applies Islamic law further confirms Saudi Arabia's image as a country at the forefront of the global struggle against Western corruption. Moreover, Saudi opposition groups are different from those in other states both because of the extreme limitations on conventional expressions of dissent within the country and because of the opposition's access to cash and the global flow of information. They are the first of the opposition groups in the Middle East to make extensive use of new technologies in communicating their message to their followers. [. . .]

In Saudi Arabia, the impact of the media on culture, politics, and society is at the forefront of the national discourse. To appreciate the complexity of this debate about Saudi society and the intrusion of these new means of com-munication, one has to understand the situation prior to their introduction. Discourse on the media, coupled with that of the state ulama (clergy), is central to the hegemony of the Saud family over competing tribes by establishing the legitimacy of the Saudi political order through a hegemony of Islamic and traditional discourse. The state must maintain itself through a web of religious and tribal discourse. If this web is weakened, the stability of the state is likely to be compromised. The preaching of the state ulama and the traditionalists' tribal discourse are mediated and propagated through mosques, state radio, television, and newspapers. This hegemony weakens during times of crisis that expose the disjunction between the legitimizing discourse of the state and the practices of the rulers. This was the case when the Saudi rulers allowed foreign troops into Saudi Arabia during the 1990 Gulf Crisis. Then, the government-owned television and radio had to broadcast the fatwas (religious edicts) of the ulama sanctioning the importation of troops to protect the holy places. The discourse of the opposition focused on a critique of the ulama's edicts and propagated its message via different means, namely books, faxes, cassette tapes, and later e-mail and web sites. For the continuation of a strong hegemony, the state has to control this alternative dissemination of information (both religious and secular) to ensure that citizens comply with the dominant order.

In this context, the Saudi state devotes a great deal of money and effort to regulate the flow of information. Some of the state's strategies to regulate information include building institutions responsible for censorship and main-taining state ownership of both radio and television. Telecommunication is also kept under state control, so the government monitors international phone calls and faxes. However, opposition forces and other social forces frequently circum-vent censorship and regulatory institutions in order to acquire or transmit alternative messages. Furthermore, state control of press, radio, and television can be circumvented through the use of satellite dishes, the Internet, and cassette tapes. [. . .]

[. . .] Saudi Arabia is currently engaged in an ambitious plan of building an information infrastructure that can be used by business and the state. However, this infrastructure can also be used by the opposition. For instance, the Saudi state took steps to upgrade its current telephone system by signing a $4 billion contract with American Telephone and Telegraph (AT &T). This contract allows AT &T to upgrade the Saudi system from traditional telecommunications to digital wireless telephones and to upgrade existing networks and satellite links. A Saudi can connect with the Internet through Gulfnet, which allows for dialup connections with other online services through a local network (al-Waseet). King Abd al-'Aziz City for Science and Technology and other Saudi universities are at the center of these activities.[2] Yet while the system will obviously serve state interests, Saudi attempts to integrate computers will also serve the opposition by opening up another media space for alternative discourse. Although currently Saudis have limited access to the World Wide Web, they can gain greater access by dialing up servers in neighboring countries, and many Saudis are wealthy enough to do so.[3] This may change the nature of Saudi opposition over time from an Islamist resistance that crosscuts many social classes into an elite opposition available only to those who can afford an international call. Currently, however, the Islamists make information available to local Saudis by providing toll-free numbers, as will be demonstrated below.

Islam-based dissent in Saudi Arabia dates back to the state's formation. The Saudi government with its traditional institutions effectively limited the appeal of its opponents by censoring their message. Groups that rebelled openly, such as those who seized the Grand Mosque in Mecca in 1979, were crushed militarily.[4] The absence of a communication structure for this group limited its supporters. Since Saudi Arabia is a very big country, revolutionaries need to disseminate their message throughout this wide space. With the advent of the Iranian revolution in 1979, the cassette tape as a new means of political communication was introduced.[5] The dissemination of Khomeini's message by tape inside and outside Iran contributed to an uprising in the Shi'a area of Saudi Arabia. However, Shi'a audiotapes did not reach the Sunni areas because of sectarian differences.

The cassette tape as a means of communicating political messages became popular in the Sunni regions of Saudi Arabia only in the mid-1980s, intensifying in 1988 and after. The debate between the modernists and Islamists prefigured the verbal war that arose between the Saudi state and its Islamist opposition during and after the Gulf War by using cassette tapes as a means of attacking the written word. The most intense debate over the role of Islam in Saudi Arabia took shape in 1989, when two major trends emerged: the liberal trend and the Islamic trend. The debate centered around the issue of modernism and its impact on Saudi society. The liberals disguised their protest in literary texts that criticized the dominant religious discourse in the country.

Islamists responded to these provocations with books, leaflets, and cassette tapes denouncing the liberal trend and asking the government to dismiss some of these writers from their positions as columnists in Saudi newspapers and magazines. [. . .]

[. . .] The Gulf War and the arrival of American troops in the "holy land" intensified the debate. New voices emerged, many of whom were embraced by large segments of the Saudi public. Two preachers who later became leaders of the Islamic movement in the Kingdom, Safar al-Hawali and Salman al-'Auda, gained prominence during the Gulf crisis as a result of their daring criticism of the deployment of American troops on Saudi soil. Due to the state monopoly of radio, television, and newspapers, the preachers used cassette tapes and occasional video tapes to propagate their messages. The tapes provided the Saudi public with well-argued religious position papers objecting to the presence of foreign troops on the holy land.[6] The Islamists were thus effective in mobilizing support against the foreign intervention and in threatening the regime. Copying machines were central to the propagation of these groups' message through print. One Saudi dissident explained,

> We used to give copies of these speeches to Indian and Pakistani workers to Xerox by the hundred and ask them to put them in the mail boxes of government officials and ordinary citizens. Since these workers didn't read Arabic, they didn't know that they were used in a political campaign.[7]

The activists also sent their messages by fax to their supporters. The Saudi government responded to all this activity by making it illegal for al-'Auda and al-Hawali to preach in the mosques. The two opposition leaders then resorted to cassette tapes as a way of circumventing the royal decree.

Existing institutions of censorship have had limited success in controlling the cassette tape phenomenon. The regulation of cassettes and the shops that sell them is covered by the Press and Publication Code, which puts the matter under the responsibility of the General Directorate for Publications. The Directorate has sought to counteract the influence of cassette tapes mainly by raiding the shops that sell them, but this has proven ineffective and tape distribution has continued to increase. In response to government raids, activists have turned to underground networks to distribute their tapes. [. . .]

Before the Gulf War, the Islamists lacked an organization but had an ideology. In fact the Islamic discourse of al-Hawali and al-'Auda is not new to Saudi Arabia; what is new is the vast increase in distribution through cassette tapes, faxes, and copying machines. Technology has created the new leadership of the Islamist movement in Saudi Arabia. [. . .]

CyberResistance

The Committee for the Defense of Legitimate Rights (CDLR)

"Everything appeared to be in place: charismatic preachers, thousands of enthusiastic followers, and a religious public. What was missing was an effective organization to channel this energy and pose a serious challenge to the regime," says Sa'd al-Faqih, one of the founding members of CDLR. Five men – Mohsen al-'Awaji, Khalid al-Hmeidh, Abd al-'Aziz al-Qasim, Abd al-W'ahab al-Trairi, and Sa'd al-Faqih – formed the basic committee and met in Riyadh to devise a plan to use these forces. In May 1991, after thirty meetings, the group drafted a letter of demands to be sent to the king in the name of the Islamic leaders. The letter was signed by many Saudi Islamists and intellectuals. [. . .] It addressed various issues ranging from corruption in the bureaucracy to the codification of laws to human rights.[8] In September of 1992, the Islamist group's philosophy emerged clearly in a forty-five-page pamphlet known as the Memorandum of Advice, which was addressed to the ulama and the king.[9] Copying machines and faxes played a very significant role in propagating the group's ideas. [. . .]

The government's response to the announcement of CDLR was to arrest its main spokesman, Muhammad al-Mas'ari. Later al-Mas'ari escaped from prison and established new headquarters for the movement in London.[10] From London, the leaders of CDLR have sent a steady stream of information critical of the Riyadh government. "Every week, via CompuServe, the CDLR faxes its newsletter to 600 distribution points in Saudi Arabia."[11] They also transmit the same information through e-mail and their World Wide Web homepage. The group uses similar means to gather news about the Kingdom. According to the leaders of CDLR, their informants include "disaffected Saudi businessmen, clerics, military officers, and intelligence officials."[12]

CDLR's homepage targets those interested in Saudi affairs in the West, namely policy makers, journalists, scholars, and Saudi students studying in the West. The latter group includes potential members of the movement whenever they return to the Kingdom, according to one CDLR activist.[13] The homepage, published in both English and Arabic, consists of four parts: the *Monitor*, a weekly publication also available in print; *ash-Shar'iyyah*, a monthly magazine, also available in print; communiqués, which respond to specific events and essentially act as press releases; and other publications, which include country reports and yearbooks. These publications differ in tone and discourse depending on the language used. For example, references to human rights in the English edition become references to Shari'a rights in Arabic. [. . .]

Although it exploits almost all available means of communication, CDLR is limited by the existing communication structure. For instance, most of CDLR's information is distributed either through the United States or Britain. This is because the Internet facilities in the Gulf area are still very limited. The only existing nodes in the Gulf area are Gulfnet and Emirates Net. Although these nets are government controlled, universities in the Gulf in general have e-mail so that one person with access to the Internet can relay information to other e-mail users. However, earlier government reaction to the CDLR suggests that the group has some influence inside Saudi Arabia.

The Movement for Islamic Reform (MIRA)

The Movement for Islamic Reform in Arabia, the group most sophisticated in using electronic resistance, is very recent. It emerged in March 1996 as a result of a split in CDLR. MIRA's director, Dr. Sa'd al-Faqih, sees the breakaway as a result of differences over "policy and methodology."[14] [. . .] He considers MIRA as the "media arm of the (Sunni) reform movement" inside the country.[15] The contents of MIRA's homepage are very sophisticated. Aside from the basic introduction about who they are and the aims of the organization, the homepage provides analytical articles on relevant subjects such as royal succession, the economic crisis in the Kingdom, and the history of dissent in Saudi Arabia. The Arabic version of MIRA's weekly newsletter, *al-Islah*, provides news from the Kingdom, foreign media reports about Saudi Arabia, and an analytical article about the current situation. Because *al-Islah* is designed to address a local audience, its discourse has the Islamic coloring of the movement but is more organized and more moderate in tone than CDLR. MIRA is trusted by the local leadership to the degree that Salman al-'Auda and Salfar al-Hawali send their writings from prison to be published in MIRA's newsletter.[16]

One may reach MIRA both by e-mail and by telephone. The homepage also provides downloadable information; some of this information is very similar to what one would download from CDLR's database. The country report is but one example of this similarity. However, MIRA provides its own information. One can also get the MIRA newsletter by dialing a telephone number in the United States. [. . .] Saudis may also dial MIRA through its toll-free numbers not only from inside Saudi Arabia but when they travel to neighboring countries such as Kuwait, Bahrain, Qatar, and Egypt. MIRA is also entertaining the possibility of providing a broadcast version of their electronic resistance via one of the satellite channels that beams radio broadcasts directly to Saudi Arabia. So far the group has met some difficulties in securing a channel due to the "nervousness of satellite companies."[17]

"Virtual Saudis" opposition

The presence of "virtual opposition" in cyberspace raises the problem of identifying participants in this discourse. Are the members of this opposition "real" Saudi citizens, non-Saudis genuinely engaged in the Saudi opposition discourse, or individuals in an unrelated category who seek, by masquerading as Saudis, to manipulate the discourse of opposition in the pursuit of ends unrelated to that discourse? These three categories (real Saudi citizens, virtual citizens, and masqueraders) overlap, to some extent. "Real" Saudi citizens may also be virtual citizens – in fact, cyberspace may provide the only place in which they can act as participatory citizens at all. The population of virtual citizens, however, is not restricted to "real" citizens with Internet access; it also includes non-Saudi participants who are engaged in and shape Saudi opposition. The possibilities are endless: It could be the state itself is masquerading as opposition; liberals as Islamists; another state; or any other interested party. [. . .]

Government responses to new forms of resistance

The Saudi government has used various strategies to cope with its opponents, be they "virtual" or real. These strategies include accommodating some of the popular demands for reform; competing with opposition in cyberspace and the "hyperreal" world of television screens; and using its financial and diplomatic power to limit the impact of opposition, both inside and outside the national boundaries. [...]

To combat the opposition's media war outside the Kingdom, the Saudi government either directly or indirectly has purchased major media outlets in different world capitals. Currently, Saudi Arabia dominates the Arabic visual and print media. The Arab media conglomerates such as Middle East Broadcasting Corporation (MBC), Orbit Communications, and Arab Radio and Television (ART), are not run or controlled directly by the government but are owned either by Saudi princes or by Saudi businessmen with close relationships to the royal family. [...] As owners of these media outlets, the Saudis control the content by punishing those who are critical of Saudi Arabia or who beam in programs offensive to Saudi social mores. For example, Saudi Arabia canceled its 150-million-dollar contract with the Arabic BBC television because it aired a Panorama program critical of Saudi treatment of foreign workers.[18] [...]

Except for having its own homepage, the Saudi government has done very little to counter the effect of the Internet-based resistance.[19] Inside the country, the government has made it difficult and expensive for Saudis to have access to the Internet. Those who want to have access to the Internet have to register with the Saudi telecommunications company which allows dialup connections with a foreign service provider. However, like the opposition, the Saudi state is likely to learn from others dealing with the Internet as a new playing field. China is one model that the Saudi government is likely to emulate. The Chinese government managed to partially limit Internet use by ordering all Internet users to register with the Ministry of Posts and Telecommunication. This "paved the way for web site blocks."[20] Chinese Internet users are also required to register with the police. Moreover, users of China's government-controlled Internet services, Chinanet, are required to sign a statement saying that they will respect China's laws and do nothing to harm the state.[21] Chinese law forbids "dissemination of information damaging to public order."[22] However, the Chinese situation is very different from Saudi Arabia, since in China few people can afford the Internet or personal computers. In contrast, many more Saudis have private telephones and the means to buy computers. They are also able to afford to pay Internet fees to servers outside Saudi Arabia, either in the West or in neighboring Gulf countries.

Analysis and implications

Analysis of the relations between the Saudi state and the opposition in the context of globalization, informatics, and late capitalism raises new questions for the state and related concepts such as sovereignty, citizenship, territoriality, and resistance. In addition to the analytical concepts, the new means of communication and the local/global dialectic have implications for the substance of the debate: the nature of Islam and Islamic governance. The interaction between the Saudi state and its opponents show that both are forced to bargain with different audiences in different scapes and contend with different hegemonies. In this process of bargaining, both the state and its opponents lose and gain ideologically and politically, at least at the level of discourse, as the analysis of the opposition homepages and government response to them shows.

The new technology and the "compression of space" have drastically altered the nature of resistance to the state by expanding the domain of political activities beyond national territories. The greater flexibility and extraterritoriality of the new modes of resistance resulting from the mobility of the site of resistance create a marked difference between this new and "postmodern" resistance and that of the "premodern" era. This is obvious in the case of cassette tapes and cellular phones and of the global flow of information on the Internet. These new developments have accorded the opposition an opportunity to communicate with similar groups and to learn new strategies from opposition movements elsewhere. The similarity of the information on the homepages and the sources of this information suggests that these new spaces allow the opposition greater coordination and communication not available at home. Even if this is not direct communication among the groups, the information is available for anyone to see, copy, or download. This information and the debate around it have the potential to provide a basis for a new "imagined community." To be part of such an imagined community, one does not have to be a "real" Saudi – "virtual" Saudis can be as much a part of this process as the real Saudi. [. . .]

A review of the cyberspace resistance homepages (CDLR and MIRA) shows that the structure of the Internet as an environment of communication, the language used, and the diversity of audience affect the substance of the message. [. . .]

Both al-Mas'ari and al-Faqih are convinced that the way they can pressure the Saudi government into accommodating their demands is to address its Western allies and patrons. In doing so, both groups anchor their criticism of the Saudi government in the discourse of metropolitan globalization. This global influence is evident in CDLR 's reformism, neoliberal economics, and human rights discourse. Saudi opposition discourse on the homepages generally does not question the regime's neoliberal economics but instead the government's mismanagement of the Saudi economy. Thus, the homepage technoscape engages both the global ideoscape and the financescape, to name but two.[23] In the human rights sphere, as they move between these multiple discourses, these two groups sacrifice certain components of their Islamic message in favor of a hybrid discourse that attempts to reconcile Islam with the Universal Declaration of Human Rights. In the process, they become an agent for globalization by introducing global discourse to a local audience. [. . .]

Although text-based messages via the Internet and faxes have proven effective in the "media war" between the opposition and the government, at least abroad, cassette tapes remain the most effective tool inside. This is because of the Saudi oral culture and the limited literacy of the Saudi public. [. . .] Although they may or may not be literate, at the very least the poor have access to radical preaching via tape-recorded messages. On the other hand, the disadvantaged in economic terms are also disadvantaged because of their limited access to higher forms of media, that is, satellite transmissions and the Internet. The elite have full access to the new global media and to the global space. Restricted to local networks, the poor find it difficult, even impossible, to partake of the globalism of concepts and systems of beliefs.

In this new global/local relationship, state media have to compete with alternative media made possible by cassette tapes, Internet connections, and the satellite dish. The Islamic message of the state ulama currently competes with other Islamic messages coming from neighboring countries or from intermediate and border line space. No authoritative discourse or hegemony is likely to convince every Saudi citizen that the moral vision of the state elite is superior to theirs, since there are so many discourses being broadcast, on tape, on the Internet that may prove superior. These alternative media will certainly have implications for the functions of traditional means of communication in Saudi society. For example, the agenda-setting impact of the news media will no longer be entirely in the hands of state officials. An alternative agenda can be set by messages coming from abroad via these alternative means of communication. The interpretation of news will no longer be the monopoly of state or government journalists but will be shared by contending forces in widening circles.

Although the intertwining of global communication structures and the discourse of globalization enhances the cause of the opposition by multiplying its access, voices, and channels, it would be a mistake to assume that cyberspace is exclusively oppositionist. In fact, the global space is still dominated by states, albeit with limited sovereignty and limited control over what their citizens are exposed to. The global space in the Saudi case also complicates the task of opposition. This is because in macropolitical terms, the Saudi state can cast itself as being an opposition to the "Western cultural imperialism" that threatens Islam and Muslims. In this sense the state can hijack the rejectionist mood and easily portray its opponents as agents of the West. Nonetheless, it is very important to review the ways in which these new means have affected the message of opposition both in substance and in form. [. . .]

The Saudi case reveals problems with the conventional understanding of resistance. It is not enough to explore hidden transcripts to "grasp potential acts."[24] One has to surf the Internet and homepages of opposition groups. The Saudi case also reveals that those who are enamored with the totalizing and homogenizing effects of modernity and globalization should take into account the local impulse that replaces grand narrative with multiple and local narratives as a way of resisting a metropolitan globalization. Nor is this the whole story, for domination and resistance in non-Western social formations such as Saudi Arabia show that, even as local society engages different trends of the global modes, some are part of the Internet and globalization; while others are part of the world of cassette tapes and faxes. Although it resists the global narrative, the local impulse simultaneously addresses the global arena by adapting the language and narrative of dominant global trends. Thus, the discourses of opposition and government interact concomitantly between the phenomenally global and the local. Here it becomes obvious that as the world "opens up," the struggle between governments and opposition is no longer merely local and that even the local is tremendously mediated.[25] [. . .]

[. . .] Geographic boundaries and notions of state sovereignty, traditionally definers of individual states, seem to dissolve in the cyberspace formed from an overriding globalization of local concepts and localization of global concepts. Mediation of the local and the global at the level of discourse, image, and lived experience poses serious challenges to such old concepts, challenges that must be taken seriously. Saudi opposition may be virtual thus far, but the dialectic of the local and the global is real, not virtual.

Notes

1 For more on the debate of the coexistence of the "modern" in the "traditional" and the traditional in the modern and even the postmodern, see Timothy Luke, "Identity, Meaning, and Globalization: Detraditionalization in Postmodern Space Time Compression," in Paul Heelas, Scott Lash, Paul Morris, *Detraditionalization* (Cambridge, MA: Blackwell, 1996), 109–33.

2 For more on the information infrastructure of the Arab world in general and Saudi Arabia in particular, see C. Bryan Gabbard and George S. Park, *The Information Revolution in the Arab World* (Santa Monica, CA: RAND, 1996). See also Hamad al-Saloom, *Science and Technology in Saudi Arabia* (Washington, DC: The Saudi Arabian Cultural Mission, 1995).

3 Interview with a Saudi professor who has used this method (Washington, November 26, 1996).

4 For more on these incidents, see Mordichai Abir, *Saudi Arabia: Government Society and the Gulf Crisis* (New York: Routledge, 1993), 79–89.

5 For more on cassette tapes and the Iranian revolution, See Annabelle and Ali Mohammadi, *Small Media, Big Revolution: Communication, Culture and the Iranian Revolution* (Minneapolis, MN: University of Minnesota Press, 1994).

6 For translation of these tapes and analysis of their contents, see Mamoun Fandy, "The Hawali Tapes," *New York Times* (November 24, 1990); see also my translation of Hawali in "Infidels Without, and Within," *New Perspectives Quarterly*, 8, 2 (Spring 1991).

7 Telephone interview with Sa'd al-Faqih (December 30, 1996).

8 For a summary of the letter, see Hriar Dekmejian, "The Rise of Political Islam in Saudi Arabia," *Middle East Journal* 48, 8 (Autumn 1994), 630–1.

9 Ibid., 633–5.

10 Al-Mas'ari's story is also recorded on a cassette tape entitled, "Al-Mas'ari and Imprisonment" (Arabic), publicized by CDLR.

11 Louise Lief, "Waging War by Fax Machine," *U.S. News & World Report*, November 27, 1995, p. 51.

12 Telephone interview with Muhammad al-Mas'ari, December 30, 1996.

13 Interview with a CDLR activist, December 18, 1996.

14 This is based on e-mail exchanges between the author and Dr. al-Faqih. This particular quote is taken from a message sent on December 13, 1996.

15 Telephone interview with Sa'd al-Faqih, December 30, 1996.

16 For a letter from Salman al-'Auda, see *al-Islah*, no. 3 (April, 1996), 1.

17 Interview with Sa'd al-Faqih, December 30, 1996.

18 Stephen Franklin, "The Kingdom and the Power." *Columbia Journalism Review* (November/December 1996), 49–51.

19 The Saudi government has its own homepage maintained by its embassy in Washington, DC.

20 Renee Schoof, "China Tightens Control of Internet, Blocks 100 Web Sites," *Associated Press*, September 9, 1996.

21 Ibid.

22 Joshua Gordon, "East Asian Censors Want to Net the Internet," *Christian Science Monitor*, November 12, 1996, p. 19.

23 For more on the specialized reports critical of the Saudi government's mismanage-
    ment of the economy, see CDLR special report, *Saudi Arabian Airlines: Prospects and
    Impacts of Privatization, an Overview* (London: CDLR Publications, 1995); also see, *Ash-
    Shar'iyyah*, no. 5 (November, 1995), 26–31.
24 James C. Scott, *Domination and the Arts of Resistance* (New Haven, CT: Yale University
    Press, 1990), 16.
25 On the impact of mediation on hegemony, see Jesus Martin-Barbero, *Communication,
    Culture and Hegemony: From Media to Mediations* (London: Sage Publications, 1993).

Part VII

Multiple Modernities

Introduction

As the Introduction to this Reader discussed, the idea of alternative modernities is a useful tool to break down the various dichotomies which have characterized debates about culture and development. In this section the readings cover a range of examples of how modernities are localized and pluralized, in the context of colonialism, postcolonial nation building, and international development.

The seminal collection, *The Invention of Tradition* (Hobsbawm and Ranger 1983), brought together a number of detailed historical studies which demonstrated that many so-called traditional practices are in fact constructions of the recent past. Terence Ranger's contribution looked at how European colonial powers reworked African social practices into a lore of "traditions" intended to bolster imperial rule. In the extract presented here, Ranger critically refines his earlier (1983) analysis, arguing that it had placed too much emphasis on colonial agency in inventing African identities. His example of the construction of Ndebele ethnicity shows that, while it was initially invented to facilitate colonial rule, it was the "Ndebele" themselves who subsequently made the label meaningful, and at various times contested its meaning.

Lata Mani's account of the debates over *sati* (or widow immolation) in colonial India demonstrates that they were less about the practice itself than its meaning in terms of Indianness. Mani argues that the crucial issue in such debates was what constitutes authentic tradition, and which of the many traditions coexisting in India represented Indian society. The status of Indian women and the debate over *sati* became crucial sites in the symbolic reworking of Indian identity between colonial and nationalist men.

Sarasawati Sunindyo complements Mani's account of colonial India. She charts the Indonesian postcolonial state's use of constructions of femininity to articulate nationalist visions of modernity which contest Western hegemony. Public discourses about women's role in the Indonesian military are revealed as contradictory. On the one hand, they portray women and men as sisters and brothers defending the nation, but on the other, they leave intact the notions of a patriarchal state and of domestic femininity.

The extract from Maila Stivens looks at how the postcolonial state in Malaysia uses the motherhood of Malay women as a signifier of a distinctive Malay modernity. British colonial authorities first focused on the parenting practices of Malay women as an indicator of Malay backwardness. The postcolonial state, intent on calibrating Malay participation in economy and society with that of Chinese Malaysians, pursued policies of urbanization and the creation of a Malay middle class. Stivens traces how Malay mothers are burdened with the responsibility of reproducing a functional Malay modernity appropriate to the government's vision.

Stacey Leigh Pigg and Lila Abu-Lughod examine the ways in which global discourses of development and modernity are refracted through national lenses to the local. Abu-Lughod considers the relation between the local and modernity in her study of the cultural politics of Egyptian television. In keeping with modernization precepts, Egyptian elites have attempted to use television as a powerful instrument to bring modernity to the masses. However, the soap operas they produce, intended to provide role models of a national middle-class modernity, lose out to apolitical American soaps of the rich and the beautiful in the popularity stakes. Abu-Lughod's ethnography of rural villagers identifies the false premise informing elite concerns that they live in a backward world of tradition. Elite efforts to educate the masses into modernity are misplaced because the villagers of Egypt already inhabit a modernity – only one that is very different from that of their national elites.

Pigg's work in Nepal also argues against the simple dichotomy of Western modernity taking over traditional cultures. She argues instead that the villagers of Nepal express a complex cosmopolitanism, in which awareness of wider worlds is a cultural capital capable of opening up the opportunities offered by the international and national development industry. What emerges out of this localization of development discourse is another version of modernity, in which indigenous practices and belief systems are pragmatically interleaved with those of national, and global, versions of modernity.

References

Hobsbawm, E. and Ranger, T. (eds.) 1983: *The Invention of Tradition*. Cambridge: Cambridge University Press.

Ranger, T. 1983: "The Invention of Tradition in Colonial Africa." In E. Hobsbawm and T. Ranger (eds.), *The Invention of Tradition*. Cambridge: Cambridge University Press, 211–62.

24 The Invention of Tradition Revisited: The Case of Colonial Africa

Terence Ranger

Introduction

[. . .] *The Invention of Tradition*[1] has been merely one of at least a score of similarly titled works.[2] Yet it has had an impact greater than most of these others. [Werner] Sollors himself regards it as providing a counter to the dangers of ahistoricity. For him it is "a model collection for applying the concept of 'invention' to a critical, yet eminently historical, study" by focusing not only on the *fact* of the invention of "essentialist categories" but also on the process and agency by which such invention is accomplished.[3] [. . .]

It is clear that this success has been achieved partly at the expense of the book's particular argument. The folklorist and many of the anthropological applicants were drawing upon it to argue that all traditions, at all times and places, are "invented." In a sense, of course, this is true and where that sense has been ignored, or denied, then its statement is liberating. But the book's argument was different. It was about a specific historical period in which, it asserted, traditions were peculiarly frequently invented rather than customs continuing to evolve. Its argument focused on the rise of romantic nationalism, the rituals of mass industrial politics, the interactions of imperialism and "scientific" classification, the production of "neo-traditional" cadres to serve the imperial states, and the counter-inventions of anti-imperial and socialist movements. My own chapter on Africa was set firmly in this context. Indeed I argued that for Africa the divide with the past was especially clear, corresponding as it did to the cleavage between precolonial and colonial societies. The colonial period in Africa, I asserted, was not only marked by the importation of European neo-traditional

Excerpted from Terence Ranger, "The Invention of Tradition Revisited: The Case of Colonial Africa." In T. Ranger and O. Vaughan (eds.), *Legitimacy and the State in Twentieth-century Africa* (Basingstoke: Macmillan, in association with St. Anthony's College, Oxford, 1993), 62–111.

inventions of identity – the regiment, the boarding school, the refeudalized country house – and the inclusion of Africans within them as subordinates, but also by systematic inventions of *African* traditions – ethnicity, customary law, "traditional" religion. Before colonialism Africa was characterized by pluralism, flexibility, multiple identity; after it African identities of "tribe," gender, and generation were all bounded by the rigidities of invented tradition. [. . .]

Modifying the Idea of the Invention of Tradition

[. . . F]or two reasons I want to return to my elementary analysis. One is that *The Invention of Tradition* may well still be where non-Africanists encounter these ideas. The other is that for me it remains a starting-point in the process of self-criticism, which generates more general critical propositions. I seek therefore to make some self-criticisms which may develop into wider criticisms of the new verities of colonial cultural and ideological invention.

I think the best place to begin with is with the word "invention" itself. Our choice of it was, of course, deliberate. It had several advantages. To "invent" tradition was yet more challenging than to invent "America" or "Athens" or even "Ethnicity," so the term pointed up the paradox of the thesis argued in the book. "Invention" was also a word appropriate to the age of industrial capitalism in which [. . .] *The Invention* is situated. Finally, it emphasized conscious construction and composition of "tradition," appropriate to the sort of situation described by Callaway:

> British officers played imperial roles with what might be seen as a talent for theatrical improvisation. Appropriate ceremonies were elaborated, drawing from numerous sources: established military and state rituals, the displays of power staged in India at the turn of the century and, in Nigeria, some of the more regal practices they found on arrival.[4]

But there are also serious drawbacks to the term "invention." It implies too one-sided a happening. An invention presupposes an inventor – and in my chapter in *The Invention* the inventors were mainly colonial administrators or missionaries, working admittedly with African collaborators but with these playing the role of laboratory assistants rather than of scientists. As Rosalind O'Hanlon remarks *à propos* of imperial India:

> The assumption seems to be made too often that the flow of power was all in one direction: that colonial knowledges intervened from above and outside to transform Indian culture and social relations.

[. . .] O'Hanlon insists that as a result of indigenous developments towards capitalism and bureaucracy Indian intellectuals were already adroit in classification and the invention of subordinate identities. She insists that "some at least of what we now call 'colonial knowledge' about India emerged from the late eighteenth century as the jointly authored product alike of officials of the East India Company and their . . . interested Indian informants."[5] [. . .]

Moreover, invention is too once-for-all an event. An invention may take some time to develop but, once made by the individual or team who have been working on it, all that is left is to apply for a patent. It is a term which makes little allowance for process, for the constant reworking of identities and the steady transformation of institutions. [. . .]

[. . .] I have come to think that the defects of the term "invention" compromise not only my chapter but also some of the later work on colonial custom. The idea can be a foreclosing one. It emphasizes, and emphasizes rightly, a contrast between precolonial fluidity and the reification of colonial classification, between mobile custom and static tradition. But, however codified and static colonial tradition was intended to be, it could never end there. To focus on the innovation of a tradition is certainly to approach it historically, but to approach it fully historically means also to study its subsequent development and the conflict over its meaning. Moreover, to say that "invented tradition was a product of the ideological needs of colonialism" foreshortens colonialism as well as tradition. Brief as it was in the overall history of Africa, the colonial period was long enough for a shifting history of hegemony. My chapter and the subsequent literature is strong on early colonialism and on the 1930s but much weaker on the period of World War II and after, when other legitimations and innovations were required. The continuation in Africa of the invented traditions of Europe, long after they had become irrelevant to governance at home (which is documented in Callaway's book), was real but deceptive. Things had changed in colonial Africa too.

So the word "invention" gets in the way of a fully historical treatment of colonial hegemony *and* of a fully historical treatment of African participation and initiative in innovating custom. I have come to prefer Benedict Anderson's word from his *Imagined Communities*. Some traditions in colonial Africa really *were* invented, by a single colonial officer for a single occasion. But customary law and ethnicity and religion and language were *imagined*, by many different people and over a long time. These multiple imaginations were in tension with each other and in constant contestation to define the meaning of what had been imagined – to imagine it further. Traditions imagined by whites were reimagined by blacks; traditions imagined by particular black interest groups were reimagined by others. The history of modern tradition has been much more complex than we have supposed.

Above all, I like the word "imagining" because, much more than the term "invention," it lays stress upon ideas and images and symbols. However politically convenient they were, the new traditions were, after all, essentially about identity and identity is essentially a matter of imagination. It is good that the growing focus on colonial ideology is beginning to be matched by an interest in African ideas.

Rethinking the Invention of Ethnicity

It seems best to begin a reconsideration of the invention of tradition in colonial Africa with the topic of ethnicity. In this way we can make a direct connection with the work of Sollors and his collaborators. It is in the treatment of ethnicity, moreover, that Africanists have begun to develop the study of intensely debated collective fictions. And the topic is central to my reconsideration of my own work because I have developed my own ideas by means of a series of studies of ethnicity in Southern Africa.

Over the eight years during which I have been seeking to resolve the problem of modern southern African ethnicity I have been changing my mind, away from the notion of "invention" and toward the notion of "imagination." The sequence of my work on ethnicity began by placing almost all the emphasis upon imposed colonial classifications of identity. Thus in 1982 I published a chapter in Robert Ross's collection *Racism and Colonialism*.[6] Its title is self-explanatory – "Race and Tribe in Southern Africa: European Ideas and African Acceptance." The argument ran that colonial administrators needed comprehensible and manageable units and so invented tribes; urban employers needed, or at any rate inevitably developed, ethnic hierarchies of hypothesized labor skills. These ready-made common-sense "inventions" were given greater legitimacy by the classifying (and sometimes frankly racist) tendencies of colonial science and social science.[7] These were the "European ideas" which Africans "accepted."[8] The emphasis was perhaps an odd one for someone as closely associated as I had been with arguments for "African initiative," especially since a sense of ethnic *identity* could hardly be simply imposed from outside or from above. There plainly had to be more than merely African "acceptance." At the least there had to be African collaboration.

This was the stage I had reached at the time of my chapter in *The Invention of Tradition* in 1983.[9] In this I took some pains to describe the essential African collaborators in the "invention" of ethnicity and of customary law. But I treated them too much as "collaborators" in an almost World War II sense. I think now that my argument was too polarized between what I identified as "admirable" flexible custom and what I defined as "deplorable" invented tradition. I associated all the positive forces in African societies with custom and all the reactionary forces with tradition. The African agents of ethnicity were all those elements in southern African society of which I disapproved – chiefs against commoners, fathers against sons, patriarchs against wives and daughters. They had their own interests, of course, but these interests were compatible with colonial hegemony. Such collaborators were building up African patriarchy within the structures of European paternalism.

This is a polarization that cannot really stand up to the abundant evidence of the key role played in the imagination of ethnicity by young migrant workers and by mission-educated catechists. Nevertheless, the same sort of argument emerges from my 1985 pamphlet, *The Invention of Tribalism in Zimbabwe*. There the inventors of Ndebele ethnicity – a self-conscious tribalism which had arisen in the twentieth century in place of nineteenth-century membership of a multi-ethnic state – were colonial administrators from Natal, who expected "the Ndebele" to be like the colonial image of "the Zulu," and salaried Ndebele chiefs, who were only too ready to accept such a glamorous and authoritarian identity.[10] Even though the Rhodesian state did not experiment with Indirect Rule and did not seek to create an Ndebele "homeland," nevertheless I argued that the invention of "the Ndebele" contributed to colonial hegemony. The salaried *indunas* – with greater wealth in cattle than they had ever enjoyed under

Lobengula – were reliable opponents of calls to revive the monarchy and reliable repressers of popular religious movements which threatened both "Ndebele" and colonial order.

I would now say that these successive formulations were not so much incorrect as incomplete. There *were* "European ideas" of ethnic classification and they did play a key role; there *was* a patriarchal alliance; there *was* one type of "Ndebele" identity which expressed particularly the interests of Ndebele *indunas*. These factors played in combination a very important part in the first stages of *inventing* Ndebele, and many other ethnic identities. But these really are very much first-stage explanations. European classifications and inventions of race, or tribe or language in effect created a series of empty boxes, with bounded walls but without contents. It was all very well to write of "the Ndebele," or "the Kikuyu," but to give *meaning* to that identity was a much more complex and contested business. Whites, in alliance with patriarchs, could suggest some very basic meanings derived from simplifications of African history or from industrial and urban occupational stereotypes. But such meanings were *too* simple to sustain and develop self-identity. And this was particularly so if, as Ekeh and Fields argue, the colonial "invention" of tribalism was less than fully hegemonic; if the production of "tribes" was essentially a device to delegate the definition and operation of social morality away from the colonial state. Under such circumstances the *significance* of being "Ndebele" or "Kikuyu" was bound to be a matter of internal struggle. Its imagination could not be left to the patriarchs, especially as they rarely commanded the intellectual tools required to shape "tribal" discourse. [. . .]

In my current work on "the Ndebele" I am seeking to go beyond the formulations of my 1985 pamphlet. It is clear that even by comparison with "the Kikuyu" or "the Shambaa" or "the Zulu" Ndebele ethnicity is a very complex business. The people who now call themselves Ndebele cover a wider area, come from more varied origins and environments, have more numerous alternative identities available to them. Whereas the clearing of the forest can be said to have created the Kikuyu, ideas about the land predated the Ndebele state, were associated with non-Ndebele cults and symbols, and could only be assimilated to an imagined Ndebele identity by strenuous ideological work. I have tried to give an account of this process, which operated at one level among Mwali cult adepts at the rural grassroots and, at another, among the cultural nationalists of the towns – two distinct, sometimes interacting, sometimes antagonistic groups of organic intellectuals.[11]

Moreover, even though the Ndebele state of the nineteenth century has often been thought of as a Zulu-style, Nguni creation, in fact its imaginative processes were very different from those described by Wright and Hamilton for the Zulu kingdom. In the nineteenth century the Ndebele state was a polity to which a great variety of linguistic and "ethnic" groups owed obedience. When early Rhodesian Native Commissioners, many recruited from Natal, tried to turn the *indunas* of the Ndebele state into tribal chiefs on an authoritarian "Zulu" model, they were bound to invent a narrow "Ndebele" ethnicity with a membership restricted to the royal clan and the *Zansi* aristocracy but excluding the great majority of the subjects of the precolonial state.

Nevertheless, despite these and other differences, there has been a steady movement of the imagination towards a wider "Ndebele" identity and away from the narrow "Zulu"-type model created by early administrators and *indunas*. I have been seeking to document two processes here. The first is the failure of the Rhodesian administration to deliver even when they had the opportunity to work with a strong chief, supported by ideological entrepreneurs who had imagined an exclusive Ndebele identity. In the case I have examined – the case of chief Sigombe of Wenlock in the 1950s – the refusal of the administration to allow Sigombe to develop his own area led to a movement in Wenlock toward a radical and inclusive definition of Ndebele identity which was compatible with participation in the Zimbabwean nationalist movement. This wider cultural nationalism allowed, among other things, for the fusion of Ndebele identity with older ideas about the landscape. Here there is material for comparisons and contrasts with Lonsdale's and Berman's accounts of Kikuyu contestations, also coming to a head in the 1950s.[12]

The second process which led to the imagination of a wider Ndebele identity was the emergence of urban ideological entrepreneurs, based mainly in Bulawayo. Here one can make something of the same use of an indigenous press as Lonsdale makes in Nairobi. In this light, Joshua Nkomo emerges as a culture-broker at least as influential as Jomo Kenyatta. As I wrote in a conference paper in February 1990:

> I have moved on to see Ndebele ethnicity in rather a different light. I see now a debate between different imaginations of Ndebeleness – the aristocratic caste-limited vision of the *indunas* vying with a succession of alternative visions; a Christian progressive imagining; an inclusive democratic vision of a greater Ndebele identity developed by urban workers and professional men in post-second-world-war Bulawayo.[13]

What emerges from all this, as from work on the Zulu and the Kikuyu, is that ethnicity, once it has been invented, cannot bear a single significance. It cannot be, *by definition*, patriarchal, conservative, reactionary – though it may well begin, or end up, by being so. Its meaning is something to be struggled for – as the uses of Zulu "tradition" are now being struggled for between *Inkatha* and the radical trade unions in Durban. In the case of Ndebele ethnicity in Zimbabwe, its potential relationship to the state has depended upon who were at any time the dominant Ndebele "imaginers," but has also depended upon the approach of the state toward regional cultural imaginations.

Thus I would at the moment propose something like the following sequence for Ndebele identity and its relationship to the state. It began, rather as I suggested in *The Invention of Tribalism in Zimbabwe*, with an alliance of administrators and *indunas*, though also supplemented by the ideological work of the first Ndebele-speaking Christian intellectuals, who were largely drawn from the aristocratic *Zansi* caste. When this narrow notion of Ndebele ethnicity spread to the towns and to labor migrants it did so defensively and as a means of beating off the competition of Shona-speakers in the Bulawayo labor market. But in the 1940s and 1950s the initiative passed from the *indunas* and aristocratic Anglicans. Many of the most successful mission-educated men were now drawn from areas which had been outside the core of the Ndebele state: they were ethnically "Kalanga" or "Nyubi." Such men, of whom Nkomo was the foremost, were simultaneously reviving Kalanga cultural nationalism – secretly visiting the shrines of the pre-Ndebele Mwali cult in the Matopos – *and* assuming leadership in the Matabele Home Society, which was defining a broader, inclusive Ndebele identity. Nkomo visited Ndebele royal praise-singers; for a time backed the call for a restoration of the Ndebele monarchy; and advocated pilgrimages to the grave of Mzilikazi. And at the same time he was a trade union leader and leader of the emerging nationalist movement.

All this was producing a rich mix of Matabeleland cultural nationalism. When the Rhodesian state sought in the 1950s to intervene in the rural areas so as to enforce massive destocking of cattle and movement of people, it alienated the "pure" Ndebele chiefs who had been its potential allies, and drove them and their people into alliance with the urban political spokesmen of the wider Ndebele identity. These urban "imaginers" stressed the compatibility of Ndebele-ness and a wider Zimbabwean nationalism. They emphasized that if Mzilikazi had founded a narrow Ndebele aristocracy, Lobengula had "imagined" a polyethnic patriotism; they argued that representation of African interest must be pyramidal, with men who thought of themselves as "Kalanga" joining in local Kalanga cultural activities, and the same men, in so far as they saw themselves as Ndebele, joining the Matabele Home Society, and the same men in so far as they shared interests with all Africans in the country, joining the nationalist movement.

Against this development, spokesmen of the old, narrow, exclusive Ndebele identity issued dire warnings of the dangers of alliance with nationalism rather than with the colonial state. But in the later 1950s and early 1960s a wider "patriotism" dominated. Nkomo was able, as leader of the Zimbabwean nationalist movement, to take even Shona-speaking colleagues to Mzilikazi's grave or to the High God shrines in the Matopos. He was, in fact, actively imagining these as resources for a Zimbabwean identity, just as they had been imagined as resources for a wider Ndebele ethnicity. Thus, in the words of John Lonsdale, "contests about tribal identity did not exclude and may have kindled a territorial political imagination . . . To rethink tribes may also be to rethink states."[14]

Such imaginations seemed ill-founded in view of subsequent events. The guerrilla war of the 1970s seemed more and more divided between "Ndebele" guerrillas of Nkomo's ZIPRA and "Shona" guerrillas of Mugabe's ZANLA. After 1980 it transpired that the imagination of a Zimbabwean national identity had been nothing like resolute or deeply rooted enough. The Mugabe state tried to equate Zimbabwean identity with a "Shona" cultural heritage; its soldiers, deployed in Matabeleland against "dissidents," tried to wean Kalanga away from the wider Ndebele identity by appealing to their older links with "Shona" culture. Commentators explained events in terms of the unchanging hostilities of primordial tribalism. But, in fact, the 1980s were a further stage of intense debate between different imaginations of Ndebele identity. Some spokesmen of the older, narrow version interpreted events as proof that they were right to warn against participation in Zimbabwean nationalism; on the ground, people responded to the preaching of Shona culture by feeling simultaneously *more* Kalanga and more Ndebele. Nkomo continued to believe that a wide Ndebele identity could be a building block for, and was not incompatible with, Zimbabwean identity. In my 1985 pamphlet I was concerned to show the artificial and narrowly based "invention" of Ndebele tribalism and to emphasize that if people had come to think of themselves as primarily Ndebele they could as readily come to think of themselves as Zimbabweans. I think now that this was correct in so far as it emphasized historicity and self-consciousness but misleading in so far as it opposed Ndebele and national identity. The issue in the Zimbabwean case – as with the Kikuyu in Kenya and the Zulu in South Africa – seems to be not so much how to move from reactionary tribalism to progressive nationalism, but how to ensure interactions between a dynamic and inclusive ethnicity and a pluralist and democratic nationalism.[15]

Notes

1   Eric Hobsbawm and Terence Ranger (eds.), *The Invention of Tradition* (Cambridge: Cambridge University Press, 1983).
2   Among these Earl Conrad, *The Invention of the Negro* (New York: Eriksson, 1967); Alvin Greenberg, *The Invention of the West* (New York: Avon, 1976); Nicole Loraux, *The Invention of Athens* (Cambridge, MA and London: Harvard University Press, 1986); Bernard Sherman, *The Invention of the Jew* (New York: Yoseloff, 1969).
3   Werner Sollors, "Introduction: The Invention of Ethnicity," in Werner Sollors (ed.), *The Invention of Ethnicity* (Oxford: Oxford University Press, 1989).
4   Helen Callaway, *Gender, Culture and Empire* (London: Macmillan, 1987), 57.
5   Rosalind O'Hanlon, "Histories in Transition: Colonialism and Culture in India," paper given at the Conference on Popular Culture in Question, University of Essex, April 1991, pp. 6 and 7.
6   Robert Ross (ed.), *Racism and Colonialism* (Leiden, 1982).
7   I treated these tendencies of colonial science and social science in "From Humanism to the Science of Man: Colonialism in Africa and the Understanding of Alien Societies," *Transactions of the Royal Historical Society* 26 (1976).
8   Terence Ranger, "Race and Tribe in Southern Africa: European Ideas and African Acceptance," in Ross (ed.), *Racism and Colonialism*.
9   Terence Ranger, "The Invention of Tradition in Colonial Africa," in Hobsbawm and Ranger (eds.), *The Invention of Tradition*.
10 Terence Ranger, *The Invention of Tribalism in Zimbabwe* (Mambo, 1985).
11 Terence Ranger, "The Politics of Prophecy in Matabeleland," Satterthwaite, April 1989; "Power, Religion and the Community: The Matobo Case," Calcutta, December 1989, forthcoming in *Subaltern Studies*, 1992; "Ethnicity and Nationality: The Case of Matabeleland," Institute of Commonwealth Studies, London, May 1991.
12 Terence Ranger, "The Origins of Nationalism in Rural Matabeleland: The Case of Wenlock," Oxford, October 1990.
13 Terence Ranger, "Ethnicity and Nationality in Southern Africa," Bellagio, February 1990, p. 9.
14 John Lonsdale, "The Moral Economy of Mau-Mau," in Bruce Berman and John Lonsdale, *Unhappy Valley* (London: James Currey, 1992), 4. Page references are to the manuscript of this chapter. The summary argument set out here on the imagining of

Ndebele ethnicity is most fully stated in my Institute of Commonwealth Studies seminar paper, "Ethnicity and Nationality: The Case of Matabeleland," May 1991.

15 For the recent reimaginings of "Kalanga" and "Ndebele" identity in Southwest Zimbabwe, see Richard Werbner, *The Tears of the Dead: The Social Biography of an African Family* (Edinburgh: Edinburgh University Press, 1991).

25 Contentious Traditions: The Debate on *Sati* in Colonial India

Lata Mani

The abolition of *sati* by the British in 1829 has become a founding moment in the history of women in modern India. The legislative prohibition of *sati* was the culmination of a debate during which 8,134 instances of *sati* had been recorded mainly, though not exclusively, among upper-caste Hindus, with a high concentration – 63 percent – in the area around Calcutta City.[1] The debate, initiated primarily by colonial officials, is regarded as signifying the concern for the status of women that emerges in the nineteenth century. Colonial rule, with its moral civilizing claims, is said to have provided the contexts for a thorough-going reevaluation of Indian "tradition" along lines more consonant with the "modern" economy and society believed to have been the consequence of India's incorporation into the capitalist world system.[2] In other words, even the most anti-imperialist amongst us has felt forced to acknowledge the "positive" consequences of colonial rule for certain aspects of women's lives, if not in terms of actual practice, at least at the level of ideas about "women's rights." [. . .]

In this essay I will argue the following: first, that tradition is reconstituted under colonial rule and, in different ways, women and brahmanic scripture become interlocking grounds for this rearticulation. Women become emblematic of tradition, and the reworking of tradition is conducted largely through debating their rights and status in society. Despite this intimate connection between women and tradition, or perhaps because of it, these debates are in some sense not primarily about women but about what constitutes authentic cultural tradition. Brahmanic scriptures are increasingly seen to be the locus of this authenticity so that, for example, the legislative prohibition of *sati* becomes a question

Excerpted from Lata Mani, "Contentious Traditions: The Debate on *Sati* in Colonial India." *Cultural Critique* 7 (1987), 119–56.

of scriptural interpretation. Contrary to the popular notion that the British were compelled to outlaw *sati* because of its barbarity, the horror of the burning of women is, as we shall see, a distinctly minor theme.

Second, this privileging of brahmanic scripture and the equation of tradition with scripture is, I suggest, an effect of a colonial discourse on India. By "colonial discourse," I mean a mode of understanding Indian society that emerged alongside colonial rule and over time was shared to a greater or lesser extent by officials, missionaries, and the indigenous elite,[3] although deployed by these various groups to different, often ideologically opposite ends. This discourse did not emerge from nowhere, nor was it entirely discontinuous with precolonial discourses in India. Rather, it was produced through interaction with select natives, though as I will show, officials clearly had power over the natives in question.

This greater power had several consequences. It meant that officials could insist, for instance, that brahmanic and Islamic scriptures were prescriptive texts containing rules of social behavior, even when the evidence for this assertion was problematic. Further, they could institutionalize their assumptions, as Warren Hastings did in 1772, by making these texts the basis of personal law. Official discourse thus had palpable material consequences, of which the constitution of personal law from religious texts is perhaps most significant from the point of view of women. The power underwriting official discourse also ensured its increasing normativity at least among the elite who were compelled, as we shall see, to take account of its key premises. I do not construe the elite as passive in this process, but as wresting these ideas to their own ends. [. . .]

Walter Ewer: An Instance of Official Discourse

Official discourse on *sati* was prompted by deliberation on whether it could be safely prohibited through legislation.[4] The concern with safety was premised on the belief that the practice had a basis in scripture and that interference in a religious matter might provoke indigenous outrage. Those opposed to abolition thus emphasized its "religious" basis and the dangers of intervention, while those in favor of outlawing *sati* stressed its "material" aspects (such as the family's desire to be rid of the financial burden of supporting the widow), and thus the safety of legislative prohibition. The two strategies were not mutually exclusive. For instance, abolitionists made both "religious" and "material" arguments for their position as did those in favor of tolerating *sati*. Indeed, the interplay between the two strategies was often quite complex.[5]

[. . .] In this essay I will draw on Walter Ewer, superintendent of police in the Lower Provinces, an abolitionist who epitomizes the official discourse on *sati*.

Ewer proposed that the contemporary practice of *sati* bore little resemblance to its scriptural model, which he defined as a voluntary act of devotion carried out for the spiritual benefit of the widow and the deceased. In reality, he argued, widows were coerced, and *sati* was performed for the material gain of surviving relatives. Ewer suggested that relatives might thereby spare themselves both the expense of maintaining the widow and the irritation of her legal right over the family estate. Also said to apply pressure on the widow by extolling the virtues and rewards of *sati* were "hungry brahmins" greedy for the money due to them for officiating such occasions.

Even if the widow succeeded in resisting the combined force of relatives and pundits, Ewer held that she would not be spared by the crowd. According to him, "the entire population will turn out to assist in dragging her to the bank of the river, and in keeping her down on the pile." Ewer thus concludes that "the widow is scarcely ever a free agent at the performance of the suttee" (*PP* [1821], 521). According to Ewer, scriptural transgressions, such as the coercion of widows or the performance of *sati* for material gain, could be the result of ignorance of the scriptures, or might reflect conscious design on the part of relatives and pundits. In the former case, *sati* could be abolished without provoking indigenous outrage; in the latter case, *sati* could not be considered a sacred act and could safely be prohibited. [. . .]

Analysis of official discourse makes it evident that arguments in favor of prohibiting *sati* were not primarily concerned with its cruelty or "barbarity," although many officials did maintain that *sati* was horrid even as an act of volition. It is also clear that officials in favor of legislative prohibition were not, as it has generally been conceived, interventionists contemptuous of aspects of indigenous culture, advocating change in the name of "progress" or Christian principles. On the contrary, officials in favor of abolition were arguing that such action was in fact consistent with upholding indigenous tradition, even that a policy of religious tolerance necessitated intervention. And indeed this was how the regenerating mission of colonization was conceptualized: not as the imposition of a new Christian moral order but as the recuperation and enforcement of the truths of the indigenous tradition. [. . .]

Indigenous Progressive Discourse on *Sati*

Rammohun Roy's first pamphlet on *sati* was published in 1818, five years after the colonial administration had authorized a particular version of the practice and three years after systematic data collection on *sati* had begun.[6] By this time the main features of official discourse on *sati* had already taken shape. Between 1818 and his death in 1832, Rammohun wrote a great deal on *sati*. Here I will draw mainly, though not exclusively, on a tract published by him in 1830, a year after the abolition of *sati*, entitled "Abstract of the Arguments Regarding the Burning of Widows Considered as a Religious Rite."[7] In Rammohun's own view this pamphlet summarizes his main arguments over the years.[8]

As the title might imply, Rammohun's discussion of *sati* is grounded from the beginning in a discussion of scripture. As he puts it, "The first point to be ascertained is, whether or not the practice of burning widows alive on the pile and with the corpse of their husbands, is imperatively enjoined by the Hindu religion?" ("BWRR," 367). Rammohun suggests in answer to his own rhetorical question that "even the staunch advocates for Concremation must reluctantly give a negative reply," and offers *Manu* as evidence:

Manu in plain terms enjoins a widow to *continue till death* forgiving all injuries, performing austere duties, avoiding every sensual pleasure, and cheerfully practicing the incomparable rules of virtue which have been followed by such women as were devoted to only one husband. ("BWRR," 367–8) [. . .]

Having demonstrated that *sati* is not commanded by the scriptures and having argued that, even where it is presented as an option, it is decidedly of inferior virtue as an act undertaken to procure rewards, Rammohun concludes his tract by considering "whether or not *the mode of* concremation prescribed by Hareet and others was ever duly observed" ("BWRR," 371). Rammohun points out that "these expounders of law" require the widow to ascend voluntarily the pyre and enter the flames. In his opinion, violation of either of these provisions "renders the act mere suicide, and implicates, in the guilt of the female murder, those that assist in its perpetration." Rammohun, like colonial officials, is here concerned with the thorny question of the widow's will. His view is similar to that of Ewer. He claims that "no widow ever voluntarily *ascended* on and *entered* into the *flames* in the fulfilment of this rite." No wonder, he says, that those in favor of *sati* have been "driven to the necessity of taking refuge in *usage*, as justifying both suicide and female murder, the most heinous of crimes" ("BWRR," 372).

It is clear even from this brief discussion that Rammohun's discourse shared key features with official discourse on *sati*. His case for abolition was grounded primarily in a discussion of the scriptures. Both his first and second pamphlets on *sati*, in which Rammohun stages dialogues between an advocate and opponent of *sati*, are debates on how the scriptures are to be interpreted. The opponent in both instances takes up, and seeks to demolish, the arguments put forward by advocates of the practice regarding its scriptural foundation. [. . .]

The Conservative Discourse on *Sati*: The Orthodox Petition to Bentinck

Whatever ambivalence may have marked "liberal" discourses on *sati* is strikingly absent from the conservative writings on the subject, which openly eulogize the practice as one willingly undertaken by devout Hindu widows. [. . .]

[. . .] The burden of the orthodox argument was to demonstrate that the India Company's criminalizing of *sati* was based on an erroneous reading of the scriptures. This is hardly surprising since, as we have seen, the entire debate turned on the issue of *sati*'s scriptural grounding. The orthodox argument did, however, differ in one respect from that of Rammohun and most colonial officials: it assigned a relatively greater weight to custom. The petition claimed that "the Hindoo religion is founded, like all other religions, on usage as well as precept, and one when immemorial is held equally sacred with the other."[9] Thus while Rammohun privileges scripture over custom, criticizing his opponents for "being driven to the necessity of taking refuge in *usage*" ("BWRR," 372), the orthodox petitioners argued that the antiquity of Hinduism implied an equal status for both. Nevertheless, despite this claim, they proceed to argue their case almost exclusively in terms of scripture. [. . .]

The petition was accompanied by a "paper of authorities" signed by 120 pundits presenting scriptural evidence in favor of *sati*, or, in the words of the petition, "the legal points declaring the practice of suttee lawful and expedient" ("Petition," 159). The enclosure sets out objections to the chief arguments of those who advocate the prohibition of *sati*: that asceticism has greater value than *sati*; that *sati* brings temporary rewards, while ascetic widowhood holds the promise of permanent bliss; and that *Manu* recommends asceticism and has priority over other Smritis since his text "is immediately originated from Sruti" ("Petition," 160).

In response to the suggestion that ascetic widowhood is more highly recommended than *sati*, the petition quotes *Manu* as cited in the *Nirnaya Sindhu*: "On the death of her husband, if, by chance, a woman is unable to perform concremation, nevertheless she should preserve the virtue of widows." Here, the petitioners claim, "the order of meaning has preference over that of reading; in other words, ascetic widowhood is a secondary option and one intended for women unable to perform *sati*. Thus they conclude, clearly overstretching their case: "It appears from the Shastra that the first thing which a widow ought to do is to ascend the flaming pile" ("Petition," 160, 161). [. . .]

The petitioners wrap up their case for regarding *sati* as a scriptural practice by returning to a consideration of interpretive principles. They suggest that the fragment from the *Rig Veda*, "let not these women be widowed" (the passage that Rammohun debunks as obscure), implies that *sati* was comfortable to Sruti, and they propose that where Sruti and Smriti conflict, "the former has preference over the latter." Thus they conclude that "it is unobjectionable that concremation, being enjoined by the Sruti, which is the most prevalent authority and original of the Smritis, must be performed" ("Petition," 162). Where Rammohun prioritizes *Manu* as a founding text containing "the whole sense of the Veda" and insists that no code be approved that contradicted it, the orthodox petition argued the absolute priority of Sruti in every case, although within the Smritis, *Manu* is conceded a premier position.

A Common Discourse on *Sati*

It is evident from the foregoing discussion of the official and indigenous arguments for and against *sati* that, whatever their attitudes to the practice, all participants in the debate on abolition held in common certain key ideas about *sati* and Indian society and employed rather similar procedures for arguing their case. Advocates both for and against *sati* grounded their case in a discussion of brahmanic scriptures, with opponents endeavoring to prove that *sati* had no clear scriptural status and proponents contesting these conclusions. One could analyze these arguments for logical consistency and conclude that, by and large, the orthodox pro-*sati* lobby had a weak case and resorted to disingenuous and facile arguments to make its point. One could also conclude appropriately that the use of scripture was strategic: each side read the texts in a manner that supported its ideological position. However, given my interest in the discursive aspects of the debate, I will adopt a different focus. I will elaborate the internal logic and parameters of the discourse, examine the kinds of arguments admissible within it and the ideological implications of these for arguing for an improved status for women.

From this perspective, what is interesting is the fact that the entire issue was debated within the framework of scripture. In other words, however clumsy or unconvincing the use of scripture in a particular argument, what is significant is the explicit coding of arguments as scriptural. Even Rammohun, commonly regarded as the first modern champion of women's rights, did not base his support for abolition on the grounds that *sati* was cruel to women. He did, of course, develop critical analyses of the status of women in India of a more "secular" variety, but these are marginal to his arguments against *sati*. [. . .]

The fundamental importance given to scripture in the debate on *sati* raises the following question: in what ways can it be regarded as an instance of a "modernizing" discourse? It is clear that the debate was not conducted along lines that are normally held to constitute the modern. It was not a secular discourse of reason positing a morality critical of "outmoded" practices and a new conception of "individual rights." To the contrary, as we have seen, at the ideological level the debate was a scriptural deliberation of the legitimacy of *sati* that was critical of its contemporary form for not being, in a sense, "outmoded enough," not true to its original principles. (One must, of course, insist on the equally mythic status of this so-called original *sati*.)

The discussion of the rights of women as individuals is also absent except insofar as it is posed indirectly in context of the widow's will. As we have seen, this will is conceded primarily in the abstract and only reluctantly, and by a few in practice, thus justifying interventions on the widow's behalf, whether by the European official or the indigenous male social reformer. However, whatever the skepticism regarding the widow's subjecthood, this concern with individual will may itself be read as suggesting the modernity of this discourse.

But the discourse on *sati* was also modern in another more important sense: it was a modern discourse on tradition. It exemplifies late eighteenth-century colonial discourses that elaborated notions of modernity against their own conceptions of tradition. I suggest, in other words, that what we have there is not a discourse in which preexisting traditions are challenged by an emergent modern consciousness, but one in which both "tradition" and "modernity" as we know them are contemporaneously produced. The modernity of this discourse on tradition needs to be recognized more fully.

Tradition in this discourse is posited as a timeless and structuring principle of Indian society enacted in the everyday lives of indigenous people. "Tradition," interchangeable for the most part with "religion" and "culture," is designated as a sphere distinct from material life. It is thus that officials can speak of returning to natives the truth of traditions that had been interrupted by the "Islamic interlude." This conception is also evident in Ewer's arguments that when Indians acted religiously they acted passively and in his legitimization of intervention in *sati*, given evidence for it as a material practice.[10]

There are two consequences to this concept of culture or tradition as a transhistorical and ubiquitous force acted out by people. First, it produces analyses of *sati* in purely "cultural" terms that empty it of both history and politics. Second, this notion of culture effectively erases the agency of those involved in such practices. However, as we noted in Ewer's description of how the widow is dragged to the river, not everyone involved in a *sati* is seen to be subjected equally to the imperatives of culture. Family members, especially the males, and the pundits present at the pyre are given alternate subject positions. The former are often seen to be acting in their own interest, the latter almost always so. Such interest is always coded as corrupt and to the detriment of the widow. Even so, within the general subjection of all indigenous people to "religion" or "tradition," men are offered some measure of will.

Not so the widow. She is consistently portrayed as either a heroine – entering the raging flames of the pyre with no display of emotion – or an abject victim – thrown upon the heap, sometimes fastened to it by unscrupulous family members or pundits. We saw both these in Rammohun's descriptions of *sati*. These poles, "heroine" and "victim," preclude the possibility of a complex female subjectivity. Indeed, given the definition of tradition operative in the discourse on *sati*, the portrayal of the immolated widow as heroine merely rewrites her as victim of a higher order: not of man but of God (or religion). This representation of the widow makes her particularly susceptible to discourses of salvation, whether these are articulated by officials or the indigenous elite. It thus comes as no surprise that both offer to intercede on her behalf, to save her from "tradition," indeed even in its name. [. . .]

Notes

1   These figures are drawn from the *Parliamentary Papers on Hindoo Widows* (hereafter *PP*). The 8,134 *satis* were recorded between 1815 and 1828. The proportion of burnings in the Calcutta region is an average for this period. Breakdown of *satis* by caste was tabulated in the *PP* for 1823: brahmin 234; kayasth 25; vaisya 14; sudra 292 (*PP*, 1825). *Sati* was proportionately higher among brahmins.

2   There is considerable debate among political economists as to whether or not colonial rule produced conditions that were favorable to the development of capitalism in India. For instance, A. K. Bagchi has argued that colonial rule deindustrialized India; see his "De-industrialization in India in the Nineteenth Century: Some Theoretical Implications," *Journal of Development Studies* 12 (1975–6), 135–64. For a critical discussion of colonial economic historiography, see the special issue *Reinterpretation of Nineteenth-century Indian Economic History* of *Indian Economic and Social History Review* 5, no. 1. This debate does not affect my argument here, for, whatever their analysis of the impact of colonialism on India's transition from feudalism to capitalism, all scholars agree that colonialism held the promise of modernity and inspired a critical self-examination of indigenous society and culture.

3   For my purposes the elite may be defined as well-to-do, urban, mercantile, and/or landed individuals whose business and social activities required them, in one way or another, to confront and negotiate the apparatus of the East India Company.

4   This discussion of official discourse draws on the more detailed analysis presented in my article "The Production of an Official Discourse on *Sati* in Early Nineteenth-century Bengal," *Economic and Political Weekly; Review of Women's Studies* (April 1986), 32–40. This article documents the legislative history of *sati* and includes a fuller discussion of the institutional context of the debate. Parts of it are included here since

my arguments in this essay build on this earlier work. For Walter Ewer's letter, see *PP* 18 (1821), 521–3.

5 "Material" in official discourse refers to anything that can be shown to be without basis in or counter to scripture. Given British colonial assumptions regarding the hegemony of scriptural texts and the passive relation to them of indigenous people, this category often included actions that represented will, whether of individuals or groups. To say more here, however, would be to anticipate my argument.

6 Rammohun, "Translation of a Conference between an Advocate for and an Opponent of the Practice of Burning Widows Alive" (Calcutta, 1818). Two years later, Rammohun published "A Second Conference between an Advocate for and an Opponent of the Practice of Burning Widows Alive" (Calcutta, 1820). See *The English Works of Raja Rammohun Roy*, ed. J .C. Ghose, vol. 2 (New Delhi: Cosmo, 1982); hereafter "PBWA."

7 Rammohun, "Abstract of the Arguments Regarding the Burning of Widows Considered as a Religious Rite," *English Works*, 367–84; hereafter "BWRR."

8 Chronology is not significant here since the nature and structure of Rammohun's arguments remained essentially the same throughout his campaign against *sati*.

9 "The Petition of the Orthodox Community Against the Suttee Regulation, Together With a Paper of Authorities, and the Reply of the Governor-General thereto" (January 14, 1830), in *Raja Rammohun Roy and Progressive Movements in India*, ed. J. K. Majumdar (Calcutta: Art Press, 1941), 156; hereafter "Petition."

10 This conception of tradition finds its clearest expression in descriptions of incidents of *sati* and in what Mary Pratt has elsewhere termed the "manners and customs," material discussion of which is beyond the scope of this essay. See Mary Louise Pratt, "Scratches on the Face of the Country; or What Mr. Barrow Saw in the Land of the Bushmen," *Critical Inquiry* 12 (Autumn 1985), 119–43.

26 When the Earth is Female and the Nation is Mother: Gender, the Armed Forces, and Nationalism in Indonesia

Saraswati Sunindyo

Introduction

The subject of women and militarism has been one of the major issues that continue to intrigue feminists across the globe. For Indonesia, a postcolonial nation that fought a colonial army for four years despite declaring its independence diplomatically, militarism has claimed a dominant role. The inclusion and the visibility of women in the military are often utilized by the Indonesian state to exemplify its claims that Indonesian women have indeed achieved equality as citizens. Yet when examining their institutional positions – within the military, within society as a whole (Sullivan 1991: 83–6), as well as within the discourses surrounding national identity – a rather different picture emerges.

Benedict Anderson suggests that nationalism is a modern phenomenon, a shared commonality and history, and is constructed and imagined by rapidly growing numbers of people. With the help of print capitalism and technology, nationhood evolves to exist as a system of signification (Anderson 1983: 40). Building upon Anderson's notion, this essay will examine how the public discourses surrounding women's role in the Indonesian military delineate the way in which women are imagined, in this imagined nation. This includes how male nationalist leaders, and nationalism in general, have imagined and conceptualized: (1) the role of women; (2) the social relations of men and women; and (3) the concept of women's/gendered citizenship. I will look at these issues both in nationalist narratives, especially as they relate to the roles of men and women in the revolutionary struggle and the military, and in actual regulatory practices within the institution of the military. I argue that the representations of women

Excerpted from Saraswati Sunindyo, "When the Earth is Female and the Nation is Mother: Gender, the Armed Forces, and Nationalism in Indonesia." *Feminist Review*, 58 (Spring 1998), 1–21.

in nationalist narratives about the military are often contradictory and, at the same time, persistently problematize and subordinate women.

In decoding the contradictory roles of women in the Indonesian military, I will analyze three different periods. The first, 1928–49, is the pre-independence era marked by an extreme nationalist spirit to overthrow the Dutch colonial government in the archipelago. The second period is the Sukarno era (1949–65), still marked politically by a nationalist rhetoric of opposition to neo-colonialism and imperialism, although Sukarno himself rose up as a paternalistic charismatic leader. The third stage (1965–present) is marked by military rule and capitalist development, characterized by both economic progress and military repression where any opposition and criticism toward the regime is easily stigmatized as anti-national and therefore anti-progress. [. . .]

The basis for my investigation of the connections between women, the armed forces, and nationalism in contemporary Indonesia can be located in three established but separate bodies of literature. The first is the study of nationalisms and sexualities (Anderson 1983; Mosse 1985; McClintock 1993; Parker et al. 1992), within which sexual, familial, and domestic iconography are often employed and manipulated in the construction of nationalisms. The second group consists of feminist perspectives on militarism and global order (Enloe 1989; Yuval-Davies and Bresheeth 1991; Yuval-Davies and Anthias 1989). These studies examine the ways in which the ideology of masculinity and gender stereotypes is maintained and placed under the doctrine of "national security." The third and final group studies gendered divisions of labor and inequality within the armed forces. These cross-cultural investigations have shown that women still occupy the lower rank, status, and economic positions in the military (Yuval-Davies 1987).

This essay argues that the national narrative none the less continues to represent not only a sexualized but also a specifically heterosexualized familial embodiment of the nation (Enloe 1989: 19). Although it is true that in times of national crisis the traditional sexual division of labor may seemingly be dissolved through the conscious encouragement and recruitment of women to participate in the war effort (in the military or through other means), these opportunities are usually limited (Yuval-Davies 1987). In most instances, once the national crisis is over and before a new crisis emerges, both the rhetoric of equality and the representation of the nation used to mobilize women's participation in the popular armed struggle are once again adjusted to fit yet another patriarchal, heterosexual familial model. This argument endures in nationalist discourse as well as in the actuality of the state's military practices.

Images of Women During the Independence Struggle and After

Since the declaration of national independence in 1945, historical women figures have been celebrated as Indonesian female role models and were awarded the state's recognition as national heroes. [. . .]

However, images of contemporary military women in Indonesia are contradictory. On the one hand, they are portrayed as symbols of gender equality and advancement, while, on the other, they are positioned as the *little daughters* in the military household. These contradictory representations need to be analyzed in light of the nationalist discourse that represents the nation as *Ibu Pertiwi* (The Motherland). Motherlands are often symbolized by nationalist and colonial writers alike as both nurturing mother and sensual maid (Innes 1994: 3–4). Instead of this iconography, during the independence struggle the Indonesian nationalist project represented *Ibu Pertiwi* more as a suffering feminine beauty.

These imaginings of the motherland are perhaps best represented in popular nationalist songs. One of the most popular [. . .] was a song called *"Kulihat Ibu Pertiwi"* ("I saw the motherland"). [. . .]

> I saw the motherland
> deeply troubled
> Tears ran down her cheeks
> remembering her gold and diamonds
> Of forests, mountains, rice-fields and oceans,
> her stored wealth,
> And now, the mother is suffering
> moaning and praying.

It is a song of summoning, intended to rally youth to the task of freeing and rescuing the motherland from her deepest suffering, suffering caused by the colonial power that had taken her dignity and dispossessed her of her wealth (i.e., the natural resources of the archipelago).

A female, even one as monumental and sacred as a "motherland," is here constructed as a fragile feminine being who needs to be rescued, protected, and guarded from the cruelty of a foreign power who has forcefully taken all her wealth away from her. [. . . I]n the case of Indonesian nationalism, *Ibu Pertiwi* is the manifestation of the feminine, whose interests, needs, and happiness must be interpreted and articulated by the masculine counterpart, the Indonesian military institution.

Some of the most enduring patriotic songs were composed by the late Ismail Marzuki, a well-respected nationalist composer. His songs are still sung today in Indonesia, and *"Sepasang mata bola"* ("A Pair of Bright Eyes") is often sung in choral presentations during Independence Day celebrations. In this song, non-combatant women are represented as inspiring, mysterious, and fragile.

> Night had nearly fallen in Jogya, when my train pulled in.
> The sky was overcast, and I was taken by surprise.
>
> They gazed at me, two bright eyes, as if she was saying:
> "Hero, protect me from the looming evil."
>
> A pair of bright eyes, through a window
> From Jakarta, headed for the front.
>
> Full of admiration, I saw them shining with valor.
> My heart has been captured, may we meet again.
>
> A pair of bright eyes, shining purely and intimately,
> Gazed at me in the Jogya station.

> A pair of bright eyes seemed to say:
> "My prayers go with you, my hero,
> Go, don't waver."

Often the women themselves never appear in the lyrics of such songs. Rather, their actions as supporters are romanticized, so that the larger struggle becomes a masculinized duty. This renders women's involvement invisible, though absolutely crucial as inspiration, support, and that which must be defended. [...]

The existence of combatant women appears to be in conflict with the masculinized image of the military as protector. This contradiction in turn generates paradoxical effects in the expectations and identity of women in the armed forces as well as in civilian women. One representation of woman as combatant, which displays these tensions, can be found in yet another popular nationalist song by Ismail Marzuki, "Jasmine Flower at the Front Line."

> Lovely young girl,
> You're like a budding jasmine.
> You offer your body and soul
> on the Bekasi front line.
>
> They call you Srikandi,
> The eternal female defender.
> You follow in the young men's footsteps
> Helping to defend the country.
>
> Oh beautiful woman defender,
> Hear the call of mother.
> The rice paddies longingly await
> Your sacred contribution.
>
> Alas, young woman,
> Price of your home village,
> Return to your mother's embrace
> We'll serve in the field.

The jasmine flower is a popular symbol of purity intermingled with femininity or true womanhood. Here, a woman freedom fighter is given the name Srikandi, a female warrior in the Javanese version of *Mahabharata*.[1] The name Srikandi is used in the Indonesian context to symbolize women fighters/heroes in general. In this song, the woman hero is praised as a capable female warrior and glorified as an object of beauty. Yet at the end of the song, she is called back to the mother nation's lap to serve behind the front lines, well within the imagined safety of the nation's borders. The song suggests that, although a woman could be a capable fighter, her place is not really at the front. The song is powerful and romantic, and its message is clear: *go back to the domestic sphere.*

[...] It is well documented that when newly independent states institutionalize their military forces, women are marginalized into non-combatant units and given tasks in any fields typically regarded as a woman's type of job.

Thus in popular nationalist songs such as "Jasmine Flower at the Front Line," on the one hand, women are acknowledged as heroes fighting alongside their brothers on the front lines of the anticolonial struggle. On the other hand, they must be reminded about their feminine duties after the war is over. [...]

National Crisis: Women as Partners?

[...] Nationalism thrives on "crisis" through which, over and over, its members have to be reminded about their imagined collective sorrows and hopes. Narratives of nationalism in crisis have to be invented and reinvented over time (Heng and Devan 1992: 343–4). Yet, in keeping with Cynthia Enloe's observation that "nationalism sprang from masculinized sorrow and masculinized hope" (Enloe 1994: 44), the narrative of nationalism in crisis must also be sexualized and domesticized.

Though Indonesia gained national independence in 1945, the spirit of anticolonialism remained quite strong throughout the 1950s and early 1960s. [...] The "father" of Indonesian nationalism, Sukarno is known for his fiery speeches against colonialism, neo-colonialism, and imperialism. He banned the use of the Dutch language as a status symbol, which the Indonesian elite were accustomed to use. He also banned Dutch-like names (*nama-nama ke Belanda-Belandaan*). Sukarno even personally gave more "native" (which in his Java-centric view translated into Javanized/Sanskritized) names to movie stars and celebrities.[2]

[...] Sukarno also attacked women's makeup.[3] He clearly stated that he did not like women with makeup who would be "dependent on imperialist products," and that he agreed with "traditional beauty makeup/tips" rather than "Western products."[4] Here, Sukarno attempted to construct an image of what he considered the "national feminine" by referring to ideas of traditional feminine beauty. Sukarno's post-independence rhetoric and actions, among other things, used images of women to help draw clear boundaries of identity between the newly liberated Indonesian nation and the advanced industrial Western nations, seen at the time as a *nekolim* (neo-colonialist and imperialist) threat to national, economic, political, and cultural sovereignty.

As the first president of the republic, Sukarno [...] fashioned himself as *Bung Karno* (brother or comrade Karno). [...] Later in his presidency he was culturally referred to as *Bapak* (father). He persistently addressed his audience as brothers and sisters in order to maintain an appearance of egalitarianism. Equality between the sexes as well as egalitarianism had been an important part of Sukarno's imagined modern Indonesian nation. The supreme proof of the cooperation that men and women, as citizens of a nation, could achieve was seen in military service (Douglas 1980: 166). Accordingly, military women were depicted as the most emancipated women.

In 1962, the media and the popular discourse were given yet another Srikandi (female warrior). This time a woman named Herlina was awarded a medal and given the name, Srikandi Trikora.[5] She was the first woman ever to have parachuted into Irian Barat in the effort to reclaim this province from the Dutch. Herlina was small, dark, and wore no makeup. Furthermore, she was energetic, vivacious, strong, adventurous, and had been a volunteer in the Irian campaign.

All in all, she was the ideal Sukarno-era picture of a perfect female nationalist. [. . .]

[. . . This was a] perfect photo opportunity, not just to create or strengthen the national narrative in crisis, but also to display the pride of independent Indonesia to the whole world. It presented, first of all, a perfect image of male and female members of the nation (Sukarno and Herlina) that could be read as father and daughter. For Herlina he is decidedly a father figure and not "brother" Karno; in her case his eloquent egalitarianism falls short. Second, the entire world is looking at them as represented by the bevy of international journalists (a white man is prominently in the frame). Finally, Herlina is looking at Sukarno, the *father of the nation*, while Sukarno looks over the top of her head at the *world*. It is as though he is once again saying: "Go to hell with your aid" and all its Western influence (see Kosut 1967: 98).

Not only does this photograph reinforce the national narrative, it also maintains patriarchal familial iconography. In the picture, Herlina, a celebrated woman warrior, is looking at Sukarno, the proud father of the nation. The construction of Herlina, therefore, is not in the image of a partner, but rather as that of a daughter. This is contrary to the revolutionary images of men and women during the war for independence in 1945–9 where social relations between men and women were defined as *bung/zus* or a brother/sister partnership.[6]

Herlina chose this picture for her book *Pending Emas* (The Golden Belt). The title referred to the physical form of the award she received from the state for her heroism during the Irian campaign. Another picture that Herlina put in her book [. . .] portrays a second powerful image of a female national hero, and was widely disseminated in Indonesia at the time. Again, the diminutive, dark Herlina appears without any makeup and in military uniform; but this time she is standing, hands in pockets, smiling, surrounded by white United Nations troops. Not only does she look powerful (in her military uniform, with a glimpse of war machinery in the background), but also sexy (her hair has been left to hang loosely). In addition, the image suggests that she has the world in her pocket: she is surrounded by uniformed white men. Herlina is shown as capable and, in contrast to the last two verses of "Jasmine Flower at the Front Line," there is no hint of the need for her to return to the rice fields. This image could only have gained popular potency and currency during the early 1960s, the era of the "national crisis" that encompassed both Sukarno's campaign to incorporate Irian Barat into Indonesia and the confrontation with Malaysia. She is the natural Indonesian woman who is simultaneously modern and professional (a trained warrior, equal to men, even white men!). While the foreign white men surrounding her do not seem to be bothered by her presence, she none the less radiates poise. She is at ease amid the wider world of nations.

Herlina was an idol who, for a limited period of time, allowed young Indonesian girls to imagine a different role for themselves aside from the domestic domain. As such, this harked back, but with more positive power, to the image of Srikandi in "Jasmine Flower at the Front Line." Yet, at the same time, the general construction of woman as daughter, and woman as natural physical marker of the nation as defined by a male leader, worked to constrain women's roles and choices during the Sukarno era.

In Time of Peace: The Sexualized and Domesticized Daughters

During Sukarno's guided democratic regime (1959–65), women's involvement in physical combat against the "nation's enemies" epitomized their already achieved equality. This was considered not only a significant advancement for women, but also a triumph of the imagined nation.

The New Order[7] military government that replaced Sukarno continues to adopt a similar discourse. In a state-sponsored book published by the Department of Information in 1968 and written in English for foreign consumption, *Indonesian Women [sic] Movement: A Chronicle Survey of the Women's Movement in Indonesia*, one subheading reads "Our women defenders." The discourse here seems to be gender egalitarianism, where both men and women can be our (the collective nation's) defender. However, the captions reveal the contradictions of the Department's (and hence the state's) project. One caption reads, "An air force pilot mounts her jet," describing a picture of a woman next to "her jet," a clearly sexualized image of how "sexy" a woman can be in military uniform and placed next to an appropriately phallic piece of machinery. Another caption reads, "After a successful jump she neatly folds her parachute" (1968: 73). A woman (again, *our* defender), who can be both hero and ultimate partner, none the less has to be represented within her *kodrat* (biological destiny). Both the women in the pictures and the English-speaking audience looking at the pictures are reminded about the nature of being a woman. In this case, a woman's nature is symbolized by the paratrooper folding her parachute neatly. There are no examples of such depictions of male counterparts.

The sexualized image of women in the military continues in more recent state-sponsored publications. Another book in English for foreign audiences was published in conjunction with the Nonaligned Bloc meeting in Indonesia in 1992. Entitled *Wanita: The Dynamics and Achievements of Indonesian Women*, the book was produced in a coffee-table format and filled with glossy pictures. The text accompanying a photo of women in the military states: "The women's corps in the military order is very important, enhancing the smooth running and efficiency of the Armed Forces' dual function" (1992: 80). Such a text contributes to the idea that the function of the women's military corps is to "smooth" things out, a traditional conception of women's role.

Thus, women in the armed forces are in a contradictory position. On the one hand, they are portrayed as the ultimate testimony to the fact that a male/female nationalist partnership has been achieved, yet again and again they are gendered and domesticized. The existence of female soldiers is used to construct them as a symbol of equality, so that the armed forces can claim that: "The Armed Forces have no problem with women's emancipation." [. . .] Issues of women's emancipation are irrelevant according to this argument, since women have already been accepted as part of the armed forces.

However, what is defined as equality in both nationalist and military discourse is an extremely gendered division of labor. Women are defined through femininity and, furthermore, that femininity is domestic. What matters for the military institution, the state, and the public is the so-called biological or female destiny of women (*kodrat*). A national newspaper headline claimed, "women of the Air Force are not exempt from female biological destiny." Ann McClintock has suggested that "nations are symbolically figured as domestic genealogies" (McClintock 1993: 44). Yet to picture the nation as female or a mother, to represent those who are protecting the nation as the extreme embodiment of masculinity, and to attempt to regulate gender relations at a discursive level prove not to be sufficient for the purposes of nationalism. These images are also constantly being constructed and reconstructed in actual practice through the policies of the institutions which circumscribe people's everyday lives. The state in this case, through the military, still feels the need to institutionalize familial imagery in practice. In order for female soldiers to keep their perceived essentialized femininity, the military must introduce a surrogate motherhood.

The Indonesian armed forces, having opened their gates to women, also institutionalized a relationship referred to as *ibu asuh* (surrogate motherhood) for female soldiers. In each branch of the armed forces (including the police force), the wife of a commanding officer – not the highest-ranking woman in that branch – plays the role of a surrogate mother to all the female members of the forces under her husband's authority. One of the main tasks of *ibu asuh* is to ensure that female soldiers retain and understand their *kodrat*.

A newspaper published by the armed forces in 1993 quoted a speech from Mrs. Rilo Pambudi, *ibu asuh* of the female members of the Air Force: "As the guardian and guide of Air Force women, she stated that women who choose a military career are expected to possess a very high degree of professionalism without having to neglect their female destiny" (*Angkatan Bersenjata*, April 16, 1993). [. . .]

All the expressions of *ibu asuh* suggest nationalist mimicry of a familial genealogy. The nation as mother is insufficient to ensure masculine ideas about the "proper" femininity within the armed forces. The claim made by McClintock, that nations are symbolically figured as domestic genealogies, is indeed true. However, the Indonesian case shows that familial mimicry is further implemented in practice. Both the construction of Herlina as the nation's "inspired daughter," and the formally institutionalized *ibu asuh* used to regulate female members of the armed forces, indicate unequal positioning between females and their male counterparts. Thus, both allegorically and practically, women are positioned as the *little daughters* of the armed forces who need to be taught how to be good daughters.

Nationalism's Femininities

Who are the nationalist women, and what are the characteristics of nationalist femininity that can be mobilized to mark the nation? These are the key questions that are being posed, answered, and modified through succeeding periods in military and state ideologies. During the revolutionary armed struggle, the nation was portrayed as a suffering feminine mother who was owned, controlled, and cruelly exploited by foreign power. Whereas freedom fighters are naturally assumed to be male, female combatants were represented as good sisters/ daughters, yet still somehow out of place. Women were also romanticized as heterosexual lovers who inspired, supported, and gave meaning to a war of independence. These images were part of an ideological discourse aimed at keeping militarism and war in the domain of protective men who drew strength from suffering, supportive women figures.

Female soldiers and volunteers who were involved with Sukarno's Irian Barata and Malaysian campaigns were, however, represented by Herlina, the Srikandi. Sukarno's showcasing of the nationalist woman, who has proved herself to be capable – side by side with all our male heroes – can be read as an attempt to differentiate Indonesia from neo-colonial nations through a demonstration of both gender egalitarianism and "natural" female beauty. Yet she too was discursively constructed as Sukarno's daughter, instead of as Sukarno's partner. Although she was a good role model for nationalist women, she too had to be confined to the role of daughter.

This ideological positioning of female soldiers as daughters continues throughout the New Order military regime, where this role is reproduced both discursively and through the institutionalized practice of the *ibu asuh*. In contrast to McClintock's analysis that emphasis is placed on the use of the ideology of family to position and control women within the nation, in the Indonesian case discursive formulations are not enough. Institutionalized practices must also be legislated for and put into place. Once again, however, the intent is to ensure that good, strong, capable daughters are those who are dutiful and containable. A tighter web has been drawn around Herlina.

One of the unique features of the Indonesian case is that there are four branches of the armed forces, the police being included as the fourth. In the late 1980s and early 1990s, an outspoken member of parliament came to prominence, Police General Roekmini, who has recently died. As a member of the Indonesian National Human Rights Committee, she was known for her outspoken critique of the military regime. She also publicly acknowledged that there was a gendered division of labor in the armed forces, particularly within the Police, which put women at a disadvantage. She is not constructed discursively as a national hero, as Herlina was, but her popularity as a retired police general, a former member of parliament, and a committed member of the National Human Rights Committee, offers an example of the different kinds of femininity not promoted by the state. As Michael Ryan notes: "Hegemony is therefore structurally unstable, a blanket thrown over a tiger rather than a windowless prison" (Ryan 1988: 485). Roekmini, as one voice speaking of the institutionalized problems that women face in the armed forces, is like the tiger of Ryan's quotation. Capable of pushing herself far enough out from beneath the confining blanket to achieve unusual professional success, she managed to use the legitimacy that her position gave her to strike back at the system which had sought to control her. Thus, while the nation is "sprung from masculinized sorrow and hope" as Cynthia Enloe claims, Indonesian postcolonial female soldiers are represented as mothers and daughters; yet they may also, by dint of unique circumstances and/or exceptional skill, come to be celebrated as national heroes and generals. In such instances, women themselves can occasionally renegotiate the boundaries of nationalist femininity.

Throughout these different periods of Indonesian national history, representations of women as nationalist subjects are often either in contradiction to the "realities" in which women have played a pivotal part (in the revolutionary armed struggle), or display mixed feelings and anxiety about women's participation in the armed forces (after independence, during Sukarno's anti-imperialist and Irian campaigns, and in the New Order era). Although sexualized, domesticized, and nativized (in this case Javanized), women were not completely invisible in the nation's history. Thus, contrary to the claim made by Heng and Devan that "women, and all signs of the feminine, are by definition always and already anti-national" (Heng and Devan 1992: 356), the feminine is not anti-national. Rather, nationalism demands a specific kind of femininity which, in this case, is dictated to women through masculine imagination. Similarly, women work to expand the options pressed on them within the confines of nationalist discourse, thereby seeking to create different possibilities of national femininity. [. . .]

Notes

1 In the Javanese popular interpretation of the Hindu epic *Mahabharata*, Srikandi is the second wife of Prince Arjuna. She is characterized as "strong-willed, warm-hearted, bright, intelligent and articulate, knowledgeable in the art of hunting and war, occasionally passing as a male warrior" (Anderson 1965: 21–2). However, in the Indian original of the *Mahabharata*, Sikhandin (Shikhandi) is a hero born a girl, who later becomes a male warrior with feminine characteristics (Rice 1934: 34; Suri 1992: 5–16). In such versions he is never described as having any sexual relationship with Prince Arjuna. What is important in the context of this essay, however, is that, within the Javanese version of the *Mahabharata*, there is a strong, articulate, female warrior. Second, in the modern Indonesian context, the name Srikandi has been used to characterize female champions in any field.

2 For example, Sukarno called Lientje Tambayong (a hybrid Dutch and Minahasa name) Rima Melati, the name she is known by today. Also, he gave the name "Lokita Purnama Sari" to a movie star who was known as Baby Huwae.

3 Sukarno was also believed to have said at one point that he would wash the face of his date if she wore makeup.

4 These sentiments from Sukarno's rhetoric became a permanent part of the "imagined national" consciousness.

5 Again, Srikandi is used to refer to the Woman Warrior or Female Hero. Trikora was the name for Sukarno's campaign to include the western part of New Guinea in Indonesia.

6 The author would like to thank Ben Anderson who pointed out that the "father" imagery did not appear until the so-called Old Order era, i.e., the time of Sukarno's presidency.

7 The military regime led by President Suharto is called the New Order (*Orde Baru*) and Sukarno's period the Old Order (*Orde Lama*).

References

Anderson, B. 1965: "Mythology and the Tolerance of the Javanese." Ithaca, NY: Modern Indonesia, Project, Southeast Asia Program, Cornell University.

Anderson, B. 1983: *Imagined Communities: Reflections on the Origin and Spread of Nationalism.* London: Verso.

Departemen Penerangan RI 1968: *Indonesian Women [sic] Movement: A Chronicle Survey of the Women's Movement in Indonesia.*

Departemen Penerangan RI 1994: *Perjuangan Wanita Indonesia 10 Windu Setelah Kartini 1904–1984.*

Douglas, S. A. 1980: "Women in Indonesian Politics: The Myth of Functional Interest." In Silvia Chipp and Justin Green (eds.), *Asian Women in Transition.* University Park: Penn State University Press.

Enloe, C. 1989: *Bananas, Beeches and Bases: Making Feminist Sense of International Politics.* Berkeley: University of California Press.

Enloe, C. 1994: *The Morning After: Sexual Politics at the End of the Cold War.* Berkeley: University of California Press.

Heng, G. and Devan, J. 1992: "State Fatherhood: The Politics of Nationalism, Sexuality, and Race in Singapore." In Andrew Parker, Mary Russo, Doris Sommer, and Patricia Yaeger (eds.), *Nationalism and Sexualities.* London and New York: Routledge, 343–64.

Innes, C. L. 1994: "Virgin Territories and Motherlands: Colonial and Nationalist Representations of Africa and Ireland." *Feminist Review* 47 (Summer), 1–14.

Kosut, H. 1967: *Indonesia: The Sukarno Years.* New York: Facts on File.

McClintock, A. 1993: "Family Feuds: Gender, Nationalism and the Family." *Feminist Review* 44 (Summer), 61–80.

Mosse, G. 1985: *Nationalism and Sexuality: Middle-class Morality and Sexual Norms in Europe.* Madison: University of Wisconsin Press.

Parker, A., Russo, M., Sommer, D., and Yaeger, P. (eds.) 1992: *Nationalism and Sexualities.* London and New York: Routledge.

Rice, E. P. 1934: *The Mahabharata: Analysis and Index.* London and New York: Oxford University Press.

Ryan, M. 1988: "The Politics of Film: Discourse, Psychoanalysis, Ideology." In Cary Nelson and Lawrence Grossberg (eds.), *Marxism and the Interpretation of Culture.* Chicago: University of Illinois Press.

Sullivan, N. 1991: "Gender and Politics in Indonesia." In M. Stivens (ed.), *Why Gender Matters in Southeast Asian Politics.* Clayton, Victoria, Australia: Monash University Centre of Southeast Asian Studies.

Suri, C. K. 1992: *Characters from the Mahabharata*, Vol. 22. New Delhi: Books for All.

Yuval-Davies, N. 1987: "Front and Rear: The Sexual Division of Labor in the Israeli Army." In H. Afsar (ed.), *Women, State and Ideology: Studies from Africa and Asia.* Albany: State University of New York Press.

Yuval-Davies, N. and Anthias, F. 1989: *Woman – Nation – State.* Basingstoke: Macmillan.

Yuval-Davies, N. and Bresheeth, H. (eds.) 1991: *The Gulf War and the New World Order.* London: Zed Books.

27 The Objects of Soap Opera: Egyptian Television and the Cultural Politics of Modernity

Lila Abu-Lughod

Circulating in Cairo in the 1980s was a joke typical for its urban contempt for the peasant from Upper Egypt:

> A Sa'idi [Upper Egyptian] came to Cairo and wanted to buy a TV set. He went to the appliance store and, pointing, asked, "How much is that TV in the window?" The owner yelled, "Get out of here you stupid Sa'idi!" He went away and dressed in a long white robe and headdress to disguise himself as a Saudi Arabian. He came back to the store and again asked, "How much is that TV in the window?" The owner yelled, "Get out of here you stupid Sa'idi!" He went away and changed into trousers and a shirt and tie, coming back disguised as a European. Again he asked "How much is that TV in the window?" The owner yelled, "Get out of here you stupid Sa'idi!" Puzzled, the poor man asked: "How could you tell it was me?" The shop owner answered, "That's not a TV, it's a washing machine."[1]

In this joke, lack of familiarity with television was made symptomatic of rural backwardness. Television represents modernity, requiring for its production advanced technology and for reception an expensive instrument. Although introduced into Egypt in 1960, it took the slow spread of electrification and labor migrants' wages in the 1970s to bring television sets to the majority of households, especially outside the major cities. [. . .]

[. . .] What, in fact, is the relationship between television and modernity?

More than any other form of mass media, especially in a place where many remain non-literate, television brings a variety of vivid experiences of the non-local into the most local of situations, the home. So when someone like Nobel laureate Naguib Mahfouz laments the decline of the Cairo coffee house, explaining "People used to go to the coffee shops and listen to story tellers who played

Excerpted from Lila Abu-Lughod, "The Objects of Soap Opera: Egyptian Television and the Cultural Politics of Modernity." In D. Miller (ed.), *Worlds Apart: Modernity through the Prism of the Local* (London: Routledge, 1995), 190–210.

a musical instrument and told of folk heroes. These events filled the role played by television serials today," he forgets that this older form of entertainment, with the imaginary non-local worlds it conjured up, was only available to men (quoted in Hedges 1992). Television gives women, the young, and the rural as much access as urban men to stories of other worlds.

In Egypt, I will argue, a concerned group of culture-industry professionals has constructed of these women, youths, and rural people a subaltern object in need of enlightenment. Appropriating and inflecting Western discourses on development they construct themselves as guides to modernity and assume the responsibility of producing, through their television programs, the virtuous modern citizen. Especially in the dramatic serials which are Egypt's most popular television fare, they seek to "educate" their public. Their faith in the impact of television is spurred by the debates their serials provoke among critics and other parts of the urban intelligentsia.

Yet a look at the place of television in these subalterns' lives suggests that this public subverts and eludes them, not because they are traditional and ignorant of the modern, as the joke about the country bumpkin would have it, but because the ways they are positioned within modernity are at odds with the visions these urban middle-class professionals promote. The nationalist message is broadcast into a complex social space where the very local and the transnational both exert powerful pulls. On the one hand, people live in the local worlds of their daily experience, of which television is only a small part. On the other hand, as multinational companies bombard the Egyptian market with their products, as Islamic political groups with broader than national identifications vie for loyalty, and as elites look to the West, television's nationalists have much to compete with.

Television in a Discourse of the Modern Nation

In the discourse of some key culture-industry professionals in Egypt, television figures in a nationalist and elitist vision of modernity. [. . .]

[. . . A] contest between the idealistic vision of television drama as the producer of a modern cultured citizen with a national consciousness and the competing tendency of Egyptian television to present "cheap" entertainment was dramatically played out during 1993 in the controversy [. . .] over the American soap opera, *The Bold and the Beautiful*. Beginning in late 1992, Channel 2, the channel that broadcasts most of the foreign programs in Egypt, began airing nightly episodes of this successful American daytime soap that has been running in the USA since March 1987 and has been exported to twenty-two countries.[2] In Egypt, cartoons in a weekly magazine caricatured its popularity; one showed a government minister on the telephone noting that the best time to raise prices on goods without anyone protesting was between 9.30 and 10.30 p.m., the time the soap was being aired.

The Bold and the Beautiful is set in the fashion world of Los Angeles and centers on two key families involved in fashion design and publishing. Nearly all the actresses are blonde and most of the actors are handsome, something that is not incidental to the success of the soap. [. . .]

The contrast between *The Bold and the Beautiful* and the highlight of Egyptian television viewing over the past five years could not be more stark. Since 1988 during successive Ramadans, the Muslim month of fasting and the television season's high point, people had been emotionally riveted by a brilliant Egyptian television serial written by Usama Anwar 'Ukasha. [...] Called *Hilmiyya Nights*, it followed the fortunes and relationships of a group of characters from the traditional Cairo neighborhood of Hilmiyya, taking them from the late 1940s, when Egypt was under the rule of King Farouk and the British, up to the present, even incorporating into the final episodes the Egyptian reaction to the Gulf War.

Although many Egyptian television serials have captured large audiences and generated discussion and affection, and the local productions are generally more popular than foreign imports, the broadcast of this unusually long and high-quality serial was a national cultural event.[3] Its popularity was not confined to the millions who regularly followed the evening serials but extended to the intelligentsia who were provoked by its political messages. The merits of the serial were debated in newspapers and magazines and a leading intellectual, Sayed Yassin, even used it as a metaphor for "Egypt's real abilities." In a brief essay in a major weekly magazine, *Al–Iqtisadi*, he contrasted the successful serial, with its excellent text, capable director, talented and devoted actors, and involved audience with the failures of current political activity in Egypt, suggesting that what Egypt needed was a better political text to guide its director (the President), more respect for its citizens, and the introduction of new political actors.[4] [...]

Hilmiyya Nights, more than most Egyptian serials, seems to be a hybrid product. Although its talented writer denied in print that he had given audiences an Egyptian *Falcon Crest* (an American prime-time soap that had aired several years earlier), there are numerous aspects of *Hilmiyya Nights* in which the influence of such American programs can be detected. [...] Strong on emotional drama, the serial focuses on the faces and feelings of its characters and intensifies its effects through dramatic music.[5] As in other Egyptian serials tears are plentiful, if balanced by laughter and anger. Like the British soap operas (and unlike the American) that take realism more seriously, the serial is set in particular neighborhoods and attempts to depict class differences and regional identities authentically and nostalgically.

What makes *Hilmiyya Nights* seem most like American prime-time soaps is that it partakes of the element of spectacle. The costumes are lavish, the sets sumptuous, and at least some of the women characters extravagantly glamorous and fashionable (Geraghty 1991: 27–8). The aristocratic central characters move elegantly among their villas and luxurious apartments, the key woman character elaborately made up and coiffured and dressed in a different outfit for each of well over a hundred episodes, trading sequined gowns for chiffon and furs, except when going in to the office when she wears stylish suits in striking colors.

In addition, the serial resembles the American prime-time soap operas in certain aspects of plot. As in *Dallas* the central action revolves around the rivalry between two wealthy men and their families, in this case an urban aristocrat and a rural mayor, both of whom become millionaire businessmen in the 1970s and 1980s. The financial wheelings and dealings of these two and the woman who at different times was married to each of them carry much of the narrative along. The adventures and love interests of their children become the focus as the serial moves into the present.

[. . .] Drawn out over five years and far more episodes than any previous Egyptian serial, *Hilmiyya Nights* allowed for the development of the kind of attachment to characters that soap-opera audiences relish. [. . .] An intimacy was created by the deep familiarity viewers came to have over time with characters' personal histories and tangled relationships, especially since old episodes of the serial were re-run each year before the new installment was aired and the whole serial, now complete, was being shown on successive Sunday evenings in 1993.[6] [. . .]

Despite these resemblances, however, [. . .] the series differed radically from any American soap opera in being historically contextualized. American soap operas have been characterized as a women's genre because they privilege the personal, depicting even the non-domestic work scenes in terms of personal relationships. This Egyptian serial similarly portrayed the personal lives of individuals but instead of having its narrative pushed along simply by events in the personal relationships among the characters, *Hilmiyya Nights* had the moral themes of loyalty, betrayal, corruption, thwarted desires, and tragic errors embedded in an historical narrative that tied individual lives to Egyptian national political events. It did what no American soap would ever do: it provided an explicit social and political commentary on contemporary Egyptian life.[7]

Above all, *Hilmiyya Nights* promoted the theme of national unity. With the exception of a very few truly evil characters, selfish and corrupt individuals out for themselves, the characters of different classes and political persuasions were shown to be basically good and patriotic. [. . . I]n the end, they saw the errors of their ways, prevented by their love of Egypt from pursuing the materialistic, immoral, or corrupt paths they had taken. Even the young religious extremist (the first to be depicted in an Egyptian television serial) was sympathetically portrayed as part of a generation that had been led astray by the lack of national spirit.[8]

Protecting the Public

Hilmiyya Nights sought to teach and enlighten. In response, intellectuals, critics, politicians, and censors sought to protect the public from its messages. Both the writer and his critics, the urban educated elite who felt it incumbent on them to protect others, assumed the power of television serials and the vulnerability of subaltern viewers. [. . .]

State censorship is exercised in Egypt in the name of protecting the public from the morally, politically, or religiously offensive. *Hilmiyya Nights* tested the limits of the more generous freedom of the press that has been President Mubarak's policy. [. . .]

Hilmiyya Nights, a serial that showed how political events at the national level affected the lives of individuals and communities, a serial in which personal histories, fortunes, and tragedies, were directly related to policies and events, battled with the censors. In contrast, several months into *The Bold and the Beautiful*, the director of censorship responsible for foreign films could still claim that there was very little to censor in the American serial. The characters are free-floating, their only real context being that created by the soap-opera world itself. This was read by many as making it "human." The censor, for example, defended the soap saying, "The serial carries general human values and debates problems that are not place specific; they are close to many of the problems of Eastern society."[9] Muna Hilmy, the daughter of the prominent Egyptian feminist Nawal El-Saadawi, defended the serial claiming that what the foreign serial offered that those "serials irrigated by Nile water" didn't was a look inside people. Instead of external events – political, economic, or social – one had people with feelings, desires, weaknesses, strengths, small wickednesses, and goodness. She defended the slowness of the serial as necessary to show the vastness of the human psyche and the politics of the serial as feminist.[10] [. . .]

Unenlightened Subjects?

[. . . T]o justify television as more than entertainment, a socially concerned and politically conscious group of culture-industry professionals[. . .] has constructed as their object "a public" in need of enlightenment. Their use of a discourse of protection is part of their patronization of their public but it also serves to reinforce among the professional classes the faith that mass media have powerful effects.

But can we determine how the television serials produced for them affect these "unenlightened subjects"? Although the answers to this are complex, on the basis of some ethnographic work in Egypt in the 1990s I will suggest how at least two groups who are the object of these professionals' efforts and discourse – poor working-class women in Cairo and villagers in Upper Egypt – seem to slip through their well-meaning nets.

[. . .] A soap directed at America's subalterns – housewives (although watched by students and many others) – has in Egypt captured instead an elite, or at least middle-class, audience that includes as many men as women. To enjoy it one must know English or be able to read Arabic subtitles and one must not be too exhausted from a hard day's work to stay awake.

[. . . M]any of the Egyptian serials [. . .] are so far-fetched or of such poor quality that audiences ignore them.

[. . . V]iewers [even] resist the nourishing social messages of [. . .] *Hilmiyya Nights*, even as they acclaim it as the best serial ever made. An example will illustrate this. *Hilmiyya Nights* had numerous important women characters, most sympathetically portrayed and shown to be facing dilemmas shared by different generations of women. Morally good older women put up with mistreatment by husbands, including secret marriages and deceptions. Younger women struggled with the tensions between career and marriage. The serial glorified education, showing most of the daughters of working-class men going on to university, the daughter of a coffee shop owner and a singer becoming a university professor, and the daughter of a factory worker and a dancer becoming a physician. In general the women were independent and able to take decisions on their own. [. . .]

However, when asked what they liked about the serial, several poor women who work as domestic servants in Cairo volunteered not the serious political or social messages but the character of Nazik Hanem, the aristocratic, conniving, magnificently dressed *femme fatale* who plays the leading female role. One young woman whose husband had left her with two children to raise suggested, "Nazik is the reason everyone watches *Hilmiyya Nights*. She's tough; she married four men. She wouldn't let anyone tell her what to do." An older woman with a disabled husband explained why Nazik was so great: "She's fickle, not satisfied with one type. She married many times. She represents what? What's it called? The aristocracy? She was strong-willed. And stubborn. Because of her desires she lost her fortune." After a short silence she added, "And Hamdiyya, the dancer, did you see her?" She laughed as she imitated a characteristic arrogant gesture of this belly-dancer turned cabaret-owner.

These were the two glamorous women characters with little nationalist sympathy who wrapped men around their fingers and wouldn't act like respectable ladies, despite the pleas of their children, their ex-husbands, and their other relatives. These were also the two who took dramatic falls. The dancer became addicted to heroin after being strung along by a man she hoped to marry. By the time she was cured she had lost everything and had nowhere to go. Nazik Hanem's end was more complex but brilliantly played. She was someone who could not accept her age, even after being swindled out of her fortune by her fourth husband, a younger man who threw her aside. She became increasingly temperamental and then began dressing up like someone half her age, with a wig covering her gray hair, to flirt with a twenty-year-old student. When scolded for this, she had a nervous breakdown.

None of the poor women who admired Nazik or the dancer ever mentioned the moral lesson of the fall; rather, they seemed to take vicarious pleasure in these women's defiance of the moral system that keeps good women quiet. These domestic workers were women whose respectability was threatened by their need to work outside the home and as servants. They struggled daily to claim and proclaim their respectability. They hid from their neighbors and sometimes even their relatives the actual sort of work they did and they had all adopted the *higab*, the headcovering of the new modest Islamic dress that, in Egypt, has come to be a sign of Islamic piety and middle-class respectability. [. . .]

Only one older woman commented on the more explicit national politics of the serial that had so exercised critics. She noted that *Hilmiyya Nights* was "against Sadat" and that was why it showed what happened with the *infitah*, or open-door economic policy: people started importing all sorts of putrid goods, like canned meat that was actually cat food. Yet she felt free to disagree with 'Ukasha's basic position adding, "In those days everyone was busy getting rich. There was lots of money around. For all of us." Various political opinions circulate in Egypt and there is no reason to assume that the "unenlightened" audiences of shows such as *Hilmiyya Nights* are waiting passively to learn from the serials what to think.

Viewers were selective in their appreciation of the messages of these television dramas. They could disagree with the politics; they could marvel at and take pleasure in the defiant characters who lived as they could not. They accepted the moral stances presented only when they resonated with their worlds. This was clearest in poor women's positive responses to the moral conservatism about family and a mother's role promoted by Egyptian serials generally and *Hilmiyya Nights* in particular. As one admirer of Nazik Hanem noted, to explain why Nazik's daughter Zohra never found happiness, "The poor thing. It was because her mother didn't take care of her. She abandoned her as a baby with her father. When the girl got sick and had a bad fever, his new wife brought her to Nazik saying, 'Here take your daughter and hold her close.' But she refused. So Zohra never knew the love of a mother. She had to depend on herself. So the man duped her [tricking her into a shameful secret marriage and a pregnancy]. Poor thing."

The villagers of Upper Egypt with whom I have worked make no more pliable subjects for the enlightening messages of the serials than these working-class urban women. This is not because they are unfamiliar with television, however. Every household in the village near Luxor where I have been working had a television set. Many were simple black and white sets with poor reception balanced precariously on rickety shelves in corners of mudbrick rooms whose only other wall decorations might be a poster of a favorite soccer club or movie star. The wealthiest families in the village had large color sets in their reception rooms – rooms that often also boasted padded couches and framed religious calligraphy. On every poor family's wish list, were they to sell a piece of land or somehow save enough for a down payment on the installment plan, was a color set.

Only on rare evenings would the television be silent; if there had been a death in the neighborhood or among one's kin, if someone was ill at home and receiving visitors. The most common reason for televisions to be silent was loss of electricity, something that happened for a few minutes almost every day and occasionally for long frustrating hours. And precisely because electric power in the village was so weak, children often had to do their homework by the light of the television sets.

Rather, the impact of serials like *Hilmiyya Nights* is deflected by the ways villagers consume television. For one thing, like their urban counterparts, villagers I knew were capable of selective readings of dramas. This was often necessary since the distance between the "realities" dramatized in the serials and the lives lived in the village was vast. The fashionable blonde stars of *The Bold and the Beautiful* in their plush offices and grand mansions are most obviously far from these hardworking people in mudbrick two-story homes with blue-painted wooden doors wide enough to allow the donkeys, sheep, and water buffaloes to pass through into the pens inside; but the characters portrayed in Egyptian serials like *Hilmiyya Nights* are hardly much closer. Most Egyptian serials are set in urban locations and deal with urban, often upper-class problems.[11]

An anecdote about watching television in a relatively poor household can illustrate the gulf between local and television lives and the selective ways women interpret what they watch. One evening, Yamna, the vivacious but exhausted mother of the family, was preparing dinner with the help of her sister when the serial, *Love in a Diplomatic Pouch*, came on. Her sister had been there all day helping this overworked woman who had bread to bake and children to be watched when she went off to get fodder for the animals. The family was miserable that night – between the fever of the eldest son, the measles that had struck all four of the little girls, the three boys' end-of-year exams, the expenses and fatigue of a recent trip to a hospital in Assiut in search of a cure for the chain-smoking father's asthmatic cough, and the government's announcement the previous day that the price of flour was to be doubled, they wondered how they would cope. Yet the serial they watched centered on a wealthy diplomat's family and included characters like ballet teachers, woman doctors, journalists, and radio personalities with career problems.

As Yamna cooked, her sister, wrapped in the black cloak women wear when they go visiting, shouted out a summary of the plot for her. She focused on the family dynamics that are the regular stuff of their own forms of telling life stories in the village. Divorces, arguments, absences, thwarted matches. She also picked up the moral message of the serial about women and family – the importance of the mother's role in raising her children and the ill consequences for their children of mothers who abandon them or put themselves or their marriages or careers first.

However, many of the "women's issues" in this serial, written and directed by one of Egypt's few women directors, were constructed in psycho-social terms that were foreign to these women: "psychological" problems like psychosomatic paralysis that love could heal, men unable to commit themselves to marry for fear of losing their freedom, mothers who cried because their children were not emotionally open with them, and psychiatrists treating drug addiction among the wealthy and educated. The women simply ignored in their discussions these aspects of the serial that were not part of their experience.

From my ethnographic work in the village, I would also suggest that the villagers make elusive targets for the cultural elite's modernizing messages for a more complex reason: through the very ease with which they have incorporated television into their everyday lives. Although it is difficult to articulate how this happens, I would argue that television created its own world, one that was for the villagers only a part – albeit an exciting one – of their daily lives. What they experienced through television added to, but did not displace, whatever else already existed. They treated the television world not as a fantasy escape but as a sphere unto itself with its familiar time slots and specific attitudes. It was a realm of knowledge about which people shared information: adolescents often had an encyclopedic knowledge of Egyptian films and serials and people knew a staggering amount about the private lives and previous roles of actors and actresses who starred in the serials. The young people read magazines but everyone had access to this knowledge through hours of viewing and the glorification of stars promoted by Egyptian television itself through interview programs and celebrity game shows.

In the villagers' attitudes toward the stars is a clue to the larger question of how television serials affect them. The villagers spoke about these stars as "ours," somehow belonging to them as viewers, but not as "us." The same mix of entitlement and distance applied to the serials. They are for "our" pleasure but they depict the lives of others who have different problems, follow different rules, and do not belong to the local moral community. What these others do, then, has little bearing on what we do or how we conduct our lives. The daily worries of trying to make ends meet, balancing a father's monthly salary of 130 LE (less than US $40) with work in the fields to grow clover for water buffaloes and sheep, of struggling to get families grown, through school, and married, of asserting rights to inheritances or extracting support from kin, of preserving one's moral reputation and standing in the face of in-laws and jealous neighbors with whom one has had disputes – these consume villagers. So do the pleasures of visits with friends and relatives, of meeting social obligations with generosity, of passing examinations, selling an animal, having a good harvest, or wearing new clothes on the religious feasts.

Even when serials try to reflect village lives, as did a 1993 serial called *Harvest of Love* about Upper Egypt written by a politically concerned progressive woman writer, people reject the problems as not theirs. In this case people enjoyed the serial and recognized the dialect and occasional bits of clothing but alleged that its central issue – the problem of revenge killings – was something that happened elsewhere in Upper Egypt. Perhaps this happens in Sohag (a city to the north), some villagers offered, even though I had heard the vivid narratives about just such a revenge killing in their village only a decade earlier.

I was most struck by the suspension of judgment people applied to the compartmentalized television others because it was so different from their critical evaluations of neighbors and kin. This response resembled the villagers' curious but neutral discussions of the foreign tourists, archaeologists, and researchers who were daily in their midst and had been since the early part of the century.

I am not arguing here that the villagers anxiously compartmentalize the "modernity" television serials (or foreigners) present in order to preserve a static traditional community somehow untouched by the global or "modernity." On the contrary, while the village appears picturesque with its "traditional" sights like mudbrick homes and swaying palm trees, donkeys, and the occasional camel carrying loads of clover or sugar-cane leaves, men hoeing fields or walking barefoot along muddy irrigation canals, and women in long black robes balancing bundles on their heads, there is not an aspect of people's everyday lives that has not been shaped by "the modern."

The modern Egyptian state determined that sugar cane be grown in the region, decides on prices, requires permits and licenses, conscripts all young men into its army, and runs the Antiquities Organization that employs so many local men, prevents people from building in certain areas, and requires that they build in quaint mud brick. It runs the schools that most children now attend, coming home weary from carrying the schoolbooks that teach about cleanliness, patriotism, and religion.

People suffer from various health problems, the result of chemicals and pesticides, too much sugar in the diet, and waste – including plastic bottles, batteries, and Raid cans – thrown into the irrigation canals. The straight-backed men in their turbans and long pale robes are savvy about the difference between local physicians and specialists who are university professors and practice in Cairo, Mansura, and Assiut. The women in black want "television examinations" of their pregnancies and want to know if you had an ordinary delivery or a caesarian.

How well people eat and whether they decide to uproot cash crops to grow wheat is determined by such faraway organizations as the World Bank and the IMF. Whether the men are away looking for work depends on the state of the Saudi Arabian economy, the decisions of bourgeois investors in the Red Sea tourist developments, French archaeologists, and wealthy Lebanese refugees setting up chicken factories on the desert road to Alexandria, 600 kilometers away. Whether children who have learned to say "Hello, baksheesh" come running home to give their mothers a few pounds, men who have developed pride in the art of carving pharaonic cats and Horus statuettes find buyers, and those who cook meals for the low-budget tourist groups visiting the tomb of King Tut on donkeys make enough to get new covers for their cushions all depends on whether the *New York Times* has reported "terrorist" attacks in Cairo.

And contrary to the joke told in Cairo, everyone knows how to operate not just television sets but washing machines, refrigerators, fans, and water pumps.

Television is, in this village, one part of a complex jumble of life and the dramatic experiences and visions it offers are surprisingly easily incorporated as discrete – not overwhelming – elements in this jumble.

This is not to say that television in general has not transformed social life or imaginaries. There are at least three areas in which careful ethnographic work might reveal significant transformations. First, in social life: there is less visiting among households in the evenings since families stay home to watch television. More important, television may have increased the number of "experiences" shared across generation and gender. Television brings families together in the evening and makes it more likely that men and women will socialize together as they sit around the single television set in the house. The focus of attention is the evening serial but families converse with each other while waiting for it, as when the start of the serial is delayed by government ministers droning on during the televised sessions of Parliament. Conflicts also arise, though, between generations and genders about which programs to watch, just as exposure to television differs by generation.

Second, television may have changed the nature of experience itself. Some Egyptian professionals rationalized to me viewers' pleasures using a discourse of continuity, suggesting, for example, that the serials are like "the stories a grandmother tells her grandchildren to send them to sleep," or "like *The Thousand and One Nights*, where the story-teller would stop at the most exciting moment to attract the audience to listen to him the next day," or the North African tradition "where the wandering poet who sings his poetry to the tune of the rababa stops every day at an exciting point in the story of 'Antar or Abu-Zeid al-Hilaly."[12] But this ignores a distinctive feature of television drama, what Raymond Williams (1989) has called, referring to the frequency with which TV viewers are exposed to it, its possible role in dramatizing consciousness itself.

The third area where television in general may be transforming experience is in its facilitation of new identifications and affiliations. Do the villagers feel part of an imagined community of citizens or consumers because they know they are watching the same programs at the same time and being offered the same goods as people across the country?

To acknowledge or explore the general effects of television on experience is not, however, the same project as the one I've been pursuing in this essay, which is to track the effects of particular kinds of public-spirited programs on their objects. Two factors conspire to undermine the impact of serials like *Hilmiyya Nights*. First, of course, the serials appear only as part of the flow (Williams 1975) of programming, sandwiched between films, pumpkin-seed serials, advertising, religious programs, children's programs, sports, news, nature programs, and countless talking-head shows. More important, their messages are evaluated from within, and hence often balanced or even contradicted by the powerful everyday realities within which villagers, like poor working women in Cairo, move. These realities are both resolutely local and transnational.

Whereas *Hilmiyya Nights* and related serials condemn the consumerism and materialism encouraged in the 1970s with the renunciation of socialism and the turn to economic liberalization, the proliferating television advertisements that precede the broadcast of evening serials and the middle- to upper-class lifestyles portrayed in most dramatic serials offer different messages. These are reinforced by local circumstances. At least among the schoolchildren, the availability of the goods in the nearby town of Luxor combines with these television messages to instill an insistent desire for specific brands of candy or running shoes (Amigo shoes with Ninja Turtles on them). For urban poor women, the availability of such goods is that much more persuasive.

[. . . T]he [. . .] enlightened professionals also exclude from their storylines any positive depiction of the various guises of the Islamic alternative being offered to Egypt's populace. Yet the Islamic identity and knowledge promoted by religious programs on television interact positively with adults' experiences in the new or refurbished mosques that are being enthusiastically supported and children's experiences in schools, secular state institutions that are, somewhat ironically, the locus of religious pressure especially in rural areas. In the village where I worked, these children, the girls forced to wear the new Islamic headcovering and all subjected to the lectures of their aggressively religious schoolteachers, even discussed in class the significance of a television serial loosely based on the Koranic story of Joseph.

Furthermore, as for poor women in Cairo, there is little to reinforce the enlightening messages about culture, social responsibility, and national unity the politically inspired culture-industry professionals are seeking to disseminate. *Hilmiyya Nights*, with its secular vision of a modern Egypt full of virtuous patriotic citizens, united across class by their love of country, sought to bring these subalterns into its modern fold.

But these subalterns are already folded into Egyptian modernity in a different way. The children who sing every morning the national anthem and memorize countless other nationalist songs from government schoolbooks may be somewhat receptive to the nationalist messages of television serials. Some, like a young village girl completing agricultural school, dream of impossible futures like being given a government plot of land in Sinai to develop. But their elders in Upper Egypt believe that their region has long been discriminated against and exploited by the north; they regularly experience the nation not through songs but through a formidable bureaucracy, a corrupt police force and army service (in which they are badly treated). The unity of rich and poor in national endeavors that *Hilmiyya Nights* idealizes is undermined by their knowledge of how the wealthy buy their way out of the army and around all regulations. For urban women who are the exploited supports of a modern class system, solving the twin demands of work and respectability through "Islamic" veiling, this vision of the nation must also find little corroboration.

The problem, finally, is that the kind of modernity these television serials depict as a vision for Egypt depends on class position and the availability of certain kinds of educational and career opportunity. The "uneducated public" at whom these serials are directed participates in the more common form of modernity in the postcolonial world: the modernity of poverty, consumer desires, underemployment, ill health, and religious nationalism.

Notes

1 Given the non-specialized readership for this essay, I have used an extremely simplified system of transliteration from the Arabic. To mark the letter *ayn* I use an apostrophe; otherwise all diacritics are absent as are distinctions between long and short vowels.
2 So popular has it been internationally that its stars have been invited to act in Italian, Spanish, and French films. They were treated as VIPs when invited to Egypt's Film Festival in December 1993, and thrilled audiences in India when they came on the air to wish Hindus well on a religious holiday. Many of these details were provided in a major magazine spread by Galal Al-Rashidy, "The Stars of the Bold and the Beautiful Behind the Camera" (in Arabic), *Sabah al-Khayr*, March 25, 1993, pp. 46–50.
3 It seems frequently the case that national productions are more widely popular than imports. For evidence from Europe, see Silj (1988).
4 Sayed Yassin, "Cultural Papers: 'Hilmiyya Nights' and Political Activity," *Al-Iqtisadi*, July 9, 1990, pp. 96–7.
5 For a stimulating discussion of the politics of television melodrama, see Joyrich (1992).
6 According to 'Abd al-Nur Khalil, "The Ramadan of Television Captured People in a Bottle" (in Arabic), *Al-Musawwar* 3518, March 13, 1992, pp. 48–9, so wedded did the actors become to their roles that, after the conclusion of the serial, many of them complained that they felt trapped by their roles in *Hilmiyya Nights*. As in American soap operas, stars also quit the show before its conclusion and had to be replaced so audiences had to cope with the separation of character from actor.
7 The only exception in recent American television was the *Murphy Brown* situation comedy that attacked the Bush family-values campaign in retaliation for Vice President Dan Quayle's attack on the protagonist's decision to have a baby out of wedlock. The fact that it was a *cause célèbre*, reported in newspapers and thought worthy of a BBC documentary, indicates how unusual the explicit inclusion of politics was in American television entertainment.
8 For a discussion of the exclusion of the perspective of the Islamic movement from television serials, see Abu-Lughod (1993).

9 Dalai 'Abd Al-Fatah (in Arabic), *Roz al-Yusuf*, 3371, January 18, 1993, p. 10.
10 The men, she argued, are not macho and they don't dominate women. The women work and make money. They want to succeed and to make their own futures. They don't give in to fate or circumstances or gossip. They use their minds and all they've got. The pleasure viewers get from *The Bold and the Beautiful*, she continues, is in seeing confrontation and hope ("*The Bold and the Beautiful*: A Serial without Male Complexes" [in Arabic], *Sabah al-Khayr*, February 11, 1993, p. 59).
11 Abdel Kader's (1985) study showed that there was a bias toward portraying the urban upper classes. Of fourteen serials and twelve short plays sampled during a six-month period in 1980, none were set in rural areas (36).
12 Nur Al-Sharif, interview with the author, July 22, 1990.

References

Abdel Kader, S. 1985: "The Image of Women in Drama and Women's Programs in Egyptian Television." Unpublished report, Population Council.

Abu-Lughod, L. 1993: "Finding a Place for Islam: Egyptian Television Serials and the National Interest." *Public Culture* 5 (3), 493–513.

Geraghty, C. 1991: *Women and Soap Opera*. Cambridge: Polity Press.

Hedges, C. 1992: "In Cairo Now a Coffee Shop is Just a Shop." *New York Times*, August 3.

Joyrich, L. 1992: "All That Television Allows: TV Melodrama, Postmodernism, and Consumer Culture." In L. Spigel and D. Mann (eds.), *Private Screenings: Television and the Female Consumer*. Minneapolis: University of Minnesota Press, 227–51.

Silj, A. et al. 1988: *East of Dallas: The European Challenge to American Television*. London: British Film Institute.

Williams, R. 1975: *Television: Technology and Cultural Form*. New York: Schocken Books.

Williams, R. 1989: "Drama in a Dramatized Society." In A. O'Connor (ed.), *Raymond Williams on Television: Selected Writings*. London and New York: Routledge, 3–13.

28 The Credible and the Credulous: The Question of "Villagers' Beliefs" in Nepal

Stacy Leigh Pigg

[. . .]

In Nepal, nowadays, your attitude toward shamans communicates who you are. My interlocutors said quite a lot in their few words. If you can laugh about dhāmis, then you do not take them too seriously. If you can find them fascinating, then obviously you do not see them every day. If you can explain what they do, then you cannot be fooled. If you know the difference between good and bad shamans, or know where and to whom their knowledge is valuable, then you know how to make the complicated judgments necessary to deal with these healers. What people said in response to my declared interest in dhāmi-jhānkris revealed little about how likely the speakers were to actually call a shaman when sick.[1] Nor did they shed much light on why shamans are so important as ritual specialists and healers in Nepal, or on why their power is compelling for most Nepalis. The responses I got indicated, quite simply, how a person chose to position himself or herself in relation to my connection to Nepal, as that person perceived it. I was taken to represent modernity.[2]

Nepal is not the only place where shamans are caught up in the meanings of modernity. In the world at large today, it is possible to be a person who is "interested in" or "not interested in" shamans. You can engage in research on shamans from any number of angles in order to explain what they do, how they do it, and why people turn to them. You can ignore them, on the assumption that they are an arcane feature of disappearing cultures. Or you can buy the experience of being a shaman's apprentice by signing up for tours and workshops. Shamans figure in the Western imagination as objects of science, obstacles to science, and alter images of science.[3] Shamans, taken to represent "tradition"

Excerpted from Stacy Leigh Pigg, "The Credible and the Credulous: The Question of 'Villagers' Beliefs' in Nepal." *Cultural Anthropology* 11, 2 (1996), 160–201.

(or sometimes "premodern" worlds), have long been handy symbols in the construction of "modernity." [. . .]

In this essay I consider why so many people in Nepal are so interested in talking about who believes what. Some of these people claim that they have a modern consciousness by associating "belief in dhāmis" with a distinct "other" who is traditional. Who does this, why, in what ways, and to what ends? Still other people embrace shamans as necessary and indispensable, but at the same time bad-mouth them in a constant tirade of skeptical criticism (as Stone 1986 has also noted). What is the nature of this skepticism, and what is accomplished through it? Is the skepticism expressed by the people most intimately involved with shamans a measure of the effects of "modernization"? Quite a number of the people I knew oscillated between these positions, adopting different stances depending on the context. What does this tell us about the lives of these people and the politics of identity in Nepal?

By being someone "interested in dhāmi-jhānkris," I stumbled upon an arena of Nepali society where the social differences created by modernity were especially at issue. There are overlapping reasons why shamans would be at the center of these concerns about identity. One cluster of reasons has to do with the way modern notions of progress infuse specific development objectives. An aim of development in Nepal is to introduce "modern medicine" (also known as "biomedicine," "allopathy," "Western medicine," and "cosmopolitan medicine").[4] In the everyday logic of development practice, "modern medicine" is positioned as the eventual replacement for existing modes of healing. "Modern medicine" thus has to combat healers like shamans. In Nepal, shamans perform rituals that placate spirits or foil witches; they generally do not give medicines or manipulate the body itself.[5] Their association with spirits and rituals makes them especially potent metaphors for tradition in juxtaposition to the "science" of "modern medicine."

Shamans are salient figures, as well, in the wider cultural politics of development in Nepal for an altogether different set of reasons. Seen from the perspective of the rural people among whom I lived, shamans and "doctors"[6] symbolize the relations between a local village world and the cosmopolitan modern world. This *social* meaning comes in part from the ways illnesses themselves are connected to place and identity. Shamans deal with problems people have because of who they are and where they live. (Spirits are attached to specific sites or social groups; witches are members of the local community.) Their divinations and rituals deal with the contingent forces working on contextualized persons.[7] The kinds of illnesses doctors treat, in contrast, are said to be "of the body," common to anyone "who bleeds when cut." Doctors' treatments address illnesses that are understood to be universal and independent of context. Whereas a shaman's actions always evoke a social context, the doctor's medicines suggest the existence of a generic individual. The sources of these healers' knowledge is associated with social spaces as well. Shamans learn "secrets" through apprenticeships and dreams, while doctors have the kind of systematic, public knowledge instilled in schools. Shamans belong to a world of local and personal relations, while doctors clearly belong to the institutions of a cosmopolitan modernity. In short, shamans mean something in both modern narratives and local understandings. Paradoxically, as I will try to show, this makes shamanic healing central to Nepali experiences of modernity.

The Idea of Modernity

Discussions of "belief" in Nepal are part of a much broader process through which local and national concerns intersect with global cultural circulations. To look at the meaning of "belief" in Nepal is to also explore the social life of the notion of the modern, in both its local manifestations and its translocal consequences. In talking about the modern here, I am concerned specifically with the vision of identity and difference embedded in the narrative of modernization. This narrative posits a rupture, a break that separates a state of modernity from a past that is characterized as traditional. Tied to the idea of progress, then, is an idiom of social difference, a classification that places people on either side of this great divide. Modernity, in this sense, is quite literally a worldview: a way of imagining both space and people through temporal idioms of progress and backwardness.

The contours of this world look different depending on the angle from which they are seen. In societies that can claim to be the home of modernity, this narrative of difference is used in myriad ways to construct a traditional "other." In Nepal, though, it is the modern that is "other." From the point of view of this small, marginal, and impoverished country, modernity is somewhere else – India, perhaps, or China. The question, for many, is how to bring modernity here, and whether it is possible to be "here" in Nepal and be "modern." "Compared to the advanced countries of the world, we are lagging about a half to a full century," wrote a contributor to an Internet discussion of Nepal's problems, expressing a widely shared sense of despair over Nepal's ranking as one of the world's poorest countries (soc.culture.nepal, 1994). In fact, development institutions are among the most important forces brokering ideas of modernity through specific projects of modernization (Adams 1995; Escobar 1995). Nepalis experience modernity through a development ideology that insists that they are *not* modern, indeed that they have a very long way to go to get there. This message has different implications and certainly different meanings for people variously positioned in Nepali society.

How, then, are we to understand the import of modernity in Nepal? Modernity is a slippery object for cultural analysis because the discourse of modernity produces the very differences that it seems to be about (Latour 1993). The dichotomy between tradition and modernity makes sense only within the narrative of modernization. We therefore have to bracket the terms "modern" and "traditional" in order to make them objects of analysis. This is not easy. Consider how anthropology has variously positioned itself within and against the modernization narrative. Again and again, these terms creep back into our vocabulary in self-consciously apologetic scare quotes, even though, for the most part, it is thought best to avoid these labels altogether. This avoidance of tainted adjectives merely evades the problem the discourse of modernity poses for cultural analysis. It will not do to look the other way simply because we now find the traditional–modern dichotomy problematic. Whether or not this dichotomy serves us well in social analysis, the fact is that these terms are thriving in the world we aim to describe and interpret.

We need, then, to track the terms of the discourse of modernity as people adopt, deploy, modify, and question it. To do so requires shifting attention from the *content* of social representations to their *use* in historically specific contexts, for it is one thing to point to the dichotomous terms characteristic of this discourse and quite another to consider who brings these categories of difference to bear on the world, through what practices, and to what effects. What at first glance appears as an ever more widespread repetition of these supposedly "Western" categories turns out to be a complicated chain of displaced differences.[8]

It is futile to try to map the boundaries of the modern, for these boundaries are redrawn every time the idea of modernity is asserted. Where, then, can anthropology begin to tackle the question of modernity? If we restrict ourselves to the description of particular social forms identified as modern we fail to address the powerful hold the idea of modernity has in a global social imaginary. But by addressing the ideological significance of modernity we are caught, by default, replicating the traditional–modern distinction and with it the presumption that modernity is quintessentially Western. Ethnography offers a strategy for dealing with this conundrum of position because, beyond discovering that there are "other" and "many" modernities, it can be a method for tracing the situated practices through which modernity is asserted while making evident the displacements such assertions produce.

Though the idea of modernity appears ubiquitous and enduring, it is not the same everywhere and at all times. We can recognize its origins in a particular historical milieu, and we can trace how it has spread through powerful ideological and political mechanisms, but we must also be cautious, as Rofel has warned, "of creating unified readings out of local Euro-American practices and allowing those to overpower interpretations elsewhere" (1992: 93). Too often, I think, we treat modernity like a robust and noxious weed whose spread chokes the delicate life out of other meanings. The strategy I employ here is to delineate points of view from which the modern and the traditional are visible. Though one aim of my ethnographic analysis is to show how the categories of modernity have indeed permeated the common sense of Nepali villagers, I do not mean to suggest simply that "our" modern ideas are taking over "their" local ones. Rather, I want to draw attention to the formation of *junctures* at which it becomes possible to communicate (or appear to communicate) across social contexts through various versions of modern dichotomies.

The question of villagers' beliefs is one such juncture. As modern social dichotomies meld with local common sense in Nepal, they also establish connections to people and places beyond the locality. This dynamic is not easily captured in the familiar inside–outside trope of anthropology. When "culture" is understood to consist of contextually dependent, situated meanings attached to places and their resident people, ideas and sensibilities are taken as features of cultural identity. In the case I discuss here, this would lead us to sort out "modern" from "Nepali" cultural orientations and to try to determine who has which and to what degree. We would end up finding "modernized" and "traditional" Nepalis.

An alternative conception begins from the premise that a locality (such as a Nepali village) is itself a translocal (or transnational) space. Locality is constituted in and through relations to wider systems, not simply impinged upon by them. We are more accustomed to noting this for economic systems – for instance, in discussing the organization of peasant household production in its relation to capitalism and markets – than for systems of signification. Through what sorts of relations do ideas, images, meanings, and ideologies become globalized? What is the relation between processes of localization and processes of interconnection? These questions are much harder to pose, let alone answer, when we look at the construction of meaning. In theorizing these relations we are caught between wanting to recognize the integrity and coherence of culturally distinctive points of view and acknowledging the impossibility of delimiting "a" culture in the face of overwhelming evidence of the cross-currents in which these points of view are positioned.

One step away from the reification of discrete cultures is to inquire into the processes that make and sustain distinctiveness. "Instead of assuming the autonomy of a primeval community," Gupta and Ferguson have argued, "we need to examine how it was formed *as a community* out of the interconnected space that always already existed" (1992: 8). By focusing on the production of difference, we stay mindful of the social relations that position people. What makes the point of view of Nepali villagers different from other perspectives in Nepal and elsewhere? More importantly, who recognizes this difference?

A second step involves looking afresh at how distinctive points of view are brought together. If difference is to be problematized by looking at how it is produced, it is equally important to ask how particular conjunctures come into existence.[9] Attention to the formation of locality also requires attention to the formation of the cosmopolitanism that transcends localities and mediates them (Robbins 1992).[10] This relation between differentiated locality and mobile cosmopolitanism is precisely the relation I address here. It seemed to me to be at the heart of the cultural tensions brought to the fore in Nepal by the discursive effects of development. The idea of the modern generates a sense of difference while at the same time holding out the promise of inclusion in a global cosmopolitan culture. To understand what this means in Nepal, it is important to realize that modernity is not cosmopolitan by definition. It has come to be so in the world we live in today. [. . .]

A State of Development

For Nepalis, modernity is not an abstraction. It is an idea rendered meaningful and concrete through their involvement with the ideologies and institutional practices of development. The salience of development in Nepali national society cannot be overemphasized: the idea of development grips the social imagination at the same time its institutional forms are shaping the society itself.[11] There is, of course, a history behind this national obsession with development. Nepal became involved as a state in postcolonial world politics without having been (directly) colonized.[12] A political upheaval in 1950–1 overthrew the Rana oligarchy, ushering in a state that legitimated itself through its declared mission to modernize Nepal.[13] This new phase in Nepali national politics coincided with the postwar emergence of the international development apparatus. For four decades, state expansion has worked hand-in-glove with foreign aid in the mission to develop the country. The post-1950 policies planted many entirely new features in the social landscape – ranging from roads to foreign development advisers, from schools and hospitals to tourists, from media images to commodities. In the process, a sense of a national society was built. Being Nepali means seeing yourself as a citizen of an underdeveloped country. Most people over the age of thirty recall quite vividly both the degree of change and the experience of realizing that they were "underdeveloped."[14] Of course, specific development policies, programs, or institutions are not the source of all social changes in Nepal. But in popular consciousness *bikās* (development) describes anything new and/or foreign. Being modern is being *bikāsi* (developed).

The intense development activity since the mid-1950s has had some tangible structural effects. First, patterns of connectedness changed. A hill population that had always traded, intermarried, and migrated became more mobile, in new ways and in relation to new places. Especially important was the opening of the Tarai (the flat land between the hills and the Indian border to the south) to colonization. The hills and the Tarai have become increasingly interconnected. In general, development, whether in the form of roads or schools, has intensified the influx of nonlocal ideas and things into hill villages. Second, the civil service has burgeoned and the government presence in the countryside has expanded through "offices" for agriculture, health, education, and development administration. Development is an industry in its own right in Nepal. It requires bureaucrats, foreign advisers, office staff, professionals, extension workers, program directors, project coordinators, trainers, trainees (who are often paid for participating), interviewers and survey enumerators, secretaries, drivers, and tea fetchers, both within His Majesty's Government and in international aid organizations. The middle class that has emerged in the last four decades sustains itself in large part from development-related employment. At the same time, subsistence farmers (estimated to be 80–90 percent of the population), who increasingly depend on the employment of one or more family members as a source of cash, look to jobs as rural schoolteachers, agricultural extension agents, village health workers, vaccinators, and office "peons" as possible local sources of income. It is important to understand that people in Nepal, at all economic levels, have a more immediate interest in the job prospects development activities offer than in the actual improvements development programs are supposed to bring. It is better to deliver development than to be its target.

In rural areas, *bikās* is associated in people's minds with social mobility.[15] There has emerged in Nepal a new kind of status that is correlated with economic advantage but not reducible to it. Being cosmopolitan, being a relatively "developed" kind of person, is a form of cultural capital. It is both a requirement for entry into other economic spheres and a result of participation in them. In hill villages, farming families attempt to place at least one member outside the household sphere of production. Circular migration between a hill home and distant employment is especially important.[16] People measure prosperity no longer just in terms of labor, land, and livestock but also in terms of connections to a wider economic sphere.[17] There is a continual peeling off of *some* people from all local social strata into different levels of the cosmopolitan economic sphere. These people remain connected to those who stay behind in the village. Though economic pressures force people into pursuing alternate sources of livelihood, what they gain from such activities is not just cash. An added payoff, even for the most disadvantaged, comes from becoming a more cosmopolitan person. This in itself has value.[18] Thus the socioeconomic changes of recent decades not only extend existing stratifications but also introduce a kind of marbling of cosmopolitan status into village society.

Whatever its economic dimension (and empirical research on this point is called for), the social salience of "being developed" or "being cosmopolitan" is striking. Being cosmopolitan means having the capacity to understand the ways of other places, to make a living away from the village, to be mobile. A cosmopolitan sensibility has a practical value, in that it enables one to manage in a wider world.[19] But more than this, it has a kind of symbolic power.[20] Obviously, the cosmopolitan–local distinction resonates for people whose livelihood is simultaneously rooted to land and enmeshed in larger, transnational economies. People in Nepal talk about this distinction through the idioms of "understanding" and "carrying loads." Cosmopolitan people say of others that "they don't understand" (*kurā bujhdainan*) or "they lack awareness" (*'conscious' chaina*), while villagers imagine "developed places" and privileged economic positions as a life of "not having to carry loads" (*bhāri boknu pardaina*) or "not having to walk" (*hidnu pardaina*).[21]

The rural area I call Chandithan, just outside Bhojpur Bazaar in the eastern hills of Nepal, is an example of the social enigma that is the "modernizing village" now emerging in Nepal. With but a few local radios, no newspapers, only a small local market, and the nearest road a two days' walk, it was in many ways a self-contained world in the mid-1980s. Yet because it lies a mere hour's walk from the district center, its people have access to offices, a high school, clinics, a veterinary clinic, a photo studio, a place to buy machine-knit sweaters and plastic buckets, and other amenities of development. (For most of the world, Bhojpur Bazaar would be a small village itself, but in the Nepali hills such places are concentrations of amenities and sophistication.) From the perspective of the most cosmopolitan of the urban elite, they are "villagers" – the kind of people in need of development. From the perspective of even more remote and isolated areas of the country, they are sophisticated cosmopolitans themselves. Situated as they are, they themselves are intensely concerned with their place as villagers in a national society oriented toward modernization – with all that entails. A discourse on belief is produced in this social context, refers to it, and is used by individuals to maneuver within it.

The Mythologies of Modernization

"It will never work to lecture villagers. That won't keep them from calling dhāmis," a nurse in Kathmandu reasoned. She was critical of what she saw as the authoritarian way many health workers scold villagers about their beliefs. She had a different approach. She tried to convince people to let go of harmful beliefs by engaging in a dialogue with them. She explained:

> When I was working at a clinic here in Kathmandu there was a woman who would come with her baby. None of the other women would speak to her; none of them would sit next to her. They ostracized her entirely. I asked why. It turned out to be because her other babies had died. They believed that if she saw their babies, she would cause them to fall ill.

I nodded. The idea that the spirits of dead infants cling to their mother and prey on other babies with whom she has contact is common throughout Nepal.

"And, seeing that, what did I do?" she continued. "I went straight over to that woman and sat down next to her. I gave her my own son, my own baby, to hold. I let her hold and play with him while I chatted with the woman!" she smiled. "Those other women were astonished. They saw that I had risked my own son to be kind to this woman. Later they asked me, 'weren't you afraid' and I said, 'No. That woman has done nothing.' I showed them with my own example that these spirits could not harm their children. That's how people have to be educated," she concluded.

We were sitting at the back table in K.C.'s, a trendy restaurant in the heart of Kathmandu's tourist district. Over cappuccino and lemon cheesecake we discussed the difficulties she experienced as a nurse working with people whose ways of explaining illness were often at odds with the kind of care she was trying to provide. She had seen a lot of misery, experienced a lot of frustration, and had thought a great deal about her own role.

"I've been to the village. I know what it is like," this urban woman told me, explaining that part of her training included several months working on a health team that toured hill villages.

"We arrived in this one village and saw a man who was on the verge of death. We *knew* we had the medicines to cure this man. But when we offered to treat him, he refused our medicines because a dhāmi had told him not to take them." She paused to let this sink in.

"But it turned out that one of the men in our team was from a village himself. He simply asked to borrow a dhyāngro, a drum, from a shaman." She chewed a bite of cake. "He sat down next to the sick man and started to beat the drum. Then he began to sing, you know, to call the spirits. And then he was trembling, shaking, the way dhāmis do. And he gave a divination instructing the man to take the medicines."

"And so he did," she smiled. "That man was cured. Other villagers flocked to the guy in our team, begging him to treat them because they were so impressed with his power as a shaman."

She was telling me this to illustrate the way health workers can "really" reach out to the people they are trying to help:

> So we stayed in that village for a couple of weeks. And when we were packing up to leave, the guy on our team showed the villagers that he wasn't really a dhāmi after all. What he did was, he just started shaking and speaking in that strange way dhāmis speak when they are giving a divination. But he had no drum, and he hadn't called the spirits.

She knew I had lived in a village long enough to know that the drum is essential to call the spirits. It is the spirits who make the shaman's body tremble and who use his voice to choke out their messages. "At first, the villagers were absolutely astonished," she continued. "They were angry with him for fooling them. But he pointed out that we had cured their neighbor. This calmed them down. And so they realized," she smiled, "that shamans shouldn't always be believed." [. . .]

At the outset, the nurse's story asserts the difference between the health team and the people she identifies as villagers. Implicitly, Nepal is portrayed as a divided society in which educated people like the health professionals travel to villages as if they were going to a foreign country with alien customs. It is precisely the neatness of this opposition that makes the mediation of the cosmopolitan man who was "from a village" necessary. In a second mediation, the forms of shamanic healing are used as a tool by the forces of its opposite, "modern medicine." The resolution of the story, in which "villagers realize that shamans can't always be believed," is a third mediation. "Modern medicine" overcomes shamanic healing by absorbing it, bringing villagers one step closer to a cosmopolitan understanding. The story is organized around the premise that cosmopolitan and village points of view are entirely different. They can be brought together in various ways, but they never blur or mix.

The story, of course, further reinforces this difference by portraying a conflict between two therapeutic approaches, presented as mutually exclusive options. The story is narrated as if the members of the health team always and only rely on "modern medicine" while villagers always and only rely on shamans. "Modern medicine" and shamanic healing are here emblematic of the broader differences in sensibility and outlook of different kinds of people.

The perfect symmetry of this social distinction is what makes a further distinction between knowledge and belief appear so clear. The health team knows more than the villagers. The health team knows that the sick man will either live or die, depending on whether he takes the medicines they have. The villagers simply hope that he will live. The health team also knows that their man is impersonating a shaman for the villagers' own good. The villagers do not know that the performance is false or that it is in their own best interest. As the story unfolds, the villagers receive two revelations: first, the divination that authorizes the taking of medicines; and second, the truth that the man they thought was a visiting shaman was in fact a fake. The health team's knowledge is doled out to the villagers. This is an economy of knowledge, in which one group holds the resources and controls their circulation.

The ruse on which the story pivots does not trouble the health team. For them, we gather, it is unremarkable that a shaman can be impersonated. That spirits choose certain people, descend on them, take hold of their bodies, and make them tremble, that this relationship allows these people to see what ordinary people cannot see and gives them power to communicate with the world of the unseen – if these fundamental truths are denied, then all shamans are, one way or another, performers. The foundation on which shamanic authority rests is not the "knowledge" villagers think it is, but the "belief" modern people know it to be. The villagers, then, in the view of the health team, are doubly deluded. They can be made to believe in a false shaman because they falsely believe in shamans in the first place.

The villagers were at first suspicious of the health team's medicine, the story hints, because it was unfamiliar. Its undeniable efficacy later convinces them. The story implies that this village will never be the same again. This, then, is a story of an encounter, a skirmish in the battle to bring "modern medicine" to villages. Stories about "introducing modern medicine" in Nepali villages share these two motifs: that "modern medicine" is entirely new to villagers and that villagers are astonished by its wondrous efficacy. It is important to grasp that these notions can appear plausible *only* from the modern point of view, a perspective that stories of medical progress themselves sustain. It is circular. Modern certainties are confirmed through experiences that are already organized from the perspective of the modern observer. Thus it is possible to assert decade after decade that "modern medicine" is coming to villages in Nepal for the very first time. Thus it seems, likewise, that the efficacy of "modern medicine" should be readily apparent despite the fact that actual medical services in Nepal are so inadequate. Neither of these basic assumptions makes sense from the point of view of villagers. They never see "modern medicine" as entirely new; they only see it as more or less accessible. Nor do they find it remarkably efficacious or always desirable ("Look how many operations doctors do, and still people die"). In villages, people do not tell stories of their wholesale conversion to "modern medicine."

Yet I consider the nurse's story to be every bit as "Nepali" as villagers' stories. Its structure, particularly the way it organizes points of view, conveys something very specific to present-day Nepal. The health team are "people who understand." They identify themselves as such merely by referring to others as "villagers." Villagers are by definition people who have not (or at least can seem to have not) been transformed by the social changes of the past decades in Nepal. They reside on the other side of the modern divide. In order for the position of "people who understand" to exist there must be a credulous "other." Differences among actual villagers must be effaced. In the nurse's story, all the "villagers" interpret the man's illness in the same way; all have utter faith in what shamans tell them; all are duped by the impersonation of the shaman; and all are equally grateful, in the end, to the health team. These moves are made again and again in modern portrayals of "villagers' beliefs."

Still, what makes the story (and the situation it describes) intriguing is the way the modern dichotomies seem to wobble even as they are asserted. As the grid of modernity is used to make sense of an interaction between a health team and villagers, the problematic ambiguities of this organizing frame become exposed. Who, for instance, is this man "from a village" who can so convincingly imitate a shaman? Perhaps he really was a dhāmi who was hiding this fact from his fellow health workers. Who fooled whom and who exactly was educated in the process? And what of the tale's implication that "modern medicine" can eventually triumph over ignorance and superstition? In order to do so, scientific knowledge must become enmeshed in the very superstitions it opposes (Prakash 1992). To make an impression on the villagers, the health team involves itself in shamanic rites. Their strategy for teaching villagers about the value of "modern medicine" involves getting villagers to transfer their (supposed) awe toward shamans to medicine instead. In the process, medicine is presented to villagers as simply another form of magical power.

My commentary on this story has taken me some distance from its teller's intention to share with me an event she really witnessed. I have drawn attention to both the dichotomies and the ambivalences evident when an event is interpreted as a sign of a transition from tradition to modernity. The heath team's interpretation of the event at the time, as well as the story she came to tell about it later, are representations. It is important to keep in mind that however much these representations draw on the imaginative tropes of the modernization narrative, they are enacted, as social practices, in a context that can never possibly fit perfectly within modern categories. What is more, this context includes other social agents who have their own ideas about things.[22]

Tradition in Development

The notion of "villagers' beliefs" plays an important role in international development thinking at present. In the 1970s, development rhetoric began to focus more on people and less on abstract economic models. Slogans such as "meeting basic needs" and "putting people first" spawned interest in "culturally appropriate development" and "indigenous knowledge." There was a sense in development circles that programs had to be tailored to specific places. Research began to be carried out on "existing knowledge, attitudes, and practices," and "social feasibility" studies began to be incorporated into the planning process (Escobar 1991). Most development professionals now would say that the "beliefs and customs" of the target population need to be taken into account for programs to succeed.

In development discourse, the word "traditional" always signals a world of shared and unquestioned beliefs. This is the realm of habit, rather than reason.[23] "Beliefs" are always associated with a group identity and taken, usually, to be a feature of ethnicity.[24] Even Shrestha and Lediard, whose advocacy for working with shamans was based on acknowledging that villagers do indeed have a perspective, objectify "belief" as a kind of collective mental prison in which villagers are trapped:

> As indicated in various social science studies, it has long been established beyond doubt that these people [shamans] possess the means of directing villagers to adopt any behavior which the practitioners see as right for the people (as ordained by the Gods who are seen to control the everyday affairs of this universe). (1980: 27–8)

It is not surprising, then, that when Stone asked rural health workers, "In what ways is local culture important in primary health care?" they responded by listing the "wrong beliefs" of villagers. As a further example of the way "cultural factors" are understood in health development, she cites a national report on Primary Health Care (PHC) in which

> illiteracy, superstition, social evils, and poverty are all listed together as one of eight basic health problems in the country, equivalent to items like malaria and malnutrition. Likewise, in PHC flow charts showing relationships between national health problems, it is common to see "ignorance" (measured as a literacy rate of 19 percent) grouped with "poverty" and linked by arrows to the ominous categories of disease, malnutrition, and underuse of health services. (Stone 1986: 297)[25]

In the implementation of development in Nepal, wider trends in international development attitudes take certain concrete forms. From Geneva and New York come policies and program designs with slots in which "local ideas and practices" are to be inserted. Accordingly, Nepali development functionaries use a language of cultural difference to pinpoint and describe the mentality of the target population. At the same time, these Nepali development workers are concerned to distinguish themselves from villagers, for it is precisely their status as "people who understand" that qualifies them for jobs in the development sector. Where the international development discourse on culture intersects with an emerging Nepali idiom of social differentiation, "villagers' beliefs" emerge as an object. This object can be perceived only from a distance. Up close, everything changes. [. . .]

Knowing Who Knows

"Dhāmile ke bhancha bhancha?" (What does it matter what shamans say?) This dismissive little remark can be heard often in Chandithan. Is the slight skepticism it conveys a symptom of "modernizing" forces that are undermining traditional institutions?

It would have to be, if we interpret this society according to the modern narrative of progress. This narrative already tells us that the traditional villagers of Nepal "believe," stubbornly, as Shrestha and Lediard would have it, in shamans. Any expression of doubt would be a sign that this belief is eroding. On the other hand, if we follow ordinary people as they interact with shamans, we see that people are always scrutinizing "what shamans say." [. . .]

Finding a shaman who "knows" is one step. By definition, shamans are people who know (jānne mānche). Unlike ordinary people, who are deaf-mutes (lātā-murkhā) in these matters, shamans have insight into an unseen dimension of the world through their ability to see spirits, hear their voice, communicate their desires, and persuade them to release their hold on bodies they are troubling. Some shamans, however, "know" more than others. I asked one dhāmi in an interview why this is the case.

"It is according to the spirit familiar, the deutā," he replied. "Some have deutā that can enable even great cures and they are able to deal with the most serious illnesses." [. . .]

People with problems form hunches about what is going on, and then seek out the specialist who might have the ability to help. To find a shaman who "knows," people must frequently consult several who do not. Shamanic mediation is fundamentally problematic. First, the spirits on whom the shamans depend for their insight are not entirely reliable. They are said to lie sometimes, and in any case they never "speak clearly" in divinations. Second, it is all too apparent to the people who live and work everyday with these shamans that they are only human. Many are the ways a shaman's interventions can go wrong. Even dhāmis themselves theorize about their limited ability to cure only some people some of the time. No wonder, then, that the question of belief in shamans is often on people's minds.

"Dhāmis can make mistakes," Chhema concluded. She had just returned from a visit to her brother, where they had recently found out that decades of misfortune in his family was the result of an inaccurate divination given some thirty years before. "You can't tell what is afflicting a person just by looking at him. Dhāmis have to make their guess. 'Perhaps it is this, maybe it is that,' they say. They aren't god, they're people just like you and me."

But realizing she might be giving me the wrong impression, she continued, "Your doctors have to examine a person too. If doctors could just know right away what the problem was, they wouldn't have to use their 'degree.'" ("Degree" is the word used locally to refer to stethoscopes and thermometers.) "Doctors have to investigate, and dhāmis have to investigate too."

People look to performances themselves to make judgments about shamanic mediation. Some shamans are widely acknowledged to be "more fun to watch." Yet people are critical of shamans they think are masking shaky ritual knowledge with energetic performances meant to dazzle. "It is not the show that counts," one man stated firmly, "it is the *riti* [ritual, spells] itself which must be big." People distinguish between what the shaman does "himself" and what is done through him by spirits. [. . .]

This equivocal fusion of shaman-as-human and shaman-as-spirit-vehicle raises two questions. How, under these conditions, do people form their judgments about dhāmis? Quite simple, I was told, "if it works, then the shaman knew. If it doesn't work, then you find another shaman." More specifically, "if a dhāmi shows your divination and gets your illness exactly right, then you believe him," I was told by many people. Typically, a divination includes a description of the symptoms afflicting the person in question.[26] [. . .]

The local shamans in Chandithan look rather unconvincing when people compare them with the purported powers of shamans of other times and places. Western folklorists might find in contemporary Himalayan shamanism the great Bon tradition of ancient Tibet, but to the jaundiced local eye they are sad examples of a devolved ritual force that no longer exists. In Chandithan, at least, there was a strong feeling that there must be better shamans elsewhere, in China perhaps, or Malaysia. My interest in meeting local dhāmis sometimes prompted passionate discussions of shamans "who know" that turned, inevitably, to the superior, but lost, knowledge of "shamans from before," *uhileko jhānkri*.

Shamans from before could sunder boulders, cut chickens outside the house while sitting inside, and transport objects from far away. They could fly. They knew how to cure tuberculosis and smallpox. They could fight off attacks from other shamans with magic spells. "They could see ghosts, *bhut-pret*," Chhema told me, "as clearly as you and I see other people. But nowadays all they can do is guess." So why are contemporary shamans unable to perform these feats? [. . .]

When people insist that authentic shamanic power no longer truly exists in their village, they position the shamanism of the here and now in relation to an absence – the absence of the best (or truest) shamanic power. Local dhāmis are being compared to something that is not there. These contrasts serve a purpose. When someone expounds on the difference between the golden age of the Satya Yug and the degraded order of the present era, the Kali Yug, or tells of the feats of a now dead shaman, this talk shows that the speaker is ready to recognize a truly powerful shaman, should he ever meet one. Through stories of displaced or absent shamanic power ordinary people establish themselves as discriminating witnesses to shamanic performances. Why is it so important to do this?

It has to do with the tension between cultural legitimation and practice. [. . . T]he dhāmi we watched earlier had retorted to his critic, "It is not your granting of respect, my child, that makes us worthy of it." Shamanic power comes from spirits; the spirits choose the body of the dhāmi and enable him or her to perform divinations and cures. Anyone can tell you this, because this is the explanation that legitimates the entire conceptual system; it is not the shaman who is powerful but the spirits who intermingle in the human world. Dhāmis must be taken seriously because spirits must be taken seriously. This is quite straightforward.

In practice, though, people are concerned not with shamanism in the abstract, but with the skills of the particular shamans on whom they can call. Calling on a shaman, confiding in him, trusting him – for the time being – is what grants that shaman authority. There must be a "someone" to make this judgment. The pervasive skepticism toward shamans reminds all concerned that it is possible to withhold belief. In the end, that is what makes shamans truly believable. [. . .]

Conclusion

That rural people are seen as credulous, naive, and superstitious by city folk who proclaim themselves modern is hardly uncommon. In Nepal, the chasm between the rural majority and an emerging urban middle class is indeed widening. The figure of the credulous villager helps mark a difference that the new elite is particularly concerned to emphasize. Yet the discourse on belief in Nepal does not boil down to the familiar dynamics of urban–rural and elite–peasant dichotomies. Attitudes and outlooks do not correspond neatly with distinct social groups.

It is all too easy to anticipate the plot of the narrative of modernization and assume that the educated urban elite have pretty much abandoned shamans in favor of "modern medicine." This has not occurred. In Kathmandu, surely the cosmopolitan center of Nepal, ritual healing thrives alongside the country's best and most readily available biomedical services. Discussion about belief in this context is as much about the ambivalence of the experience of modernity in

Kathmandu as it is about Kathmandu's difference from villages.[27] In the accounts of the urban elite, ritual healers can step in where "modern medicine" inevitably falls short, whether because Kathmandu's diagnostic and treatment facilities are inadequate or because even the most advanced medical knowledge has its limits. In these situations, they, like villagers, position themselves as modern believers who carefully choose which healers to rely on in particular circumstances. But whereas villagers are concerned that others see them as credulous and ignorant, the Kathmandu elite are concerned with a state of modernity they fear is partial or second-rate compared to that of the developed world. Cosmopolitan and local meanings exist simultaneously in every social location. In Chandithan and Kathmandu, a narrative of modernization is being assimilated, but it is also being refashioned to various local purposes.

There is no monolithic modernity expanding, inexorably, into new social spaces. To insist on this is not to deny that the social formations we call modern (such as capitalism, bureaucratic rationality, and certain forms of state control) do not have an impact. They do, and their forms and consequences in various societies should be understood. But we should not confuse the label social science uses to signal the complex relation among these forms – modernity – with an essential, immutable, and uniform quality of the social forms themselves. "The worlds of capitalism and modernity are complexly multilinear rather than straightforwardly unilinear," Pred and Watts observe in their study of local modernities (1992: xv). Further: they "are characterized not only by temporality but also by spatiality – by simultaneous diversity" (1992: xv). Among the simultaneously diverse aspects of modernity is the *idea* that being modern can be a social identity, distinct from other identities. The idea of the modern posits difference, but it is not the same difference for everyone, everywhere, every time.

There is no coherent local counterideology that "resists" modernity, even though there are many aspects of local life that do not fit easily within it. It is not possible to recover a pure, authentic indigenous belief system that is clearly separate from someone else's modern ideas. Nor, if this were our goal, would this tell us much about the local "culture" of Chandithan, for cosmopolitanism is itself now an aspect of that local culture. Clearly, by displacing the traditional onto someone somewhere else, some people in Chandithan are able to construct themselves as cosmopolitan villagers. In the process, tradition itself emerges as an object of self-conscious attention. The local – as local, as marginal, as parochial – comes into being through engagement with the wider systems of many beyonds (Tsing 1993). Local and cosmopolitan are socially constructed positions. My goal has been to trace practices that construct them.

Talking about belief is an activity that enables local meanings to intersect with cosmopolitan ones. The skepticism built into all relationships with shamans blurs easily into a modern skepticism toward any belief in them. No one in Chandithan is called upon to differentiate between a traditional and a modern skepticism. For them, this is a productive ambiguity. Any local talk about belief lends itself to presentation and/or interpretation in the dichotomizing terms of modernity. This is a convergence that can be solidified into a connection. Positioned speakers, each with their agendas and their real and imagined interlocutors, act as if, and can be understood as if, they are all speaking the same *lingua franca*.

Ambiguities and slippages of meaning, even misunderstandings, create a chain of translatability that allows talk about belief to have complex local meanings while simultaneously lending itself to a discursive cosmopolitanism.

The idea of the modern similarly operates as a node of connection, a representational adaptor kit suitable for international travel. It becomes cosmopolitan not because "Western" ideas spread through the world, homogenizing it, but because heterogeneous meanings and social concerns can be organized through it. This is why it is not enough to simply observe how widespread Western notions of modernity are or to insist that in every locality modernity has its own shape. For the idea of the modern has become a modality for engagement within and between social locations, and it is the forms and practices of that engagement that need to be understood.

If we want to talk about the power relations organized through the idea of the modern, we must begin by realizing that this is not the power of a dominant ideology imposed upon other views (the image is of a power acquired by "conquering" more and more "territory"). It is the power of a network whose extensive reach depends on a web of linkages rather than its ability to be everywhere at once. The idea of the modern exists in a network of translatable social maneuvers that are not reducible to a single thing. One, but only one, of these maneuvers is the explicit ideology of modernization that legitimates so many national and international institutions. This ideology can both propagate and play on ideas of the modern, but it is neither the only source of local ideas of the modern nor the only form such ideas take. Ideas of the modern are not simply manifestations of an expanding Western hegemony. In order to account for the symbolic power, the social effects, and indeed the imputation of "Westerness" to the idea of the modern, we must begin by paying close attention to the specific ways this idea is alive in the world.

A central issue here concerns how we understand the realm of culture and how we approach both global culture and situated analyses of localities. Here I turn to yet another metaphor, one taken from optics. To analyze the social processes at work in this place, we must combine a close-up, high-magnification view of the micropolitics of local life with a wide-angle picture of global interconnections. When we focus on the village level, social differences that are slight by aggregate measures of stratification come into high relief. The traditional–modern dichotomy replicates within communities, within families, perhaps even in the ways individuals think about themselves. It generates ambiguities and displacements. The apparently smooth surface of a village where people rely on shamans turns out to be bumpy and uneven. It is important to remember that this uneven surface is the ground of everyday life for people in Chandithan. It can appear smooth only at a distance.

A wide-angle view shows that the minutiae of this textured local life is simultaneously part of a much, much bigger picture. When someone in Chandithan makes a claim to modern consciousness by positing a credulous other, that person has tapped into a deep global reservoir of ideas and images. These images include notions of progress and development, of rationality and science, of beliefs and culture – protean ideas of modernity that have life and uses in some of the most powerful discourses and institutions around. The key modern

concepts are cosmopolitan concepts not just because for Nepalis they are associated with the rest of the world but because *the concepts themselves are mobile*.
Being cosmopolitan in Nepal means being able to draw on and maneuver with
these notions. Being modern advantageously distinguishes a person in Nepal
from others in the same village or the same country. At the same time, it signals
distant alliances. The *lingua franca* of modernity allows one to move, to speak
with more people, to establish far-reaching connections. To claim a modern
consciousness in Nepal is to claim membership in a transnational community of
modern people.

Notes

1 *Dhāmi-jhāṅkri* is a generic term that covers a range of ritual specialists. In central and
    western Nepal, the words *dhāmi* and *jhāṅkri* indicate distinct ritual practitioners. In
    eastern Nepal, the terms *dhāmi* and *jhāṅkri* are used interchangeably. I follow the
    usage of the people of Bhojpur in this essay.
        In addition to shamans (who experience trance/possession) there are many other
    kinds of ritual healers in Nepal. These include people who can "blow spells" (*phukne
    mānche*), various ritual officiants, astrologers, Brahmin priests, and Buddhist lamas.
2 I learned this through the many ways people informed me what I "must be thinking"
    about events I witnessed.
3 See Atkinson (1992) for an overview.
4 I use the term "modern medicine" in this essay because I want to emphasize the
    symbolic connection between biomedicine and modernity that is operating in Nepal.
    Tellingly, just how to "name" this kind of medicine has been a persistent difficulty in
    medical anthropology. As Leslie (1976) notes, to call it "modern medicine" suggests
    a contrastive relationship to some conservative "traditional medicine"; to call it
    "scientific medicine" obscures its nonscientific dimensions and suggests that other
    medical systems are unscientific; to call it "Western medicine" is to overlook its
    transcultural dimensions. Leslie (1976) and Dunn (1976) prefer the term "cosmopoli-
    tan medicine."
5 In many cases, the sufferer need not even be present in order to be diagnosed
    (through divination) and treated (through ritual).
6 I use the word "doctor" because that was the way people in the village where I lived
    referred to "modern medicine." Few of these people will ever come face-to-face with
    a university-trained physician in their lives. In 1988–9 there were 879 doctors for a
    population of just under 18 million. Even auxiliary health workers – health assistants,
    nurses, village health workers, vaccinators, malaria field workers, and so forth – are
    few and far between in the hills (there were a total of 20,565 auxiliary health workers
    in 1988–9). These statistics are from His Majesty's Government of Nepal (1994). No
    one knows how many dhāmi-jhāṅkris there are in Nepal.
7 I am arguing that shamanic healing is tied to locality through these associations.
    Shamans themselves do not need to be members of a local community to heal,
    however. In fact, people prefer shamans from other places.
8 I find a parallel in Homi Bhabha's observations on the semiotic instabilities in colonial
    discourse, though Bhabha posits these relations for discourse in the abstract and I am
    concerned as an ethnographer to show how they structure social practice. Bhabha has
    shown that in the course of being asserted and reasserted, the essentialist and self-
    evident nature of colonial distinctions is revealed as problematic. Rather than fixing

the world once and for all according to its naturalized categories, colonial discourse paradoxically produces a hybridity that escapes classification. Colonial categories of difference are displaced through the very acts that attempt to replicate them. This displacement occurs because the idea of difference on which colonial authority is based is also a "mode of address" that structures interactions between actual historical subjects. Bhabha reminds us that there is always a gap between a representation and that which is represented. "Paradoxically ... an image [of colonial authority] can never be 'original' – by virtue of the act of repetition that constructs it – nor 'identical' – by virtue of the difference that defines it," notes Bhabha. Consequently, "the colonial presence is always ambivalent," he insists, "split between its appearance as original and authoritative and its articulation as repetition and difference. It is a disjuncture produced within the act of enunciation" (Bhabha 1994: 107–8). Bhabha's insights suggest that a formal reading of the structural oppositions of this discourse is inadequate to account for the proliferation of meanings left in its wake (see, for instance, the accounts in Comaroff and Comaroff 1993 and Pred and Watts 1992).

9   These questions are especially salient as we try to find a point of analytical purchase on the moving terrain of global cultural interconnections. There is a sense often expressed in vague, hyperbolic evocations of "new" and "dizzying" forms of interaction across space – that relations of cultural differentiation and diffusion have accelerated or changed in some fundamental way. Most discussion of the transnational character or cultural processes has focused on the media, communications, and information technologies; on commodification and consumption; or on mobile, displaced, or diasporic communities. These are practices, things, and conditions associated with modernity or postmodernity. People who mainly stay put in villages that lack television sets, and whose lives include what seems like stereotypically traditional involvement with shamans and their rituals, fit less obviously into these discussions. Yet as Tsing (1993) shows, the very marginality of these "out-of-the-way places" both arises from particular forms of global engagement and generates a situated commentary on them.

Appadurai has attempted to formulate a vision of the convergences and divergences he calls "cultural flows" by suggesting that "the complexity of the current global economy has to do with certain fundamental disjunctures between economy, culture, and politics which we have only begun to theorize" (1990: 6). The metaphor of "cultural flows," while helpful in focusing attention on the multiple pathways through which "globality" is achieved, risks calling up a vaguely diffusionist imagery of ideas that spread of their own accord between fixed locations. Latour's criticism of diffusionist models in the sociology of science is pertinent here. Diffusionist models, he argues, imply that facts and technologies are endowed with inertia. "[I]t seems that as people so easily agree to transmit the object, it is the object itself that forces them to assent. It then seems that the behaviour of people is *caused* by the diffusion of facts and machines" (1987: 133). When ideas are thought of as compelling in and of themselves, what is "forgotten are the many people who carry them from hand to hand" (1987: 133). Latour proposes an alternative perspective that attends closely to the practices that construct the associations, linkages, and translations through which ideas and technologies move: "*there are always people moving the objects along but they are not the same people all along*" (1987: 137–8; emphasis in original). My attention to conjunctures in the creation of cosmopolitanism borrows from Latour's methodological discussion of "associations" and "translations."

10 Writes Robbins: "Instead of renouncing cosmopolitanism as a false universal, one can embrace it as an impulse to knowledge that is shared with others, a striving to transcend partiality that is itself partial, but no more so than the similar cognitive

strivings of many diverse peoples. The world's particulars can now be recorded, in part at least, as the world's *discrepant cosmopolitanisms*" (1992: 181; emphasis in original).

11 In the 1980s, *bikās* (development) was *the* idiom in which virtually all social debate took place. When I returned to Nepal for a few months in 1992, after the 1990 People's Movement overturned the politically repressive panchayat system of government, I had the sense that the terms of public debate had broadened somewhat. *Bikās* was still important, but "democracy" and "privatization" were also important organizing themes. My sense was that in the more open political climate, previously repressed concerns could be expressed more directly. This seems to have contributed to a wider and more critical debate about development itself.

12 Nepal's relations to British India were extremely complex. I do not mean to suggest that Nepal was unaffected by its relations to British India. Burghart (1984) argues that Nepal was not ruled as a "nation-state" (in the modern sense) until after 1951.

13 Rana rulers systematically extracted labor and resources from the countryside, investing little in public welfare or improvement.

14 Nanda Shrestha, a geographer, has begun writing about development ideology in Nepal through his own memoirs of the experience of "becoming a development category." [. . .]

15 In the 1950s and 1960s (when these processes were in their earliest stages), it was mostly the very few literate people (most often, high-caste Hindus) in rural areas who were able to take advantage of new opportunities. Newer merchant families and some of the soldiers retired from the British Army (mainly Gurungs, Magars, Rais, and Limbus) also appear to have been advantageously placed to take advantage of new opportunities.

16 Shrestha (1990) discusses the general patterns of circular migration. Shrestha suggests that a new trend may have begun: instead of reinvesting in their home village, circular migrants are starting to buy land and move to towns and cities instead, thus further impoverishing the countryside.

17 Though economic pressure leads men to go to India in search of employment, this employment raises their status and the status of their families, not just economically but in terms of the cultural capital associated with being cosmopolitan.

18 This includes a reinvestment value, because it can potentially be brokered into further opportunities.

19 Note that for hill villagers, being able to cross a street with car traffic is a cosmopolitan survival skill. (I heard many funny self-mocking stories about people's first trips to Kathmandu: trying to cross a street, figuring out how to drink fizzy beverages such as Coca-Cola, buying a ticket for a movie.) For Sherpas, for instance, learning to anticipate the desires of foreign tourists and "be" the kind of Sherpa Westerners will pay to be around is a sophisticated deployment of a cosmopolitan sensibility (Adams 1995).

20 Tsing (1993) writes about a similar association of travel with power in her analysis of "the cultural construction of marginality" in Kalimantan.

21 See Pigg (1992) for a longer discussion of the ways these phrases are used in a relativistic imagining of difference in relation to development.

22 "There exists a disjuncture," Gyan Prakash says of colonial discourse, "between meanings articulated and the processes and conditions that make their articulation possible" (1992: 154).

23 Mainstream development research on local attitudes rarely takes into account the reflexivity people have about their own society, much less their perceptions of the messages, institutions, and programs thrust at them in the name of development.

24 For instance, in development-related research in Nepal, sites are chosen for the ethnicity of the population.

25 Invocation of the "ignorance" of villagers by more educated Nepalis has many meanings. Though Linda Stone and I have remarked on the ways it stereotypes and blames villagers, denies them agency and silences their voices, the denunciation of villagers' ignorance has another, political meaning as well (Pigg 1992, 1995; Stone 1986). It serves as shorthand for the complex social, political, and economic factors that limit most villagers' access to information, education, and opportunity. Thus, speaking of villagers' ignorance can be intended as a condensed and oblique way of denouncing social inequality.

26 The sick person does not necessarily have to be present for a shamanic treatment.

27 I am grateful to Pratyoush Onta for suggesting the importance of "the ambivalence of modernity" (his phrase) in Kathmandu for my argument about the place of villages.

References

Adams, V. 1995: *Tigers of the Snow and Other Virtual Sherpas: An Ethnography of Himalayan Encounters*. Princeton, NJ: Princeton University Press.

Appadurai, A. 1990: "Disjuncture and Difference in the Global Political Economy." *Public Culture* 2 (2), 1–24.

Atkinson, J. 1992: "Shamanisms Today." *Annual Review of Anthropology* 21, 307–30.

Bhabha, H. 1994: "Signs Taken for Wonders: Questions of Ambivalence and Authority under a Tree outside Delhi, May 1817." In *The Location of Culture*. New York: Routledge, 102–122.

Burghart, R. 1984: "The Formation of the Concept of Nation-State in Nepal." *Journal of Asian Studies* 44 (1), 101–25.

Comaroff, J. and Comaroff, J. (eds.) 1993: *Modernity and its Malcontents: Ritual and Power in Postcolonial Africa*. Chicago: University of Chicago Press.

Dunn, F. 1976: "Traditional Asian Medicine and Cosmopolitan Medicine as Adaptive Systems." In Charles Leslie (ed.), *Asian Medical Systems*. Berkeley: University of California Press, 133–58.

Escobar, A. 1991: "Anthropology and the Development Encounter: The Making and Marketing of Development Anthropology." *American Ethnologist* 18, 658–82.

Escobar, A. 1995: *Encountering Development: The Making and Unmaking of the Third World*. Princeton, NJ: Princeton University Press.

Gupta, A. and Ferguson, J. 1992: "Beyond 'Culture': Space, Identity, and the Politics of Difference." *Cultural Anthropology* 7, 6–23.

His Majesty's Government of Nepal, Central Bureau of Statistics 1994: *Statistical Pocket Book*. Kathmandu.

Latour, B. 1987: *Science in Action: How to Follow Scientists and Engineers through Society*. Cambridge, MA: Harvard University Press.

Latour, B. 1993: *We Have Never Been Modern*, trans. Catherine Porter. Cambridge, MA: Harvard University Press.

Leslie, C. 1976: "Introduction." In Charles Leslie (ed.), *Asian Medical Systems*. Berkeley: University of California Press, 1–12.

Pigg, S. L. 1992: "Inventing Social Categories through Place: Social Representations and Development in Nepal." *Comparative Studies in Society and History* 34, 491–513.

Pigg, S. L. 1995: "Acronyms and Effacement: Traditional Medical Practitioners (TMP) in International Health Development." *Social Science and Medicine* 41, 47–68.

Prakash, G. 1992: "Science 'Gone Native' in Colonial India." *Representations* 40, 153–78.

Pred, A. and Watts, M. 1992: *Reworking Modernity: Capitalisms and Symbolic Discontent.* New Brunswick, NJ: Rutgers University Press.

Robbins, B. 1992: "Comparative Cosmopolitanism." *Social Text* 31/32, 169–86.

Rofel, L. 1992: "Rethinking Modernity: Space and Factory Discipline in China." *Cultural Anthropology* 7, 93–114.

Shrestha, N. 1990: *Landlessness and Migration in Nepal.* Boulder, CO: Westview Press.

Shrestha, R. and Lediard, M. 1980: *Faith Healers: A Force for Change. A Preliminary Report of an Action-Research Project.* Kathmandu. Educational Enterprises.

Stone, L. 1986: "Primary Health Care for Whom? Village Perspectives from Nepal." *Social Science and Medicine* 22 (3), 293–302.

Tsing, A. L. 1993: *In the Realm of the Diamond Queen: Marginality in an Out-of-the Way Place.* Princeton, NJ: Princeton University Press.

29 Modernizing the Malay Mother

Maila Stivens

[. . .]

Exploring Malay Mothering

To examine "modern" mothering in Malaysia, we need first to attend to the particularities of modernity in the country. As I suggest elsewhere (1994b, n.d.b), imported Eurocentric models of "modernization" project ideas deriving from Western social developments directly on to analyses of Malaysia. I argue that we cannot unproblematically apply assumptions about a standard linear progression from "tradition" to the rationalization, bureaucratization, industrialization, and secularism of mainstream Western models of modernity; this is to ignore both the specificities of the development process in the country and the problems within contemporary social theory with the increasingly unstable category of modernity itself.[1] Malaysian colonial and postcolonial processes have been marked by a highly directive state, with a reconstitution of the Malay peasantry through land legislation in the colonial period, continuing agricultural interventions (Lim Teck Ghee 1977; Stivens 1985, 1996) and an increasingly managerial state role in the economy with the implementation of the New Economic Policy in the 1970s.[2] Most particularly, the colonial reconstitution of a Malay peasantry cast as a "yeoman idyll" has reverberated down to the present politically and economically, forming a core imaginary for Malay nationalism: this core imaginary is only now being challenged by the multiplying and fragmented meanings about Malayness produced in relation to the new industrial and globalizing orders.[3] In the context of resurgent Islam, the idea of modernity is rendered even

Excerpted from Maila Stivens, "Modernizing the Malay Mother." In K. Ram and M. Jolly (eds.), *Maternities and Modernities: Colonial and Post-colonial Experiences in Asia and the Pacific* (Cambridge: Cambridge University Press, 1998), 50–80.

more unstable, because it is located within a series of tensions surrounding the role of religion in the modern Malay world and its relationship to "tradition," "family," and critiques of modernization and Westernization. For a sizeable minority of contemporary Malays, modernity and its future is understood solely within a narrative about a hoped-for Islamic modernity.

We have similar difficulties if we look against the masculinist grain of the many debates about modernity (and postmodernity) from a gendered stand-point. I have argued elsewhere that feminist theory's profound critique of the main assumptions of masculinist social theory can be applied to the category of modernity, revealing it to be a thoroughly masculinist construct, based on a series of highly dubious, socially and historically specific and gendered binary oppositions that pose women, woman, and the female as always negative: in such theorizing the processes producing modernity are seen as taking place in a male public sphere from which women are excluded (cf. Felski 1995; Stivens 1994b, n.d.b).

A dominant storyline about the development of mothering in Malaysia within government and some social science rhetoric accepts such linear models of modernity. It sees ever-increasing health arising from colonial and postcolonial medical and infant welfare services, and, with industrialization, increasingly nuclearized urban families and individual mothering replacing the allegedly more collective earlier patterns and a new purposive parenting replacing the previous overindulgence and nurturance. For most commentators, such devel-opments have been seen as *effects* of the larger forces of modernization. But as Lenore Manderson's work has shown (1981, 1982, 1987a, 1987b, 1989, 1992), in fact the colonial state largely allocated the task of producing "modern" health for the Malayan populace to women, with a range of pressures and exhortations applied to them. Other versions growing in importance recently pose a dystopic vision, seeing the "problems" produced by women going out to work – the failings of mothers – as directly responsible for some of the ills of modernity, especially oversexed and lazy youth "hanging out" and "loafing."

The Malaysian context poses a particular tension for would-be feminists in writing about mothering because of the explicit critique of Western feminist perspectives by some recent Islamic commentators there. *Dakwah* groups in Malaysia (missionary, so-called fundamentalist groups, although they disown the term) argue that women's true vocation is motherhood and child care. Islam, it is held, upholds and values motherhood and child rearing as part of women's full participation in society, while the West devalues such activities. Some scholars have also argued that Western feminism is inappropriate in the Malay-sian context, and that the veil and Islamic practices confer equal but separate power. In this account, then, a somewhat different "public" and "private" is created from that argued for by the modernists, with women more firmly located within the "private." It is debatable, however, how far such avowedly Islamic "womanist" discourses (e.g., Roziah Omar 1996) will be "free" to distance themselves from hegemonic North Atlantic perspectives. Some Islamic feminists have worked for a reinterpretation of "fundamentalist" ideas, through a reread-ing of the Koran (e.g., Mernissi 1991, writing from a Middle Eastern context; Amina Wadud-Muhsin 1992, writing from Malaysia). They suggest that the

Koran can be read as a text setting out a social justice agenda whose gender egalitarianism has been suppressed historically. Many of my present middle-class informants' representations of their everyday lives are deeply embedded in religion in its highly specific local manifestations.

The *Dakwah* critique rightly objects to the ways Islam has been represented in some Western feminist discourse. This has sometimes pictured the veiled Muslim woman, in a highly Orientalist and reductionist way, as representative of all that is oppressed (cf. Lazreg 1988).[4] But the various versions of a supposedly purer Islam, both in modernist and revivalist versions, have great appeal for modern Malay women of both the middle and working classes (cf. Ong 1987). This is apparent in the mass of writing by middle-class women – journalists and others – within the proliferating magazines aimed at the modern Malay market. For example, there are large numbers of articles outlining the correct ways to conduct Muslim family life. For some middle-class Malay women, some of the greatest adherents to the model of modern Muslim womanhood, the veiling and covering of their bodies has become a potent symbol not only of "modern" womanhood but of ethnic and class situation. In the contemporary period, the veiled Malay woman has become a significant site of (Malay) nationalist symbolization (cf. Ong 1990), the very embodiment of a highly specific Malay modernity, although there are many veils and as many versions of the new Malay woman (see Stivens n.d.b). The long development of this discursive production of the Malay woman within Malay nationalist thought and education is apparent in Malaysian history (see Manderson 1980). [. . .]

The Modern Mother in the Malay Imaginary

I want now to look at the very specific and limited ways in which the Malay mother has been imagined in popular culture. Mothers figure prominently in some of the contrasting images of the march towards modernity, as chaste, modern Muslim wives, glamorous and/or energetic business and career women, hard-working housewives, doting mothers and keepers of the family, particularly of the family's health, and indeed of Malay modernity. A major arena for these representations is the growing number of magazines targeted at the middle-class market. Random selections from the plethora of images picturing women to themselves illustrate the representations of mothers: a back cover of *Ibu* (Mother) magazine in 1991 shows a boy, probably Indian (although his ethnicity seems to be deliberately fudged), astride the picture, neatly dressed in gray school pants, with blocks of flats in the middle distance. The caption celebrates the Selangor Development Corporation, taking part in a government campaign exhorting "happy families," "We build housing, you build happy families." *Jelita*, a more up-market production, ran a special issue on mothers and children in May 1993, featuring a folio of beautiful mothers and their children of varying ages pictured in "designer" clothes – Western and up-market refigured Malay "traditional" dress, with only one of the women veiled – and articles about how a safe house makes for a happy family. The multiplying and diverse images of women are clearly not simply reflections of a monolithic state or Islamic ideology or discourse governing the lives of women, in spite of the many crude state messages about the happy family making for a happy country. They express, rather, the very clear tensions between the varying versions of state, market, and religious modernities.[5]

However diverse popular representations of contemporary women are, they are notable for their emphasis on the energy and industry of mothers and women in general. [. . .] The ever-growing cultural production of "domesticity" suggests that women (as wives-mothers) are being groomed to take a crucial role in producing the everyday practices of modern Malays. The detailed instructions on household decor, advice bringing women up-to-date (sic) with "modern" views about child rearing and interpersonal relationships, and the reinvention of cuisine all apparently accord women a key part in the "domestic" construction of Malay middle classness. This may seem predictable to observers of consumer capitalist culture in the West, where women are seen to occupy a similarly focal role as coordinators of consumption and the producers of an elaborated domesticity. But, as noted, the embeddedness of a range of Islamic practices in the material manifestations of becoming modern lends a highly specific set of meanings to women's place in producing domesticity. Thus magazine articles (often written by male "experts") regularly instruct women on the duties of Muslim parents and give full instructions, complete with numerous glossy pictures, to help readers produce all the reworked trappings of preparations for Muslim holy days and festivals.

The commoditization of child care accompanying the emergence of the recently modern mother is remarkable. To be a modern mother is to be an active consumer under great pressure to acquire all the commodities necessary for the satisfactory performance of motherhood. The smaller number of children has coincided with an enormous expansion of expenditure on children. Today, the market for baby goods has boomed dramatically, with cots, pushchairs, disposable nappies, a huge range of feeding equipment, toys, and clothing sold in glossy new stores in the postmodern shopping centers in urban areas, including the giant US toy chain Toys R Us. Disposable nappies and pushchairs were rare even in 1982, when I took my first child, then nearly two years old, to Malaysia: now disposable nappies are ubiquitous. The relative absence of footpaths in 1982 made the use of a pushchair difficult even in Petaling Jaya (the "satellite" area of Kuala Lumpur), and ours was constantly commented on. The commoditization of child care is expressed in a number of ways, including masses of new shops and the growing role of servants (often allegedly Indonesian illegal immigrants), childminders, and nurseries. As noted, many middle-class women have become avid employees, backed up by complex and sometimes fraught arrangements of kin help and servants and childminders. But we need to be careful about generalizing these patterns for all sections of the middle class: only a minority of the sixty middle-middle-class households interviewed on a Seremban housing estate, for example, actually employed servants, although over 80 percent of the Kuala Lumpur sample had some form of paid domestic help.

The expansion of women's magazines and advice books has brought a whole new arena for the cultural production of ideas about childbearing and child rearing. Again, these ideas have become closely linked to other burgeoning cultural productions surrounding religion and nation building. There is a strong strand of exhortation: a recent publication for example is titled *Mengapa Anak Anda Malas Belajar?* (Why is Your Child Lazy about Studying?),[6] which is amusingly illustrated with cartoons almost all featuring boys, although the cover shows a picture of a girl. This and the earlier example of the link between nation and happy families both feature maternal efforts as being directed at sons in particular. I suspect this focus on boys may be general, but my analyses of the magazines are still in process. My present informants tell me that they have usually not consulted the "bibles" of Western child rearing such as Dr Spock and Penelope Leach (available in all the big bookstores), but do rely heavily on newspaper and magazine articles. The discourses of the latter are very much in line with the imported modernist psychological ideas of those books, however, stressing the development of the child in a loving, child-centered atmosphere, but not one of "overindulgence." It is notable that such ideas represent a marked contrast to the state school system's emphasis on relatively disciplinarian practices that appear to be a direct descendant of the quasi-military school practices of the British colonial era. This suggests some disjunction between the actual child-rearing practices of home and state, although both are addressed in the state discourses about a direct and necessary link between family, child rearing, and nation building.

It is worth stressing the simultaneous creation of and living in and criticism of their own cultural forms by the contemporary Malay middle classes. The "authentic" voice of the middle-class woman herself will always be a mediated one: the journalists, doctors, writers, lawyers, TV producers, teachers, and academics who are part of the elaborate production of the "modern" mother are simultaneously living the processes that they are imposing on other women who lack their voice – for example, nurses, secretaries, clerks, and housewives.

Power, "Tradition," and Modernity in Malay Mothering

Some feminists have interpreted the continuing growth of modernist interventions in the mothering process, especially state interventions (both in Malaysia and elsewhere), as elaborate male-dominated mechanisms of social control (Laderman 1983; Manderson 1987a; Oakley 1980). Such interventions can be seen as only partially effective, however; women have not simply acquiesced or been complicit with such impositions, although these resistances often brought new contradictions. The power of "expert" advice has not been uniform: thus while much advice about infant care seems to have been imposed, most notably by the maternal health clinics, pregnant women have sometimes been able to successfully resist the new regimes. [. . .]

Some of the ideological contests about managing life-cycle events were well illustrated by the ceremonial display which I observed of the baby of a Rembau schoolteacher who had flown home from Sabah to her village to give birth.

> Like other newborns, her baby was presented for visitors in a highly uniform ritualized display of newly acquired "modern" consumer goods. He was placed on

a cushion on the floor, flanked by one or more plastic laundry baskets stacked with cloth nappies, Johnson's baby powder, other items of clothing, and a feeding bottle (*nota bene!*). In this case, the mother had left hospital after one day, because she could not get any sleep. A number of neighbors and the government midwife were in attendance to visit the new arrival. The government midwife on her daily visit saw to the mother's perineum and the baby's umbilicus and then tried unsuccessfully to get the baby's swaddling loosened. The mother was observing all the food taboos which are "traditionally" supposed to preserve women's health under the humoral system of beliefs. "You must eat dry foods," said a thirty-seven-year-old neighbor. "The *orang tuo* [old folk] are very much against fruit and vegetables" (which are believed to cool the body). The government midwife retired, defeated. The *bidan* (village midwife) later made her appearance, supervising the binding and massage of the mother's abdomen.

My informants represented the relationship between the two midwives as a simple division of labor, with the government midwife there to look after the child, the village midwife to look after the mother, which was not strictly the case. The scene represented an interesting conjunction of the impositions of commoditization and modernizing state control, only some of which were being resisted.[7]

The new "modern" mothers among my informants were decidedly ambivalent about the control exercised by the *orang tuo*, the "old folks," in spite of the apparent success of the latter in imposing food taboos. Some of the young women grumbled a lot about these taboos, saying that they felt unable to resist the social pressure within the village. This ambivalence was also manifest in the case of the young schoolteacher mentioned above. She had planned to leave her baby with her mother while she and her husband went back to East Malaysia, but her husband persuaded her to take the baby with them, because he had become very attached to him. She was not feeling very confident:

> I'm worried about looking after the baby myself. My sister's baby who's a month older weighs fifteen pounds and mine still only weighs seven pounds. It's because she breast-feeds. Mine is bottle-fed, because I thought that I was leaving him. The doctors prefer you to breast-feed. I'm very worried about taking him. My mother knows how to stop him crying. He cries every night. What if he cries on the plane? I can't stop him. I would have liked to leave him for a few months longer.

These anxieties suggest to me that romantic naturalizing views about the supportiveness of the women's community are not necessarily apposite. They can overlook the considerable ambivalence present about the older women's control and competence. The younger woman in this case obviously felt that her competence as a mother had been called into question by the failure of the baby to thrive like her sister's, and by her mother's much greater ability to stop the baby crying. That this anxiety was to be resolved by leaving the baby with her mother also suggests an absence of "modern" ideologies and subjectivities about "maternal deprivation." We might, however, see her lack of confidence overall as deriving from the loss of maternal power through the medicalization of childbirth and by the new conjunctures in which mothering after the birth period has become an activity carried out in individual households often removed from kin support.

The management of childbirth in the industrializing era has been marked by a series of conflicts – between, on the one hand, the pronatalist "old" ways with a high level of female control over everyday events and, on the other hand, the state's zealous efforts in first limiting, then, later, encouraging fertility, medicalizing birth, and improving nutrition. I do not think, however, that we can see the "persistence" of the "old" ways as merely a cultural transmission from the past. Rather, the "traditional" ways can be seen as constantly recreated within "modern" cultural practices. There has obviously been some undermining of women's ideological control of biological reproduction with attempts to strengthen modernist health practices. Women's "traditional" knowledge has been more and more devalued by "moderns" and the state, although we also see many of these practices still firmly adhered to. In Negeri Sembilan in the 1970s, for example, the placenta was often retrieved in hospital births, so that the home-delivery-based ritual surrounding it could be performed. But not everyone bothered, although some reportedly still bring the placenta home even from urban centers. Some religious officials and *Dakwah* groups have also been attempting to discredit such practices as un-Islamic, which ties religion again into a version of modernity and against "un-Islamic," premodern tradition. Those attached to the modern ways, whether the "young," representatives of the modern sectors (such as nurses and teachers), or migrants to the city, marshal ammunition from the media and their experience of the urban world about vitamins and "correct" ways of looking after babies. But even young proponents of some of the new ways among my informants have found their contacts with modern medicine profoundly alienating; for example, one young mother deeply resented the episiotomy and stitching with her first baby, feeling it was worse than the whole labor. She also found the government midwife *sombong* (arrogant) and in fact resolutely refused all the vitamins and iron given to her at the *mukim* (young women engaging in "free sex") maternal health clinic during the pregnancy. On the other hand, stories are widespread of the battles some urban middle-class parents have engaged in to follow the new ways in having the father present at the birth.

The sexual politics of child care has been another important aspect of the power relations surrounding mothering. It appears that women have done and continue to do much of the work in looking after children, although it is possible that there was some spreading of this labor to men and other children in the more communal contexts of village life in the past. This is not simply a "traditional" sexual division of labor. It has, of course, been endlessly reconstituted. As in the past, power in household relations can be seen as linked to the larger forces of economy and polity. It is clear that the social changes of the industrial era have imposed enormous new strains on women. The elaboration of child care and the consumption necessary to motherhood have produced complex new domestic regimes. Such work often has to be carried out within a period of time strongly circumscribed by paid work regimes. School arrangements were a real headache for the Seremban households interviewed, for example: one neighboring couple, with four children at four different schools on different shifts (Malaysian schools run two shifts) and with no servant, had complex and often fraught arrangements for both parents and some friends to pick up the children. On the other hand, my village study showed how many middle-class migrants have relied on grandmotherly care of children sent back to the village over the last few decades – about a quarter of all village households had been involved in such care at some point (see Stivens 1996). Such kin care obviously has often helped out, but has provided full care for only a small proportion of working parents in the middle-class populations I studied in Seremban, Kuala Lumpur, and Penang.

The politics of child care has other dimensions. The absence of proper maternity leave has left many salaried women returning to work after six weeks. This gives them little respite from the pregnancy and birth and forces many of them to hand over some of the child's care to kin and servants long before they actually wish to. (There are as yet few well-run nurseries.) They have also experienced problems with breast-feeding because of this. The absence of any developed state ideology of maternal deprivation over the last couple of decades is especially interesting, compared to its force in the West, for example. Thus there seemed to be little public discussion about the supposed guilt that "working mothers" might feel until recently, although there has been much publicity about problems with servants and their care of children. (There is very little discussion, however, about the problems servants have with their employers.) And it is only comparatively recently that we have seen a developed campaign about working mothers and their effects on teenage children, although ideas of maternal deprivation have been deployed in some of the Muslim critiques of modern life.

The extent of the sheer hard work (and mostly female work) that goes into child rearing cannot be exaggerated. The extended family, mainly mothers or sisters, can also provide some help, but it is less clear that they actually provide sustained periods of relief from the hard slog of motherly care, apart from cases where the grandmother was looking after the children. It is significant, for example, that only a small number of interviewees were living in extended family households, and the majority had kin living far away in other states.

Some Malaysian feminists have been expressing real despondency about the potential for men to change, particularly on the domestic front. While I know of some academic men doing a larger share of domestic labor, and some of the magazines are now running stories about fathers cooking and doing night feeds for their bottle-fed babies, there appears to be little evidence of real changes in urban housework patterns. Among my Kuala Lumpur sample, for example, most informants – male and female – thought that fathers should "help" with child care and feeding. It is much harder to measure how much they actually did do, however. The forces of conservatism are not just the national production of the housewife or intransigent, individual men, however. In Rembau older women occasionally disparaged a few such pioneers. It is also possible that the availability of servants for some sections of the middle class has lessened the pressures on men to "help" their harassed "working wives," forestalling renegotiation of domestic masculinity.

The postcolonial state has clearly seen mothers as having the power to build happy families and a happy nation. Such attributions of power carry with them [. . .] equal potential for the state's blaming mothers. These interweave in interesting ways with the received everyday ideologies and practices of mothering, which also attribute considerable power and blame. In Rembau, for example, people told me that a mother was to blame if her children quarreled among themselves. Whether we can see this particular development as a move towards an increasingly individualistic "modern" attribution of blame and responsibility within a rural context of growing individualization of production is debatable and probably outside the scope of this discussion.[8] But the state and media campaigns at the national level to exhort parents – both fathers and mothers – to greater efforts in raising their children suggest some elaboration of these ideas. This has been especially noticeable in recent moral panics about *boh sia* (young women engaging in "free sex") and *lepak* (loafing, hanging out): the behavior of teenagers has become a site for the negotiation of anxieties about the possible ills of modernity, the embodiment of parental and societal failures to produce the right kind of Asian family values and Islamic modernity, or at least to be able to resist the worst of "Westoxification."[9] Child abuse, which has also received a lot of attention recently from academics, journalists, and government, is similarly represented in some quarters as one of the by-products of "development," collapsing family values, and general social decline.

Conclusions

I have suggested that the unrecognized gendering and specificities of Malaysian modernity have been embedded in writing about the "family," motherhood, and childbearing in the country. We cannot simply and authoritatively pronounce about the "effects" of successive stages of Malaysia's divergent modernity on women's mothering. Women have had complex and multiple relationships as mothers to the modernizing patterns and practices described: these relationships have been open to various interpretations, positioned differently by different sets of commentators.

Earlier models of Malay mothering were constructed within the colonial discourses of mothers and others as indulgent, loving, and nurturant, but perhaps too indulgent and [. . .] unhygienic, fatalistic, and somewhat unindustrious. Much of this body of earlier work presumptuously claimed to be providing authoritative accounts of the relationships between parents and children and their respective subjectivities. Yet for all this authoritativeness, there was comparatively little about the conditions and experiences of mothering in this work. These views led directly to a contemporary modernist storyline that sees increasingly nuclearized urban families arising with industrialization, individual mothering replacing the more collective earlier patterns and a new purpose in life replacing the previous overindulgence and nurturance. Women are to be transformed into energetic creators of happy families and a happy nation.

A different version of contemporary narratives of motherhood, however, sees "traditional" child rearing as peculiarly vulnerable to the ills of Westoxification, collapsing family values, and general social decline. This scenario is prominent in some resurgent Islamic versions of "modern" discourse, which to some extent collapse family and society into each other, granting family a central place as the building block of society. The "Asian Family" of government rhetoric becomes a nostalgia-laden repository for reinvented versions of family life, motherhood, and morality.

A third, feminist version can pronounce that modernity and modern mother-hood mean a loss of earlier female power or autonomy, that ever-increasing modernity and commoditization erodes women's situation in multiple ways. Women are seen as suffering under their responsibility for increasing production of the commodity-like product, the happy, smiling, clever, industrious, religious, and indeed nation-building child, while on occasion slowly going mad in their expensive, if not especially large, town houses or burning out with the dual demands of work and home. The child in such accounts, however, can veer dangerously towards being depicted as the main villain, as in Barrett and McIntosh's account of the "tyranny of motherhood" (1982: 62). The child *per se* can appear to be held responsible for the institution and the woes it may confer on women.

These competing claims to give an authoritative account of Malay mothers' experiences of mothering return us to the opening remarks about the problems facing any such account. It is clear that scholarly and media agendas have often mirrored the overt impositions of first colonial, then nation building, and now resurgent religion's and globalizing culture's concerns and agendas. The compet-ing narratives about the transformations of mothering from "traditional" to "modern" and the place of mothering in the modernizing process echo the tensions in women's lived experiences of modernity. I highlighted in particular the embeddedness of much discursive production of Malay mothering in the tensions surrounding the relationship of Malaysian Islam to modernity. Thus some of my informants in the present study have been living the religious resurgence in very intense ways, finding religion to be their main support in such stressful situations as negotiating single parenthood after divorce. I am not happy about representing these experiences as simply a governance of women as "victims" by an ultimately repressive religion (as Ong 1990 does). Indeed, we could equally see their religious practice as representing a form of social and political agency: the support for revivalist Islam among sections of the new middle classes, especially university students (Narli 1986), can be seen as a means for women to confront Malaysian modernity on terms somewhat more of their own making.[10]

The dominant representation of the many tensions surrounding the modern-izing process as a conflict between the purported "old" and the "new" creates a false duality out of what are in fact shifting meanings. This opposition is represented as a straightforward temporal one: the "traditional" is posed as some relic of the "premodern" "past," which "progress" – in whatever version is favored by the observer – will displace. I would see "tradition" rather as a highly complex, continuous development of discursive and social practices, constantly recreated in the "present." The discursive opposition between "tradition" and "modernity" has constantly shifted, tying one or other or both terms to various other areas of discourse, as in the widespread linkage of "modernity" with "Westernization"/"Westoxification." For my informants, these shifting instabili-ties are ever-present as they negotiate the complex intersections of mothering, class, nation, and religion.

Notes

1 There is clearly a growing instability surrounding the category of modernity, produced mainly by the debates around postmodernity and postcolonialism. Elsewhere, I have argued that we have many problems in theorizing Malaysian modernity, especially the all too common conflation of modernity and Westernization in much of the development literature (1994b, n.d.a, n.d.b). This is a further twist on the undoubted Eurocentrism of most of the sociological debates about modernity and postmodernity.

2 The New Economic Policy, introduced in 1970 after communal riots in 1969, has been particularly important in subsequent restructuring of the economy: this aimed to progressively redistribute wealth to the poorest sections of Malaysian society, the Malays. The target of the New Economic Policy was a 30 percent *bumiputra* (Malay or indigenous) ownership of the economy by 1990 (compared to 2.4 percent in 1970, and 10.3 percent in 1978). Other Malaysians were to own a 40 percent share and foreign interests 30 percent (compared to 63.3 percent in 1970; Majid and Majid 1983: 69).

3 See Stivens (n.d.b).

4 Lazreg (1988) has argued that this is common in writing on the Middle East (cf. Ahmed 1992; Sabbah 1988). Mather (1985) is a clear example of this demonizing of Islam. See Stivens (1992).

5 Elsewhere I look at what we might see as a postmodernization of the many images of women within contemporary Malay cultural productions (Stivens n.d.b).

6 This book was published in 1991 in Kuala Lumpur, but the author, Heryanto Sutedja, appears to be Indonesian from his name. The front cover has a different title from the frontispiece, namely *Anak Anda Malas Belajar*.

7 See Karim (1984) for a descriptive account of Malay midwives. See Manderson (1981, 1982, 1987a, 1987b, 1989, 1992).

8 See my book *Matriliny and Modernity* (Stivens 1996) for discussion.

9 "Westoxification" is, I understand, a term first used by the Ayatollah Khomeini, which has some currency in the region. There was, in fact, a conference exploring its meanings in Singapore in December 1993.

10 See, for example, Akbar Ahmed (1992), who argues for an understanding of Islamic resurgence as a quintessentially postmodern form of political practice. See Sabbah (1988); Stivens (n.d.b).

References

Ahmed, L. 1992: *Women and Gender in Islam: Historical Roots of a Modern Debate.* New Haven, CT: Yale University Press.

Akbar Ahmed 1992: *Postmodernism and Islam: Predicament and Promise.* London: Routledge.

Amina Wadud-Muhsin 1992: *Qu'ran and Woman.* Kuala Lumpur: Penerbit Fajar Bakti.

Barrett, M. and McIntosh, M. 1982: *The Anti-social Family.* London: Verso.

Felski, R. 1995: *The Gender of Modernity.* Cambridge, MA: Harvard University Press.

Heryanto Sutedja 1991: *Mengapa Anak Anda Malas Belajar?* (Why is Your Child Lazy about Studying?) Kuala Lumpur: Syarikat S. Abdul Majeed.

Karim, W.-J. 1984: "Malay Midwives and Witches." *Social Science and Medicine* 18 (2), 159–66.

Laderman, C. 1983: *Wives and Midwives: Childbirth and Nutrition in Rural Malaysia.* Berkeley: University of California Press.

Lazreg, M. 1988: "Feminism and Difference: The Perils of Writing as a Woman on Algeria." *Feminist Studies* 14 (1), 81–107.

Lim Teck Ghee 1977: *Peasants and their Agricultural Economy.* Oxford: Oxford University Press.

Majid, S. and Majid, A. 1983: "Public Sector Land Settlement: Rural Development in West Malaysia." In D. A. M. Lea and D. P. Chaudhri (eds.), *Rural Development and the State: Contradictions and Dilemmas in Developing Countries.* London and New York: Methuen, 66–99.

Manderson, L. 1980: *Women, Politics and Change: The Kaum Ibu UMNO Malaysia, 1945–1972.* Kuala Lumpur: Oxford University Press.

Manderson, L. 1981: "Traditional Food Beliefs and Critical Life Events in Peninsular Malaysia." *Social Science Information* 20 (6), 947–75.

Manderson, L. 1982: "Bottle Feeding and Ideology in Colonial Malaya: The Production of Change." *International Journal of Health Services* 12 (4), 597–616.

Manderson, L. 1987a: "Blame, Responsibility and Remedial Action: Death, Disease and the Infant in Early Twentieth Century Malaya." In N. Owen (ed.), *Death and Disease in Southeast Asia: Explorations in Social, Medical and Demographic History.* Singapore: Oxford University Press for the Asian Studies Association of Australia, 257–82.

Manderson, L. 1987b: "Health Services and the Legitimation of the Colonial State: British Malaya 1786–1941." *International Journal of Health Services* 17 (1), 91–112.

Manderson, L. 1989: "Political Economy and the Politics of Gender: Maternal and Child Health in Colonial Malaya." In P. Cohen and I. Purcal (eds.), *The Political Economy of Primary Health Care in Southeast Asia.* Canberra: Australian Development Studies Network and ASEAN Training Centre for Primary Health Care Development, 79–100.

Manderson, L. 1992: "Women and the State: Maternal and Child Welfare in Colonial Malaya, 1900–1940." In V. Fildes, L. Marks, and H. Marland (eds.), *Women and Children First: International Maternal and Infant Welfare 1870–1945.* London: Routledge, 154–77.

Mather, C. 1985: " 'Rather Than Make Trouble, It's Better Just To Leave': Behind the Lack of Industrial Strife in the Tangerang Region of West Java." In H. Mshar (ed.), *Women, Work and Ideology in the Third World.* London: Tavistock Publications, 153–80.

Mernissi, F. 1991: *Women and Islam: An Historical Enquiry.* Oxford: Blackwell.

Narli, A. N. 1986: "Malay Women in Tertiary Education: Trends of Change in Female Role Ideology." Ph.D. thesis, University Sains, Penang.

Oakley, A. 1980: *Women Confined: Towards a Sociology of Childbirth.* Oxford: Martin Robertson.

Ong, A. 1987: *Spirits of Resistance and Capitalist Discipline: Factory Women in Malaysia.* Albany: State University of New York Press.

Ong, A. 1990: "State Versus Islam: Malay Families, Women's Bodies, and the Body Politic in Malaysia." *American Ethnologist* 17 (2), 258–76.

Roziah Omar 1996: *State, Islam, and Malay Reproduction.* Working Paper No. 2. Canberra: Gender Relations Project, Research School of Pacific and Asian Studies, The Australian National University.

Sabbah, D. A. 1988: *Woman in the Muslim Unconscious.* New York: Pergamon Press.

Stivens, M. 1985: "The Fate of Women's Land Rights: Gender, Matriliny, and Capitalism in Rembau, Negeri Sembilan, Malaysia." In H. Mshar (ed.), *Women, Work and Ideology in the Third World.* London: Tavistock Publications, 3–36.

Stivens, M. 1987: "Family and State in Malaysian Industrialisation." In H. Mshar (ed.), *Women, State and Ideology: Studies from Africa and Asia.* London: Macmillan, 89–104.

Stivens, M. 1992: "Perspectives on Gender: Problems in Writing about Women in Malaysia." In I. Kahn and F. Loh (eds.), *Fragmented Vision: Culture and Politics in Contemporary Malaysia*. Sydney: Allen and Unwin, 202–24.

Stivens, M. 1994a: "The Gendering of Knowledge: The Case of Anthropology and Feminism." In N. Grieve and A. Burns (eds.), *Australian Women: Contemporary Feminist Thought*. Melbourne: Oxford University Press, 133–41.

Stivens, M. 1994b: "Gender and Modernity in Malaysia." In A. Gomes (ed.), *Modernity and Identity: Asian Illustrations*. Bundoora: La Trobe University Press, 66–95.

Stivens, M. 1996: *Matriliny and Modernity: Sexual Politics and Social Change in Rural Malaysia*. Sydney: Allen and Unwin.

Stivens, M. n.d.a: "Introduction: Theorising Gender, Power and Modernity in Affluent Asia." In K. Sen and M. Stivens (eds.), *Gender and Power in Affluent Asia*. London: Routledge (forthcoming).

Stivens, M. n.d.b: "Sex, Gender and the Making of the Malay Middle Classes." In K. Sen and M. Stivens (eds.), *Gender and Power in Affluent Asia*. London: Routledge (forthcoming)

Index

impact on Lesotho, 96, 99
impact on Turkey, 3–10
theory, *see* development theories
values, 12–17
Mohanty, C. T., xviii
Morris, M., xiii
multiculturalism, 129
Myrdal, G., 1–2, 11–18

Nana, figure of, 71–3
Narayan, U., xviii, 209, 225–38
national identity, *see* identity
nationalism, 204, 232–3, 258, 288–90,
300–9, 345, 347
and class, xvii, 315–22
ethnonationalism, 264
and tradition, 200–4, 231–6, 304
nation-state, 14–15, 157–66, 263–6, 352–3
nativism, 112–13, 304
Nehru, J., 18 n.9
Nelson, D., 210, 257–69
Nepal, 77, 90, 103–14, 282, 324–43
new social movements, 130, 239–40, 242,
245–6, 249–53, 258–66
Norval, A. J., 128–9

Olympia (Manet), 66–7, 69, 71–2
Ong, A., xviii–xix
organization
charitable, 40–1
nongovernmental (NGO), xx–xxi, 88,
106, 109–11, 118, 145–7, 245–7, 250,
262, 273–4
Orient, 47–8, 53
Orientalism, xv–xvi, xix, 45, 47–55, 189,
218–19, 221
definition of, 45, 47–9, 51–2
"Other," the, 54, 63, 73, 128, 163, 189, 206
n.2, 326, 333
and exoticism, 47, 73, 110, 135

Pacific, 144–54
Pakistan, 13
Palestine, 61–2, 162
Parent-Duchatelet, A. J. B., 69–70
patriarchy, 85, 137, 184, 229, 242, 301,
304–5
peasantry, 220–1
and agriculture, 189, 214–15
Philippines, 156, 182–92
Picasso, P., 72

Pieterse, J. N., xx–xxi
Pigg, S. L., 282, 324–44
Pol Pot, 212–13
politics
of difference, 123–32, 134–43, 163, 166,
196–8, 202–5, 225, 251, 326–8
international, 19–20
popular culture, 38–41, 312–22, 347–9
postcolonialism, studies of, xvii–xix
post-development, discourse of, xx–xxi,
77–92, 96–7, 103, 111
poverty, 77–92, 98, 103–5, 109, 111–12, 115,
118–19, 136
economic definition of, 81
and governmentality, 80–90
power, 85, 169
power/knowledge, xiv–xxi, 45, 49–54,
56–64, 82, 88, 90, 172–8, 247, 262–3
Pred, A., 155, 168–81, 338
Preis, A.-B., 121–2, 132–43
progress, development as, 86, 89, 109, 140,
325–6
prostitution, 69–73, 75, 162–3
psychoanalysis, 58–9, 73
psychology, 58–9, 73

race, 45, 85, 266–7 n.3
cultural constructions of, 66, 107–8, 190,
286
racial prejudice, xvi, 107, 183–4, 187–90
and sexuality, 65–75
white racism, *see* whiteness
racial inequality, and Third World, 107–8
Rahnema, M., 79
Ranger, T., 281, 282–91
Ransom, J. S., xvi–xvii
relativism, 63, 101
religion, 20–1, 37–41, 104–5, 293–5, 297,
351, 354
religious sects, 39–41
see also Christianity; Hinduism; Islam
research methodology, 51, 103–4
actor-oriented approach, 140–1
interview-based, 3–6
textual analysis, 97
resistance, 113, 128–31, 131 n.1, 137, 171–8,
179–80 n.24, 184, 197–9, 239–54, 270–8
concept of, xvii–xviii
from colonized peoples, xvi, 126, 213,
215–16, 260–6, 288–9, 304